KU-005-978

THE DYNAMICS OF EMPLOYEE RELATIONS

Second Edition

Paul Blyton

and

Peter Turnbull

1449618

CHESTER COLLEGE

ACC No. 01089588 DEPT OWL

CLASS No. 658.315 BLY

331.0941 BLY

LIBRARY

palgrave

© Paul Blyton and Peter Turnbull 1994, 1998

All rights reserved. No reproduction, copy or transmission of this publication may be made without written permission.

No paragraph of this publication may be reproduced, copied or transmitted save with written permission or in accordance with the provisions of the Copyright, Designs and Patents Act 1988, or under the terms of any licence permitting limited copying issued by the Copyright Licensing Agency, 90 Tottenham Court Road, London W1P 0LP.

Any person who does any unauthorised act in relation to this publication may be liable to criminal prosecution and civil claims for damages.

The authors have asserted their rights to be identified as the authors of this work in accordance with the Copyright, Designs and Patents Act 1988.

First edition 1994
Reprinted 4 times
Second edition 1998

Published by
PALGRAVE
Houndmills, Basingstoke, Hampshire RG21 6XS and
175 Fifth Avenue, New York, N.Y. 10010
Companies and representatives throughout the world

PALGRAVE is the new global academic imprint of
St. Martin's Press LLC Scholarly and Reference Division and
Palgrave Publishers Ltd (formerly Macmillan Press Ltd).

ISBN 0–333–67985–7

This book is printed on paper suitable for recycling and made from fully managed and sustained forest sources.

A catalogue record for this book is available from the British Library.

10   9   8   7   6   5
06   05   04   03   02   01

Copy-edtied and typeset by Povey-Edmondson
Tavistock and Rochdale

Printed in Malaysia

For Matthew (1985–96)

He filled our hearts with love
enriched our lives
and lifted our souls

The first edition of this book was dedicated to our children, Barley, Matthew, Stephanie and Bryony, who endured our obsession with the text for almost a year with a mixture of curiosity and disdain. When we discussed our preoccupation, their response was to ask whether the 'story' was illustrated, whether it featured dramatic tales of dinosaurs or the adventures of pirates, and whether, ultimately, there was a happy ending. Some people say trade unions are industrial dinosaurs and that 'fat cat' managers behave like modernday pirates in pinstripe suits, but figures are not pictures and no matter how hard we tried we could not conjure up a happy ending. Our children, not surprisingly, lost interest.

Shortly after we agreed with Macmillan to write a second edition of the book, Matthew died suddenly and unexpectedly from septicaemia. Words cannot express our love for Matthew nor our sense of loss. There can be no greater suffering for any parent than the death of a child. There can be nothing so incomprehensible to a child than the death of a sibling or close friend. And what do you say to someone who has lost a child? Many of my colleagues have found words and offered their support. My friendship with Paul Blyton is constant in all things. Other friends and colleagues from Cardiff, both past and present, have supported me throughout, and my heartfelt thanks are extended to Rick Delbridge, Tom Keenoy, Miguel Martinez Lucio, Nick Oliver, Michael Poole, Vicki Wass, Syd Weston, and Barry and Julia Wilkinson. Many more comrades deserve special thanks, in particular John Kelly, David Sapsford, Brian Towers and all our friends in Australia. Even when there can be no happy ending, never lose faith in love and friendship.

PETER TURNBULL

Acknowledgements

The authors and publishers wish to thank the following for permission to reproduce copyright material: Blackwell for Figure 4.1 from J. Storey, *Developments in the Management of Human Resources* (1992); Blackwell and *Journal of Management Studies* for Figures 4.2 and 9.2 from J. Purcell and A. Gray, 'Corporate Personnel Departments and the Management of Industrial Relations: Two Cases in Ambiguity' (1986) and I. McLoughlin and S. Gourlay, 'Enterprise without Unions: The Management of Employee Relations in Non-Union Firms' (1992); Prentice-Hall for Figure 4.3 from M. Marchington and P. Parker, *Changing Patterns of Employee Relations* (1990); Blackwell and *British Journal of Industrial Relations* for Figure 5.2 from J. Kelly and E. Heery, 'Full-Time Officers and Trade Union Recruitment' (1989); Organising Works for Figure 5.3 from *Organising Works*, no. 2 (1995); Blackwell and *Industrial Relations Journal* for Figure 9.3 from P. Willman, 'The Logic of "Market-Share" Trade Unionism: Is Membership Decline Inevitable?' (1989); Sage for Table 4.2 from L. D. Goodstein, 'A Case Study in Effective Organizational Change toward High Involvement Management', in D. B. Fishman and C. Cherniss (eds), *The Human Side of Corporate Competitiveness* (1990); Ashgate for Tables 7.1, 7.2, 8.1 and 10.3 from N. Millward *et al.*, *Workplace Industrial Relations in Transition* (1992). Every effort has been made to trace all the copyright-holders, but if any have been inadvertently overlooked the publishers will be pleased to make the necessary arrangement at the first opportunity.

Accession no.
01089588

MANAGEMENT WORK

University of Chester CHESTER CAMPUS
LIBRARY
01244 513301

This book is to be returned on or before the last date stamped
below. Overdue charges will be incurred by the late return of
books.

CANCELLED	- 7 DEC 2007
2 1 NOV 2007 CANCELLED	CANCELLED
1 3 DEC 2007	2 8 NOV 2007

2004

One Week Loan

If you wo
make use
your boo
name and
to begin
have the
publisher
Customei
Houndmi

Other books by the authors include:

P. Blyton and P. Turnbull (eds) *Reassessing Human Resource
Management*
P. Blyton (with A. Dastmalchian and R. Adamson) *The Climate
of Workplace Relations*
P. Blyton (with M. Noon) *The Realities of Work*
P. Turnbull (with C. Woolfson and J. Kelly) *Dock Strike:
Conflict and Restructuring in Britain's Ports*

Contents

Part 4   Summary and conclusions

List of figures

List of tables

Preface to the first edition

When we began the preparation for this book we had two main thoughts in mind. Could we write a book which held students' interest, and could we write one which demonstrated the continuing importance of employee relations in contemporary industrial society? To make the subject-matter more accessible we have leavened the general analysis of trends, themes and issues with a series of seven case studies which depict both the reality of employee relations and the diversity. Employee relations occur wherever people work, be that in a hospital, garage, shop or factory. The cases reflect this diversity. They are drawn from a range of industries and types of employment: from ambulance drivers to steel workers, car workers to shop assistants, dockers to garment makers, TV assemblers to airline flight attendants. They are intended to give a flavour of the way work and employee relations are organised in the public, private and recently privatised sectors, in manufacturing and services, in manual and non-manual activities. Above all, they illustrate that employee relations embraces much more than the world of male-dominated industrial unions seated around the negotiating table with management, or shop stewards threatening to take the rank-and-file out on strike. Employee relations is as much about the 'customer care' programme in the high street retailer or airline as the disputes procedure in an engineering factory, and is as much about the personal relations between management and staff in the small non-union workshop as the formalised union–management relationship in a large company. We hope that the cases will be used as a basis for seminar discussion, to provoke argument and debate. To assist this we have included notes on additional reading for the cases at the end of the book.

In addition to conveying the reality and diversity of employee relations, we have used the cases to introduce each of the themes in the central section of the book, and to draw on them throughout the relevant chapter to illustrate and illuminate our argument. And an argument is what students will find when they read the book. After many years of teaching, researching and writing on employee relations, we have formulated views which we believe it is important to set down. One view of a text is that above all it should be detached, providing information and summarising different arguments, while leaving readers to draw their own conclusions. While we agree that it is important to have balance in any academic work, we also believe that there are some important things to say and lessons to be drawn from the current state of employee relations, not least the continuing importance of those relations in contemporary industrial society.

One recurring theme, for example, is the problem management encounter when seeking to engender a highly committed and a more flexible workforce in a context generally characterised by low trust relations, low productivity and low wages; another is that facing trade unions when attempting to recruit and effectively represent employee interests in a hostile environment. That environment is heavily influenced by the policies of the state, which are also examined in some detail. In many ways the central message from the book is the importance of appreciating the reciprocal nature of employee relations. Within those relations it is essential to recognise the inherent tensions and the way both state and managerial approaches to competitiveness are important in shaping the character and development of employee relations. It is no good management embracing the jargon of 'continuous improvement', 'world-class' manufacturing and 'total quality management', for example, if they are constructed on the shifting sands of low trust, low skill and low wages.

As Britain falters towards greater European integration, and as industry becomes more heterogeneous in its character and ownership, it is a critical time to look at the nature of employee relations, the environment in which they take place and the forces shaping their development. Moreover, in societies where unemployment affects one in ten or more of the working population, where millions of people work not only for wages which do not support a decent standard of living but also in jobs which provide only low-quality work and poor protection, then something is wrong. Throughout the book we have sought to elaborate what the dynamics of employee relations hold for the individual employee, the 'missing subject' of so many texts on management and industrial relations. If we are to appreciate the importance of employee relations in modern society, what better place to start than the reality of people's working lives? If we can elucidate these arguments, hold students' interest as we do so, and encourage them to think more about the breadth of employee relations, the factors that shape those relations and the issues which confront the individual actors taking part, we will be more than satisfied.

Several of the cases stem from more extensive research work the authors have been engaged in, while others developed through a mixture of published accounts and additional fieldwork by one or both of us. Peter Turnbull would like to acknowledge funding from the ESRC for the study of dock-working, while Paul Blyton would like to acknowledge the financial assistance of the Anglo-German Foundation for its funding of a research project on the steel industry. In addition, both authors would like to thank the many managers, union officials and employees who have given freely of their time to provide us with the additional insights which have helped enormously in the writing of the cases. We have also benefited from the helpful and stimulating comments of several colleagues who have read the chapters in draft form, notably Tom Keenoy, Miguel Martinez Lucio, Mike Noon, Chris Rowley and Paul Stewart, together with those from one of the series editors, Mick Marchington. Stephen Rutt at the publishers showed patience with our delays, while Karen Trigg and Pauline Welsh battled gamefully with two sets of handwriting. We also asked our students to read some of the chapters and have learned much from them, not least the need for teachers to convey ideas effectively and to do so in a way which is both lively and stimulating.

June 1993

PAUL BLYTON
PETER TURNBULL

Preface to the second edition

The second edition of *The Dynamics of Employee Relations* has been written at a time of both significance and anticipation for those who teach, research, study or work in the fields of employee relations, human resource management, personnel management and industrial relations. It is a time of great significance because 1997 marked not only the end of eighteen years of Conservative government but the termination of a programme that had sought to reconstitute the very nature of employment relationships in the UK. Anticipation is occasioned by the election of a new Labour government that has likewise placed employee relations at the heart of its agenda, most notably through the introduction of a statutory minimum wage and trade union recognition procedure, a commitment to 'fairness at work', education and training, and the social dimension of European integration. This is, therefore, an opportune time to reflect on the past and review the current state of employee relations.

The first edition took the analysis of employee relations up to 1993. All the case material, statistical data and large sections of the text have been updated to 1997 in this second edition, which incorporates all the most significant research findings in the field since the publication of the first edition. In addition there is a new case study in Chapter 5 on trade union recruitment and organising, reflecting the renewed emphasis on recruitment by the union movement. Most importantly, the opportunity to prepare a second edition has enabled us to refine the argument and incorporate valuable comments from reviewers, colleagues and students who have read the book, debated the cases and dissected our analysis. Nick Bacon and John McGurk deserve particular thanks for their comments on the British Steel and British Airways cases respectively, and Miguel Martinez Lucio and Syd Weston have offered comments and made available several research reports on European Works Councils that have been incorporated in the final chapter. We would also like to thank officials of the T&GWU for sharing their recruitment and organising experiences with us, the Leverhulme Trust for its support of our current research on the European airline industry, and the ESRC for its continued support of Peter Turnbull's research on the port transport industry. Finally, we extend our thanks to Penny Smith for her assistance in preparing the text.

August 1997

PAUL BLYTON
PETER TURNBULL

List of abbreviations

AA	Automobile Association
ABP	Associated British Ports
ACAS	Advisory, Conciliation and Arbitration Service
ACTT	Association of Cinematography, Television and Allied Technicians (now BECTU)
AEEU	Amalgamated Engineering and Electrical Union
AEU	Amalgamated Engineering Union (now AEEU)
APEX	Association of Professional, Executive, Clerical and Computer Staff (now GMB)
ASLEF	Associated Society of Locomotive Engineers and Firemen
ASTMS	Association of Scientific, Technical and Managerial Staffs (now MSF)
BA	British Airways
BBC	British Broadcasting Corporation
BR	British Rail
BECTU	Broadcasting, Entertainment, Cinematograph and Theatre Union
BEA	British European Airways (now BA)
BETA	Broadcasting and Entertainments Trade Alliance (now BECTU)
BIFU	Banking, Insurance and Finance Union
BOAC	British Overseas Airways Corporation (now BA)
BS	British Steel
BSC	British Steel Corporation (now BS)
CAA	Civil Aviation Authority
CBI	Confederation of British Industry
CEGB	Central Electricity Generating Board
COHSE	Confederation of Health Service Employees (now Unison)
CPSA	Civil and Public Services Association
CSEU	Confederation of Shipbuilding and Engineering Unions
CSU	Civil Service Union

CWU	Communication Workers Union
DTI	Department of Trade and Industry
EEF	Engineering Employers' Federation
EETPU	Electrical, Electronic, Telecommunication and Plumbing Union (now AEEU)
EPOS	Electronic Point of Sale
ETUC	European Trade Union Confederation
EU	European Union
EWC	European Works Council
FTO	Full-time (union) official
GCHQ	Government Communications Headquarters
GDP	Gross Domestic Product
GMB	General, Municipal and Boilermakers' Union
GPMU	Graphical, Paper and Media Union
HCU	Hotel and Catering Workers' Union
HMSO	Her Majesty's Stationery Office
HP	Hewlett Packard
HRM	Human Resource Management
IBM	International Business Machines
IRSF	Inland Revenue Staff Federation
ISTC	Iron and Steel Trades Confederation
ITF	International Transport Workers' Federation
JIC	Joint Industrial Council
JIT	Just-in-Time
LFS	Labour Force Survey
LSB	Lump Sum Bonus
M&S	Marks & Spencer
MDHC	Mersey Docks & Harbour Company
MEBO	Management-Employee Buy-Out
MSF	Manufacturing, Science and Finance
NALGO	National and Local Government Officers' Association (now Unison)
NAPE	National Association of Port Employers
NAS/UWT	National Association of Schoolmasters/Union of Women Teachers
NATFHE	National Association of Teachers in Further and Higher Education
NCU	National Communications Union
NDLB	National Dock Labour Board
NDLS	National Dock Labour Scheme
NEDO	National Economic Development Office
NGA	National Graphical Association (now GPMU)
NHS	National Health Service
NUM	National Union of Mineworkers

NUPE	National Union of Public Employees (now Unison)
NUR	National Union of Railwaymen (now RMT)
NUS	National Union of Seamen (now RMT)
NUT	National Union of Teachers
NUTGW	National Union of Tailors and Garment Workers (now GMB)
OECD	Organisation for Economic Cooperation and Development
Offer	Office of Electricity Regulation
Ofwat	Office of Water Services
ONS	Office for National Statistics
OPEC	Organisation of Petroleum Exporting Countries
POEU	Post Office Engineering Union
PTC	Public Services, Tax and Commerce Union
RMT	National Union of Rail, Maritime and Transport Workers
SCELI	Social Change and Economic Life Initiative
SCPS	Society of Civil and Public Servants
SIC	Standard Industrial Classification
SOGAT	Society of Graphical and Allied Trades (now GPMU)
SPC	Statistical Process Control
SBU	Strategic Business Unit
TASS	Technical, Administrative and Supervisory Section (now MSF)
T&GWU	Transport & General Workers' Union
TQM	Total Quality Management
TSB	Trustee Savings Bank
TUC	Trades Union Congress
UCATT	Union of Construction, Allied Trades and Technicians
UCW	Union of Communication Workers
USDAW	Union of Shop, Distributive and Allied Workers
WIRS	Workplace Industrial Relations Survey

PART 1

THE THEORY AND CONTEXT OF EMPLOYEE RELATIONS

Employee relations

Introduction

Our point of departure in writing a book about employee relations can be summarised in a few short statements. First and foremost, work dominates the lives of most men and women. Aside from the domestic sphere, the vast majority of those who work are employees rather than employers. The terms and conditions under which we undertake that work are of central importance to us all. These terms and conditions include both the 'market exchange' that we enter into with an employer and the 'managerial relations' to which all of us are subjected. The former evokes notions of fairness and equity in the remuneration of labour. According to an old Proverb, 'in all labour there is profit', but how much profit should the employer derive from our labour? The latter, managerial relations, are equally important because 'there can be no employment relationship without a power to command and a duty to obey' (Kahn-Freund, 1972:9). We are all concerned about the authority of the employer to direct and (ab)use our labour.

Secondly, the management of employees, both individually and collectively, remains a central feature of organisational life. Despite the competitive gains that may be secured from sources such as product innovation, technological change, and the more efficient utilisation of energy and raw materials, the manner in which (and the terms under which) a workforce performs its functions will normally have a major bearing on the organisation's long-term success. As Alfred Marshall wrote in his *Principles of Economics*, 'the most valuable of all capital is that invested in human beings'. The modern-day versions of this truism, voiced by company directors and personnel managers alike, are that 'employees are our most valuable asset' or that 'people are the key to success' (see, for example, Storey, 1989:2). The significance of the way employees perform their roles is particularly visible in those service-related activities where employees interact directly with the public, the so-called

3

'pink-collar' occupations. However in manufacturing too the social aspects of organisation remain a key feature on which organisational effectiveness turns.

Thirdly, within organisations a common interest between management and workforce cannot be assumed, willed, or 'managed' into existence. On the contrary, the nature of employment relations, and the basic relationship between profit and wages, authority and compliance, creates a persistent (albeit often latent) tension between employers and employed, management and workforce. The objectives of employees at work – be they for income, security, satisfaction, career, companionship – are not synonymous with the objectives of management or company shareholders. It is due to this under- lying tension and potential source of conflict that the management of employ- ee relations remains problematic. Conformity and consent cannot be assumed. In capitalist systems, capital and labour maintain both diverging and conver- ging interests, centred upon interdependence. Interdependence, however, does not equate with common interest.

Finally, it is misguided to assume that developments over the recent past such as the decline in trade union membership, the increased legal circum- scription of industrial conflict and the greater prominence being given to 'human resource' techniques of employee management, signal the demise of the collective aspects of the employment relationship (see Blyton and Turn- bull, 1992). Almost all work in contemporary industrial society is a coopera- tive endeavour. Individuals rarely work in complete isolation, and almost all rely on the work of others to complete their own tasks. Indeed in many work settings the division of labour discerned by Adam Smith in *The Wealth of Nations* more than two centuries ago is even more in evidence today (see Braverman, 1974), creating a 'natural' interdependence and common interest among those who extract raw material from the earth, manufacture goods in the factory, or provide services in the office, shop or bourse. The natural affinity and common interest of work groups are invariably reflected in some form of collective representation and action, usually, though not always, through the medium of trade unions. Even where management seek to foster greater individualism among the workforce, the conflict that is implicit in the relationship between capital and labour cannot be eradicated, nor can the (periodic) expression of that conflict through collective action.

At first sight these 'position' statements, reflecting the basic importance, problematic nature and contemporary significance of employee relations may appear almost too obvious to warrant restating. We believe, however, that the tendency for them to be discarded or overlooked in some of the recent management literature may have led to a misconception about the continuing significance of collective employee relations in contemporary work organisa- tions. Coupled with this conviction about the continuing importance of the subject, we also hold views on the study of employee relations, and particu- larly the place of a core text within that scheme. It may be useful to outline these briefly, for a browse along library shelves and college bookshop displays reveals the presence of a number of other texts in this area. So why another one? One reason is because many previous texts have tended to rely too much on aggregate information: there is an undue focus on overall patterns and trends in the various 'indices' of employee relations, such as the level of trade union membership, the number of strikes or general trends in collective bargaining activity. Clearly such approaches have value – indeed we too will consider such trends. At the same time, at its core employee relations is not about general trends, social aggregates or institutions but about *people*: people interacting with one another, pursuing objectives, reaching agreements, engaging in cooperative and conflictual behaviour. As such an enquiry into the nature of employee relations will be significantly enhanced by examining specific cases as well as general trends and developments.

Many existing texts have sought to do this by reference to the findings of other studies. We feel, however, that this needs to be taken further. The dryness of texts which so many students complain about is not an inevitable or inescapable feature of industrial or employee relations. In some respects the subject has acquired 'a deserved reputation for being dull' (Nichols, 1980:12), but only because it has too often failed to relate in any meaningful way to the reality of people's working lives, how these were formed, how they are constrained and how they might be changed. In important part it is a question of how one approaches the subject. The student is certainly no longer required to enter the field like a botanist, discovering facts and falling back on theory only when the relevant data are unavailable (McCarthy, 1992:2). In fact, from being a subject formerly criticised for its apparent (or at least explicit) absence of theory, there is now an entire literature on different theoretical approaches to the subject (see for example Adams and Meltz, 1993; Dabscheck, 1983; Guille, 1984; and Winchester, 1983b). Theory enables the student to understand and not just appreciate the complexity of the subject, which in reality has few clearly defined boundaries. What is needed, therefore, is a central focus around which to organise ideas, present data and provide an explanation. The focus of this text is the *employment relationship*, which as Fells (1989:471) points out need not be an abstract notion but one of practical significance, being the basis of the parties' own interactions and the relationship upon which all other aspects of employee relations develop.

Even though there are now several routes over the 'mountains of facts' accumulated in the study of industrial and employee relations (Dabscheck, 1983), students nevertheless complain about the scenery *en route*, the way the facts are presented and the balance between the general and the specific. We have sought to overcome this in part by introducing each chapter in the central sections of the book with a case study. The cases have been chosen for the way they encapsulate some aspect of wider developments. They are not meant to signify 'leading edge' or 'best practice' examples of the so-called 'new industrial relations', such as that presented by Wickens (1987) or the examples cited by Bassett (1986). As Kelly (1990:30) points out, the absence from these studies of a theoretical framework means that there is no basis upon which to discern whether the cases cited therein are prototypical or exceptional. Inevitably the cases we present are not, and cannot be, wholly 'typical' of the developments under discussion; single cases alone can rarely convey all aspects of a broader pattern of development. Rather they have been chosen to illustrate, and in many respects exemplify, the way that broader issues operate in practice: to provide a more tangible feel for the various issues of employee relations. At various points in the text of each chapter, therefore, we refer back to and elaborate upon the opening case study to illuminate the argument and ground the analysis in a more concrete setting. Clearly we cannot explain every nuance of the cases or explain them in great detail; to do so would require a separate book for each case. Given that such books or more detailed articles exist, we have sought to write these cases in such a way that they may be used as the basis for separate group discussions, with references to allow further exploration of the cases themselves. To this end we have provided an annotated list of readings and other sources of information at the end of the book to enable readers to examine the cases in greater depth.

One reason why case study material has not figured more prominently in previous texts is no doubt a simple lack of space. Typical conceptions of a text are that it should provide a comprehensive guide to a subject, summarising both its historical development and the different aspects of its current nature. In the present volume, it is true that by devoting a significant amount of space to the case studies, something else has had to be sacrificed in order to keep the book to a reasonable (and readable) size. In this instance it is some of the historical aspects of the subject, which at times are sketched in less detail than we might have wished (although extensive references are provided through-out the text to enable students to explore particular topics in more depth). Our emphasis is more focused on recent and contemporary developments, though at the same time we endeavour to provide sufficient historical context against which to judge the significance of more recent events. It is often said that history casts its shadow forward, so we must understand the past if we are to comprehend to present. The need for at least some historical knowledge of the subject is particularly relevant for those studying the subject in the UK, where the institutions of employee relations did not undergo major reconstruction as occurred in the United States under the New Deal in the 1930s or as in Germany and Japan after the Second World War. In the UK, institutional continuity is much more evident – for example in the structure of trade unions – with the result that a full understanding of the contemporary situation needs some appreciation of its historical roots (see Fox, 1985; Hyman, 1995; Kessler and Bayliss, 1995:1–37; and Ursell and Blyton, 1988).

Before embarking on this investigation, this introductory section needs to address two further questions. First, what do we mean by the term *employee relations* and how does it differ from other expressions applied to workforce management, such as industrial relations, personnel management and the increasingly popular human resource management? Second, why are we concerned with the *dynamics* of employee relations? Over the last two decades, much discussion in the employee relations field has been dominated, implicitly or explicitly, by a debate couched largely in terms of change versus continuity. Although the notion of dynamics is typically used to convey the idea of change, it is important that this does not exclude due consideration of underlying continuities.

Why 'employee relations'?

The title 'The Dynamics of *Employee Relations*', rather than 'The Dynamics of *Industrial Relations*', was chosen for a purpose. In one sense we hardly need to worry about the distinction for neither bears close scrutiny in terms of its literal meaning. Just as Hyman (1992:7) poses the question 'what is an industrial relation?' to highlight the vacuous nature of the actual label, the same question could also be asked of an 'employee relation'. However while some authors use the terms 'industrial relations' and 'employee relations' interchangeably (for example Beardwell, 1996), and while we too should say at the outset that we see no hard and fast distinction between the two, there is nonetheless a tendency for each to place the subject's focus within somewhat different boundaries. In particular industrial relations has, over time, acquired a particular set of meanings both in the sphere of work and among academics researching and teaching the subject (see Dunn, 1993). As Miliband comments, industrial relations is 'the consecrated euphemism for the permanent conflict, now acute, now subdued, between capital and labour' (1969:80). Among the general public and much of the media, the typical view also seems to be that industrial relations is about trade unions and strikes. A popular (mis)conception of industrial relations is that the entire subject can be reduced simply to the Winter of Discontent (1978–9) and the year-long miners' strike of 1984–5 – constituting the zenith and nadir of trade union power – and the subsequent emergence of a new industrial order. Using the term 'employee relations' is a way of circumventing these prior (mis)conceptions about the subject, as well as a device to broaden that set of meanings in the light of significant developments that have occurred since the academic field of industrial relations was first mapped out.

A common criticism of industrial relations enquiry in the past, for example, was that it had too strong a tendency to view the world of work as if composed of unionised male, manual workers, working on a full-time basis. The proletarian stereotype was the muscular male hewing coal, hammering metal or swinging a docker's hook. Industrial relations itself appeared to equate with the institutions of collective bargaining between trade unions and employers in manufacturing and extractive industries. As we illustrate in Chapter 3, however, changes in industrial structure and workforce composition are increasingly making this subset a progressively less accurate index of the overall workforce, not that it ever was so (the UK has never had a majority of its workforce employed in the manufacturing sector). Using the term 'employee relations' represents an acknowledgement that 'industry', as it has been traditionally defined (that is, goods production or manufacturing), is an increasingly less prominent employer of labour (less than one quarter of the workforce are now employed in manufacturing). More than seven out of ten of the UK workforce are now engaged in service sector activities, and the proportion is likely to grow even higher. Reflecting the nature of many service activities, the majority of the workforce are now employed in white-collar jobs in which traditionally their holders have been referred to as 'employees'. Furthermore, almost one half of the employed workforce are female and over one quarter of the workforce are engaged on part-time contracts.

Moreover the majority (approaching seven out of ten) of the workforce do not currently belong to trade unions. While in some sectors these non-members are 'free-riders' (not members of a union but covered by union negotiated terms and conditions), in others – most notably in the private service sector – trade union recognition remains sparse. Yet it is precisely in some of these sectors, where many workers are poorly paid, face health and safety hazards and arbitrary and unjust disciplinary practices, that the need for adequate trade union representation is at its most pressing (see Chapter 9). Hence it is important to incorporate non-union as well as unionised settings into our analysis in a way that only a small number of texts have previously done (e.g. Beaumont, 1990), and more generally to reflect the diverse nature of contemporary work and employment. If nothing else, the analysis of non-union work settings illustrates that the determination of pay and conditions, and the direction of labour at work is not solely achieved through collective bargaining. A feature of employee relations in non-union firms, for example, is their highly personalised nature. Elsewhere, as the study of British Airways in Chapter 4 demonstrates, the control of labour can equally be sought through customer care campaigns: a far cry from the popular image of the 'two sides' confronting each other across the negotiating table, locking the factory gate or manning the picket line.

In the United States, Kaufman (1993) identifies the changing structure of employment, the decline of collective bargaining and the concomitant rise of human resource management as contributing to the 'hollowing out' of industrial relations. Other factors contributing to the difficulties faced by the subject, which are also evident in the UK (Kelly, 1994), include the (deductive) science-building of related disciplines such as labour economics and organisational theory which have 'encroached' on traditional areas of industrial relations research, and equally important the lack of any integrating theory in industrial relations itself. Echoing Kaufman's conclusion that industrial relations must return to the core focus of yesteryear, namely *all* aspects of the employment relationship, Paul Edwards (1995a:40) has argued that, 'In order to survive, industrial relations needs to change its focus to "employment relations", examining not just institutions but how the employment relationship operates in practice, and exploring the outcomes for efficiency and equity'. A concern with efficiency and equity, and in particular the dependence of the former on the latter, is one of the features of our analysis in Part 3 of the various interactions and outcomes in employee relations. More immediately, Chapter 2 presents an integrated theory of the employment relationship that provides the foundation for the entire text.

Although we have forsaken the label 'industrial relations' in favour of 'employee relations', and although we are concerned to include non-union, 'non-traditional' workers in our analysis, it is the *collective* aspects of relations between workforce and management that we take as our focal point. In this, employee relations is distinct from personnel management and human resource management (HRM), though again the distinctions reflect differences of emphasis rather than separate, watertight compartments. Most texts and courses on personnel management and HRM recognise the presence of trade unions, but place their primary focus on the individual at work. Personnel management, for example, focuses principally on the way individuals are selected, recruited, trained, developed, supervised, motivated, rewarded and retrenched. The traditional distinction between personnel management and industrial relations was tolerably clear: the former dealt with individual aspects of the employment relationship while the latter addressed the collective aspects.

In more recent times the distinction between the two fields of study has become rather more blurred as a result of the attention claimed by HRM, particularly since its rise in prominence has coincided (not unconnectedly) with a period of decline in trade union power (for an analysis of HRM see Blyton and Turnbull, 1992; Guest, 1989, 1991; Legge, 1995; and Storey, 1989, 1992). Whilst, as already noted, HRM contains certain 'collectivist' notions, its overall approach has been centred squarely on the individual and the way individuals may be managed to enhance the achievement of broader organisational objectives. Within this perspective, the role of trade unions and collective bargaining tends to be marginalised, and the existence of separate interests scarcely acknowledged, if not ignored altogether. We will seek to demonstrate that while the employment relationship comprises important individual aspects, it is only by recognising the simultaneous existence of collective aspects in the employment relationship that an adequate picture can be constructed of how a workforce is constituted, and the nature of relations between managers and employees. The focus of HRM on the individual, and its general unwillingness to acknowledge the existence of distinct interests within the workplace, has created a picture of simple common interest among managers and managed, an interest supposedly centred solely on the organisation's success in the market place. This is both too narrow and too simplistic an account, reflecting a managerial ideology rather than an objective summary of organisational reality (Blyton and Turnbull, 1992). As such it needs to be countered in order to understand more clearly the dynamics of workplace relations.

The dynamics of change and continuity

An overarching debate within employee relations is whether the developments occurring over the past two decades signal a fundamental change in those relations or whether they remain characterised by an essential continuity. On the one hand, developments such as the decline in trade union membership, changes in workforce composition, the withdrawal by Conservative governments from tripartite discussions with employers and trade unions, the increased legal circumscription of industrial conflict and the rise of managerial approaches less wedded to constitutionalism and collective bargaining, have combined to challenge existing patterns of employee relations. While several of these factors have been present for a much longer period, their coincidence with others during the 1980s is seen by many to have created the conditions for a long-term change in relations between managers and managed. Thus when reviewing the historical evolution of British industrial relations, Hyman (1995:28) notes that from 1979 Conservative governments 'presided over the most radical changes in British industrial relations since the industrial revolution'.

Yet on the other hand, many of the macro-surveys undertaken in the 1980s failed to show any marked change in terms of the institutions of employee relations: the extent to which employers recognise trade union representatives, the existence of joint machinery, and so on (Batstone, 1984; Gallie *et al.*, 1996; Marginson *et al.*, 1988; and Millward and Stevens, 1986). Despite specific examples to the contrary, these surveys indicated that most employers had not used the changed context to dismantle existing institutions of employee relations. Indeed this institutional robustness has encouraged some commentators to argue that employee relations remained essentially intact despite the adverse conditions facing trade unions over this period (e.g. MacInnes, 1987). Even in more recent surveys, where change has been more evident, much of the developments taking place can be accounted for in terms of the changing composition of workplaces (e.g. a decline in the number of very large establishments) rather than a dismantling of established arrangements (Millward *et al.*, 1992). Thus in concluding his review of the historical evolution of British industrial relations, Hyman (1995:48) insists that 'the heritage of the past still exerts a profound influence on contemporary employment relation-ships'. How then can change and continuity be reconciled?

Our own views on this debate can be outlined at two levels. First, in terms of the specifics of the last two decades we would argue that the 'change' and 'continuity' schools of thought may be synthesised: it would seem that while the *form* has broadly remained in the majority of workplaces, the *content* of collective relations has changed. That is, while surveys have revealed the widespread maintenance of structures of union–management relations, the survey method, as Morris and Wood (1991) have pointed out, represents too blunt an instrument to identify the more subtle changes in patterns of influence taking place within those relations (see also McCarthy, 1994). This argument holds that it is at the level of influence, rather than institutional structure, that most change has occurred, with trade union power becoming marginalised in a growing number of decision-making areas, both at the national and the organisational level.

However there is also a second and more general point here. It is a truism that in any field of activity, *all* periods are characterised by elements of change and continuity. Part of the problem in evaluating the respective significance of each, however, is that by their nature changes tend to receive more attention:

> Academic researchers appear to pay more heed to change than continuity: change is widely perceived as more exciting, more newsworthy, more likely to be judged 'relevant' by policy-makers, and probably more appealing to research-funding bodies. The danger in this of course is that, compared to continuity, change comes to be scrutinized disproportionately. Thus in the study of work organization, just as in other areas of social science, warning bells should ring when all the talk is of the new and excludes what remains from before (Dastmalchian *et al.*, 1991:11).

The danger is also that by adopting too short a time scale or too narrow a perspective, any changes taking place mask underlying continuities in atti-tudes and behaviour. In contrast, by adopting a very long view, emphasis is placed on the continuities present, with a danger of overlooking or minimis-ing the significance of periods of change and turbulence. Thus while a focus solely on the 1980s and early 1990s might indicate a period of rapid and marked change in employee relations, a perspective encompassing the entire era of Western capitalism might demonstrate that relations between capital, labour and the state display a high degree of continuity in their basic pattern – a continuity that in part reflects the persistent imperative of capitalism to secure profits.

The need, then, is for a model that adequately encapsulates both continuity and change in the relations between employers and employed. For an insight into how such a model might look, we may usefully draw parallels from a discussion in organisational analysis concerning the way 'time' in organisa-tions may be adequately conceptualised (Burrell, 1992). The issue centres on whether time is best viewed as following a linear, cyclical or some other pattern. Linear time conveys the idea of time as standardised, calculable and invariable, based upon clock time and the overriding notion that time is moving forward in an orderly progression. This view has implicitly informed most of the assumptions behind organisational theory and enquiry. In contrast a cyclical view of time emphasises the way times 'return' upon one another – in the way that day follows night, spring follows winter, tides ebb and flow, and so on. Thus while a linear conception of time places emphasis on change, progress, the short term, the uniqueness of the moment and the finite commodity of time (encapsulated in such sayings as 'time is money', 'buying time' and 'losing time'), the latter stresses continuity, the longer term and the unchanging rhythms of life.

Yet the problem with giving primacy to one of these conceptualisations at the expense of the other is clear: while linear time places undue emphasis on the uniqueness of the moment, cyclical time overemphasises the unchanging nature of things temporal. Whereas the latter view tends to subsume events, in the former view events appear to be almost random. In seeking a way to avoid the limitations of each of these extreme positions whilst at the same time deriving insights from both for the study of organisation, Burrell (1992) develops a third view, based on Filipcova and Filipec's (1986) notion of 'spiral time'. The spiral can incorporate elements of both linear and cyclical time: movement along the spiral involves travelling away from the original point of departure but not in a simple linear fashion. The trajectory also contains cyclical elements or reversal. By combining aspects of progression and return in this way, Burrell argues that spiral time 'breaks free from linear and cyclical patterns with the assumption of the march of progress in the former and that of the overarching repetitive stability of the latter' (1992:169). Burrell uses this notion of spiral time to argue against the assumption that organisational forms simply *progress* from one to another over time in a unilinear fashion. He incorporates this into a case for reevaluating historical developments and the contemporary insights they may provide, once the assumption is dropped that organisational development follows a straight line.

This question of the nature of time and the study of organisations can provide fresh insights for the study of employee relations, and the more satisfactory situating of the 'change versus continuity' arguments that have unfolded over the last decade. While parallels can be drawn between the 'change' lobby and the notion of linear time, the 'continuity' argument has at least some aspects in common with the notion of the cycle. Hence, by similarly adopting the notion of a spiral, we may be equipped with a more adequate metaphor with which to understand the way employee relations are developing – a development that simultaneously displays aspects of change and continuity, progression and reversal. In this way we can avoid the trap of thinking narrowly or having to choose between change *or* continuity as portraying the nature of employee relations in the recent past, present or future. It is the relative strength of each, rather than the presence of one and the absence of the other, that is likely to characterise a particular period. The use of the spiral also allows short- and long-term patterns to be located within the same model – the short term representing a single twist of a longer-term spiral.

Many of the following chapters demonstrate the interplay between change and continuity, between short- and longer-term developments in employee relations. Overall our aim is to identify and analyse the dynamic nature of those relations – both influencing and being influenced by the external environment and the internal work context – and to examine the factors affecting the structures, processes and outcomes of relations between employers and employed. A key objective in this is to elucidate the *core* aspects of workplace relations, thereby equipping students with a framework with which to judge any particular approaches (or fashions) to the (re)structuring of those relations.

To this end the following chapter lays the basis for this enquiry by critically reviewing the utility of the main conceptual approaches taken in the past to employee relations. We advance an argument for a distinct approach to understanding the employment relationship and employee relations that recognises the need to return to basic questions such as: what is the *raison d'être* of firms in capitalist economies? What are management's overall objectives in the organisation? What are their specific objectives in managing labour? What responses are available to employees and their representatives? Recognising that there is no *one* theory of industrial or employee relations, the main purpose of Chapter 2 is to establish a conceptual understanding of the subject by developing an integrated theory of the employment relationship. Any account of social life depends not only upon *what* one looks at but also upon *how* one looks. The 'answers' therefore depend upon the questions asked and the methods by which one 'solves' the questions. Put differently, the theoretical approach one adopts will in large part determine the questions to be asked, the way in which the solution is derived, and ultimately the construction of an answer. The central problematic of employee relations is the 'labour question' – the dual problem of social welfare (providing an adequate standard of living for the working classes) on the one hand, and social order (the regulation of industrial conflict) on the other (Hyman, 1989a:3). Our concern, in other words, is not simply the efficiency of organisations, the control of labour and the resolution of conflict, but also the interests of workers, the conditions of their labour and the remuneration of their effort.

The third chapter of Part 1 identifies the changing contexts in which employee relations are taking place. Of course the state of employee relations cannot simply be 'read off' from the socioeconomic context of a particular time and place, but equally cannot be understood other than in relation to those contexts (see Marchington and Parker, 1990:85). This requires a wide-ranging, though necessarily summary review of developments in product and labour markets, including the changing fortunes of individual sectors, the overall intensification of competition, including that stemming from increased multi-national activity and enlarged trading blocs, the changing character of the public sector along with changes in labour force composition, including the growth in female and part-time employment and the growing heterogeneity of work patterns. In reviewing contextual developments, however, account must be taken not only of the changes in the external environment but also the significance of changes within the workplace itself, including changes in technology and the impact of recent developments in production control techniques such as just in time (JIT) production and total quality management (TQM). In seeking to draw together the implications of changes in internal and external contexts, consideration is given to the extent to which, in contrast to many European economies, a low-cost, low-productivity approach to securing competitive advantage characterises the overall direction of change in the UK, and the implications this has for the character of employee relations.

Part 2 (Chapters 4–6) examines the principal actors in employee relations – management, employees and trade unions, and the state. The three chapters draw on three very different cases – British Airways, the Transport & General Workers' Union, and dockwork – in order to focus on the aims, objectives, strategies and actions of the different parties, especially their ability to exercise control over the other parties to achieve their desired goals. The actual exercise of influence and control is a major underlying theme of the four chapters in Part 3 (Chapters 7–10) on 'Interactions and Outcomes in Employee Relations'. The cases of British Steel, Nissan and Marks & Spencer (together with one of its suppliers) are used to illustrate and assess three different approaches to the (re)structuring of employee relations, based on a decentralisation of bargaining arrangements, the use of non-bargaining forms of involvement (such as quality circles and consultation committees) and the operation of employee relations in the absence of trade union recognition. The final chapter in Part 3 (Chapter 10) examines the theme of industrial conflict, one of the most controversial 'outcomes' of employee relations. The case of the 1989 ambulance workers' dispute is used to illustrate the issue and to highlight important themes such as the growth in industrial conflict in the public sector, the role that the media and public opinion can play in conflict situations and the relationship between different forms of conflict. Finally, in Part 4, we look to the future and examine the increasing influence of European integration on employee relations in the UK. This final chapter also draws together some of the main arguments from earlier chapters and examines the case for a reconstitution of UK employee relations founded upon greater equity, trust and reciprocity; enhanced employment standards, including a decent living wage for all and the right to work in a safe and healthy environment; greater employment security; more shared influence over a broader range of organisational decisions; individual and collective employment rights enshrined in law; and a commitment to developing a more inclusive and extensive system of vocational education and training.

CHAPTER 2

The theory of employee relations

Historical roots

The empirical roots of employee relations enquiry lie in the coincidence at the end of the nineteenth century of the two faces of the 'labour question': the issues of social welfare and social control (Hyman, 1989a:3). The theoretical roots of the subject can be traced principally to the clash between Marxian political economy and the emergent neoclassical economics at around the same time (Marsden, 1982:236–8). In terms of empirical enquiry, the problematic nature of the 'labour question' was epitomised at this time by two significant disputes: the Match Girls' strike of 1888 and the Great London Dock Strike of 1889. At that time, being a match girl 'rated somewhere practically below prostitution in the social scale' (McCarthy, 1988:57–8), their conditions of work dangerous and unpleasant, their pay meagre. The match girls' victory in the 1888 dispute, however, secured with public opinion on their side, had a significance beyond the strike itself. It 'turned a new leaf in Trade Union annals. . . . It was a new experience for the weak to succeed . . . [and] The lesson was not lost on other workers' (Sidney and Beatrice Webb, quoted by Stafford, 1961:79). The following year, the social convulsion sparked by the match girls at Bryant & May's reached the river Thames and the men who worked on the docks and wharves. The dockers' strike became the 'symbol of new unionism' that emerged at the end of the nineteenth century (Clegg *et al.*, 1964:55), not only a great victory for the dockers but a dispute that 'changed the whole face of the Trade Union world' (Webb and Webb, 1920:401). For radicals such as Henry Champion, one of the leaders of the strike, the dispute was won 'despite our socialism' (quoted by McCarthy, 1988:50), but for others, such as Frederick Engels, lifelong companion of Karl Marx, the strike was the movement of the greatest promise we have had for years. . . . If these poor downtrodden men, the dregs of the proletariat, these odds and ends of all trades, fighting every morning at the dock gates for an engagement, if *they* can combine, and terrify by their resolution the mighty Dock Companies, truly then we need not despair of any section of the working class. . . . If the dockers get organised, all other sections will follow. . . . It is a glorious movement (Marx and Engels, 1975:399, original emphasis).

The dockers, like the match girls, had attracted widespread public sympathy and substantial financial donations, due partly to their own efforts during the strike itself but also to the work of social reformers such as Beatrice Potter (later Webb) and Charles Booth, whose *Life and Labour of the People in London* demonstrated to the public and ruling classes alike not only the problems of poverty and degradation among casual workers such as the dockers, but also the wider threat to the stability of society from an 'underclass' deprived of a basic standard of life. The question of social welfare, it appeared, was inseparable from that of social control. Or more precisely, the latter appeared to be largely dependent on the former.

The theoretical origins of the subject can be traced to the 'Achilles Heel' of the emergent neoclassical economics, namely the analysis of labour and labour markets in general and the theory of wage determination in particular. The break between classical economic thought or political economy and neoclassical economics was marked by very different questions being asked about what constituted the subject matter of economics. Classical political economy was concerned, first and foremost, with the conditions that make possible the creation of an economic surplus (or as Adam Smith put it with *The Wealth of Nations*), and in particular how society had been transformed from a situation of subsistence to one of accumulation. Neoclassical economics, in contrast, is concerned with the allocation of scarce resources between competing ends, with questions of supply and demand, pricing and allocation. As a result the focus of economics shifted from the production of wealth to its consumption, from the division of labour and social relations between classes to the market mechanism and individual decision making.

On the question of wages, classical economists such as David Ricardo (1817) had developed 'subsistence' theories to explain the remuneration of human labour. Wages would tend to remain at a level that sustained and reproduced human labour but did not provide that labour with any degree of affluence. Thus, although Ricardo allowed for the influence of 'custom and habit', such that the subsistence wage might increase to reflect what is deemed 'customary' or 'necessary' at any given time (the 'standard of living'), the theory nonetheless presented a rather bleak future for the financial well-being of the working class. Similarly, Marx (1976) too proposed a subsistence theory of wages, but with the added twist of the analysis being grounded explicitly in a theory of capitalism, wherein the wage labourer was subject to exploitation by the employer. Furthermore, even though the subsistence wage might increase over time, Marx put forward the notion of 'absolute impoverishment' for the working class, reflecting the progressive 'deskilling' and 'alienation' of labour. For Marx, workers under capitalism would gradually but inexorably lose control over the process of production, as greater division of labour would create not only unskilled but also highly fragmented work, with workers becoming, as a result, more and more estranged from the product of their labour. At the risk of oversimplification, the working class would thus cease to be a passive class *in itself* and become mobilised into a class *for itself*, ultimately seeking to overthrow capitalism and replace it with socialism.

But what has all this got to do with employee relations? Simply put, neoclassical economics sought to take the 'political' out of political economy by developing a theory of wage determination and income distribution based not on the social relations between classes but on the concepts of marginal productivity and individual choice. According to this new economics, wages were not determined by a (political) power struggle between classes but by the marginal productivity of the worker. To explain the theory, imagine a situation where capital (buildings, machinery, and so on) is in fixed supply and the firm increases the number of workers employed. As more and more workers are engaged there will be less capital per worker, and consequently the output of each additional worker will be less than that of the original workforce. In other words the productivity of each successive employee to be hired (output per worker) will be lower. What matters is not whether total output is increasing but what the *marginal* increase to output is, for according to neoclassical economics it is the productivity of the final worker to be hired that determines the wage. To be sure, the last worker to be engaged adds less output than that created by the original workforce, but more than any future or potential workers because of declining marginal productivity. So if any of the original workforce demanded a higher wage the employer could sack them and engage the marginal worker in their stead. Each and every worker is therefore worth to the employer only what the last (marginal) worker engaged can produce, and so the employer will continue to employ additional workers only up to the point where their cost (wage) is equal to the value of their marginal product. As each and every worker receives a wage equivalent to the amount of wealth he or she creates, there can be no exploitation. In short, the politics has been taken out of political economy, and the socialist movement theoretically defused.

Unfortunately for the new economists, as Alfred Marshall pointed out in his *Principles of Economics*, first published in 1890, marginal productivity is an incomplete theory of wages. In fact it is not a theory of wages at all. Rather it is a theory of labour demand. It tells us how many workers an employer will hire at a given wage in order to maximise profits (suggesting that the higher the wage, the fewer the number of workers that will be employed, and vice versa). But what determines the actual wage that prevails? To complete the picture, the theory of wage determination requires an explanation of the supply side. Again the theory is based on individual decision making, this time the choice made by individual workers between income and leisure. Higher wages, up to a point, will induce workers to work longer hours (or sacrifice more hours of leisure), or alternatively will induce more people of working age to offer themselves for employment. The result is an upward sloping labour supply curve that intersects the downward sloping labour demand curve at what neoclassical economists call the 'market clearing wage' (that is, the wage at which there are neither shortages nor surpluses in the labour market, the wage at which every individual who wants to work can in fact find a job). The problem of wage determination has thus been solved without even a whiff of exploitation or a whisper of power. Or has it?

Even neoclassical economists, for all their heroic assumptions about the labour market, cannot ignore the presence of monopoly, combination and collective action on the part of both employers and employees. If the firm is a monopsonist (single buyer) in the labour market, then neoclassical theory predicts that the firm will pay a lower wage than would prevail in a competitive market. On the other hand, if a trade union is a monopoly (single seller) in the labour market then it will seek a wage above the market clearing rate by restricting the supply of labour. In other words, in a situation of bilateral monopoly there will be no unique 'solution' to the problem of wage determination but rather a *range of indeterminacy* between what the union demands and what the employer is prepared to pay (for a formal exposition see Sapsford, 1981:102–4). In Marshall's words, 'if the employers in any trade act together and so do the employed, the solution to the problem of wages becomes indeterminate . . . there is nothing but bargaining to decide the exact shares in which this [surplus] should go to employers and employed' (1930:627–8). For some neoclassical economists, such as Edgeworth (1881:20), the fact that 'contract without competition is indeterminate' meant that such matters were beyond the scope of economics. Not only had the 'politics' been removed from 'political economy' but the analysis of production, labour relations and social relations more widely were now matters to be left to other disciplines.

One such discipline was industrial relations, arguably founded by Beatrice and Sidney Webb. The Webbs have been credited with being the first to coin the phrase 'collective bargaining', which for many years was the central subject matter of industrial relations. The term itself, however, was clearly derived from Marshall, with whom they agreed 'absolutely in economics' (Marsden, 1982:237). Theoretically therefore, the analysis and study of industrial relations largely grew out of a concern to explain the supply and sale of labour. 'The concern with collective bargaining did not materialize out of thin air, it was given by economics' (Marsden, 1982:238; see also Clegg, 1979a:447). But henceforth it was to be an area of study largely *separate* from economics. As Hugh Clegg (1979a:34) put it, there is 'not much to be gained by looking to economics for a theory of industrial relations if economists have to go outside economics to find an explanation for wage determination'. This separation not only narrowed the field of economics, it effectively forestalled the development of any political economy of industrial relations. Unfortunately, in this separation of industrial relations from economics the work of the earlier classical economists and that of Marx was also ignored, arguably to the detriment of both economics and industrial relations (Brown and Nolan, 1988). A consequence of this was that one of the first explicit 'theories' of industrial relations, developed by the American labour economist John Dunlop (1958), centred on a (largely self-contained) 'system' of industrial relations that was *not* part of a society's economic system but a distinctive subsystem of its own, only partially overlapping the economic and political decision-making systems with which it interacted. The three subsystems themselves were seen to be contained within an overall 'social system'.

The industrial relations system

For Dunlop, heavily influenced by the functionalism of Talcot Parsons (1952) and the core Parsonian question of how the elements of society interacted to produce social continuity, the industrial relations system is seen to be 'comprised of certain actors, certain contexts, an ideology which binds the industrial relations system together and a body of rules created to govern the actors at the workplace' (Dunlop, 1958:7). The actors include a hierarchy of management and their representatives, a hierarchy of non-management employees (workers) and their representatives, and specialised third party agencies such as governmental bodies. The environmental contexts that influence the decisions and actions of the actors include the technological characteristics of the workplace and the nature of the work community, market or budgetary constraints, and the locus and distribution of power in the larger society. Interaction between the parties within different environmental contexts is governed, in large part, by an ideology or common set of beliefs that 'defines the role and place of each actor and that defines the ideas which each actor holds towards the place and function of others in the system' (ibid:16). But the definition of industrial relations as 'the complex of inter-relations among managers, workers and agencies of government' (ibid:v), as Marsden (1982:239) notes, was quickly and quietly switched to the formation and maintenance of the *rules* of the system: 'The central task of a theory of industrial relations is to explain why particular rules are established in particular industrial relations systems and how and why they change in response to changes affecting this system' (Dunlop, 1958:ix).

At one level, systems theory might be viewed as a useful means of classifying variables relevant to industrial relations, but it is hardly an explanatory approach in its own right. If anything, it is 'more a set of questions than a theoretical statement' (Strauss and Feuille, 1978:267). Indeed both theoretical and substantive criticisms of Dunlop's model abound (for a review see Poole, 1981). As Poole (1988:13) in a later discussion argues, the relationship between variables in the framework are assumed to be interlocking and interactive, which runs counter to genuine explanatory analysis: it is very difficult to disentangle central from peripheral variables, to identify causal sequences, to isolate independent variables, and to attach explanatory weights to such variables. At best systems analysis is a *description* of industrial relations, not a theory, an abstraction from the 'known facts' arranged into a coherent model or system (Marsden, 1982:239). More importantly, the very notion of a 'system' of industrial relations implies a functional integration of component institutions (Hyman, 1992:7), especially when a common ideology amongst the actors is assumed. When combined with a focus on rules, the implication is that 'what industrial relations is all about is the maintenance of stability and regularity in industry' (Hyman, 1975:11). While subsequent expositions of systems theory (e.g. Craig, 1986) have considerably elaborated Dunlop's original schema, introducing a far more extensive range of variables and a greater awareness of feedback relationships between variables over time, the emphasis on order and stability remains. Only in those models that cast conflict as a possible *outcome* of relations rather than simply a temporary aberration en route to agreed rules are there signs of a move away from functionalist assumptions of order and stability (see, for example, Dastmalchian et al., 1991:43–6).

The influence of Dunlop's systems analysis and the focus on stability and order in the study of industrial and employee relations is clearly evident in the work of prominent UK academics in the field, most notably Allan Flanders, Hugh Clegg and (the early work of) Alan Fox, often referred to collectively as the 'Oxford School':

> Economics deals with a system of markets, politics with a system of government . . . a system of industrial relations is a system of rules. These rules appear in different guises: in legislation and in statutory orders; in trade union regulations; in collective agreements and in arbitration awards; in social conventions; in management decisions; and in accepted 'custom and practice'. This list is by no means exhaustive, but 'rules' is the only generic description that can be given to these various instruments of regulation. In other words, the subject deals with certain regulated or institutionalised relationships in industry (Flanders, 1965:9–10).

Similarly Hugh Clegg (1979a:1) argues that industrial relations 'is the study of the rules governing employment, together with the ways in which the rules are made and changed, interpreted and administered'. The rules themselves 'cannot be understood apart from the organizations that take part in the process', namely trade unions, employers' associations and government/ public bodies, and 'each of these organizations has its own sources of authority' (ibid:1). As a result, rules can be made jointly (through collective bargaining or custom and practice) or unilaterally (through managerial prerogative, trade union regulation or statutory imposition). But to define industrial relations as 'a study of the institutions of job regulation' (Flanders, 1965:10) is to conceive the subject in terms of relationships between agencies rather than between people, to ignore the real, active men and women whose activities *are* industrial and employee relations (Hyman, 1975:13; and Nichols, 1980:12). And there remains the overriding concern with the 'problem of order', diverting attention away from the structures of power within the workplace and beyond. In sum, such a focus has relegated the problem of social welfare to the periphery, 'while the preoccupation with job regulation brought the problem of control to the centre of the agenda' (Hyman, 1989a:8).

Unsurprisingly industrial relations became problem focused, issue driven and policy orientated (see Strauss and Feuille, 1978). In the UK this was reinforced in the 1960s by governments identifying industrial relations as a 'problem', contributing to low productivity and increasing strike activity. This placed an emphasis on the practical need to study industrial relations institutions in order to recommend policy reform. The role of industrial relations academics in this was epitomised by many of the contributions to the Royal Commission on Trade Unions and Employers' Associations (Donovan, 1968), and in particular in most of the research papers written to inform that Commission.

Research on the subject was thus predominantly empirical, characterised by the aphorism attributed to the Oxford School of 'a pound of facts and an ounce of theory' (Cappelli, 1985b:91). To study industrial relations was to be a detective, for as Sir Arthur Conan Doyle wrote in *The Memoirs of Sherlock Holmes*, 'it is a capital mistake to theorize before one has data'. Hugh Clegg made this orientation quite clear in his book on *The Changing System of Industrial Relations in Great Britain*. Having described 'what appear to be the main elements of, and developments in, British industrial relations', it is 'only after that have explanations been offered – where they were available, and as they seemed to fit in' (1979a:446). The question of theory was in fact left until the final chapter of his book, the reader having been presented with the option in the introduction of reading the final chapter either first or last – for Clegg it made no difference.

Methodologically, the approach of the Oxford School, and indeed industrial relations research dating from the Webbs (Brown and Wright, 1994:155–8), can be characterised as essentially one of induction, where 'theories or rules are suggested by behaviour in specific examples and are used to make inferences about the general case' (Cappelli, 1985b:91). The classic example of this approach was Allan Flanders' (1964) investigation of *The Fawley Productivity Agreements*, a single case study that suggested the structure of collective bargaining could have a powerful influence on the conduct of industrial relations at the plant level, and on the behaviour of management and trade unions. This analysis, and the prescription that followed, was then extended to much of British industry in the form of 'productivity bargaining'. But as Cappelli warns, the inferences generated by induction do not follow logically or necessarily from the phenomena to be explained. They are 'at best probable explanations that must be supported by empirical arguments in order to be judged reasonable' (1985b:91). Empiricism is therefore perpetuated, but more importantly there is a tendency for any general laws to come from the same level of analysis that is employed, which in turn is largely determined by the questions being asked. Put differently, if the focus is the 'institutions of job regulation', an inductive theory will place heavy emphasis on institutional detail, frequently to the detriment of other levels of analysis or explanatory variables, consequently leading to an emphasis on order rather than disorder in employee relations.

An important illustration of the shortcomings of this approach was the work of the Donovan Commission (Donovan, 1968) which, as already noted, was heavily influenced by the Oxford School. Prior to the Royal Commission it was widely believed that Britain had only a single system of industrial relations, based on a formal system of collective bargaining between trade unions and employers' associations, conducted largely at the national level (see for example Flanders and Clegg, 1954). The reality proved to be somewhat different, but rather than abandon the idea of an industrial relations system the Royal Commission's approach was to describe an additional one, an informal system of negotiations involving workers, shop stewards and management at the workplace level. The prognosis was that the informal system was in conflict with the formal system, or more precisely that the former had undermined the stability of the latter. But to say that the formal and informal systems were in conflict was 'equivalent to saying that systems theory cannot explain reality, fact is in conflict with reality' (Marsden, 1982:242). In order to maintain the integrity of the system, the Donovan prescription was inevitably to bring about closer integration of component institutions in order to curtail 'disorder'. More elaborate, formalised, systematic procedures at the local level were deemed necessary, as were stronger industrial relations management and a closer integration of shop stewards into (official) trade union structures. These recommendations not only reflected the failure of systems theory to adequately explain the problems of UK industrial relations, but also highlighted the hold that the pluralist perspective, as propounded by the members of the Oxford School, had gained.

Pluralism and industrial relations orthodoxy

Pluralism is far from being a homogeneous body of analysis and prescription (see Hyman, 1978 for a discussion), but the central tenets of the dominant influence in UK industrial relations enquiry – what might be termed 'institutional pluralism' – can be briefly stated. Organisations are viewed as 'a miniature democratic state composed of sectional groups with divergent interests over which the government tries to maintain some kind of dynamic equilibrium' (Fox, 1966:2). Recognising the reality of separate interests within industry, and the legitimacy of their organised expression, pluralists argue that from the organisation of competing interests will develop a stable 'negotiated order'. In other words, conflict is accepted as both inevitable and legitimate within any organisation, but the dominant preoccupation of pluralists is with establishing structures and procedures within which those legitimate conflicts of interest can be contained and prevented from damaging the interests of all. As Brown (1988:49) notes, this 'institutionalisation of conflict' requires a recognition of both the existence and legitimacy of conflicting interests; the effective representation of those interests; some flexibility of objectives and central direction of policy; a climate where sectional interests can be realised; a semblance of power balance between the parties; and, as a second line of institutional defence, a system of mediation and arbitration. In short, not only must management be prepared to *recognise* and *accept* a conflict of interests with their workforce, but be prepared to *negotiate* with (strong) trade unions in a climate of 'give-and-take'.

Pluralism is usually contrasted with unitarism, where the organisation is viewed as a team 'unified by a common purpose' (Fox, 1966:2), namely the success of the organisation. With a single source of authority (management) and all participants sharing the same goal, harmony and cooperation are the predicted outcomes. For unitarists, conflict is not inevitable but pathological, the outcome of misunderstanding or mischief. Either management has failed to communicate its goals effectively, causing temporary friction until the message 'gets home', or there must be troublemakers deliberately stirring up problems where none would otherwise exist. Writing in the mid 1960s, Fox held that unitarism 'has long since been abandoned by most social scientists as incongruent with reality and useless for the purpose of analysis' (1966:4), but the view is still widely held by many UK managers (Poole *et al.*, 1981:82–3; and Poole and Mansfield, 1992, 1993) and underpins many of the recent developments encapsulated in the term 'human resource management' (see Blyton and Turnbull, 1992). Consequently unitarism 'is not simply to be dismissed. It is important to try to understand why "practitioners" hold the views that they do instead of treating them as wrong' (Edwards, 1986:20–1). But then we must treat unitarism as a *perspective* rather than a theory. The same can be said of pluralism.

Although pluralists recognise that there is an imbalance of power within organisations and that no single interest group will be able to dominate totally all other interest groups, when it comes to employee relations, where there are effectively only two parties (management and labour), there is nonetheless a tendency to assume (at least implicitly, if not explicitly) that an approximate balance of power exists, with the state acting as a neutral referee. As a result, many pluralists very quickly move from a statement that conflict is natural, rational and inevitable to an assessment of how conflict is organised, channelled and ultimately 'managed'. In other words the pluralist approach 'does not tackle the problem of the nature or the basis of conflict, and merely concentrates on what happens when organizational expressions of conflict have already been articulated' (Edwards, 1986:24). Thus the focus is on the *resolution* of conflict rather than its *generation*, or in the words of the pluralist on 'the institutions of job regulation'. This in turn 'encourages a segregation of "industrial relations" as an area of analysis from the underlying social relations of production, and hence facilitates an uncritical orientation towards managerial priorities of cost-effectiveness and technical rationality' (Hyman, 1978:35). Thus issues of social control tend to predominate over those of social welfare.

Furthermore, by asserting the autonomy of industrial relations (ibid:20) and rejecting existing theories derived from the social sciences in favour of an inductive approach (Bain and Clegg, 1974:107), pluralist industrial relations has simply replicated many of the problems of systems analysis. There cannot be a coherent theory of industrial relations when almost every situation is believed or portrayed to be a special case, inexplicable by existing laws and therefore requiring detailed empirical, institutional analysis. For it is a truism, not a theory, that conflict is inevitable. Pluralism offers no comprehensive explanation for such conflicts, beyond acknowledging that different interests prevail in the workplace. In fact, by failing to elaborate the bases of conflict within organisations, pluralism serves more to mystify than to illuminate. As Richard Hyman has argued,

> understanding would be better assisted by a radically different approach: a sensitivity to the contradictory dynamics of capitalist production, the antagonistic structure of material interests within the labour market and the labour process, and the consequent and persistent generation of conflict and disorder within the very institutions and procedures designed to bring order and stability to employer–employee relationships (1978:35).

Hyman is one of a number of Marxist theorists who have posed broader questions about the nature of the employment relationship, and in so doing have rejected the accepted orthodoxy of British industrial relations and its tacit support for the *status quo*.

Marxism and the issues of control and resistance

Just as there is no homogeneous body of pluralist thought, the same is true of Marxist analysis. In particular, because Marxism became a movement, there has been a tendency to focus on the political agenda derived from Marx's writings, rather than what he contributed to our understanding of society. As capitalism has not been superseded by socialism, many writers assume this to be sufficient to dismiss Marxist thought outright. Thus, Farnham and Pimlott (1990:16–17) write,

> To Marxists, industrial relations are essentially politicized and part of the class struggle . . . the Marxist stress on the inevitable and polarized class struggle in industry and society between capitalist and proletariat, whilst probably a valid interpretation of nineteenth-century Victorian capitalism, does little to explain the complex, economic and social conflicts of late twentieth-century Britain.

However this is to miss the point and to ignore the insights that can be derived from Marx's analysis of the nature of capitalism, and how these illuminate aspects of the relationship between employers and employed. To focus on the Marxist *movement* rather than Marxist *thought*, and to reject the theory out of hand (as Farnham and Pimlott seem to advocate), is to throw the baby out with the bath water. If nothing else,

> the major contribution of Marxists has been as much in the questions asked as in the answers given or the methods of their attainment. It is the framework of what is taken for granted or what is regarded as problematic that most clearly differentiates Marxists from conventional 'industrial relations' analysts (Hyman, 1989a:128).

For Marxists, industrial and employee relations can *only* be understood as part of a broader analysis of (capitalist) society, in particular the social relations of production and the dynamics of capital accumulation (Hyman, 1994:171). That is why, strictly speaking, there can be no such thing as a Marxist 'theory' of industrial relations: the project is a contradiction in terms (Marsden, 1982:245). As Hyman notes, for Marxists 'the activities of employers and unions are to be construed in terms of such concepts as relations of production and class struggle; the term "industrial relations" is at worst vacuous and at best incoherent' (1989a:124). What Marxian analysis offers is a different perspective from which to understand society, a theoretical approach that emphasises totality, change, contradiction and practice (Hyman, 1975:4). Totality reflects the idea that all social phenomena are interrelated, and that no one area can be analysed satisfactorily in isolation. Unlike systems analysis, however, Marxists not only seek to construct a political economy of industrial relations, in which industrial relations are *integrated with* and not *separated from* the political and economic spheres, but also to assign causal priority to the social relations of production – that is, 'the way in which economic activity is organised in any society' (ibid). In other words the material, productive base of society will shape political institutions, legislation, modes of thought and even the nature of the family. As Marx himself put it, 'the mode of production in material life determines the general character of the social, political and spiritual processes of life' (1972:11). Furthermore an emphasis on stability is rejected in favour of change and contradiction. Social relations are judged to be not only dynamic but also characterised by the opposing interests of different classes. These contradictions present opportunities for change, but actual changes reflect the choices made by the different actors – what Marx referred to as praxis. In Marxist analysis the material features of social life, especially the economics of production, limit the possibilities available for the organisation of human existence, but do not determine behaviour. A dialectical, not a deterministic process takes place.

It is this broader approach to the study of employment relations that most usefully distinguishes Marxism from systems theory, pluralism and unitarism, and it is through this approach that Marxists have sought to dig beneath the surface elements of employee relations such as collective bargaining, management decision making, legislation, trade union regulations and workplace custom and practice. Thus in contrast to any implicit or explicit assumptions about a balance of power in industry, Marxists emphasise the *asymmetry* of power between employer and employee, derived primarily from the ownership or non-ownership of capital. That is, at the most basic level an employer is able to survive longer without labour than the employee can survive without work. Of course the employee has a degree of freedom to choose for which employer he or she wishes to work, but as Marglin (1974:37) points out, 'it is a strange logic of choice that places its entire emphasis on the absence of legal compulsion'. The employee, by definition, must sell his or her ability to work in order to subsist.

Ownership acts as a source of power and control, bestowing on employers not only the 'right' to hire and fire labour but also to direct that labour in the process of production. Moreover if employers can convince employees that they not only have a legitimate (property) right to control certain decisions but also a moral right or duty, they exercise not only power but authority (see Gospel and Palmer, 1993:189–97). For Marxists, the exercise of power and the achievement of authority is a key dynamic in all employment relationships, because the employer can never secure total control or achieve complete authority. The capacity to work may be bought and sold in a (labour) market like any other commodity, but the object that is sold (the mental and physical capabilities of individuals) cannot be separated from the subject of the actual exchange (the individuals themselves). When the employee agrees to work for so many hours per week at a given wage, that is not the end of the matter but the start. Unlike other 'factors of production', the precise nature of the labour input, or more accurately the precise tasks the worker is expected to perform, both in a quantitative and qualitative sense, can never be perfectly specified in advance by the employer. The labour input involves 'a continuous bargain every day and hour, renewed either in the prices that are to be paid or the amount of product that the worker turns out' (Commons, 1919:24). The 'wage–effort bargain' is therefore contended and in a continuous state of flux, 'an invisible frontier of control . . . which is defined and redefined in a *continuous* process of pressure and counterpressure, conflict and accommodation, overt and tacit struggle' (Hyman, 1975:26, original emphasis). For Marxists, then, the 'negotiation of order' is an unceasing power struggle between capital and labour: the frontier of control, at any point of time, 'represents a compromise unsatisfactory to *both* parties' (ibid:27, original emphasis).

Since first elaborated against the backcloth of nineteenth century capitalism, many subsequent events have challenged aspects of Marx's anticipated development of capitalist society. For example the growth of a substantial proportion of the labour force occupying 'intermediate' positions in the occupational structure – administrative, middle managerial and professional positions, for example – is not easy to square with Marx's prediction of the general polarisation of the two principle classes within capitalism. Moreover, because much of Marx's analysis was directed at the societal level – identifying the basic nature of capitalism and the sources of its instability – in practice the concepts that he developed have often proved to be somewhat blunt instruments for analysts seeking to understand the nature of employment relations within different work contexts. Even at the societal level it must be acknowledged that Marx's analysis was developed in the context of 'competitive capitalism', whereas today we live in an age more appropriately characterised as 'monopoly capitalism'.

Nevertheless it is the questions that the Marxian analysis poses, and the situating of employee relations within a broader conceptual framework, that represents its significance to contemporary enquiry. With its emphasis on the 'unceasing power struggle' between capital and labour, it follows that 'industrial relations is the study of *processes of control over work relations*' (Hyman, 1975:12, original emphasis), both inside the workplace and beyond. But the distinctiveness of this definition, and that of the Marxist approach to the subject, is often lost. Clegg (1979a:450–2), for example, tries to play down the differences between Marxism and pluralism in both a literary and a theoretical sense. By contrasting the definitions of Flanders ('the institutions of job regulation') and Hyman ('the processes of control over work relations'), Clegg concludes that:

> 'Job regulation' is to be preferred *for its greater elegance and precision*, but if students of industrial relations had to rub along with 'processes of control over work relations' they would probably manage fairly well. (ibid:452, emphasis added).

In terms of their theoretical approach, Clegg suggests that since both are concerned with conflict and stability, and as both regard conflict as inevitable and seek to explain how it is contained, students adopting either approach 'will come to much the same conclusions at the end of the day' (ibid:452). The divergence, if any, is 'to be found mainly in their attitudes' (ibid:455). Here again, therefore, we are back to a focus on Marxism as a movement rather than a theory. Not only is this a misrepresentation of the different theoretical approaches to the subject, it presents a persistent and significant source of confusion for students. This confusion is compounded by the tendency to draw on different elements of the various perspectives in a generally *ad hoc* manner, resulting in a lack of theoretical coherence and clarity. Coherence is essential if we are to traverse successfully the 'mountains of facts' and penetrate beneath the surface of the day-to-day activities that make up the practice of industrial and employee relations.

A theory of employee relations

Industrial relations has always been a specialist area of study. From its origins in the late nineteenth century it has been studied predominantly as a separate, autonomous area of material life. But as the industrial relations 'system' in Britain was seen to disintegrate in the 1960s it was necessary to cast the subject's net more widely, to incorporate the informal as well as the formal processes of industrial relations. Pluralists suggested that Britain now had two systems of industrial relations, but following the dramatic changes of the 1970s and especially the 1980s (as outlined in the following chapter), very few commentators would insist that there are two identifiable systems in Britain today, let alone one. Just as the boundaries and content of the subject changed in response to events and circumstances, it also responded to theoretical criticism. Indeed the very term 'industrial relations' has been brought into question, as have the underlying assumptions that inform much of the research and teaching in the area (see for example Edwards, 1995a:40). Using terms such as employee relations rather than industrial relations reflects a redrawing of the boundaries of the subject to include *all* employment relationships, rather than just those involving unionised male, manual workers in manufacturing, and also a change in the underlying assumptions that now inform theoretical perspectives on the subject. Thus it is possible to discern a growing tendency to focus on and define the distinctive characteristics of the *employment relationship*; to locate that relationship within the broader *nature of economic activity*; to analyse the *structural bases* of conflict and accommodation between employer and employee; to consider the influence of the *wider society*; and to develop an *interdisciplinary approach* using concepts and ideas derived from sociology, economics, psychology, history and political science.

It has become commonplace, for example, for academics in the field to argue that the jurisdiction of industrial and employee relations embraces 'all aspects of the employment relationship' (Strauss and Feuille, 1978:275; see also Fells, 1989; and Kaufman, 1993). Strauss and Feuille (1978:275) go on to argue, however, that this is much too broad because the 'employment relationship' encompasses such diverse fields as selection and testing, health and safety, equal employment rules, career paths, government labor market programs, and the entire field of organizational behavior. Pulling this conglomeration together under a single head would be intellectually meaningless.

But this would only be the case if research followed the traditionally empirical, inductive approach of earlier generations of writers. As it is impossible to ignore these diverse factors, the question becomes how to order, prioritise and understand such a complex range of variables, rather than how to limit the subject to a manageable range of analysis. In other words, having defined the boundaries of the subject it is necessary to assign priority to particular variables or relationships, to identify causal links and to produce (testable) hypotheses.

To focus on the employment relationship has the advantage of homing-in on the (material) basis of the interaction between employer and employee, and the relationship from which all other aspects of employee relations stem. As already noted, to focus on a system of rules or the institutions of job regulation is to ignore the foundations underpinning such rules and regulations in the sphere of production, to run before one has learned to walk (and without an adequate map of which direction to run). So what is the nature of the employment relationship? What do management and workers seek from such a relationship? And how does each party attempt to achieve its goals?

At its most basic level, every employment relationship is an *economic exchange*, an agreement between employer and employee over the latter's capacity to work (commonly referred to as labour power). But the employment relationship is also a *power relationship* as the worker, by virtue of being an employee, agrees to submit to the authority and direction of the employer. The exchange of labour power is therefore unlike that of any other 'commodity'. As Brown (1988:55–7) points out, the employment relationship is a *continuous relationship*, not a 'one off' exchange; the employment contract itself is *open ended*, in that the wage might be agreed in advance, but effort is not and cannot be specified explicitly or exactly; the employment relationship is necessarily an *authority relationship* between super- and subordinate, where the employee agrees to accept and follow the 'reasonable' instructions of those in positions of authority; the parties are *interdependent*, creating patterns of both conflict and cooperation; but the employer is in possession of greater power resources than the employee, creating an *asymmetrical* relationship between the parties. Each of these points warrants further elaboration as they provide the foundations upon which a theory of employee relations can be built.

The demand for labour, to borrow a term from economics, is a 'derived demand' because the employer is not interested in labour *per se* but in the contribution of the employee to the production of goods and services. In other words the employer has no interest in the talents and needs of the employee unless they are useful in the process of production. But what the employer purchases in the labour market is the *capacity* of men and women to work (labour power), whereas what the employer is actually interested in is the *performance* of work (physical, mental and in many cases emotional labour). As Edwards (1986:35) notes, 'in the labour contract what the employer wants is not a capacity but its exercise'. This creates an on-going relationship between the parties, but also a pattern of conflict and accommodation because while the wage may be agreed the level of effort is not. Even if employees are paid by the piece, their diligence and/or the quality of the product is invariably difficult, if not impossible, to specify precisely in advance.

Conflict will thus emerge from the 'exploitation' of labour, but as Edwards (ibid:31–2) argues, exploitation does not exist solely because the employer takes part of the product but also because of the way the product is actually produced. As already noted, the employer hires the mental and physical attributes of employees, not the employees themselves. In effect labour bears no market price, because it is *labour time* and not work itself that is purchased. Put differently, paid working time is not necessarily equivalent to time worked. What determines efficiency (and profitability) is not simply the (technical) combination of different 'factors of production' but also the degree of congruence between potential and performed labour. Since in large part, the latter depends on the power and authority of the employer over the employee, firms can be expected to organise work in a way that reproduces the authority and control of capital over labour (Bowles, 1985; Gordon, 1976; and Marglin, 1974). This may result in, for example, improvements in productivity being sought in changes that involve work intensification, the subdivision of operations, the deskilling of jobs and outright job losses, all of which are likely to invoke worker and/or trade union opposition (Turnbull, 1991c:141). Employees may submit to the authority of the employer but will always retain a very strong interest in the (ab)use of their labour. Indeed the study of work group behaviour shows how workers combine and cooperate with each other not only to bargain over wages and working conditions but also to control or influence the pace of work, to create meaning in otherwise alienating work processes, and to protect themselves not just from 'overwork' but particularly from 'unremunerated overwork' (Turnbull, 1988b:101). Thus the use of labour power within the process of production encapsulates within it important sources of potential conflict (see Edwards, 1986:35).

The task of management in this process is not to hope or assume that worker and union interests coincide with those of their own, but rather to structure workplace relations in the manner that is most conducive to the attainment of higher productivity, lower unit costs and improved profitability (Turnbull, 1991c:141). Those holding a unitary perspective of work relations simply assume that the only goal of the employee is furthering the profits of the firm, such that management need only apprise the worker of the 'needs' of the organisation to elicit worker cooperation and optimum performance.

Pluralists, while accepting a 'conflict of interest' between the parties, do not explore the material base of those conflicts. Clearly, what distinguishes the employment relationship from other types of exchange is 'the attempt by employers to reconcile . . . two problems – of securing workers' cooperation and a surplus product' (Nolan, 1983:303). It is in this respect that the concept of interdependence plays a crucial role. The interests of capital may dominate the organisation of work, and employers will hold the balance of power in any employment relationship by virtue of their ownership of capital and the authority this imparts. But ultimately it is the workforce that actually performs the detailed activities of the work process. Even unskilled workers hold the power to frustrate the efficiency and profitability of the organisation by failing to cooperate actively in the work process. The required level of cooperation needs to go beyond mere compliance with rules if work is to be performed efficiently. Indeed a common form of worker insubordination is 'working to rule', whereby employees are able to undermine the manufacturing process or the quality of service provided merely by doing exactly and precisely what is (officially) required, rather than exercising a level of discretion not covered by the rules. Essentially then, management want workers to follow the spirit, not the letter of the rules. Employers cannot rely on coercion or even compliance to secure high performance; they also need to secure active employee consent and cooperation.

Power is typically understood as the ability of one party to compel another party to do something they otherwise would not undertake of their own volition. In the employment relationship, employers seek to enjoin and entice workers to comply with their demands and cooperate with their instructions. To do otherwise would run the risk of overt conflict between capital and labour. For their part, one reason why workers do not simply resist management control is that they identify with and define themselves in relation to their work. The fact that many people seek intrinsic reward from their work indicates that there is likely to be at least a latent degree of cooperation with management. The nature of the employment relationship, then, is not simply one of (management) control *versus* (worker) resistance, but a more problematic mix of dissent and accommodation, conflict and cooperation. In the past, one of the major criticisms of industrial relations research, and in particular the juxtaposition between pluralism and Marxism, was that 'industrial relations writings, overall, seems polarized around the two problematics of "how is order achieved" and "why is disorder not rampant"' (Guille, 1984:486). But in reality

> It is not a matter of employers gaining what workers lose, or vice versa, but of the coming together of the two sides in a relationship which is inherently contradictory: employers need workers' creative capacities, but cannot give them free rein because of the need to secure a surplus and to maintain a degree of general control; and workers, although subordinate, do not simply resist the application of managerial control (Edwards, 1986:6).

It is these features of the employment relationship – the creation of an economic surplus, the coexistence of conflict and cooperation, the indeterminate nature of the exchange relationship and the asymmetry of power – not the institutions of trade unions, employers' associations or government agencies, that makes the subject matter of employee relations distinctive. The activities of institutions, such as collective bargaining or other 'rule-making' processes, in fact *arise from* the employment relationship and cannot be understood in isolation from it. Thus trade union activity is first and foremost the organised expression of the grievances, deprivations and wider interests of employees that arise from their (subordinate) role in the process of production or the provision of services. Given the asymmetry of power that exists, collective action is invariably essential if employee interests are to be represented effectively. Likewise the need for management control derives from the tensions that exist between employer and employee within the employment relationship, giving rise to the development of a variety of control strategies. These activities can be grounded in a theory of the employment relationship, which has the added advantage of accommodating both sides of the labour question, namely the achievement of social welfare on the one hand, and social control on the other.

Having emphasised the distinctive nature of the employment relationship and the process of production, it is also important to acknowledge that the employment relationship does not take place in isolation. What occurs in the workplace is also influenced by the wider society. Indeed it is a maxim of industrial sociology that to understand what goes on inside the workplace it is also necessary to look at what goes on outside it, to consider such factors as the structure of power in society, the nature of communities and the degree of occupational solidarity (Lockwood, 1966). The labour forthcoming from a worker depends, in addition to biology and skills, on such factors as states of consciousness, degrees of solidarity with other workers, labour market conditions, and other societal influences such as schooling, welfare provisions and family life (see Gintis, 1976; and Lazonick, 1978). Thus workers 'learn to labour' (Willis, 1977) and generally enter the workplace with a 'work ethic', a respect for private property and a general willingness to accept authority:

> explaining the nature of the employment relationship necessarily involves considering the culture, the values and norms of the wider society and the institutional arrangements which ensure that appropriate normative obligations are internalized, and developed and reinforced by each generation (Brown, 1988:61).

In short, social attitudes and socialisation play an integral, not an accidental role in shaping the relationship between employers and employees (Lazonick, 1978:5).

This framework of analysis is set out in a simplified form in Figure 2.1. As illustrated, the core of our analysis is the employment relationship. At the most general level, the nature of economic activity has a direct bearing on the essential structure of this relationship: the ownership or non-ownership of capital gives rise to an authority relationship characterised by hierarchy and control. But this cannot be achieved simply by using the coercive power that ownership imparts. Thus in order for management to achieve their objectives they must secure the cooperation and consent of the workforce. The outcome is one of struggle and accommodation, as those employed seek to improve the wages and general conditions of their employment. The end result is the many and varied employment relationships that we observe in the real world. Again, however, interaction is a dialectic rather than a deterministic process, as indicated by the influences (arrows) in Figure 2.1 flowing out from, as well as into, the employment relationship.

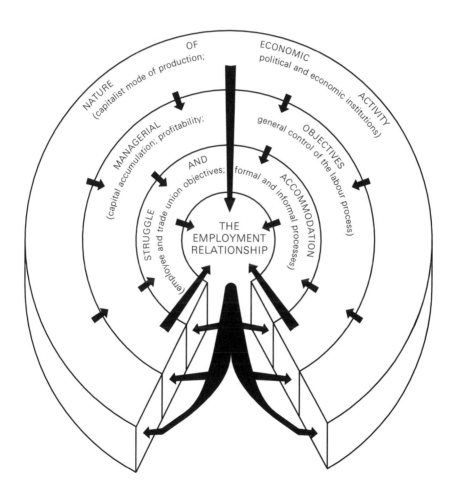

FIGURE 2.1   A framework of employee relations analysis

Four further points need to be made about this framework. First, it is not meant to represent a highly deterministic pattern of relationships. For example, despite the influence of the economic context, a series of strategic choices remain open to management, such as seeking profitability through a high-skill, high-wage, high-productivity route or via a low-skill, low-wage, low-productivity one (see Chapters 3 and 4). Other areas of indeterminacy include the principal level at which employee relations are focused and the main processes of those relations: for example the extent to which employee relations are pursued through institutionalised relations with trade unions based on collective bargaining (Chapter 7), or non-bargaining forms of worker involvement (Chapter 8), or via relations based on non-unionism (Chapter 9).

Secondly, and following on from this last point, although Figure 2.1 represents a 'cross-section' of society, it is clearly the outcome of historical processes – in the first instance, the evolution from feudalism to capitalism, and more recently the transition from competitive to monopoly capitalism. In the 1990s the employment relationship increasingly bears the imprint of globalisation and the progressive internationalisation of capitalist economic relations. Any account of contemporary employee relations must therefore combine synchronic and diachronic analysis – describing a subject as it exists at one point in time, whilst at the same time incorporating the historical evolution of the subject. Though our emphasis is on contemporary employee relations, we do not neglect history. The key task, however, is not historical *description* for its own sake, but the *conceptualisation* of historical processes. In an 'event-driven' view of history, as Franzosi (1995:371) points out, 'the emphasis is on the unique and the unrepeatable', whereas in a 'structure-driven' view of history 'the emphasis is on regularities, patterns, repetitions, and sequences, with occasional disruptions and discontinuities conjecturally introduced by events of particular significance'. The notion of spiral time, as a metaphor, helps us to understand how these two views of history can be combined. But metaphors do no more than heighten our intuitive grasp of a particular phenomenon by comparing two 'objects' (in this case an employment relationship and a spiral) that are not normally associated with one another (for a discussion of the role and utility of metaphors in industrial relations see Dunn, 1990; and Keenoy, 1991). Theoretically, therefore, our analysis seeks to combine history and sociology, focusing on the dialectics of (capitalist economic) *structures* and *agency* relationships (the interests, choices and actions of the different parties involved in employee relations).

Thirdly, the framework is mute on the role of the state. As the employment relationship is based fundamentally on 'property rights' enforced by the state, the latter is a 'silent partner' in all contractual exchanges between employer and employee. In modern capitalist economies, however, the state has become increasingly 'vocal' in the employment relationship and an ever more active participant in the public sector, as discussed explicitly in Chapter 6 and in several other chapters. Moreover, the state in large part determines the 'type' of capitalism that prevails: Anglo-Saxon capitalism is very different from the 'social market' capitalism of Western Europe and Scandinavia, and different again from East Asian capitalism (see Best, 1990; Dore 1992; Hampden-Turner and Trompenaars, 1994; and Hutton, 1996:257–84). The 'peculiarities' of the UK economy (Fine and Harris, 1985; and Hutton, 1996) – for example the primacy accorded by the state to finance over industry, consumption over production, and competition and contract over cooperation and commitment – have a profound impact on employee relations that can neither be 'taken for granted' nor assumed to be an ineluctable feature of capitalist socioeconomic relations (since all market economies are socially produced and politically governed).

Finally, we have sought to portray the central elements of the framework in Figure 2.1, rather than show all the possible influences on the employment relationship. We recognise that in reality there is a wide range of factors influencing employee relations, not least the nature of product markets, types of technology employed and size of organisation. The influence of such factors is examined in subsequent chapters; at this point it is more important to clarify the central elements of our theoretical framework, to which other factors may be incorporated at a later stage.

Thus far our analysis of the employment relationship has necessarily been somewhat abstract, since it is essential from the outset to understand the fundamental principles and defining characteristics of the labour exchange. These principles and characteristics will inform and underwrite the analysis of employee relations in subsequent chapters. But to understand the reality and variety of employment relations, how and why they differ over time and across industries, occupations and organisations, it is necessary to deploy more concrete levels of analysis. Edwards (1986:60) distinguishes between three levels of analysis: the *mode of production* in general; the broad principles of the *organisation of the labour process*; and the *concrete operation* of the labour process in the real world. Clearly, much of the preceding analysis has been focused at the level of the (capitalist) mode of production, with only passing reference to some of the broad principles of the organisation of the labour process. For Edwards (ibid:60–1), a mode of production is simply the way in which people are brought together in social relationships in order to produce goods and services. The key features of the capitalist mode of production – the creation of an economic surplus, the asymmetry of power between employers and employed, *inter alia* – have already been identified. To this can be added the general *instability* of the capitalist system: the fact that capitalist economies are subject to the incessant fluctuations of the trade cycle – booms interrupted by crisis and slump, prosperity followed by recession. Both short and long waves of capitalist economic development are closely associated with many of the key facets of employee relations – management strategy, union membership, collective bargaining, strikes – and their impact is explored in subsequent chapters.

The organisation of the labour process takes the analysis into the realms of management control strategies and employee and union response. The subdivision of tasks and the deskilling of jobs have already been identified among the broad principles of work organisation that are characteristic of the capitalist mode of production. To these may be added supervision, bureaucratic rules, even the surrender (to a limited degree) of control to the workforce, as elements of the variety of management control strategies that have emerged (see Braverman, 1974; R. Edwards, 1979; and Friedman, 1977). These strategies and the response of trade unions are discussed in Part 2 (Chapters 4 and 5), together with the changing role of the state (Chapter 6) in structuring the broader context in which the labour exchange takes place.

Finally, there is the actual operation of the labour process in the real world. As a first step, the general characteristics of employment in the UK economy are outlined in the following chapter. Then in Parts 2 and 3 each chapter begins with a case study that represents an example of the varied labour processes, and their interaction with wider society. We start with this level of analysis as it is the most accessible. However a deeper understanding of the issues and processes covered in each of these chapters can only be derived from the higher, more abstract levels of analysis identified above, and which underpin our analysis throughout the remainder of the book. This theoretical framework informs the questions we pose, the structure of the analysis, the inferences drawn and the conclusions reached in each of the remaining chapters.

CHAPTER 3

The dynamic context of employee relations

Introduction

Employee relations do not take place in a vacuum. They are situated within, influenced by and in turn impact upon many other aspects of the work organisation. Variables such as the size and structure of companies, the technologies they use, their patterns of ownership and control, and the character of their product markets have increasingly come to be recognised as important influences on the processes and outcomes of employee relations. Just as significant is the nature of the workforce and the composition and conditions prevailing in the broader labour market from which individual workforces are drawn. Important changes have been occurring in the composition of the labour force in the UK and elsewhere, the types and location of industries that the labour force is employed in (or, if unemployed, excluded from) and the patterns of ownership, organisational structures and interorganisational linkages found in those industries. Moreover many organisations find themselves operating under very different market conditions from those pertaining two decades ago. What is more, intensified competition in the private sector has been mirrored by greater financial stringency in the public service sector, as the state has sought to commercialise, and ultimately privatise, public sector organisations (see Chapter 6). Within organisations, too, changes have been taking place at an accelerated pace in the way jobs are designed and performed. New technologies, coupled with operational techniques emphasising production that is 'just-in-time' and reflects 'total quality management', are contributing to significant changes in what jobs are undertaken, in what way, at what pace, by how many people and in what relationship to one another.

It is not possible here to rehearse in full all the changes taking place in industrial societies over the recent period that may impact on the experience of work. Further, the significance of particular developments such as the changing role of the state in influencing labour market conditions will be dealt with in more detail in later chapters. What is necessary, however, is to note some of the most pertinent developments taking place at the organisational, industrial and societal level, and to draw out their significance for the analysis of employee relations. In order to highlight some of the many contextual developments impacting upon employee relations, this chapter begins with a brief review of some of the broader changes in the economic context. This is followed by sections considering developments in the nature and composition of the labour force and changes occurring within individual work organisations. These are then combined to demonstrate the practical interaction and theoretical integration of product and labour market processes.

Changes in the economic context

In recent years commentators have increasingly used the term 'globalisation' (the integration of spatially separate locations into a single international market) to summarise a range of developments in the world economy. Central to this has been the diffusion of multinational activity, with individual companies establishing operations in a widening range of 'host' countries. Multinational operations are nothing new, of course. In vehicle production, for example, for more than half a century companies such as Ford and General Motors have produced outside the United States, including several plants in the UK. In fact by the late 1970s the UK was host to just over a quarter of the world's foreign affiliates (with the United States hosting around a third), compared with less than 7 per cent for West Germany and 3 per cent for Japan. What *is* new about multinational activity in the 1980s and 1990s is the pace at which companies in the more recently industrialised countries – primarily Japan and other Far Eastern countries – have established production facilities across the world. Almost two hundred Japanese companies had located in the UK by the early 1990s, including major employers such as Honda, Nissan, Sony, Toshiba and Toyota, and this is typical of many other Western industrial countries, although the UK (now firmly established as the 'sweatshop of Europe') has secured a disproportionate share of such investment: in 1994, for example, the UK secured 40 per cent of all Japanese investment in Europe, over 50 per cent of all Korean investment and 57 per cent of all European investment made by Taiwanese multinationals. Furthermore this multinational presence has been extended by the growth of alliances and joint venture activities, with companies joining forces to design and produce a wide range of manufactured goods. The automotive industry has witnessed many such joint venture activities, with UK examples including Honda-Rover, Bedford Vans-Isuzu, Iveco-Ford, NP Echo-Kanto Seiki, Hoover International-Ikeda Busan, TI-Nihon Radiator, and TI Fulton-Sano. As Amin and Dietrich (1990) note, joint venture activity within the European Union increased almost two and a half times in the six years from 1982 to 1988, with intra-EU joint ventures increasing in relative importance at the expense of joint ventures between companies from a single country. The upshot has been a growing presence in the domestic economies of industrial countries of a growing proportion of the labour force working directly for, or indirectly associated with, multinational companies based elsewhere. Indeed by the early 1980s 40 per cent of employment in industry in nine of the wealthiest industrial nations was accounted for by multinationals (ILO, 1981:1). In the UK, foreign-owned firms currently employ around 800 000 workers in over 2500 enterprises; a quarter of UK manufacturing capacity is foreign-owned (Hutton, 1996:8).

The implications of globalisation for employee relations are readily apparent. Potentially, the global mobility of capital (and increasingly labour) will force a *downward* harmonisation of terms and conditions of employment. Of course globalisation is unlikely to create a single unregulated world market. The global economy remains dominated by three large trading blocs – the United States, Japan and the EU – which between them account for around three-quarters of all foreign direct investment flows, 70 per cent of world trade flows and 70 per cent of world gross domestic product. But within Europe the potential for all economies to be pulled down to the lowest level (that is, that of the UK in the 1990s), rather than up to a minimum accepted standard, remains a very real danger. More directly, foreign companies bring to the host country their own ideas and methods of production and labour management, the result of which is not only a greater diversity of employee relations practice but also pressure on indigenous firms to adopt similar 'best practices'. Thus the Ford Motor Company brought more formalised collective bargaining procedures to the British motor industry than those being practised by domestic manufacturers at the time (Beynon, 1984). Conversely, McDonald's brought its own brand of non-unionism to Britain's shores and beyond (Lamb and Percy, 1987; and Ritzer, 1996).

More recently Japanese automotive and electronics companies have brought 'new' employee relations practices, ranging from single-union, no-strike agreements to company uniforms and a morning workout (accompanied in some cases by the company song!) (Oliver and Wilkinson, 1992; for a more general discussion of foreign-owned firms see Purcell *et al.*, 1987). Equally important, but often overlooked, are the deficiencies in UK management that have been highlighted by the presence of overseas companies. For example a 1970s study of US companies based in the UK found that not only did they achieve much higher rates of return on capital than their UK counterparts, but that recorded productivity levels were almost a third higher where production and management methods had been shaped by the parent company (Dunning, 1976). Similar reports have accompanied the arrival of Nissan and other automotive companies to the UK (Turnbull, 1991a:169–71). Rather ingenuously, Nichols (1986:168) argues that 'it does seem that British managements have not been doing their jobs very well', a conclusion echoed in a study commissioned by the Department of Trade and Industry (*The Sunday Times*, 14 March 1993). Williams *et al.* (1988:23) similarly castigated UK managers as 'specialists in the disorganisation of production':

> The British management problem is that, within their area of discretion, British managers consistently take poor decisions about the priority of different problems and execute their strategy in a way that is generally inept (ibid:22).

Whilst detailed discussion of the management of employee relations is reserved for a later chapter, the implications for the performance of the UK economy and the causes (and causality) of employee relations 'problems', should be noted:

> the lack of sophistication in management organisation both in relation to labour relations and the more technical aspects of production . . . not only led directly to low productivity, but also exacerbated industrial relations problems. . . . To a significant degree, therefore, rather than poor labour relations leading to production problems, production problems lead to poor labour relations and low productivity (Batstone, 1986:41).

It is widely acknowledged that the globalisation of capital has brought about a marked intensification of competition in many industrial and service sectors over the past two decades. Other factors too have been adduced to account for this intensification. These include the shake-out effect of the 1980–2 world recession (leading to a high level of plant closure), the accelerated diffusion of new technologies (partly reflecting the adaptability of microelectronic technology) and the move towards larger trading blocs (such as created by the North American Free Trade Agreement and the Single European Market). The resulting intensification of competition in both home and export markets is widely perceived to have exacerbated an already difficult economic situation in the UK, as indicated by the decline of its share of world trade in manufactured goods and total world exports (Crafts, 1991; House of Lords, 1985; and Porter, 1990:494–6) and marked by several decades of 'slippage' in productivity relative to major industrial competitors. This has had a marked effect on the UK's competitiveness. Despite the emphasis successive governments have placed on wages and the rate of increase of average earnings as a key factor in the 'competitive equation', the UK is in fact a comparatively low-wage economy (see Beaumont, 1995:167). In addition 'social charges' or non-wage labour costs (such as holiday pay, medical allowances, sick pay, pension

TABLE 3.1 Unit labour costs in manufacturing

	Total hourly labour costs				Labour productivity (output per hour)				Unit labour costs			
	1980	1984	1986	1989	1980	1984	1986	1989	1980	1984	1986	1989
United States	126	194	161	130	273	262	267	232	46	74	60	56
Japan	80	109	129	127	196	177	176	195	41	62	73	65
France	121	114	122	113	193	179	184	166	63	64	66	68
West Germany	165	153	173	165	255	232	178	195	65	66	97	85
Italy	108	117	127	n/a	173	156	155	n/a	62	75	82	n/a
Belgium	176	140	149	n/a	207	200	154	n/a	85	70	97	n/a
Netherlands	160	142	156	n/a	269	267	205	n/a	59	53	76	n/a
UK	100	100	100	100	100	100	100	100	100	100	100	100

Labour costs are compared at current market exchange rates; 1989 figures are provisional.
Sources: Ray (1987), Neale (1992)

contributions, vocational training, and welfare) as a percentage of earnings are much lower in the UK than most other industrialised economies, and a larger proportion of the workforce are excluded from such entitlements (in 1996, for example, almost 11 per cent of the workforce, over 2.3 million workers, did not receive any paid holidays). Yet despite relatively low *hourly* labour costs, as illustrated in Table 3.1, *unit* labour costs are significantly higher in the UK *due to poor productivity*.

In the more difficult trading conditions of the 1980s, the UK became a net importer of manufactured goods for the first time ever (in 1983), and the relative weakness of the UK economy – arising from poor productivity growth and the decline of manufacturing industries – became even more evident. For example the balance of payments deficit was £4.8 billion in 1983, but this figure had doubled by 1987 and then doubled again in 1988 to over £20 billion, the highest deficit ever recorded. Even in the depths of the recent recession, the UK's (non-oil) balance of payments deficit was over £15 billion in 1992, more than £10 billion of which was attributed to the manufacturing sector. As Coutts and Godley (1989:150) concluded in their review of the UK's economic performance during the 1980s, what distinguishes the UK economy most sharply from that of other countries, and indeed from previous periods in its history is that, 'despite its relatively slow rate of growth, total demand has run beyond our capacity to produce' (see also Coates, 1994; and Hutton, 1996). In other words the productive base of the economy has become too small to support the consuming population, hence the record levels of imports (UK manufacturing output today is barely higher than two decades ago). At the macro level, the previous Conservative government redoubled its efforts to keep wage inflation down, especially in the public sector, while at the micro level managements have placed even greater emphasis on improving productivity and competitiveness. This 'wage–effort' bargain, as we demonstrated in Chapter 2, is a central focus of employee relations.

Responses to competitive pressures

New market circumstances, according to many analysts, require a new basis for organising and controlling productive activity. Changes will include intraorganisational developments involving, for example, the introduction of new technology and the adoption of new manufacturing techniques, and interorganisational changes such as new subcontracting arrangements or vertical re/disintegration. These developments are discussed in more detail in a subsequent section. At this point it is more instructive to focus on general trends at the level of the economy as a whole, especially as it is now well established that the UK is a comparatively low-wage, low-productivity, low-investment economy. This 'unholy trinity' has important ramifications for employee relations and the social welfare of the working population:

> for many inefficient, low productivity enterprises low wages and low social charges have become a pre-condition for survival. Indeed, it is reasonable to conjecture that over time low wages and low productivity have become self-reinforcing. . . . At issue is the difference between an organisational and economic environment which is conducive to a virtuous circle of high productivity and high levels of remuneration and an environment characterised by a vicious and self-perpetuating spiral of low wages, low morale and low productivity (Nolan, 1989:84).

Put differently, with productivity lagging far behind, UK industry has only remained internationally competitive by cutting wages relative to other industrialised economies (Fine, 1990:140).

Not surprisingly, it is in industries where non-price factors such as quality, reliability, product innovation and technological sophistication are an important determinant of competitiveness that the UK's competitive position has been most seriously eroded. Conversely, industries characterised by low research intensity and the preponderance of price factors have been more successful in international markets (Smith, 1986). The crucial variable appears to be investment, both in physical and human 'assets'. Here again, the UK's record on manufacturing investment is deplorable. Not only does the UK invest less, as a percentage of its gross domestic product (GDP), than other industrialised countries, but the effectiveness of that investment (as measured by incremental capital–output ratios) is often inferior (House of Lords, 1985:25–6). During the recession of the early 1980s, when manufacturing output recorded the largest ever twelve-month decline – greater even than during the Great Depressions of the 1870s and the interwar years – total fixed investment fell by 36 per cent between 1979 and 1983. Further, in the period 1982–6, when gross trading profits in manufacturing industries increased by 55 per cent, total manufacturing fixed investment as a percentage of gross trading profits actually fell to 27 per cent, compared with over 35 per cent in 1982 and over 50 per cent in both 1979 and 1980. During the 1980s investment increased by 2 per cent per annum, while profits on average rose by 6 per cent per annum and dividends jumped by 12 per cent per annum (Hutton, 1996:8). Whereas the world's top 200 companies as a whole spent three times more on research and development than on dividend payments, the UK's top innovators' research expenditure was a mere two thirds of what they paid out in dividends (ibid:8). By the mid 1990s business investment had fallen to a 30-year low (ibid:181). Lest readers think this emphasis on manufacturing is undue, it should be recalled that manufacturing is both the engine of economic growth (known as 'Kaldor's Law') and a major creator of wealth (see Kaldor, 1966; and Cornwall, 1977). In other industrial countries the growth of GDP has been led by the *growth* of manufacturing. In the UK the decline of the economy has been led by the *decline* of manufacturing (Aldington, 1986:7). Service industries may have grown in recent years, as the following section documents, but there must always be something to service. If nothing else, the 'value added' of manufacturing exports is three times that of services, such that a 1 per cent fall in manufacturing exports requires a 3 per cent rise in services to compensate.

The inadequacy of UK investment in human assets is long-standing and has been well documented (see for example the *Oxford Review of Economic Policy*, 1988, number 3). In the mid 1980s, for example, the rate of participation in education among 16–18 year-olds (around 30 per cent) was lower in the UK than in any of its major competitors (almost 60 per cent in France, around 70 per cent in Japan and 79 per cent in the United States) (*The Times Educational Supplement*, 11 October 1985; see also Layard *et al.*, 1994). Participation rates have increased significantly in recent years, but the UK still lags behind. In 1987, for example, the proportion of 20–24 year-olds in education in France was only slightly higher than in the UK, but by 1995 the percentage had risen to 43 per cent in France compared with less than 25 per cent in the UK. Among the under–20s in education, France increased its proportion to over 90 per cent during this period, compared with less than 75 per cent in the UK. Furthermore, despite the increased participation in education, one in five 21 year-olds in the UK are innumerate and one in seven are illiterate (Hutton 1996:2).

Almost two thirds (64 per cent) of the UK workforce have no vocational qualifications, compared with 26 per cent in Germany (Hutton, 1996:8). In industry the number of apprentices in training halved from 218 000 in 1970 to 102 100 in 1983. Following the Conservative government's reform of the apprenticeship system in 1983, substituting tested standards for traditional time-serving, the numbers fell further to 53 600 in 1990 (Keep and Mayhew, 1995). As Mayhew (1991:5) concludes, 'too many of those who go into jobs receive inadequate training, whilst the provision of training and retraining for adults is pathetically inadequate'. But the problem is not just the *level* of education and training, but a much deeper *structural* problem:

> Not only is there a failure to treat training as an investment in human capital in the same manner as investment in physical capital; training decisions are often taken at the wrong management level and at the wrong stage in a company's decision-taking process. Only if they are taken simultaneously with strategic decisions about which products to produce and about the techniques with which to produce these products, will training expenditures be efficiently made (ibid:5).

After 1979, successive Conservative governments progressively dismantled legislative backing (compulsion) for training and abandoned all notion of social partnership or tripartite control of training design and delivery (see Keep and Rainbird, 1995). Consequently, the UK now has a market-based, employer-led training system that is not only failing to produce a sufficient level and quality of training, but is effectively encouraging firms *not* to train: in the absence of compulsion, the rational policy is to minimise training investment (and associated costs) and simply poach skilled workers when market conditions demand it (see Hutton, 1996:187–92). One consequence is that the UK is currently trapped in a 'low skill/low quality equilibrium' (Finegold and Soskice, 1988; and Stevens and MacKay, 1991).

At several points throughout this book the implications of the UK's overall approach is examined in more detail – for example in relation to the state's approach to the labour market and the effect of trade unions on wage levels. Here, however, we may note three outcomes that influence the general context in which employee relations take place. First, relatively low wages have acted as a stimulus to inward investment in the UK. The country's membership of the EU and comparatively low wage rates (at least compared with other countries in northern Europe) has attracted many multinational investors, most notably in the past decade from the Far East. This is despite the potential drawbacks of the UK as a location, in particular its island status, its position on the periphery rather than at the core of the EU, and the equivocal attitude of successive Conservative governments during the 1980s and 1990s to full participation in the EU project. One such inward investing company, Nissan Motor Manufacturing (UK) Ltd, is the subject of our opening case in Chapter 8.

Second, the UK's low wage levels have contributed to high levels of (relative) poverty. According to Labour Force Survey data, nearly one quarter of all jobs pay less than £4 per hour (TUC, 1997:3). Among the long-term unemployed finding work, almost half (49 per cent) took jobs paying less than £4 per hour. Using the Council of Europe's 'decency threshold', which measures whether countries are complying with Article 4 of the European Social Charter to provide 'fair remuneration', by the early 1990s the UK had over 10 million employees on adult rates (six million of whom were women) that were below the decency threshold (the figure is calculated as 68 per cent of all full-time mean earnings) (Pearson and Quiney, 1992:1). This represented nearly a quarter of all Europeans living below this threshold, *and almost half (47 per cent) of the UK working population.* Low pay is a long-standing problem in the UK, but the 1980s witnessed an increase both in the number of low paid workers (the figure stood at just under eight million or 38 per cent of the workforce in 1979) and in the inequality of income distribution. In fact the lowest paid 10 per cent now earn less in relation to the average wage than they did in 1886, when statistics were first collected, while the highest paid 10 per cent now earn more in relation to the average wage than at any time since records began (Pearson and Quiney, 1992:5; see also Atkinson, 1996). In other words, while the higher paid have been getting better off, the lower paid have been falling even further behind (this is not to argue that living standards are

CHESTER COLLEGE LIBRARY

worse than they were in previous generations, only that *inequalities* in pay are greater now than at any time in the past century). In one fifth of households in 1993 with an adult man and woman, neither partner had paid work, whereas in three fifths of such households both adults were working – giving rise to the distinction between 'work poor' and 'work rich' households, and contributing further to the growing inequality between different groups in society.

Having been implored by Margaret Thatcher to 'glory in inequality', the UK is now the most unequal country in the western world (United Nations, 1996). According to the economic philosophy of the political right, 'There needs to be fear and greed in the system in order to make it tick' (Hutton, 1996:173), the former to prevent dependency and the latter to encourage enterprise and efficiency. But even the World Bank and the OECD now recognise that low wages fail to create jobs, while inequality actually hinders economic growth, amplifies the boom and slump of the economic cycle and destroys social cohesion (ibid:175–81; and OECD, 1996). In sum, equality and efficiency are *complementary*, not alternatives.

Third, in an attempt to improve unit labour costs attention has been focused on increasing labour productivity principally through more flexible forms of working. But UK employers have made only very modest strides towards greater functional flexibility or multiskilling (Cross, 1988; and Elger, 1990). One reason for this is the lower priority given to training, which has already been documented. It is difficult to improve functional flexibility in the absence of a suitable pool of skills or a willingness to invest in appropriate (re)training programmes. The result has been a greater tendency to pursue numerical forms of flexibility through such means as part-time and temporary work (including 'hire and fire' policies) or subcontracting, rather than extending the skills of the workforce. Where job content has been made more flexible, this has tended to come more in the form of semiskilled workers increasing the range of tasks they undertake (task flexibility), rather than through an extension of skilled activities. Boyer (1988) and others have characterised the pattern of flexibility pursued in the UK as essentially defensive and short term, representing reactions to market fluctuations. In contrast, extending the skill range of employees is viewed as a long-term, offensive flexibility strategy by creating a more adaptable labour force, capable of responding to longer-term changes in job requirements.

The development of the UK economy along a trajectory of low wages, low productivity and low investment has important implications for the structure of the labour market. In a period of intensified international competition, the long-term decline of the manufacturing sector has accelerated, creating widespread unemployment and job insecurity. At the same time the growth of service sector employment and part-time work has changed both the character and composition of the labour force. It is to these and other changes in the labour market that we now turn.

Changes in employment and the labour force

Broad shifts in employment can be identified in all mature industrial societies. Many aspects of these developments have been occurring for several decades, though the conditions prevailing since the late 1970s appear to have fuelled the pace of change along several dimensions. Consequently it is in discussions on the labour market that one encounters directly the debate on continuity versus change (e.g. Hakim, 1990). For instance, manufacturing employment declined dramatically during the 1980s, but the manufacturing sector has been in relative decline since 1966 (Thirlwall, 1982). There has been an increase in the number of part-time workers over the past two decades, but such employment has always been a feature of the UK industrial landscape. There are more women in the labour market today, but female participation rates have been increasing since the end of the Second World War.

Emphasising continuity has led some authors, such as MacInnes, to argue that the policies of successive Thatcher governments in the 1980s

> did not produce intensified restructuring. Rather it drowned its effects by a recession. Its policies appear to have stifled rather than stimulated economic change in the sense of restructuring. . . . There is therefore little evidence that Thatcherism has transformed the economic environment of British industrial relations through changing the nature of economic activity and therefore the institutional environment in which unions operate. Most of the changes in the composition of the workforce and the sorts of workplace in which they are found have been developing for some time (MacInnes, 1987:78–9).

Even MacInnes (ibid:79), however, recognised the importance of the massive increase in unemployment brought about by the collapse of manufacturing. Metcalf (1989:10) takes this as his starting point to argue that it is possible that 'industrial relations are not amenable to incremental "reform". Perhaps only a climacteric – like the loss of 1 million full time manufacturing jobs (1-in-7) in the first eighteen months of the 1980s – does the trick'. As we identified in Chapter 1, the dynamics of economic development cannot be reduced to a simple dichotomy between continuity or change. Rather it is essential to recognise the mutual coexistence and interaction of both. Clearly the time period one focuses on is of crucial importance. A short time scale (or in terms of the earlier metaphor, one twist of the time spiral) may suggest a magnitude of change that appears much more modest when viewed over a longer time span (several turns of the spiral). Whilst not losing sight of the continuities, however, it is nonetheless important to highlight the main dimensions of change, since it is these changes that have overlain patterns of continuity to produce a markedly different context for employee relations. Six aspects of change are particularly noteworthy: the decline of employment in production industries; the increase in service sector employment; the growth of female and part-time work; changes in the location of production and employment; the increase in self-employment; and rising unemployment, increased redundancies and a fall in the level of job security.

Decline of employment in production industries

Since the mid 1970s and particularly during the 1980s, there has been a marked decline in employment in the production industries in Britain (this sector covers manufacturing plus the energy and water supply industries). The fall has been especially marked in manufacturing and coal extraction. Long-established industries such as steel, coal, textiles and shipbuilding have dramatically cut the numbers they employ. The biggest steel producer, British Steel, for example, employed over 165 000 people in 1978, but by 1996 the figure had fallen to below 54 000. In British Coal (formerly the National Coal Board) employment more than halved between 1979 (232 400) and 1987 (109 900) and more than halved again to only 44 000 by 1992, while that in British Shipbuilders fell from 82 000 to just 7000 between 1979 and 1987 (see Ferner, 1989). This decline, however, has not been confined to a few industries, but has been widespread. Manufacturing employment as a whole fell by more than half between 1971 and 1996. As Table 3.2 illustrates, more than half of that reduction took place in the first half of the 1980s, with another sizeable fall in the early 1990s.

In 1971, 36.4 per cent of all employees in employment in Britain worked in manufacturing; by 1996 this had halved to 18.1 per cent. Table 3.3 shows that no branch of production has been immune from a reduction in employment since 1971, though the severity of the decline has been far greater in some sectors than others, with five industry groups (coal, oil and gas extraction; electricity, gas and water supply; mechanical engineering; transport equipment; and textiles, leather, footwear and clothing) seeing their job numbers fall by two thirds or more during this period. This decline is by no means unique to Britain (see OECD, 1994), but what is unusual is that it is more a result of output loss (negative deindustrialisation) than of productivity growth (positive deindustrialisation) (see Coates, 1994). Some of the implications of manufacturing decline for employee relations have already been noted. A further point to make at this juncture is that it is in these industries that trade unions have traditionally been well organised.

Increase in employment in service industries

Whilst almost four million employees left manufacturing between 1971 and 1996 and over 4.5 million left the production industries as a whole, the service sector in Britain experienced a corresponding rise in employment of just over five million between these years (see Table 3.2). Service sector employment grew almost continually during that period, the two exceptions being 1981–2 and 1991–4. By June 1996, 76.1 per cent of all employees were employed in the service sector, a marked rise from 52.6 per cent in 1971. Again, such growth is not unique to Britain. Throughout the OECD member countries employment in services grew by an average of 2 per cent per annum throughout the 1970s, and while this growth slowed to 1.5 per cent during the early 1980s it had picked up again to over 2 per cent by 1984 (Blyton, 1989:37–9). Even before the 1960s the service sector had been the main source of job creation throughout the OECD; from the 1970s onwards, however, it became the *only* sector to be a net creator of jobs in most countries (Japan and the United States being notable exceptions) (see OECD, 1994b).

TABLE 3.2   Changes in employment in the manufacturing and service industries, 1971–96 (thousands)

Year (June)	Manufacturing industries	Service industries
1971	7890	11 388
1974	7722	12 240
1978	7143	12 859
1979	7113	13 222
1980	6808	13 345
1981	6107	13 102
1982	5358	13 475
1983	5052	13 502
1984	4946	13 825
1985	4895	14 089
1986	4777	14 261
1987	4713	14 549
1988	4754	15 166
1989	4747	15 563
1990	4628	15 931
1991	4215	15 802
1992	3995	15 808
1993	3814	15 783
1994	3827	15 894
1995	3992	16 184
1996	3919	16 450
Actual change, 1971–96	−3971	+5 062
% change 1971–9	−50.3%	+44.5%

Source: *Employment Gazette* (Historical Supplement 4), October 1994 (1971–81 figures); *Labour Market Trends*, February 1997 (1982–96 figures).

TABLE 3.3   Change in employment in production industries in Britain, 1971–1996

Sector	% change 1971–96	No. employed in September 1996 (000s)
Coal, oil and gas extraction	−84.3	63
Electricity, gas and water supply	−68.2	124
Metal manufacturing	−32.5	555
Chemicals and manmade fibres	−43.3	249
Mechanical engineering	−64.6	401
Office machinery, electrical engineering	−51.3	500
Motor vehicles and parts	−58.8	208
Other transport equipment	−63.9	153
Food, drink and tobacco	−42.4	446
Textiles, leather, footwear and clothing	−64.9	354
Timber, wooden furniture, rubber, plastics etc.	−50.7	302
Paper products, printing and publishing	−22.6	444

Sources: Calculations based on Department of Employment and Department for Education and Employment data.

In Britain, as Table 3.4 opposite indicates, the strongest growth in service employment has taken place in the finance, real estate and other business activities sector, together with hotels and restaurants, health activities, and other services (the latter covering, among other areas, social work, personal services and employment in recreational and cultural services). In contrast to manufacturing and other production industries, unions have traditionally been less well organised in many areas of the service sector, particularly in private sector services. These and other non-union firms are examined in more detail in Chapter 9.

Increase in female employment and part-time work

Of the various other changes in patterns of employment that are associated with the changing proportions of those working in manufacturing and services, the most marked is the growth in female employment and part-time work.

Women's share of total employment increased from just over one third in the late 1950s to almost one half by 1996 (Table 3.5). In June 1996, 87 per cent of female employees worked in the service sector (compared with 65 per cent of male employees). Female employees considerably outnumber their male counterparts in services: women made up 57 per cent of all employees in

TABLE 3.4   Change in employment in service industries in Britain, 1971–96

Industry sector	% change 1971–96	No. employed in September 1996 (000s)
Wholesale retail and repairs	+26.9	3714
Hotels and restaurants	+83.7	1262
Transport	−21.0	866
Post and telecommunication	−1.1	431
Finance real estate and other business activities	+185.0	3756
Public administration	−23.0	1332
Education	+39.7	1777
Health activities	+64.3	1549
Other services	+90.1	1859

Source: Calculations based on Department of Employment and Department for Education and Employment data.

service sector employment in June 1996. In some parts of the service sector the proportion of female employees is considerably higher, for example hotels and restaurants (where 62 per cent of the total employees are female), education (71 per cent), and health and social work (81 per cent). Moreover, within these industry groups employment in particular occupations is even more highly feminised: in hairdressing and beauty treatment, for example, 84 per cent of employees are female. Overall, more than half of all women in employment work in catering, cleaning, hairdressing and other personal services, or in clerical and related jobs. This tendency for women to be concentrated in some industries and occupations is an issue we shall return to below.

TABLE 3.5   Change in the number of males and females in employment in Britain, 1959–96* (thousands)

	1959	1971	1979	1992	1996
Females	7174	8207	9435	10 395	10 693
Males	13 817	13 433	13 176	10 911	10 916
Total	20 991	21 640	22 611	21 307	21 609
Proportion of females in total (%)	34.2	37.9	41.7	48.8	49.5

* June figures, adjusted for seasonal variation.
Sources: Department of Employment and Department for Education and Employment.

Much of the increase in female employment in Britain over the past two decades has been concentrated in the public sector, particularly in education, health and social services (Edwards *et al.*, 1992:48). However total employment in the public sector declined from almost 30 per cent of total employment in 1977 to only 22 per cent in 1990. Overall, six million men and women were employed in the public sector in 1990, just under three million of these in local authorities, 1.2 million in the National Health Service and around three quarters of a million in central government and in public corporations (ibid:48). The fall in the proportion of total employees in the public sector in the 1980s and 1990s principally reflects privatisation policies and job cuts in those organisations that remained nationalised.

A substantial proportion of female employees work part-time (46 per cent in June 1996). One effect of the expansion in service sector employment has been to contribute to this growth. In 1971 the 3.3 million part-time workers comprised 15.4 per cent of the total workforce in Britain. By June 1996 the number of part-timers had risen to 6.1 million, representing more than one quarter (28.4 per cent) of the total number of employees in employment. Labour Force Survey data show that the number of full-time jobs fell by 69 000 from 1992–5 and the number of permanent jobs by 109 000, while part-time jobs increased by 175 000 (temporary jobs increased by over 300 000). In Britain, the level of part-time working is comparatively high (though lower than in Sweden and Norway). An increase in the proportion of part-time employees is evident, however, in most other industrial countries (Bamber and Whitehouse, 1992), although a larger proportion of part-timers in Britain work fewer hours (26 per cent of those in part-time work in 1995 worked 10 hours or less a week compared with 19 per cent in Germany and 10 per cent in France). The vast majority of all part-time employment in the UK is in the service sector (93.4 per cent in 1996). Sectors particularly reliant on part-time workers include retail distribution (56 per cent of all employees in 1996), hotels and restaurants (56 per cent), health and social work (47 per cent) and education (44 per cent). Within individual occupational groups the highest rates of part-time working are among cleaners and bar staff. Four fifths (79.9 per cent in 1996) of part-time workers are women. Although this proportion has changed relatively little since the early 1970s (in 1971 the proportion of female part-timers was just over 82 per cent), the number of part time workers on low pay rose by over a third (36 per cent) between 1979 and 1991. In fact over 70 per cent of all part-timers in the UK earn less than the Council of Europe's decency threshold, and 84 per cent of these are women (Pearson and Quiney, 1992:6–7; and Rubery, 1995:547).

Changes in the location of employment

As well as shifts in gender composition and the proportion of part-time and full-time workers, changes have taken place in the location where people work.

In particular the decline in traditional manufacturing employment is reflected in overall employment growth in locations outside the main industrial conurbations, as many new manufacturing and service concerns have chosen to set up their operations on 'greenfield' sites, in semirural areas (Lane, 1982).

The decline of industrial conurbations accelerated in the 1980s but has been occurring for over a generation. Between 1960 and 1978, for example, manufacturing employment in rural areas (districts in which all settlements have less than 35 000 people) increased by 38 per cent; this contrasts with a fall of over 26 per cent in manufacturing employment in the six major industrial conurbations during the same period (Massey, 1988:61; see also Sayer and Walker, 1992). Parallel declines have occurred in other countries, such as in parts of northern France and north-eastern USA (Hudson and Sadler, 1989; and Hoerr, 1988). Thus not only are the arenas of employee relations increasingly likely to be found in the service sector rather than in manufacturing, those arenas are also increasingly likely to be located away from industrial regions with more extensive trade union traditions than the semirural districts in which 'greenfield' and other developments are being located. The problems these developments present for trade unions are discussed in Chapters 5 and 9.

Self-employment

Up to now this chapter has focused on changes taking place among the employed workforce. This group represents around four fifths of the total labour force, the remaining fifth being those who are unemployed (see below), those serving in the armed forces (218 000 in September 1996), those on government training programmes (176 000 in September 1996) and the self-employed. Self-employment increased only slightly between 1961 and 1981, but thereafter the number of self-employed rose by almost one half to over three million by mid 1990, representing 11.6 per cent of the total labour force in Britain (Table 3.6). In the early 1990s the level of self-employment fell slightly (as did the number in employment), reflecting the economic recession. However by 1996 the growth in self-employment had recovered to the point where almost one in eight of the labour force was self-employed. Men comprise around two thirds of the self-employed. More than four in five self-employed people work full time, with self-employed women more likely to work part time than men. More than two thirds of the self-employed in 1991 had no employees (Campbell and Daly, 1992) and few own a business (many are 'labour-only subcontractors', whose employers have shifted their jobs from 'employee' to 'self-employed' status in order to reduce costs) (see Dale and Kerr, 1995:462).

TABLE 3.6   **Changes in the level of self-employment in Britain, 1961–96 (thousands)**

	1961	1971	1981	1991	1996*
No. of self-employed	1665	1953	2058	3066	3290
Total labour force	24 221	24 637	26 028	27 614	27 387
Self-employed as percentage of total labour force	6.9%	7.9%	7.9%	11.1%	12.0%

* September
Sources: Department of Employment and Department for Education and Employment.

Unemployment and redundancy

Unemployment levels in the 1980s and 1990s have been far higher than during the two previous decades. Precise comparisons are hindered by the many changes that have been made to the basis on which unemployment figures are compiled, but bearing this qualification in mind, official unemployment increased steadily following the oil price rises and resulting economic setbacks of the mid 1970s. By the late 1970s the average level of unemployment was around one and a quarter million, or 5.6 per cent of the UK workforce (Table 3.7). However a marked acceleration in unemployment occurred during the early 1980s. By 1983 unemployment had climbed to over three million, peaking eventually at 3.21 million in February 1986 (officially 11.9 per cent of the workforce, based on the revised definition of unemployment then in operation). In the late 1980s unemployment fell steadily, yet despite substantial economic growth during this period it only fell to around one and a half million (in June 1990) before rising again as economic recession reappeared and then deepened. By January 1993 more than three million people were registered unemployed, or over 10 per cent of the workforce. Despite an overall fall in unemployment in recent years, by the end of 1996 over 1.8 million people remained on the official unemployment register (6.6 per cent of the workforce), and among certain groups the rates were much higher. Almost 27 per cent of Pakistani–Bangladeshi workers and over 22 per cent of those of Afro-Caribbean origin were unemployed in 1996 (based on Labour Force Survey statistics). Unemployment among black workers aged 16–24 years was particularly acute, with one third out of work in 1996.

In reality, however, unemployment is much higher than the official figures suggest. For example a recent study by HSBC, the parent company of the

TABLE 3.7   Unemployment rates in the UK, 1945–94 (five year averages)

	Yearly average (%)
1945–49	2.1
1950–54	1.7
1955–59	1.7
1960–64	1.9
1965–69	2.1
1970–74	3.1
1975–79	5.6
1980–84	11.1
1985–89	9.7
1990–94	8.7

Source: Calculated from Denman and McDonald (1996).

Midland Bank, suggests that unemployment may actually be as high as four million if various 'hidden' jobless categories are taken into account (*Independent on Sunday*, 13 April 1997). The unemployment statistics are based on the number of people who are out of work and claiming benefit, but since May 1979 the basis of these statistics have altered as many as thirty two times. Groups who are jobless but are excluded from the unemployment figures include the following: women who are unable to claim means-tested benefits because they have a working partner; men over the age of 60, who are not required to register as job seekers; recipients of sickness or invalidity benefit; and those who have exhausted their entitlement to the Jobseekers' Allowance after six months but fail to qualify for the means-tested allowance. The higher official rate of unemployment in the 1990s compared with the period before the late 1970s is despite a marked reduction in the number of young people entering the labour market, as a result of both demographic trends and an increased tendency for 16 and 17-year olds to remain in full-time education.

Alongside the rise in unemployment in the early 1990s was a sharp rise in declared redundancies. It appears that the reasons for redundancy have changed in recent years: whereas redundancies in the past were overwhelmingly the consequence of economic difficulties, latterly there has been a tendency for redundancies to be announced as a cost-cutting measure even at times when the business and economic outlook are buoyant (Cappelli, 1995b). According to Cappelli, a major reason for this is that cutting workforce numbers – euphemistically described as 'downsizing' – is invariably seen by stock markets as a significant cost saving and a likely source of improved profitability. The upshot is that redundancy announcements can improve share prices (ibid:571; see also Cameron, 1994:183–4; and Worrell *et al.*, 1991), although US evidence suggests that this is no more than a short-term palliative (no company ever shrunk its way to success). In the UK, an editorial in *Management Today* on 'The unbearable lightness of business' declared that,

> Too many companies today are preoccupied with the benefits to the bottom line that can come from paring away at fixed costs. This has become an obsession, like anorexia. Management eyes the already feeble corporate frame, and continues to slash at yet more pockets of what it perceives to be fat (*Management Today*, February 1995).

Only a proportion of all those made redundant receive any severance pay, as employees must satisfy criteria relating to age and length of service before they are entitled to statutory compensation (see Chapter 6). It has been estimated that for every redundant employee who is eligible for statutory redundancy pay there is another redundant employee who does not qualify for such a payment (Turnbull, 1988a:204–5). Nonetheless around £30 billion was spent on redundancy payments in the 1980s alone, with disproportionate sums expended in traditional industries such as coalmining and steel (see Turnbull and Wass, 1997). Like unemployment, the number of (confirmed) redundancies fell sharply in the late 1980s, but likewise increased significantly during the recession of the early 1990s (Labour Force Surveys indicate that between 1990 and 1995 over four million redundancies took place in Britain). Although it is very easy for employers to declare workers redundant and select the employees they want to dismiss (see Turnbull, 1988; and Turnbull and Wass, 1997), many firms find that 'the survivors are the real problem . . . although the corporate fitness regime broke no law, it scuppered the psychological contract on which the whole idea of career rests' (Caulkin, 1995:28–9). Those who survive corporate downsizing often experience feelings of guilt and fear, in many cases leading to an acute sense of job insecurity (see ISR, 1996:19). In 1983, Ron Todd (then chief negotiator at the Ford Motor Company and later General Secretary of the T&GWU) summed up the effect of unemployment and redundancy on employee relations when he declared that 'we've got 3 million on the dole, and another 23 million scared to death' (quoted by Bratton, 1992:70). David Metcalf (1989:19) identified fear of job loss as a key factor facilitating the higher levels of productivity that resulted from an intensification of work effort during the 1980s. Work effort in fact peaked in 1983, but the 'fear factor' endured in a diluted form for several years thereafter and appears to have intensified again in the 1990s.

Widespread redundancies account for the insecurity felt by a substantial number of the workforce since the early 1980s. As Gregg and Wadsworth (1995:74) point out, it is those who have been through the experience of job loss once who are most likely to continue to experience job insecurity. Since 1992, 8.7 million different people have suffered at least one spell of unemployment, including one in three men of working age. In 1995, 52 per cent of all those on the unemployment register who found a job were back on the dole within a year (12 per cent were back on benefits after less than four weeks in work). For such workers, employment has become 'a much more precarious affair with insecurity, redundancy, temporary contracts and unemployment contributing to an overall experience of a fragmented, rather than a unified, working life' (Noon and Blyton, 1997:32–3). In the 1970s the 'average' person had six to seven jobs in their working lifetime; by the 1990s this average had risen to eleven to twelve jobs. In sum, these data help explain one of the apparent contradictions of employment in the UK today, namely the fact that while average job tenure is little different now than in the late 1970s, workers report a greater (and increasing) degree of job insecurity (see, for example, ISR, 1996). Not only is the experience of unemployment widespread and the threat of redundancy ever present, even for the middle classes, most workers are no longer protected by trade unions or the certainty of seniority, career hierarchies or the principle of 'last in, first out' (see Turnbull and Wass, 1997).

These various developments in the labour market – growth in the proportion of females, part-timers, and self-employed in the workforce, an increase in the proportion working in service rather than manufacturing activities, away from the traditional industrial heartlands, the persistence of high levels of unemployment even in periods of economic growth, and increasing job insecurity – indicate the extent to which employee relations in the UK have altered from those prevailing a generation ago. Not only has the typical arena changed, but also the nature of the typical employee constituency has altered significantly. Moreover, the widespread experience of redundancy, unemployment and job insecurity has had a considerable effect on how employees view work, the employment relationship and their relations with employers. The structure of the British labour market is depicted in Figure 3.1, which subdivides the labour force into three broad categories: (1) a core of full-time employees, (2) a 'periphery' of part-time, temporary and home-workers, together with the self-employed, and (3) the unemployed, differentiated between the short- and long-term unemployed.

As well as the broader economic developments and overall shifts in labour market activity identified above, important changes in the intra- and inter-organisational context have been taking place. It is to these that we now turn.

Organisational changes

Several developments relating to the structure of organisations, interorganisational relations and the nature of production processes, impact directly upon the contexts within which employee relations take place. First, in terms of patterns of *ownership and control* we have already noted certain prominent

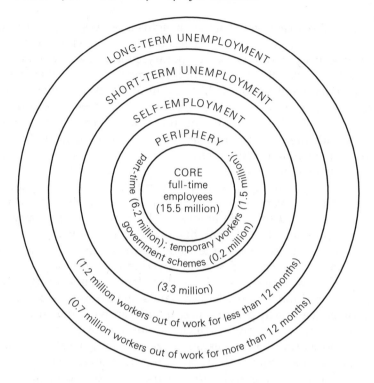

Source: Department for Education and Employment.

FIGURE 3.1   The British labour market, 1996–7

trends, such as the expansion of multinational operations and the spread of joint venture activity. One of the employee relations issues raised in later chapters is the extent to which multinational 'transplants', such as the expansion of Japanese companies in the UK, may act to stimulate more widespread changes in managerial approaches to employee relations. Furthermore, as Beaumont (1992a) comments, where joint ventures involve organisations from different countries, this raises significant questions not only about the ability of venturers to accommodate different employee relations 'styles' but also the extent to which joint venturing may stimulate change in the parties' approaches to those relations.

Other changes in the ownership and control of organisations are also highly relevant to the analysis and experience of employee relations. As companies have sought to position themselves more effectively in their existing product markets or enter new ones, any resulting concentration or diversification strategies, and any related acquisition and/or divestment activities, create not only greater uncertainty among employees regarding the form of ownership and control, but in many cases has resulted in the breaking of long-standing ownership relations. One effect for employees is that their representatives are increasingly having to deal with new management cadres and employers, whose main business may well lie in other spheres of activity, frequently in another country. Nor is this situation faced only by workers in large organisations, such as Jaguar employees following the company's purchase by Ford, Rover employees after the company's acquisition by BMW, and ICL when taken over by Fujitsu. For example, the experience of the two hundred or so employees at a plant manufacturing industrial components just outside Cardiff is not untypical of thousands of employees in similar work contexts elsewhere. Having been part of a UK business for several decades, the employees in the Welsh plant found themselves taken over, hived off and taken over again in the space of three years, the second time by a US company whose main activity was brewing beer! Takeover activity is far greater in the UK than other comparable economies: in the 1980s, for example, three quarters of all hostile takeovers in the EU occurred in the UK.

To date, structures of ownership and control have been studied more by those concerned with corporate strategy and organisational analysis than those focusing on employee relations – though notable exceptions include the work of Purcell (1991; and Purcell and Gray, 1986), and the surveys conducted by researchers at Warwick University (Marginson *et al.*, 1988, and 1993; and Purcell *et al.*, 1987). But research on employee relations conducted during the 1980s indicates many of the dominant forces for change during the decade were *beyond* the traditional boundaries of the subject (e.g. Ahlstrand and Purcell, 1988; Hendry, 1990; and Marchington and Parker, 1990). As Purcell (1991:38) notes, developments in business policies and corporate strategies concerned with the structure, shape and control systems of the firm have forced personnel and industrial relations managers, often reluctantly, to restructure their collective bargaining arrangements and other traditional methods of managing the workforce. This is especially so among the large companies that dominate the UK economy, where there has been a devolution to profit centres within the organisation, a focus on 'strategic business units' (SBUs) and greater independence of subsidiaries from head office administration.

The process, however, is one of both disintegration *and* integration, as operations are often broken down into smaller units but within the context of large firms retaining overall control and command (Amin and Dietrich, 1990; and Blackburn, 1990). In other words, although large firms still dominate the economy, 'what has changed is the *way* in which they dominate' (Turnbull and Weston, 1993a:118). Instead of controlling productive activity through vertical integration, for example, many large firms, especially in the automotive sector (Turnbull, 1991a), have subdivided their core operations into SBUs and moved towards a system of 'quasi-vertical integration'. As Purcell (1991:38) notes, SBUs 'have tougher requirements to meet in terms of performance targets. The emphasis is placed on performance and productivity within the business unit and greater monitoring of results from corporate and divisional head office through the performance control systems'. The effect of decentralisation on employee relations, as Purcell indicates, is likely to be pressure for both quantitative and qualitative improvements in performance under the more watchful eye of corporate management. This pressure is likely to be particularly acute in those industries where product market competition is more intense, but similar pressure is evident in the public sector as a result of financial management initiatives and cash limits (see, *inter alia*, Bailey, 1994, 1996; Beaumont, 1992b; Blackwell and Lloyd, 1989; Ferner, 1989; and Pendleton and Winterton, 1993).

Intraorganisational developments such as these represent a shift to *organisation-based* employment systems, rather than an industry or occupational base (Dore, 1989). Essentially, the organisation is seeking to insulate itself from the external labour market but *not* from the product market. For some this represents 'the replacement of class struggle with the struggle for markets. No longer us workers against them management, but us Company X against them Company Y people' (*Financial Times*, 7 September 1985). Greenfield sites are an extreme example of this broader-based development, where many companies have sought to reach an agreement with a single trade union before production even begins, and therefore before any workers are even hired, in order not only to dictate terms but also to create a *firm-specific* relationship with the union in question. In general, as Purcell (1991:41) cautions, it is difficult to judge how extensive or how effective the development of organisation-based employment systems will be, but what is clear is that managerial *intentions* are markedly different from in the past. This is perhaps best illustrated by management attempts to engender a form of psychological as well as economic dependency from employees (ibid:40). The emphasis is on winning the 'hearts and minds' of the workforce, epitomised by the growing rhetoric, if not yet the reality, of new 'human resource management' practices (see the contributions to Blyton and Turnbull, 1992; Legge, 1995; see also Chapter 4 below).

In addition to changes in the structure of individual organisations, the last decade has seen some significant changes in interorganisational relations. We have already noted the acceleration of joint venture activity as organisations join forces to spread risk, share research and development costs, rationalise production and marketing activities, and strengthen market position. Also important in some sectors has been the further growth of franchising arrangements, whereby franchiser organisations secure a greater presence in a market without incurring significant capital costs to fund expansion or increases in direct employment (Felstead, 1993). Much comment has also been made on the growth of subcontracting arrangements for service activities (such as catering, cleaning and transport) and production-related work. Subcontracting is believed to be one of the factors behind the growth of small firms during the 1980s and 1990s and is generally viewed as being functional for larger companies, who are able to dominate and to a large extent determine the environment faced by small firms. As a result, pay and conditions of employment are likely to be inferior at smaller firms. Size, however, is secondary to the relationship with the client company and the wider economy (Curran, 1990:130; and Chapter 9 below). Thus, Holmes (1986:89–95) suggests that subcontracting can be used to accommodate structural and temporal instability in product markets, different levels of 'minimum efficient scale', and the structure and nature of labour supply conditions. The last has understandably been the main focus of research in employee relations, where subcontracting arrangements are used to minimise and control labour costs; to ensure that labour is a truly variable rather than a fixed cost of production; to enhance managerial control over the labour process, as the withdrawal of a commercial contract is arguably more potent a weapon than the termination of an employment contract; and to ensure an adequate supply of labour, especially where reserves of labour not normally available can be mobilised.

In the economic climate of the 1980s and 1990s, as one might expect, the use of subcontracting arrangements has increased, although it must be recognised that such practices are well-established in many industries and that many firms report 'no change' (Marginson *et al.*, 1988:88–9). Nevertheless, as a significant number of people are not directly employed by the organisation in which they work, important employee relations issues such as comparability and job security are likely to arise (see Keenoy, 1985:1–26). At a number of points in later chapters (for example in the British Steel case in Chapter 7) we shall see how the threat of putting additional work out to subcontractors has had a direct bearing on employee response to managerial initiatives in recent years.

Shutt and Whittington (1987) have summarised these intra- and interorganisational changes as processes of decentralisation, detachment and disintegration (which are not necessarily mutually exclusive). The first refers to operations that are broken up into smaller units but are retained under the same ownership. Detachment refers to those situations where large firms cease to own units directly but still maintain commercial links with them through some form of franchising or licensing agreement. Finally, disintegration arises where large firms cease to own units of production but maintain control through market or contractual power (e.g. subcontracting) and/or the ability to repurchase. As with decentralisation and detachment, this need not imply a loss of control, often quite the opposite. In each case, product market development plays a key role, but the importance of employee relations cannot be overlooked. In Britain's docks, for example, new ownership structures and intra- and interorganisational relations can only be explained as part of a process through which capital has sought to regain or strengthen control over the labour process and to offset the (highly variable) costs of fluctuating labour demand in the port transport industry (Turnbull and Weston, 1993a). Similar conclusions have been drawn for construction (Evans, 1990) and steel (Blyton, 1992c, 1993; and Fevre, 1986).

In addition to these general developments in organisational ownership and control and interorganisational relations, more specific developments in *production* and work processes are worthy of note, for these encapsulate a range of issues relevant both to the context and the content of employee relations. The spread of microelectronic technologies into a broad range of manual and non-manual work in both goods production and services has had (and continues to have) a quantitative and qualitative impact on jobs, though it is clear from the many studies now conducted that the actual effects have varied considerably between different work contexts (see Clark, 1993; Daniel, 1987; and Ramsay et al., 1992). In quantitative terms, the issue has been the extent to which jobs have disappeared and/or been created as a result of technological changes in both products and work processes. Qualitative issues, on the other hand, have focused primarily on questions of skill and control. Earlier debates on whether new technology results in deskilling or enskilling (e.g. Wood, 1982) have been superseded by subsequent empirical studies indicating a less clearly defined reality. While clear cases of deskilling and enskilling can be found, it is evident that in many cases, as Ramsay et al. (1992:176) conclude, 'the evidence on skill is largely indeterminate', not least because 'jobs are often just different, gaining and losing skill elements in ways that are not readily commensurable'.

Similarly, the extent to which the introduction of new technology is associated with any change in the level of control (either towards greater centralisation or decentralisation) is influenced by a number of possible factors, including the extent to which employees or work groups exercised control prior to the technological change and the degree to which in practice the technology performs to specification or requires additional operator intervention (Ramsay et al., 1992). While in some cases it is apparent that new technology entails a transfer of control from supervisors to work groups, in others – for example checkout operators using electronic point-of-sale (EPOS) equipment, or clerical employees working on computer terminals – the new technology enables greater centralised monitoring of time keeping and performance.

As well as issues of skill and control, new technology has wider relevance for employee relations, for example in relation to the nature of its planning and implementation, and the potential for different technological developments to alter patterns of work organisation by combining former discrete tasks into single jobs, thereby undermining traditional job boundaries. This last aspect can be particularly significant for those trade unions that have traditionally organised their recruitment along occupational or skill lines, basing their power on exclusive representation of an individual craft or occupation (see Chapter 5).

New technologies have also influenced developments in production control techniques, most notably in terms of using more powerful information systems to achieve a closer integration of different stages of production. Key aspects of this, for example, have been the closer matching of customer orders to production and an improvement in work flow, with materials and components being delivered just-in-time to be incorporated into products, which are in turn completed and delivered just-in-time to the market place. Improved information on production processes, together with the closer integration of different production stages, enable management to reduce stocks of materials and work-in-progress and remove reserve 'buffer' stocks of part-finished items. Just-in-time (JIT) operation, however, requires a high degree of employee cooperation to maintain the work flow and prevent production bottlenecks. Moreover the tendency to link JIT with teamworking and the quest for total quality based on both minimising resource waste (human, capital and energy) at every stage of production and maximising output quality, further heightens the degree to which contemporary production systems rely on worker compliance with managerial objectives and active cooperation within the production system itself. This need to secure employee cooperation with JIT and total quality management (TQM) systems indicates the relevance of employee relations for production developments. Indeed these developments highlight not only management's need to use those relations to ensure minimum disruptions to work flow, but also employees' potential power because of the relative vulnerability of JIT systems to disruption (see, for example, Turnbull, 1988c; and Wilkinson and Oliver's 1990 account of a strike at Ford in 1988).

The integration of product and labour markets

Although it is now commonplace for commentators to note the importance, and occasionally the interaction, of product and labour markets, this is rarely integrated into the analysis of employee relations. A key feature of product market pressures in the UK is that they are mainly transmitted through price, 'and when this is adverse the employers simply lay off workers' (Wilkinson and White, 1994:126). In other words, where market pressures are manifest through price competition rather than non-price competition (e.g. quality, design, reliability, after sales service), firms will tend to 'reap' instead of 'sow', to cut assets (capital and labour) rather than grow or diversify the business (e.g. identify new markets, invest in new products and/or processes, improve the quality and performance of products and services, and of course invest in the education, training and development of human resources) (see Hamel and

Prahalad, 1994). The firm's employee relations policies are therefore a product, *and also a determinant*, of the wider business strategies through which the organisation seeks to compete (Marchington and Parker, 1990).

To understand the potential interaction of product and labour markets, consider the situation where firms are faced with flexibility in their access to the external labour market but must accept strong rigidities with respect to internal (re)deployment and (re)training. Such a combination is characteristic of the UK: firms can hire and fire with comparative ease (Emerson, 1988:791), and increasingly employ labour on short-term, part-time, temporary or subcontracts that can more easily be terminated, but in the internal labour market employees have traditionally sought to protect their status, and secure a degree of employment security, by preserving job demarcations, manning levels and working methods. Hence, the more limited uptake of functional as opposed to numerical forms of flexibility in recent years. As Streeck (1988:417–18) argues, flexibility in the external labour market combined with rigidity in the internal labour market is better suited to the (mass) production of standardised goods. As already noted, it is precisely in industries that are characterised by low research and development intensity and the preponderance of price factors that UK firms have traditionally been more successful (Smith, 1986; see also Porter, 1990). Under such circumstances, where firms compete predominantly on the basis of price, management will continually seek to 'strip out' labour costs in order to remain competitive.

This combination of flexibility and rigidity, and its association with particular product market strategies, is depicted in Figure 3.2, where it is contrasted with flexibility in the internal labour market and rigidity in the external labour market. Where employees have a rigid 'entitlement' to employment security, whether as a result of legislation (as in Europe) or social obligation (as in large Japanese corporations), it is more difficult for firms to simply hire and fire as demand in the product market dictates (see Turnbull and Wass, 1997:42). Where management's recourse to the external labour market is more rigid, however, the 'trade-off' is invariably greater flexibility in the internal labour market: workers who enjoy a rigid entitlement to job security are more prepared to concede greater flexibility in adapting to new technology, new working methods, changing job requirements, retraining and even relocation (see Dore, 1986, 1988; and Streeck, 1988). As rigidity and flexibility, like equity and efficiency, are not mutually exclusive but rather part and parcel of the same organisational and economic dynamic, the key question is how different combinations of rigidity and flexibility in the internal and external labour markets shape and constrain different outcomes, and whether particular combinations are more or less effective given the prevailing economic and social conditions. According to Streeck (1988), as illustrated in Figure 3.2, flexibility in the internal labour market and rigidity in the external labour market is more conducive to serving volatile markets with

EXTERNAL LABOUR MARKET

		Flexibility	Rigidity
INTERNAL LABOUR MARKET	Flexibility	Anomic conflict	Diversified quality production
	Rigidity	Standardised production	Uncompetitive firms

Source: Adapted from Streeck (1988:417–18).

FIGURE 3.2 **Rigidity and flexibility in the internal and external labour market**

diversified, high-quality products. Under these conditions, exogenous shocks (e.g. a sharp decline in product demand) are generally diffused rather than magnified, because firms are required to keep workers on the payroll and are therefore encouraged to devote resources to 'reconversion' (that is, producing new, differentiated, high-quality products utilising the functionally flexible skills of the workforce, who are well paid and highly productive).

Many employers, and certainly the Thatcher and Major governments of the 1980s and 1990s, have argued that UK firms were uncompetitive in the 1970s because they were enveloped in both external and internal labour market rigidities. Consequently 'rigidities' in both markets – especially those 'imposed by' or 'attributed to' trade unions – were a prime target for Conservative government reforms (Chapter 6) and a succession of management initiatives in recent years (Chapters 4 and 7). However, trying to impose greater flexibility in both labour markets – for example by extending the qualification period for statutory employment protection, undermining statutory and practical support for collective bargaining and trade union representation, extending subcontracting and franchise agreements, and embracing human resource management, JIT production and TQM – simply 'involves firms in unending anomic conflict as it deprives workers of both employment security and the protection offered by standardized work roles and the external tradability of associated skills' (Streeck, 1988:417). The clearest indication of anomie, already alluded to, is the growing insecurity and associated stress now regularly reported by UK workers in countless studies (e.g. CBI, 1997; Demos, 1995; and ISR, 1996). Anomie frustrates the successful adaptive behaviour of individuals and organisations alike, as workers have no incentive to learn skills and employers no incentive to offer training. Instead management relies on outmoded techniques, or bastardised versions of the latest initiatives in production control or service provision, combined with a poorly paid and inadequately trained labour force, to produce standardised, low-quality goods. The organisational and economic dynamic that ensues, as subsequent chapters will demonstrate, is inherently *ill*-suited to prevailing economic and social conditions.

Conclusion

The foregoing analysis has highlighted both continuities and a number of significant changes in the context of employee relations. The latter include more intense product market competition, changes to the ownership and control of organisations, the problems associated with relative economic decline, the changing balance between employment in goods production and service provision, the growing prominence of female, part-time and self-employment, the importance of high levels of unemployment, redundancies and insecurity, and developments in technology and production techniques. Together these represent the intricately woven backcloth against which the day-to-day interactions that comprise employee relations must be assessed. These developments, of course, should not be seen as *determining* the precise nature of those relations but they have helped to *shape* those relations, and as a result a full understanding of employee relations can only be obtained by incorporating these broader contextual changes into the analysis. Many of these facets of the world of work have traditionally been seen as beyond the remit of employee relations enquiry. This chapter has demonstrated both their interaction and their integration with employee relations. As subsequent chapters show, employee relations can *only* be understood in relation to, and not in isolation from, these broader developments in industrial society.

PART 2

THE ACTORS IN EMPLOYEE RELATIONS

CHAPTER 4

Management and employee relations

The management of employee relations in British Airways

'Flying to Serve' with emotional labour

Having 'flown the flag' on a British Airways (BA) intercontinental flight, passengers arriving at London Heathrow are canvassed about the service they enjoyed. Did the check-in staff use your name? Did he or she look you in the eye? Did they smile? If yes, did the smile seem genuine or forced (on a scale of one to four)? As Dr Nick Georgiades, a former Director of Human Resources at BA and previously a professor of industrial psychology at the University of London, made quite clear,

> We are maintaining a commitment to customer service which transcends merely being nice. It demands more than a plastic smile and 'have a nice day'. . . . As well as using their brains, they are going to need to use their hearts and engage in what we call 'emotional labour' (quoted in Corke, 1986:114).

In the 1980s BA embarked on a major programme of cultural change in its quest to become 'The World's Favourite Airline', a programme designed to transform the company from being operationally driven to one that was market led (Höpfl *et al.*, 1992:25). In short, the company's business was redefined from transportation to service. The way to improve service, and thereby custom, revenue and profits, was 'to treat every single customer as though the entire airline is at his or her service, as indeed it must be. . . . The simple fact is that what we have to sell is a service to our customer' (Sir Colin Marshall, now BA chairman, quoted in Corke, 1986:91). As the new logo on the company's coat of arms boldly proclaimed, 'We Fly to Serve'.

Quality of service became not only a key factor for BA, but in the words of Sir Colin Marshall, the airline is 'entirely dependent upon the performance of our own people for the quality of service we give' (quoted in ibid:135). Clearly this brings the issue of management's direction and control of employee attitudes and behaviour to the fore. In BA this issue was particularly acute, as extensive market research had revealed significant gaps between customer and staff expectations regarding the delivery of service. In short, staff tended to focus on routine and procedural aspects of the job (such as getting everybody on the plane before it takes off, preferably with all their baggage), while for customers this was the minimum they expected (see Höpfl *et al.*, 1992:26). On many occasions passengers, as they were formerly called before they became customers, didn't even get this. Disputes and stoppages were frequent occurrences. In 1976–7 for example, BA experienced eighty seven disputes and fifty two actual stoppages of work, while in the following year industrial disputes accounted for the loss of 59 000 working days, equivalent to one day per employee (Corke, 1986:66). In a survey conducted in 1980 by the International Airline Passengers Association, 33 per cent of customers put BA at the top of the list of airlines to be avoided at all costs, ahead of Aeroflot, Nigerian Airways and even teetotal Arab carriers (Campbell-Smith, 1986:11). BA's policies, according to one commentator,

> had resulted in a 'peasant class' of travel on BA's European flights, repackaged catering arrangements which amounted to 'doggy-bag specials' and a general subservience to trade union pressure which had the management running to the pilots' union headquarters for routine meetings (ibid:2).

BA thus had to employ 'emotional labour' and 'Fly to Serve' simply in order to survive, but in the early 1980s there were more pressing concerns.

BA – from Bloody Awful to Bloody Awesome?

At the end of the 1970s BA faced intense competitive pressure on a number of its routes, in particular from Laker's 'Sky Train' service to the United States. On top of this, OPEC oil price rises doubled fuel costs, sending BA into a tailspin and the international economy into recession. Losses of over £140 million were recorded by the company in 1981 as money drained away at the rate of £200 per minute (Corke, 1986:82). The flag-carrying company that was to be the flagship of Tory privatisation plans was in a financial crisis, with a fifth of its international routes losing money. 'BA stood for Bloody Awful, said the wags. . . . As for the Speedbird on the side of the fuselage, a dodo would be more appropriate' (Campbell-Smith, 1986:8).

Management's initial response was to cut costs. Fuel costs were effectively beyond the company's control, so the axe fell on labour. Employment declined by almost 2500 between 1979 and 1981, but a more dramatic cost-cutting exercise was to follow. In February 1982 Lord King of Wartnaby (then Sir John) was appointed chairman with a brief 'to knock the airline into shape for take-off to the private sector' (ibid:27). Sixteen international passenger routes were suspended, aircraft sold off, two engineering bases disposed of, the training college axed, administration pruned and 9000 redundancies announced. '[T]here were emotional scenes, with BA girls [*sic*] openly in tears at the check-in counters at Heathrow and many senior managers expressing genuine dismay' (ibid:28). Lord King was once asked how, as a captain of industry, he sought to motivate his employees. ' "Fear", he replied' (ibid:24).

As a cost-cutting exercise, Lord King's strategy proved successful, reducing the company's labour force from 53 600 in 1981 to 39 700 by 1983, and increasing profits to £77 million over the same period. But BA's policy of voluntary redundancy on very generous terms – what the human resources director subsequently described as a 'hosing down with money strategy' (Nick Georgiades, quoted in Corke, 1986:111) – left the company with skill shortages in certain areas. Furthermore, the adoption of a tougher line with the unions (as during the baggage handlers' dispute at Heathrow during February–March 1982) and the rather 'high-handed' management style (Hamil, 1993:221) simply exacerbated a deeper malaise that afflicted BA, namely 'the appallingly low morale of the workforce' (Campbell-Smith, 1986:85). Profits had certainly improved, which was essential if the airline was to be privatised, but BA was still '*not* a very efficient airline' (Ashworth and Forsyth, 1984:7, emphasis added). In fact whichever way one looked at it (historically or in comparison with domestic or international competitors) 'the much publicised view of a dramatic improvement in efficiency is not borne out by the evidence' (ibid:9). With the labour force cut back and profitability rising, the tendency was to link the two, but in fact BA's recovery was predominantly founded on an improvement in yields, mainly brought about by favourable exchange rate movements (ibid:55, 124–5). Management themselves soon realised 'that "very determined management" could only go so far. To sustain further progress, BA had to win the employees' positive involvement and support' (Heller, 1992:53). A change of approach was signalled by the arrival in February 1983 of Colin Marshall, former chairman of Avis, the US car-hire company, and the subsequent appointment of Nick Georgiades as the director of a newly created human resources department.

A new approach towards employees

For many commentators, 'British Airways provides the best instance of intensive and ambitious commitment to culture change in the UK in the last ten years' (Höpfl, 1992:5–6, 1993; see also Anthony, 1994:11–16; Colling, 1995a;

and Storey, 1992:15–16). The company's culture, according to the consultants, changed from being bureaucratic and militaristic to one that was service-orientated and market-driven (Goodstein, 1990:180–1). According to Sir Colin Marshall, 'the purpose was to get all of us to understand how better to relate to other people and that our first obligation was to our customers, not to a series of practices and rules laid down in a manual' (1989:74). 'Customer contact staff', such as check-in and cabin crew, were the first to be targeted in BA's 'Putting the Customer First' campaign launched in November 1983, through a programme called 'Putting People First' (PPF). This was then extended to non-customer contact staff such as baggage handlers, whose 'customers' were identified as other BA employees (principally the customer contact staff). The final stage of the campaign was 'A Day in the Life', which rather than focus on the individual, emphasised the benefits of collaborative working on *all* aspects of BA's operations (see Corke, 1986:112–15; Goodstein, 1990; Höpfl, 1992, 1993; and Höpfl *et al.*, 1992). BA employed the same Danish consultants (Time Management International) as the Scandinavian airline SAS, whose aim had been 'to get the SAS girls [*sic*] smiling sweetly, come what may' (Campbell-Smith, 1986:147). The TV ads for the British Caledonian Girls might have been embarrassing to some, but BA got the message. Along with the 'cultural change' programme came five-year contracts and an upper age limit of 26 years for all new cabin crew: 'Elderly BA matrons were to be a thing of the past' (ibid:148). So too are cabin crew deemed to be too fat (BA tries to enforce svelteness by insisting that uniforms would not be available above size 14), or indeed too thin. According to a company spokesperson, BA's strict height/weight limits – some up to 9lbs below the levels recommended by the Department of Health – are set to ensure that staff are up to the rigours of the job: 'if you are a beanpole or a fatty you are probably going to flag out' (quoted in the *Daily Express*, 11 October 1996).

According to most accounts BA's programme was a resounding success (e.g. Goodstein, 1990; and Heller, 1992), although other analysts were prepared to settle for *behavioural* change, such as 'a well-mixed in-flight martini' (Thomas, 1985:27), rather than *cultural* or *attitudinal* change (e.g. Campbell-Smith, 1986:147–8). The programme certainly demanded a massive commitment to training and communications, and Sir Colin himself made every effort to attend all the PPF courses (part of what he called 'visible management'). The more critical dimension of the change programme, however, as is widely recognised, was to change the style of managers and management (Heller, 1992:53; Höpfl, 1992; and Sisson, 1989:24). First and foremost the 'Customer First' programme projected a 'shared vision' and thus a clear sense of direction for a restructured BA (now decentralised into eight profit centres for passenger operations, defined by geographical area, and three additional centres for cargo, charter and package-tour operations). Managers were expected to share this new vision. Indeed, the massive commitment involved sent a clear and symbolic message to all staff, but in particular to managers, that it was *necessary* to 'fall in' with the initiative (Storey, 1992:43). Consequently, 'out came the tumbrils once again', only 'this time, tears were not the monopoly of the check-in girls [*sic*] at Heathrow' (Campbell-Smith, 1986:103–4). Over seventy senior managers were to take 'permanent retirement', while the rest were to learn how to 'Manage People First' (MPF). The key themes of MPF were urgency, vision, motivation, trust and taking responsibility (Höpfl, 1992; see also Anthony, 1994:11–16; and Colling, 1995a). The latter – being in charge of, and responsible for, one's own behaviour – was to be evaluated through a new performance appraisal system for all managers, and rewarded through a new performance-related pay system.

Along with these changes came the requirement to be more 'visible' (which many managers simply equated with working longer hours) and to attend outward-bound courses. Watching managers dangle upside down on an abseil rope 'may be helpful in knocking a little of the pomposity out of them' (*Financial Times*, 21 December 1983), but its value back in the workplace has been questioned (James, 1989; and Lowe, 1992b). It not only created considerable stress among middle management, but also considerable cynicism towards the new training programmes and the evangelical message which the company now proclaims. Commenting on the presentation of one training session, one manager asked, 'Does this remind you of the Live Aid concert? It's all Save the World togetherness – like Coca Cola' (quoted in Höpfl, 1992). Another expressed his feelings more personally: 'I hated a lot of the "touchy-feely" stuff. . . . If it achieved anything it gave me the experience of shared humiliation rather than shared self-esteem' (ibid). Of course this is not to deny that changes in management attitudes and behaviour were achieved, but it also illustrates a resistance among employees at all levels. BA certainly experienced dissension on both an individual and collective basis.

A pragmatic approach towards trade unions

Prior to its privatisation in 1987, BA had a statutory duty under the British Airways Board Act 1977 to negotiate the terms and conditions of its employees through collective bargaining. As the major employer in the civil aviation industry, BA was the principal actor on the employers' side of the National Joint Council for Civil Air Transport (NJCCAT). The NJCCAT agreements covered such areas as statutory holidays and payment during sickness and absence. Negotiations on other items were covered by National Sectional Panels (NSPs), where separate agreements would be reached for each airline represented on that panel. BA recognised seventeen unions covering the different occupations and groups represented on ten NSPs, such as cabin

crew, engineering, maintenance and administrative staff. Collective bargaining was therefore complex, sectional and fragmented, with several groups
occupying strategic positions within the airline's operational structure, most
notably pilots. In responding to pressure and demands from these different
groups, management's approach to employee relations could best be described as pragmatic and opportunistic. As a result 'industrial peace was
only maintained at the price of significant concessions to the union side'
(Heller, 1992:53).

During the 1980s, while BA management developed a whole range of
employee relations initiatives directed at the individual, such as PPF and
Customer First Teams (quality circles), collective bargaining structures were
maintained intact. There was a tendency to play down collective relations, and
on several occasions management bypassed the usual trade union channels
and sent letters direct to each employee's home to explain the company's
position on key issues or disputes. But consultation was still handled on a
corporate basis through management–union committees at various levels
within the company. In many respects, collective interests were reinforced
by the reorganisation of the company and the programme of 'cultural change',
which in the words of one union official 'forced' a series of disputes
throughout the 1980s (interview notes). In addition to industrial disputes
involving baggage handlers (1982), cabin crews (1982, 1984, 1989 and 1997),
engineers (1984, 1986, 1988 and 1990), and pilots (1985 and 1987), latent
discontent among *all* grades of staff was revealed in a survey conducted by
BA, which indicated that while employees were certainly committed to the
company, many felt that the 'World's Favourite Airline' did not care about
them as much as it should (*Financial Times*, 2 December 1991; see also Höpfl,
1992). Trade unions continue to vent such frustrations.

Hence, as in other British 'mainstream' organisations (Storey, 1992:242–3),
BA was effectively operating 'dual arrangements' for most of the 1980s. As
Storey (ibid:259) argues, in many companies 'the old-style industrial relations
"firefighting" was disavowed and even scorned', but in the majority of cases
'there was hardly an instance where anything approaching a "strategic"
stance towards unions and industrial relations could be readily discerned as
having taken its place'. However all this altered in 1989 when BA proposed to
change its collective bargaining structure from ten NSPs to thirteen separate
bargaining units, which would reflect the various business interests of the
company. This new approach, however, is not indicative of a new synergy
between individual programmes and collective or institutional arrangements,
where the latter are geared towards reinforcing the corporate mission. Rather
the changes represent an attempt to undermine trade union influence within
the company. The emphasis on human resource management shifted discern-
ibly from quality to cost, and changes to collective arrangements within the
company are geared to facilitating what is visibly a more hard-nosed,
commercially focused approach.

An airline transformed?

Although the theme of 'caring' has been evident throughout BA's cultural change programme of the last two decades, so too has the 'bottom line'. Senior BA managers in fact caution against the caring image that is often portrayed in the media: 'Don't be deluded into thinking the change was about being nice to each other. It was about effectiveness, performance and survival' (BA manager quoted by Höpfl *et al.*, 1992:34). In the late 1990s BA is operating within a rapidly changing industry context – one marked by increasing privatisation of former state-owned carriers and growing deregulation of the air transport sector. In 1997, for example, the EU completed a process aimed at creating a more liberalised air transport system by easing restrictions on which carriers can fly which passengers to, from and within different member states. This development follows a move by the United States in the late 1970s to deregulate its own air passenger industry. As the market for passengers and cargo has become increasingly open, two of the key responses by the main European carriers, including BA, has been to develop an increasingly 'global' presence, and to launch a process of significant restructuring and cost cutting (see Blyton and Turnbull, 1996; and Warhurst, 1995).

In 1996 BA displaced Singapore Airlines as the world's most profitable carrier. In the same year Robert Ayling, BA's chief executive, announced a three-year £1 billion cost-cutting exercise, which translated into 5000 job losses in the 'backroom' areas of the business such as maintenance, cargo and other ground handling activities, accompanied by a two-year pay freeze for existing ground staff and lower rates of pay for any new staff recruited to 'frontline' jobs. Union officials complained bitterly about the plan, warning of increasing mistrust and falling morale among the workforce. In a document entitled 'Step Change – Keeping Staff on Board', the unions expressed the view that 'the company has set the new £1 billion efficiency target simply to please investors with no regard for the views of staff. [Staff] are concerned that the new target is unattainable, unnecessary and counter-productive'. Customer discontent and employee disputes have continued. An example of the former was the decision by the British Standards Institute to withdraw quality accreditation (ISO 9002) from BA's Heathrow cargo business in April 1996. The most recent examples of the latter were the pilots' dispute in the same year, when 90 per cent voted for strike action (on a turnout of 94 per cent of those eligible to vote), and the strike by cabin crew in 1997.

Overall, then, it is evident that BA employees continue to experience the inconsistency of what appear to be irreconcilable objectives, namely improved quality of service and lower costs (achieving the former with ever fewer resources). Union officials believe that if it comes down to a choice, cost will prevail over quality (interview notes). Changes to collective bargaining arrangements, and indeed the very operational structure of the company itself, are now geared to 'resolving' these inconsistencies. Or more accurately, they are geared towards undermining effective collective resistance. Bill Tate, a former BA human resource strategist, believes that the so-called transformation of BA during the 1980s has turned sour. In a less than subtle play on words, Tate (1991:112) noted that 'Some say Sir Colin Marshall worked a miracle at BA', but asked 'can he stem the tide that has turned against British Airways? King Canute thought he could. But wasn't it just his sycophants? A myth.'

The management of labour: control, confrontation and competition

As this brief account of BA indicates, despite the importance ascribed to collective bargaining, strikes and other activities of trade unions, the principal actor in employee relations is in fact management. Indeed, the employment relationship itself is fundamentally an *individual* exchange between employer and employee. Furthermore, the importance of management must be acknowledged if only because management is ubiquitous whereas trade unions in the UK have at best organised only a little over half the working population. Unions themselves are in fact 'secondary' organisations, as their members have already been engaged and organised into distinctive groups and relationships by employers (Offe and Wiesenthal, 1980:72). In this respect employers exert a strong influence over both individual and collective relations with employees. More importantly, management holds the 'balance of power' by virtue of its control over the means of production and the authority this imparts (see Chapter 2). And yet analysis of management played little part in industrial relations texts until after the Donovan Report in the late 1960s. Today no textbook on employee relations would be complete without at least one chapter specifically focusing on management.

The change was partly brought about because management, at the behest of the Donovan Commission and leading authorities on industrial relations such as Allan Flanders, were adjured to take responsibility for the much-needed reform of British industrial relations. For Flanders (1975:62), for example, the most important lesson from his influential study of *The Fawley Productivity Agreements* was that management must accept full responsibility for the human aspects of its job, or what is sometimes called 'man-management'. Subsequent research, however, indicated that company directors in particular devoted little attention to employee relations issues (Winkler, 1974:197–202; see also Hickson *et al.*, 1985:30; and Hill and Pickering, 1986). Even today,

Serious though the labour control problem may appear to senior managers, it tends to take a back seat in comparison with other issues at most times, at least in its *explicit* contribution to strategic decisions . . . managers operate in a manner which implicitly expects labour to conform to management plans, chosen in the 'best' interests of the company (Marchington and Parker, 1990:56–7, original emphasis).

In the light of extensive research since the early 1980s, Clegg's (1979a:164) assertion that 'the study of management in industrial relations is in a primitive state' could nowadays be rejected, but the argument that management strategies in employee relations remain in a primitive state would doubtless occasion considerable support.

For most managers 'industrial relations only becomes a consideration when it becomes a problem' (Keenoy, 1992:97). The absence of any coherent, let alone strategic approach towards the management of labour has often been noted (e.g. Hyman, 1987a:25–6; Kessler and Purcell, 1995:362; Purcell, 1987:545–6; Rose and Jones, 1984; and Sisson, 1989:3), and yet so too has the importance of management control over the actions and activities of labour. If control is so important, why is it that most British firms are characterised by a pragmatic, opportunistic and *ad hoc* approach towards labour? Three reasons are commonly cited. The first of these is the weight of history and key structures inherited from the past (Sisson, 1989:3). In combination, early industrialisation, growth by merger and acquisition, the late development of professional personnel management, greater importance attached to the finance function and the control of large shareholdings by investment trusts that demand immediate returns, 'constitute a major barrier to managements in Britain investing in the long term and, in particular, in people' (ibid:16; and Edwards *et al.*, 1992:20). The persistence of these features in the UK economy today represents an on-going but not insurmountable problem for effective management control.

The second and more important reason is the 'dynamic of confrontation . . . a dialectical interplay between control and resistance' (Storey, 1985:196), which Hyman (1987a:28–30) simply refers to as contradiction. Contradiction exists both within and between the various managerial specialisms, as well as between capital and labour. Given the open-ended, indeterminate nature of the wage–effort bargain, firms organise work in ways that reinforce and reproduce the authority and control of management over labour. But here is the rub:

Control has to be constructed in a fashion which also 'manufactures' consent . . . however imbalanced the distribution of power, the controlled always have some leverage on the terms of exchange. No matter how extensive the controls, in the final analysis, management is reliant on employee co-operation (Keenoy, 1992:93–5).

Capital owns and has the 'right' to control both the means of production and the labour it has hired, but at the same time capital must 'surrender' the means of production to the control of the worker for their actual use in the labour process. 'It is precisely because capital must surrender the use of its means of production to labour that capital must to some degree seek a cooperative relationship with it, unite labour with the means of production and maximise its social productivity and powers of cooperation' (Cressey and MacInnes, 1980:14; see also Burawoy, 1979). It is this underlying contradiction inherent in management control over labour that 'creates potential for worker initiative in ways which further adapt and qualify the strategies of management' (Hyman, 1987a:49).

Finally, management must continually respond to the external environment, in particular the pressures of competition. Almost every new development in employee relations during the 1980s and 1990s appears to have been initiated, if not justified or explained, by reference to more intense (international) market competition. In reality, of course, employee relations are not simply, automatically or directly adjusted in line with contingent circumstances. In fact the trajectory of monopoly capitalism has been to secure greater influence over markets, rather than simply respond to them. According to Nolan and Brown (1983:272),

> this is precisely the defining characteristic of competition; firms struggle to overcome existing impediments to profitable expansion, both in their input and product markets, by creating new economic opportunities and by redefining existing ones on terms more favourable to themselves.

Of course this is not to say that managements no longer respond to market signals, nor to suggest that they are able to control product and labour markets. As demonstrated in the previous chapter, it is the *interplay* of these different forces that must be considered, where management action is 'viewed as both a cause and a consequence of environmental influences' (Marchington and Parker, 1990:99; and Marchington and Harrison, 1991).

Each of these three factors has played an important part in the unfolding pattern of the management of employee relations in both British Airways and the British economy as a whole. To continue with the example of BA, historically the company has grown through a process of merger and acquisition, the most significant being the merger of BOAC and BEA in 1972 to create BA. At the time it was said that two airlines had been amalgamated into three, as not only did the merger bring together two companies with very different histories and cultures, which carried over into the 1980s (Campbell-Smith, 1986:10), but management itself was not fully integrated until four years after the merger (Corke, 1986:60). BA's acquisition of British Caledonian in 1988 presented further problems, not least that created by the formation of a break-away union, Cabin Crew '89, from the T&GWU cabin crew section (the British Airlines Stewards and Stewardesses' Association) which gave rise to considerable animosity and ill-feeling among the crew, especially as BA decided to recognise the new union. More recent takeovers (e.g. of Dan Air and Brymon), mergers and link-ups (e.g. with Qantas, USAir and Air Russia) have presented additional problems (not least industrial action in 1993 and the grievance at the centre of the pilots' dispute in 1996) and could act to undermine the corporate identity that BA has worked so hard to create. Finally, financial crisis, the political pressure to restore profitability in readiness for privatisation, and of course deregulation of the industry itself, have all created strong environmental pressures. In order to weather the storm of competition and exert greater influence over its product market, BA has recently sought a strategic alliance with American Airlines, which involves the combined control of 60 per cent of all flights between the UK and the United States and 70 per cent of all traffic between London and New York. As a result of all these developments, management policy towards labour has changed markedly since the early 1980s, if not in purpose (to make a profit) then at least in practice. And yet doubts are still being expressed about the success of past policies and the prospects for the future.

These doubts apply with equal force to the UK economy as a whole. The failure of management to secure control of the labour process, to develop a coherent approach to the management of employee relations, to respond effectively to competitive and other environmental changes, and ultimately to develop a high-wage, high-productivity, high-investment, high-growth economy, are the key themes in the remainder of this chapter. Following a review of various management control strategies, a number of distinctive management styles, and how these have changed over recent years, are identified. Noting that most UK companies have adopted an essentially pragmatic and opportunistic style of employee relations management, relying largely on compliance rather than on more effective forms of cooperation, the key factors that account for the failure of UK management are examined.

The management of control

For some organisations, control appears to be the *sine qua non* of all management action. Michael Edwardes' account of his chairmanship of British Leyland (now Rover) is a case in point:

> The real problem was that management was still striving to get into the driving seat, having been out of it for many years . . . we needed to re-establish management authority. . . . We could either regain control of the company, or in the event of failure, concede that closure was the only viable option (1983:78–85).

Usually, however, labour is only one of several management problems, and arguably not even the most important (Wood and Kelly, 1982:77). Having produced goods and services in a cost-effective manner, firms must then sell those goods and services on the market in order to realise a profit. For British Leyland/Rover this proved to be a continuing problem after Edwardes' departure, as product design, marketing and other aspects of the management function had been woefully neglected (Williams *et al.*, 1987). Employee relations must therefore take its place alongside, or preferably be integrated with, other management functions and the organisation's overall business strategy.

As organisations and their managers are ultimately judged in the only terms that count in a capitalist economy, namely a good return on capital, some have argued that management is not interested in control *per se* (Littler and Salaman, 1984:64). Thus according to the former Personnel Director of Nissan Motor Manufacturing (UK) Ltd, 'companies are not in the employee relations business they are in business to sell profitably a product desired by the consumer' (Peter Wickens, quoted by Marchington and Parker, 1990:55). While this statement is self-evidently correct, management control of labour is nonetheless a *precondition* for the production and subsequent sale of a product or service desired by the consumer. Some authors go further, suggesting that management will actually forgo technically superior (quantitatively more efficient) methods of production unless they maintain, and preferably re-inforce, management control over labour and the process of production (qualitative efficiency) (see Gordon, 1976; and Marglin, 1974). If profits are based on the exploitation of labour, as Marxists suggest, then this statement is equally self-evident (see Chapter 2).

Anglo-Saxon capitalism, as distinct from the 'social market' capitalism of Western Europe or Japanese and Asian (familial) capitalism, has always given preeminence to shareholder interests, but the emphasis on profitability and the consequent neglect of employee and other stakeholder interests, has arguably intensified in recent years (see Hutton, 1996). For example, in its 1987 annual report ICI described itself in the following terms:

> ICI aims to be the world's leading chemical company, serving customers internationally through the innovative and responsible application of chemistry and related sciences.
>
> Through achievement of our aim, we will enhance the wealth and well-being of our shareholders, our employees, our customers and the communities which we serve and in which we operate.

As John Kay (1997:22) points out, however, following Hanson's abortive attempts to buy ICI the company's description of itself changed significantly: 'Our objective is to maximise value for shareholders by focusing on businesses where we have market leadership, a technological edge and a world competitive cost base'. Whereas the 1987 statement emphasised *operational* activities, recognising all *stake*holders in the company, the new portrait emphasises *financial* activities and recognises only *share*holders. With this reorientation ICI is no longer forward looking, seeking instead to restrict activities to what it is already doing, and profit is no longer a means but an end in itself (ibid:24). Evidence suggests, however, that companies that embrace a stakeholder rather than a shareholder view of their business actually perform better (Wheeler, 1997), and for very good reasons. As Kay (1997:23) argues, an emphasis purely on shareholder interests undermines the very factors – trust, commitment and flexibility – that have been central to the competitive advantage of many successful firms such as ICI. British Airways is another case in point.

In BA, management control over employee behaviour, or in management's terms the exercise of 'emotional labour', was identified as a key element of corporate reorganisation and cultural change. As in all industries, but more so than most, management in the airline industry is highly dependent on employee initiative, cooperation and ultimately autonomy if work is to be performed quickly, efficiently and to the required standards. Unlike the provision of physical goods, however, where standards can be defined according to *technical* dimensions, in the service sector, where the level of involvement with customers is much greater, quality and other standards tend to be defined in *functional* and *expressive* terms. In fact the technical dimensions of the service are almost taken for granted: customers expect the plane to fly and to be conveyed to their chosen destination, along with their baggage! But what about reliability (did the plane depart/arrive on time?); the responsiveness of the staff (are they willing to help customers?); assurance (the knowledge and courtesy of staff and their ability to instil confidence and trust?); and of course empathy (do staff provide caring and individualised attention?) These factors tend to be the key determinants of service quality in 'high contact' industries such as hotels, catering and air transport, and each provides a measure of customer perception or satisfaction with the service. Of particular significance in the service sector are 'system failures' or 'critical events' and how employees handle such incidents, because every service encounter has the potential to lead to a satisfactory experience for the customer. Should a passenger develop acute appendicitis on a flight from London to Sydney, for example, and have to be taken off the plane in Bangkok for an emergency operation, if the airline provides medical support, rear-ranges flights and arranges hotel accommodation for convalescence, then a negative event can be turned into a positive experience (for a discussion of service quality, see Bitner *et al.*, 1990; Grönroos, 1984; and Zeithaml *et al.*, 1985). Clearly the role of front-line personnel (cabin crew, airport adminis-trative staff, airline doctors and so on) is critical in such situations, one of the everyday events that airline chief executives describe as 'moments of truth' (Carlzon, 1987).

In a detailed study of Delta Airlines, the US carrier with a world-wide reputation for service quality that BA and other airlines have sought to emulate, Hochschild (1983) describes in great detail the pressures on customer contact staff. In fact the term 'emotional labour', as sometimes used by BA, is derived from Hochschild's study, defined as the management of feelings to create a publicly observable facial and bodily display. Such labour involves 'acting', but 'it is not a resource to be used for the purposes of art, as in drama, or for the purposes of self-discovery, as in therapy, or for the pursuit of fulfilment, as in everyday life. It is a resource to be used to make money' (ibid:55). Emotional labour, in other words,

> requires one to induce or suppress feelings in order to sustain the outward countenance that produces the proper state of mind in others. . . . This kind of labor calls for a coordination of mind and feeling, and it sometimes draws on a source of self that we honor as deep and integral to our identity (ibid:7).

Maintaining a difference between feeling and feigning over long periods inevitably leads to strain, especially among female flight attendants, who also have to deal with sexual harassment, perhaps partly a result of their own status (or lack of it) (ibid:90–4), but more notably as a result of expectations created in the past by company promotional campaigns (Continental Airlines, for example, hired Playboy bunnies for a short period, while a naked woman implored customers to buy cheap Virgin Airline tickets in a Danish TV commercial) and airline advertising ('Fly me, you'll like it' and 'We really move our tails for you to make your every wish come true' are just two of the slogans previously used by carriers) (see Noon and Blyton, 1997, ch. 7).

Stewardesses are just part of an increasing number of 'pink-collar' workers (around a third of all employees, the majority of whom are women) who must engage in emotional labour at work. In a major supermarket chain, for example, as checkout operators walk onto the shopfloor they are confronted by a sign which reads 'Smile, you are going on stage', and a major UK food retailer issues each employee with a plastic card that summarises key points for action (Marchington and Harrison, 1991:294):

- Acknowledge eye contact and smile at your customer.
- Say Hallo/Good Afternoon etc.
- Be smart. Impress your customer.
- Thank your customer and say Goodbye.
- Remember! Customers always have a choice.

At another store, one checkout operator complained that 'there are times when I just want to look up angrily and tell [customers] to shut up but I have to be busy and keep smiling' (Ogbonna, 1992:91). If they fail to exercise emotional labour, employees are reprimanded by supervisors: 'We are able to detect when a checkout operator is not smiling or even when she is putting on a false smile . . . we call her into a room and have a chat with her' (ibid:85; see also Ogbonna and Wilkinson, 1988, 1990; and Noon and Blyton, 1997). Along with the 'stick', one high street retailer offers the 'carrot' of store gift vouchers for 'best grin of the day' (see Turnbull and Wass, 1998).

BA employed management consultants and appointed a professor of industrial psychology to effect the desired changes in employee behaviour. Generally, management scientists consider the problem of labour control in terms of employee motivation, involvement and job satisfaction. In contrast to the assumptions of scientific management – that employees have an inherent dislike of work and must therefore be coerced, controlled, directed and threatened with punishment if they are to exercise the required level of effort, with financial reward acting as the only motivator – Maslow (1943) and other psychologists suggest that individual behaviour is determined by a 'hierarchy of needs' ranging in ascending order from physiological needs, safety, love, esteem and self-actualisation. The quest for fulfilment of these needs is governed by a ratchet mechanism, such that once individuals have secured basic physiological needs such as food and shelter (or when employees have secured acceptable physical working conditions), they then seek higher-order needs. In a similar vein, Douglas McGregor (1960) distinguishes three major classes of need, namely physiological, social and self-fulfilment, arguing that self-fulfilment is especially important but that conventional organisational structures and practices totally ignore it. Thus managers tend to assume that employees dislike work, are passive, unambitious, indolent and resistant to change, and therefore prefer to be directed (follow orders and obey the rules) rather than be self-directed at work. Managers therefore reap what they sow: this attitude is self-defeating, bringing about resentment, dissent and resistance to change.

This approach, which McGregor calls 'Theory X', is contrasted with 'Theory Y', which is based on very different assumptions about human motivation and behaviour. In effect Theory Y is the reverse image of Theory X. Employees are assumed to welcome self-direction and self-control at work and to be capable of personal psychic development. Hence, there is perceived to exist a reservoir of creativity that can be harnessed by management to meet the goals of the organisation. The contrast, then, is relatively straightforward: 'people need whipping versus people are better at whipping themselves, as someone once mischievously put it' (Thompson and McHugh, 1990:133). The consultants claim that British Airways has opted for the latter (e.g. Goodstein, 1990), although the case study demonstrates that autocratic management still exists. As one pilot complained during the recent dispute, 'We are professional men [*sic*] being treated like children. We want the management to treat us with trust, respect and fairness' (*The Independent*, 9 July 1996).

Theory Y, however, is in fact a *programme* rather than a theory (Rose, 1975:189), a prescription for change rather than a framework for understanding employee behaviour and management action. In particular, there is a fortuitous concurrence between individual and organisational needs: if management adopt structures and practices that facilitate self-fulfilment, employees will work harder, efficiency will improve and profits rise (ibid:193). As a result there is a very narrow interpretation and understanding of industrial conflict. As we argued in Chapter 2, these conflicts are inherent in the very structure of the employment relationship. A more fruitful approach is to follow labour process theories of management control that actually *start* from the structured antagonism between capital and labour. As with the motivational theories of McGregor, a range of possible control/motivation strategies are identified as available to management. Friedman (1977), for example, distinguished between 'direct control' and 'responsible autonomy'. The former conforms to the principles of scientific management and is characterised by the fragmentation of tasks and the deskilling of work, accompanied by close supervision and tight discipline (what is sometimes referred to as the '3B' system of 'Bark, Bollock and Bite'). Responsible autonomy, on the other hand, is characterised by managerial attempts 'to harness the adaptability of labour power by giving workers leeway and encouraging them to adapt to changing situations in a manner beneficial to the firm' (ibid:78; see also Melman, 1958). In other words, employers grant discretion but surround this with policies designed to encourage the employee to identify with the goals of the organisation, a policy that was clearly evident in BA's 'Putting the Customer First' programme.

Other control strategies have been identified in the labour process literature, such as Richard Edwards' (1979) distinction between simple/direct control (via close supervision), technical control (achieved through technology and the production process itself) and bureaucratic control (adherence to rules and administrative procedures). The problem with Edwards' analysis, however, like that of Gordon *et al.* (1982), is that these different control strategies are linked to different stages of capitalist development, suggesting that at any given time there is a single, or at least predominant strategy of control that will ensure continued accumulation of capital. In addition there is a tendency to cast management in the role of monolithic, omnipotent, omniscient strategist (Thompson and McHugh, 1990:157). 'Managers too often are simply regarded as essentially unproblematic agents of capital who dispatch their "global functions of capital" in a rationalistic manner' (Storey, 1985:195). Yet conflicts between different management groups have already been noted (see Armstrong, 1984; and Whipp and Clark, 1986:213), as has the *variety* of 'means of control' that coexist at any one time (see Storey, 1985:198). Furthermore the presence of a particular strategy, such as 'responsible autonomy', may reflect management neglect (allowing control to drift away) rather than a deliberate policy of ceding control to the workforce to elicit cooperation, motivation and self-actualisation. Reality, as Paul Edwards (1986:41) illustrates, is far more anomalous:

> Firms will develop their practices of labour control with whatever materials they have available. They are unlikely to have explicit strategies and more likely to react to particular circumstances as best they can. Even when they have fairly clear goals

they are unlikely to follow a policy which conforms to an ideal-type: they will proceed according to their own needs. In particular, they are likely to use a variety of means of controlling the labour process and tying workers to the firm. Reliance solely on arbitrary power or technology or rules would be a very limited and dangerous approach.

Labour control is therefore of crucial importance, but management are not simply confronted with a (strategic) choice between different types of control. Ultimately, choice is not entirely in their hands, because control is the product of past and present struggles within the social relations of production. Because of this *constrained choice*, a contradictory array of structures and practices is invariably the outcome. In particular, as Storey (1985:201) notes, managers frequently want both to use labour instrumentally and to tap cooperation and initiative. In other words, 'employers require workers to be both dependable and disposable' (Hyman, 1987a:43), which in the case of BL/Rover, for example, produced 'an inconsistent amalgam of the disciplinary practices seen as necessary for high productivity and cost minimisation and the employee-involvement exercises seen as necessary for high-quality output' (Willman, 1986:315). Thus the result is often a Theory X structure and Theory Y management. This suggests a separation of individual and collective relations with labour, where managers pursue an array of employee relations policies to elicit individual cooperation and commitment, while at the same time referring to external organisations such as trade unions to handle the inevitable conflicts of interest that arise from the very structure of the employment relationship itself (as discussed in Chapter 2).

Given the limits to any rational choice of a coherent 'means of control', and the tensions inherent in the very purpose of management control, namely to secure the cooperation of labour and at the same time make a profit, it is hardly surprising that most firms display a distinctly *un*strategic approach towards employee relations. In general, management practices are found to be 'opportunistic, habitual, tactical, reactive, frenetic, *ad hoc*, brief, fragmented and concerned with fixing' (Thompson and McHugh, 1990:137). To return to employee relations in British Leyland and the account of Michael Edwardes, management 'were still fire-fighting, running from dispute to dispute without tackling the root of the problem' (1983:80). British Leyland was not alone in its approach, as the account of British Airways clearly demonstrates. Nor was either company alone in its determination to change its style of management during the 1980s.

The management of employee relations

There are two fundamental dimensions to the management of employee relations. First, there are the terms on which labour is hired: substantive terms such as wages and hours of work that are adjusted periodically to reflect changes both in the external environment (such as inflation and the relative pay of other workers) and internal conditions (in particular, profitability or the 'ability to pay'). Determination of these terms and conditions in union and non-union environments is discussed in Chapters 7 and 9 respectively.

Second, there is the general control and direction of labour that is exercised by management on a day-to-day basis. Frequently referred to as 'managerial relations' or the company's employee relations 'style', this second dimension can be seen 'as a set of proposals and actions which establishes the organization's approach to its employees and acts as a reference point for management' (Brewster et al., 1983:62), or is simply 'the preferred way of dealing with employees individually or collectively' (Purcell and Gray, 1986:213). The most obvious distinction is between a unitary and a pluralist perspective (Fox, 1966), where three basic areas of difference can be identified:

1. management acceptance and recognition of trade unions.
2. views about managerial prerogatives and employee participation.
3. the perceived legitimacy of, and reactions to, conflict at work (see Marchington, 1982:38–47; and Chapter 2 above).

Fox (1974:297–313) subsequently developed this unitary–pluralist dichotomy to distinguish six different patterns of employee relations management, based on the frame of reference (unitary or pluralist) held by the parties. The utility of this approach is limited however, since the vast majority of managers display a pronounced preference for unitarist values (Poole et al., 1981:82–3; and Poole and Mansfield, 1993). This is only to be expected, as such values 'have been strongly inculcated in their own training and development, they are uncomplicated in their implications, and they are self-reassuring' (Purcell and Sisson, 1983:113). And yet most larger companies recognise trade unions and are involved in collective bargaining. Clearly, the values of individual managers are insufficient datum with which to distinguish different styles of employee relations management.

In a series of articles John Purcell and Keith Sisson have identified five ideal-typical styles of industrial/employee relations management (Purcell and Sisson, 1983; Purcell and Gray, 1986; Purcell, 1987; Purcell and Ahlstrand, 1994; and Sisson, 1984). These styles are summarised in Table 4.1. Briefly, *traditionalists* display forceful opposition towards unions and openly exploit labour. *Sophisticated paternalists/human relations* refuse to recognise trade unions, 'but do not take it for granted that their employees accept the company's objectives or automatically legitimise management decision-making; they spend considerable time and resources ensuring that their employees have the right approach'. *Sophisticated moderns* recognise unions and legitimise their role *in certain areas* of joint decision making, either through a *constitutionalist* approach, where the limits to trade union activity are codified in collective agreements, or through a *consultative* approach where, in contrast to the constitutionalists, 'every effort is made to minimise the amount of collective bargaining especially of a "conflictual" or "distributive" kind. Instead, great emphasis is placed on "cooperative" or "integrative" bargaining: "problems" have to be solved rather than "disputes" settled'. Finally, the *standard modern* approach can best be described as pragmatic or opportunistic, such that employee relations tend to be viewed primarily as a 'fire-fighting' activity (Purcell and Sisson, 1983:113–16).

A priori, one would expect a company's employee relations style to be defined, or at least promulgated by personnel managers. As Table 4.1 indicates, however, the role of personnel managers varies according to which employee relations style is adopted. In fact, in many organisations, and not just among the traditionalists, there is unlikely to be a personnel specialist as such employed by the company. Despite the increased importance of the personnel management function in the 1970s, due in large part to government employment legislation (Brown, 1981:33; and Sisson, 1989:25), the majority of establishments do not employ a personnel specialist. Thus the three Workplace Industrial Relations Surveys found that senior people dealing with industrial relations, employee relations or personnel matters (the principal management respondents in the survey), were unlikely to have 'personnel' in their job title – only 15 per cent of management respondents in 1980 and 1984 were 'personnel managers', and 17 per cent in 1990 (Millward *et al.*, 1992:27–8) – and despite all the HRM rhetoric there were even fewer 'human resource' specialists (Guest and Hoque, 1993; and Sisson, 1993:201). Personnel managers are not even universal in the divisional and head offices of the large corporate enterprises that dominate employment in Britain (Marginson *et al.*, 1988:52–4). This does not mean, however, that employee relations issues are necessarily handled by inexperienced or unqualified staff. For example, there has actually been an increase in personnel qualifications among non-designated staff responsible for industrial and employee relations (Millward *et al.*, 1992:35–7). The more important distinction to make, therefore, is between different functions and roles, rather than simply the presence or absence of personnel managers. This has a direct bearing upon, and will help us to distinguish between, different employee relations styles.

In an analysis of contemporary management practice in Britain, Storey (1992:167–8) locates the role and function of personnel specialists along two dimensions. The first is the degree of intervention in overall management policy (for example whether personnel managers exercise a high or low degree of discretion). The second dimension is the type of intervention (strategic or tactical) that personnel managers engage in. This generates a four-fold typology of personnel practice as illustrated in Figure 4.1.

Both advisers and hand-maidens play a reactive role. The former perform a more consistent role as 'internal consultant' while the latter are predominantly

TABLE 4.1 Management styles in employee relations

Title	Description	Dominant frame of reference	Most likely to occur in these circumstances	Examples	Expected role of central personnel management
Traditional	Labour is viewed as a factor of production and employee subordination is assumed to be part of the 'natural order' of the employment relationship. Unionisation opposed.	Unitarist	Small owner-managed companies (or franchise operations). Product markets often highly competitive, emphasis on cost control.	Grunwick Processing Laboratories Ltd, Port of Tilbury, Sew & Son (see Chapter 9).	Few personnel specialists.
Sophisticated human relations	Employees are viewed as the company's most valuable resource. Above average pay. Internal labour market structures with promotion ladders are common; internal grievance, disciplinary and consultative procedures; extensive networks and methods of communication. The aim is to inculcate employee loyalty, commitment and dependency. Companies seek to make it unnecessary or unattractive for staff to unionise.	Unitarist	Large, American-owned, single industry, financially successful firms with a high market share in growth industries (electronics/finance sector).	IBM, Hewlett Packard, Kodak, Mars, Marks & Spencer.	Strong central personnel departments developing policies to be adopted in all areas of the company.
Consultative (sophisticated modern)	Similar to the sophisticated human relations companies except that unions are recognised. An attempt is made to build 'constructive' relationships with the trade unions and incorporate them into the organisational fabric. Emphasis is also placed on techniques designed to enhance individual employee commitment to the firm and the need to change (share option schemes, profit sharing, briefing or cascade information systems, joint working parties, quality or productivity circles/councils).	Pluralist	British/Japanese-owned single industry companies that are large and economically successful, often with a high market share. Companies with relatively low labour costs (process industries) often adopt this style.	ICI, Esso, Cadbury-Schweppes.	Central personnel departments produce policy guidelines or precepts providing advice and central direction when required.

Constitutional (sophisticated modern)	Unions have been recognised for some time and accepted as inevitable. Employee relations policies centre on the need for stability, control and the institutionalisation of conflict. Management prerogatives are defended through highly specific collective agreements. The importance of management control is emphasised with the aim of minimising or neutralising union constraints on both operational (line) and strategic (corporate) management.	Single industry companies with mass production or large batch production requiring a large unit size of operation. Labour costs form a significant proportion of total costs. Product market conditions are often highly competitive.	Ford	Relatively strong emphasis on the central personnel auditing/control function.
Standard Modern	The approach to employee relations is pragmatic and trade unions are recognised. Employee relations are viewed as the responsibility of operational management. The importance attached to employee relations policies changes in the light of circumstances. There can be marked differences of approach between establishments or divisions and between various levels of the hierarchy.	Most common in conglomerate, multiproduct companies that have grown through acquisition and diversification, especially in the engineering and heavy manufacturing industries with long traditions of unionisation.	General Electrical Co., GKN, Tube Investments, Lucas Industries, British Leyland, British Airways.	Relatively weak central personnel departments. Personnel specialists operate at unit level, have a fire-fighting role, and react to union claims and the impact of labour legislation.The personnel function tends to have a chequered history: sometimes strong, sometimes weak.

Also pluralist labels: Constitutional = Pluralist; Standard Modern = Pluralist.

Source: Adapted from Purcell and Gray (1986:214–15). Examples from Purcell and Sisson (1983:113-16), Smith *et al.* (1990), Sisson (1989:9–11), and authors' own research.

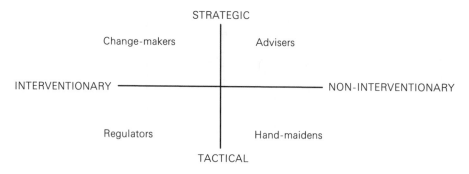

Source: Storey (1992:168).

FIGURE 4.1   Types of personnel management

'customer led' in the service they offer, largely performing a subservient, attendant role to line management. The regulators are more interventionist. In other words, they operate within a traditional industrial relations paradigm as the 'manager of discontent', seeking order through temporary, tactical truces with organised labour (ibid:168–9). The change-makers, in contrast, have higher ambitions, seeking to put relations with employees on a new footing, namely the 'needs of the business'. Typically this means eschewing the regulative approach in favour of a management style that engenders employee commitment and a willingness to 'do the extra mile' (ibid:169), or in the words of British Airways management, 'use their hearts'. Storey's research evidence, however, drawn from fifteen UK 'mainstream' organisations, indicates that this particular approach is rare. Only two of the fifteen companies approximated to the change-maker type, and even then changes were not always initiated by personnel managers (ibid:186–7). In BA, despite the creation of a new Human Resources department, personnel staff acted as internal consultants (advisers) rather than change-makers, with initiatives for customer care and the like originating predominantly in the marketing department (see Goodstein, 1990). These results are not inconsistent with other evidence (e.g. Legge, 1988, 1995; Marginson *et al.*, 1988; Millward *et al.*, 1992:350; and Sisson, 1989:38). The limited role of personnel management is a key characteristic of many UK companies and a major reason for the widespread absence of any coherent or strategic approach to the management of labour, and the observation that management style tends to wax and wane in the light of changing circumstances. This is true of personnel management itself (Hart, 1993), as Legge (1995:14) explains:

The fact that personnel specialists oscillate between the 'personnel' and 'management', between 'caring' and 'control' aspects of the function, can be attributed to their role in mediating a major contradiction embedded in capitalist systems: the need to achieve both the control *and* consent of employees (original emphasis).

What, then, have been the major changes in employee relations over the past decade? Why has management style changed? And why have the changes at companies such as BA often failed to achieve the desired results?

Although the standard modern approach identified by Purcell and Sisson (1983:116) is the most inconsistent and least coherent, it is nonetheless the *predominant* management style in Britain (see also Deaton, 1985; and Marsh, 1982). For most companies, employee relations are assumed to be unproblematic until events prove otherwise, such that the importance of labour issues – and of course the organisational status of those specialists who are normally charged with responsibility for them – will vacillate over time (Purcell and Sisson, 1983:116). Not surprisingly, in the recession of the early 1980s 'a new breed of tough managers, almost contemptuous of union and negotiating procedures, seems to have emerged. . . . The spirit is almost of the divine right of managers to manage, to broach no argument and get on with the job of directing, controlling and enforcing order over a demoralised workforce' (Purcell, 1982:3). 'Macho management' had arrived in the public and private sectors alike, epitomised by a new firmness and determination to manage, even if this meant direct confrontation with the workforce (ibid; Ferner, 1989; and Mackay, 1986). For macho managers at British Leyland, British Airways and elsewhere, market power was preeminent, with changes forced upon the workforce on the grounds of 'common sense' and the 'economic facts of life' (Purcell and Sisson, 1983:117).

Beyond the well-publicised examples, however, there was uncertainty about the extent of macho management. Mackay (1986:25) argued that 'the macho manager is alive and kicking in a surprisingly large number of organisations', but larger-scale surveys found very little evidence of direct attacks on trade unions or shop steward organisation, nor a reassertion of the right to manage or even a more aggressive policy in the event of industrial action (Batstone, 1984; see also Edwards, 1987:146; and Chapter 5 below). The confusion, according to Legge (1988:55), might be resolved by recognising that '*"macho" management is far more generally apparent in strategies to change work practices than in deliberate attempts to undermine union organisation*' (original emphasis). Widespread changes to working practices during the 1980s have in fact been documented (e.g. Elger, 1990; and Ingram, 1991a), and it has been suggested that 'managements appear to have no need to "take the trade unions on". All they need to do is ignore them – for the moment' (Mackay, 1986:27). Alternatively macho management could be seen as an attempt to break the old *status quo*, to convince the workforce, in the words of Michael Edwardes, 'that the new management had a level of commitment, a determination that was fundamentally different' (1983:80). In other words macho management was never likely to be a long-term strategy, but rather a transitionary phase in the development of a new approach. In BL, for example, Edwardes' punitive style was increasingly seen as inappropriate to the emerging business strategy of concentrating on more upmarket, quality cars (Storey, 1992:271). Consequently, Paul Edwards (1987:150) suggested that a more subtle approach had emerged, since to treat workers simply as an expandable resource may work in the short term under conditions of financial stringency, but was unlikely to have much success in the longer term. A more 'enlightened' approach was called for, where

> managers assert not so much the right as the need to manage; they stress 'business realities', but they try to take workers along with them, and indeed must do so if they are to retain the flexibility that is increasingly necessary in new competitive conditions (ibid.)

As Edwards cautioned, however, this new approach may be just the latest fad, born of recession and crisis rather than long-term planning. The arrival of a new management rhetoric, that of human resource management (HRM), confirmed these suspicions.

It is evident that HRM has fared little better than macho management or enlightened managerialism before it. Not only is the concept itself unclear – the 'soft' approach to HRM grounded in the human relations school emphasises the potential input of resourceful *humans*, whereas the 'hard' approach to HRM grounded in the theories of manpower planning and organisational development emphasises the control of human *resources* – but the four key policy goals of high commitment, high quality, flexibility and strategic integration (Guest, 1987) have been demonstrated to be theoretically and empirically inconsistent if not contradictory (Blyton and Turnbull, 1992; and Legge, 1995). Most UK firms, especially in the wake of the early 1990s recession, have opted for hard (cost control) HRM rather than soft (caring) HRM, although even then the adoption of sophisticated HRM policies of any description has been limited, opportunistic and partial, and their implementation problematic (for a review of the literature, see Blyton and Turnbull, 1992; Legge, 1995; Sisson, 1994; and Storey, 1989, 1992, 1995). The reason is not difficult to find: HRM demands that managers change their habits of a lifetime, as proponents of this latest management fashion argue that it is only when a coherent strategy is applied, directed towards all four policy goals, fully integrated into business strategy and fully sponsored by line management at all levels, that the high productivity and related outcomes sought by management will be achieved. This is simply asking too much of most UK managers.

In defining management style, Purcell (1987:533) suggests that it is 'a *deliberate choice* linked to business policy' (emphasis added). Consequently,

> Pragmatic, reactive responses to labour problems cannot be classified as management style. Style implies the existence of a distinctive set of guiding principles, written or otherwise, which set parameters to and signposts for management action in the way employees are treated and particular events handled. Management style is therefore akin to business policy and its strategic derivatives (ibid:535).

In other words management style must not only be deliberate, but also ubiquitous, coherent, integrative, consistent and long term (see also Poole, 1986:43). Having eliminated the standard modern approach through this definition, the different management styles can then be categorised along two dimensions, namely individualism and collectivism. The former expresses the extent to which the firm gives credence to the feelings and sentiments of each employee and seeks to encourage each employee's capacity and role at work, while collectivism indicates the extent to which management recognise the collective interests of employees, their collective involvement in the decision-making process and the legitimacy accorded to the collective by management. As individualism and collectivism are not opposites but two facets of the managerial belief or value system with regard to employees, this leads to the four remaining styles of management being arranged as in Figure 4.2.

At one level, this framework is a useful device with which to distinguish the different styles of those companies that heavily inform much of the research and literature on employee relations (e.g. M&S, IBM, Ford, Esso, ICI and so

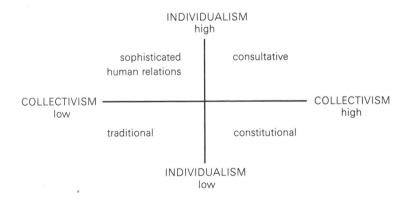

Source: Purcell and Gray (1986:213).

FIGURE 4.2   Individualism, collectivism and management style

on). At another level, however, its utility is clearly limited since it effectively excludes the majority of standard modern (opportunistic) UK firms. Furthermore, it is evident that employers view labour as a cost while also seeking to tap into employee cooperation and initiative, which makes the precise location of many organisations within the grid of Figure 4.2 very difficult to determine. Additionally, management's approach is not necessarily one of individualism *per se*, but whether or not they are prepared to invest in employees (the company's 'investment orientation') (Marchington and Parker, 1990:235). Similar problems apply to collectivism, where the *existence* of collective bargaining structures or employee participation arrangements conveys little in terms of the actual *operation* of such structures, or indeed management's approach towards them (see also Storey and Bacon, 1993). Using an X–Y axis rather than a grid, Marchington and Parker (1990:235–8) relabel individualism as 'management's approach to employees', and collectivism as the degree to which a 'partnership orientation' with trade unions is pursued by management. This is illustrated in Figure 4.3. Such an approach allows for much greater variation and nuance in management style to be identified. In the case of British Airways, for example, management's approach shifted from somewhere in the region of point A in the late 1970s towards point B in the mid 1980s, although the current emphasis on cost-cutting, the decentralisation of collective bargaining and the (attempted) policy of union exclusion signals a further movement towards point C (clearly these points represent broad rather than precise movements).

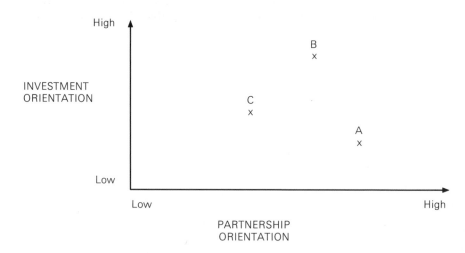

Source: Marchington and Parker (1990:238).

FIGURE 4.3   **Mapping management style in employee relations**

Movements such as these can more accurately depict changes in the management of employee relations. Thus subtle (and not so subtle) shifts within any given style can be more readily depicted. Kessler and Bayliss (1992:95–6), for example, suggest that companies adopting a consultative style have reduced the scope of collective agreements compared to the 1970s, in order to get management solutions to problems more readily accepted. At Cadbury's, for example, where management have described the employee relations style as 'democratic consensus: slow persuasion and very mild coercion' (Smith *et al.*, 1990:177), changes in employee relations have been more of a variation on a theme than a totally new approach:

> Coercion, coupled with continual striving after the desire to build consensus, continued to animate Cadburyism as a management philosophy. . . . It was not that consensus gave way to coercion as some permanent break, but rather that a new managerially derived understanding of consent had to be rebuilt with different ingredients and constructed *against* custom, service and the tradition of job security that formed the basis of earlier employment practices (ibid:217, original emphasis).

At Esso, in contrast, management recently completed a process of union exclusion (derecognition) that was initiated in the early 1970s (Claydon, 1996:164–5). Although Esso is typically cited as a 'sophisticated modern' (consultative) organisation (see Table 4.1), Ahlstrand (1990:161) has dismissed the assumption that the company ever genuinely sought to integrate trade unions into management decision making. Thus it is important to map changes in the *practice* of employee relations over time, and certainly to look beyond managerial rhetoric, but we must not lose sight of the fact that in the vast majority of cases the changes adopted by most firms still do not constitute a new 'style', as defined by Purcell (1987:535). The significance of this, according to Purcell, is that many initiatives are 'like the seed on stony ground', having only 'a short life because there is no underlying accepted standard of treatment for employees beyond pure short-run commercial logic' (ibid:546). As at British Airways, then, the management of employee relations continues to wax and wane in the light of changing circumstances, invariably in a reactive rather than proactive manner. The question that remains is whether the mismanagement of employee relations is inevitable.

Competition, confrontation and the failure of UK management

Throughout the 1980s and 1990s managers have used the rhetoric of market forces to expedite changes in both collective bargaining arrangements and working practices: the argument has been that unless changes were made, the company would become uncompetitive, orders and jobs would be lost, and ultimately the company could go out of business. In short, firms could no longer guarantee stability or security, if indeed they ever could. Competition from rival capitalists in international markets where UK firms perform most poorly would see to that. Managers at plant level in particular tend to view employee relations as being subordinate to the market (Marchington and Parker, 1990:86–9), and yet considerable research exists that illustrates the importance of (strategic) management choice (ibid:96–100). In the airline industry, for example, the effects of deregulation appear to be propelling carriers along the route of ever more aggressive cost-cutting: 'Labour cutbacks, reductions in wages, increases in working hours and workload, cross-utilisation of manpower, and contract work are going to be the order of the day' (ITF, 1992:12; and Gil, 1990:327–9). In the Unites States, however, where the industry was deregulated in 1978, changes to labour relations have not been a function of deregulation *per se* but the interaction of more competitive market pressures and the structure of collective bargaining. As collective bargaining was traditionally conducted on a craft basis and, more importantly, on an independent basis at each carrier, there was no protection for labour from competitive market pressures (put differently, if wages and conditions had been negotiated on an industry-wide basis, this would have taken wages out of competition). As Cappelli (1985a) demonstrates, collective bargaining became extremely sensitive to varying situations within individual carriers, who were each hit very differently by competition (depending on, for example, their scale of operations, route networks, financial situation and age of aircraft).

Market pressures, in other words, are mediated by the dynamics of conflict, accommodation and cooperation identified in Chapter 2. US airlines in fact developed very different strategies in response to common environmental conditions (deregulation), and it was not necessarily those carriers that met competition head on that ultimately proved successful. In fact two companies that avoided competition and stuck to their regional markets, namely Northwest and USAir, survived the initial upheavals in the US air transport market better than some of their rivals, despite (or perhaps because of) making few changes to their labour relations (ibid:324–5). What appears to have been of fundamental importance in the restructuring of the industry was not so much the changes to labour relations but the development of a 'hub and spoke' route network, whereby each major carrier came to dominate one or two major airports (the hub), flying passengers in from regional airports on domestic routes (the spokes) to link up for onward domestic or international flights. Prior to 1978 not a single US airport was dominated by a single carrier. By the early 1990s there were eighteen major (hub) airports where one carrier held 60 per cent or more of all slots (ITF, 1992:26). When combined with computer reservation systems linking the carrier to the travel agents, this had given the four major US airlines 70 per cent of the domestic market by that time.

The 'power' of product markets over the employer, and therefore the extent to which employers, on balance, are reactive or proactive in their policies towards labour, will clearly be influenced by both competitive pressures (the degree of monopoly power) and customer pressure (the extent of monopsony) (Marchington and Parker, 1990:240–6). In the US airline industry there are now fewer competitors and entry is prohibited both by the capital costs of aircraft and other equipment, and by the inability of new carriers to secure slots at the major airports. The overall level of demand is obviously beyond the control of individual carriers, but customer choice is now restricted (controlled) by the hub and spoke system and by computer reservations, giving carriers more predictable demand at any given time. Thus both monopoly and monopsony power have been enhanced, contrary to the expectations of the proponents of deregulation (see Gil, 1990:320; and ITF, 1992). By reducing the power of the market, or alternatively gaining more control over the market, the successful US airlines were able either to trade job security for concessions on work practices (United and American Airlines) or to make relatively few changes to employee relations (Northwest and USAir) (see Cappelli, 1985a). Neither Pan Am nor TWA could offer promises of job security and neither could secure the concessions they wanted from the workforce. Pan Am collapsed in December 1991, while TWA entered a state of financial crisis in the early 1990s, re-emerging as a much scaled-down organisation after 1994 (Wilson, 1995; and Cappelli, 1995a).

The power of individual organisations over their product and labour markets is clearly a key variable in whether or not a distinctive 'style' of employee relations will emerge and persist over time. This is quite different from financial success, which as Purcell and Sisson (1983:116) note is insufficient to explain whether or not firms have a specific management style, or indeed any identifiable style at all if we exclude the standard moderns. As the examples in Table 4.1 indicate, financially successful companies can be found in each category, but those in the sophisticated human relations, consultative and constitutional categories are either market leaders or major (oligopolistic) players in their respective product markets. Obviously, not all firms can secure oligopolistic control over their product markets. Equally, however, not all oligopolistic organisations display a uniform, consistent and coherent management style. British Airways is a case in point.

Where companies grow through merger and acquisition – as in BA's case and most other major British firms – rather than 'organically', management are usually faced with a wide variety of traditions, practices and approaches to employee relations throughout the organisation. Consequently, 'it is not difficult to understand why most of them opt for pragmatism' (Purcell and Sisson, 1983:117). But this is the symptom rather than the cause of the problem: 'British companies not only suffer one of the highest cost of capital in the world, but the febrile stock market compels them to earn a very big mark-up over even that cost of capital to fend off the threat of take-over and keep their shareholder base stable' (Hutton, 1996:157). Thus companies aim to keep their financial returns high in the short term, principally by maintaining downward pressure on pay and other terms and conditions of employment, to ensure that the company is a predator rather than a victim in the event of a hostile takeover bid (ibid:327). With the booms and slumps of business cycles amplified by the demands of financial capital, human resources are inevitably treated as a cost rather than an investment on the accountant's ledger. It is hardly surprising, then, that so few UK companies are able to establish or maintain a clear and consistent management style.

Nonetheless some organisations clearly do have a recognisable management style, which Purcell and Sisson (1983:116–17) attribute, in the first instance, to the presence of strong personalities at an early stage in the company's development. The 'founding fathers' often establish a pattern that continues to influence subsequent developments, such as 'Cadburyism', the 'HP Way' or being an 'IBMer'. But then it is very difficult for other companies to imitate the management style of these successful companies. Len Peach, the former personnel director of IBM, when asked how other companies could emulate IBM's personnel style, replied, 'you start thirty years ago' (quoted by Bassett, 1986:170). Not surprisingly, in the case of standard modern companies key personalities are more notable for their absence, at least in terms of their contemporary influence on management practice. Even when key figures emerge or are appointed, such as Michael Edwardes at BL, their ability to impose an overriding approach or style is constrained both by what has gone before (Purcell and Sisson, 1983:117) and by the resistance that is almost inevitably encountered (to a greater or lesser extent) from other managers, but especially from labour.

The inability of key figures or the management team as a whole to change the employee relations style of an organisation is somewhat at odds with press and other reports in the 1980s that hailed new 'captains of industry' as the driving force behind corporate reorganisations. John King and Colin Marshall are often cited in this context, having been lauded by the press and honoured by the government. The management of change at BA is now presented as a blueprint for other organisations to follow. Goodstein (1990), for example, presents an almost mechanistic picture of organisational change at BA using Lewin's (1958) model to depict change taking place at three levels and through three stages. The former include individuals (skills, values, attitudes and behaviour), structures and systems (rewards, work design, *inter alia*) and climate (interpersonal style, conflict management and decision-making). The change process itself involves 'unfreezing' the existing pattern of behaviour as a way of managing resistance to change, 'movement' or actual changes that elicit different (the 'right') response from all employees, and finally 'refreezing' to stabilise or institutionalise the changes that have been made. The process is then neatly summarised in tabular form for ease of consumption (reproduced as Table 4.2).

TABLE 4.2   Organisational change in British Airways

Level	Unfreezing	Movement	Refreezing
Individual	New top management. Downsizing of top and middle management (59 000 to 37 000). 'Putting People First'.	Acceptance of concept of 'emotional labour'. Personnel staff as internal consultants. 'Managing People First'. Peer support groups.	Continued commitment of top management. Promotion of staff with new BA values. 'Top Flight Academics'. 'Open Learning' programmes.
Structures and systems	Use of diagonal task forces to plan change. Reduction in levels of hierarchy. Modifications of budgeting process.	Profit sharing (3 weeks pay in 1987). Opening of Terminal 4. Purchase of Chartridge as training centre. New 'user friendly' MIS.	New performance appraisal system based upon both behaviour and performance. Performance-based compensation system. Continued use of task force.
Climate/ interpersonal style	Redefinition of the business: service, not transportation. Top management commitment and involvement. Off-site team-building meetings.	Trend toward decision making at lowest possible level. Greater emphasis on open communications. Data feedback on management practices.	New livery and uniforms. New coat of arms. Development and use of cabin crew teams. Continued use of data feedback on management practices.

Source: Goodstein (1990:183).

The 'success story' of British Airways has yet to turn sour as John Egan's did at Jaguar, although continuing outbreaks of industrial action in the 1990s and the uncovering of a 'dirty tricks' campaign against Virgin Airlines has tarnished BA's image (see Gregory, 1996). However, the change process itself at BA was less straightforward than the consultants portray, not least the timing of events and the lack of control by BA management over certain key events, such as the opening of Terminal 4 at Heathrow. Quite simply, reality was somewhat different, as a former BA manager notes:

> no change process lasting several years can be mapped out in advance at the top and then adhered to by those below. It meanders along a course that responds to the various pressures, energy levels, ideas, past experiences and new hires and promotees encountered along the way in the system. . . . To satisfy our need for rationality, we fabricate the pieces of the jigsaw puzzle after admiring the finished picture (Tate, 1991:111).

This brings us back to the question of whether management can *ever* take rational, strategic decisions in the face of market uncertainty, internal management factions and worker opposition. To impute, *post hoc*, rational intent to all management action is clearly fallacious, but that does not mean that managers always act without strategic intent. As Tate makes clear in the case of BA, it is invariably the implementation and actual practice of employee relations policy on the shopfloor (or in the cabin) that creates a disparity between intentions and actions (see, *inter alia*, Marchington and Parker, 1990:258; Kessler and Purcell, 1995:347; Storey, 1985:203; and Storey and Bacon, 1993:669). As Friedman (1987:294) points out, *failure* is perhaps a more useful concept to introduce when considering management action towards its workforce.

A major factor underlying the weakness of UK management is poor education and training (see Constable and McCormick, 1987; Handy, 1987; and Mangham and Silver, 1986). According to Handy *et al.* (1988:168), 'the conclusion is inescapable that in Britain management education and training is too little, too late for too few'. A reliance on 'status' rather than 'occupational professionalism' has facilitated and supported an 'expert' division of labour *within* management, which in turn encouraged and legitimated hierarchical specialism of a particularly rigid kind (Reed and Anthony, 1992:593). The lack of what Batstone (1986:40) calls 'management sophistication', essentially the extent to which the internal organisation of management allows it to act in a manner consistent with its objectives, has led to basic failures in the organisation of production (see also Cornfield, 1979; Daly *et al.*, 1985; Finniston, 1980; Neale, 1992; Nichols, 1986; and Pavitt, 1980). As noted in Chapter 3, this has not only led to poor productivity but has also exacerbated employee relations problems. For example, if management fails to ensure the prompt delivery of parts and materials from suppliers, or fails to coordinate the production process effectively, this might lead to disputes with employees over their (in)ability to earn bonus payments. 'British workers', notes Theo Nichols (1986:168), 'give like for like, inefficient management fostering less than helpful workforces.'

Of particular concern is the continued fixation of UK managers with the question of wage costs and labour utilisation. As New and Myers (1986:10) point out, direct labour costs account for only 18 per cent of total product costs for most manufacturing firms, whereas bought-out items such as materials and components account for over 50 per cent. This is not to deny the importance of unit labour costs, merely to illustrate the limitations of such an approach in what is, after all, a comparatively low wage economy (see Chapter 3). Thus taking the share of wages to be 15 per cent, Rubery *et al.* (1987:132) demonstrate that the average British firm would at best secure a relative price advantage of 3 per cent if wage costs fell by 20 per cent. Clearly, not only is this approach limited in terms of the savings that can be achieved, it is also myopic in that it assumes that cost is the prime determinant of competitive advantage. While competition has obviously intensified in recent years, so too has the emphasis on non-price determinants of competitiveness, most notably product development and differentiation, and of course quality. In the UK's low-skill, low-wage, low-productivity, low-investment economy, however, where financial interests prevail, pressure for change invariably manifests itself as a further assault on those factors (wages and labour utilisation) that make the transition to a high-wage, high-growth economy more difficult to achieve: organisations inevitably encounter worker opposition and resistance to change (or at least less than full cooperation) when they attempt to shift the wage–effort bargain in management's favour.

Over the past two decades the predominant response of UK managers to more intense international competition has been to intensify the work process rather than attempt to improve the skills and functional flexibility of the labour force – working harder rather than smarter – and noisily to reclaim the prerogatives they had given up (often willingly) in the 1960s and 1970s (Edwards and Whitston, 1991; Elger, 1990; Neale, 1992; Nichols, 1986; and Waddington and Whitston, 1995b). However not only has work practice reform been too narrowly focused to reverse the UK's relative economic decline, but even the policy of cost-cutting has been pursued in an opportunistic (non-strategic) fashion (Hakim, 1990:168–78; and Rubery, 1988:271). That managers in companies such as Jaguar, Rover, BA and countless others (e.g. Scott, 1994) have failed to win the 'hearts and minds' of their employees is hardly surprising. The failure of British managers to secure the most basic of all objectives – the active cooperation of the workforce as distinct from mere compliance or coerced consent – arises from the fundamental tension that exists, and persists, between employer and employee. Inevitably there is no 'one best way' to manage these conflicts, 'only different routes to partial failure. It is on this basis that managerial strategy can best be conceptualised: as *the pragmatic choice among alternatives none of which can prove satisfactory'* (Hyman, 1987a:30, original emphasis).

Conclusion

Under capitalist employment relations, management are the predominant though by no means the exclusive agents in the determination of employee relations. Thus central to an understanding of the employment relationship is an appreciation of the needs and objectives of management. Simply put, management need to secure a productive and cost-effective workforce. But control and compliance is often insufficient to secure the rate of return on capital that management (and shareholders) demand. Increasingly this requires the active cooperation and commitment of the workforce. At BA, for example, the difference between compliance and commitment was reflected in the quality of a smile. Whether such emotional labour appeared 'forced' or 'genuine' was seen as a critical aspect of a broader competitive strategy.

Management face a variety of options and routes to secure their aims. During the 1980s and early 1990s, the decline of union membership and the policies of successive Conservative governments appeared to offer UK managers a unique opportunity to reconstitute the bases upon which they structured and conducted employee relations. But as the example of BA and countless other organisations aptly demonstrate, the majority of UK firms are still characterised by a style of employee relations management that is based on pragmatism and opportunism, rather than on any coherent philosophy or standards of behaviour. The piecemeal adoption of HRM is just one illustration of this.

Of course, while the previous two decades provided an opportunity for managers, the period also presented severe constraints on management action and the development of any long-term strategy. Economic recession, heightened international competition and the demand for improved quality have all militated against long-term policies. More importantly, management seem to have been unable to break out of the low-trust dynamic that has been an enduring feature of UK employee relations (see Fox, 1974). This in part stems from feelings of job insecurity among many workers and from the fact that the UK remains a comparatively low-wage, low-productivity economy where investment in employee skills and training have been woefully neglected (see Chapter 3). Equally important, however, is the 'dynamic of confrontation' between capital and labour. Not only do workers continue to resist management attempts to intensify the work process and shift the wage–effort bargain in management's favour, but trade unions continue to provide collective support for employee resistance. It is to the activities of trade unions that we now turn.

CHAPTER 5

Unions and their members

Organising for strength: rebuilding the Transport & General Workers' Union

Working for union

'We came out of the workplace, and I just thought, "YES"! What a feeling', enthused Louise Chinnery, 'there's nothing else like it. We've enabled people to change their lives, to look after themselves at work. There's no other job I know of where you get that kind of feeling' (interview notes). Louise is a women's recruiter for the T&GWU in Region 1 (South-East and East Anglia), having previously worked as an assistant development manager at Homes for the Homeless People in Luton after graduating from Essex University with a degree in History and Politics. Along with Karen Hannant, who previously worked for Britannia Airways and was a shop steward at Servisair, Louise's job is to recruit and organise non-union workers, especially women and young workers. To date they have been highly successful: of the 187 new members recruited by the two women during the first five months of their one-year contracts, 65 per cent are female and well over half are below 30 years old. Of course the process of recruitment is by no means automatic: 'It's a myth that just because we're women that we'll automatically be able to recruit other women. It's not just a case of showing your face and expecting people to sign up. If anything, they're rather surprised when we turn up – I don't think they expect people from the Union to look like us' (Karen Hannant, interview notes). Karen and Louise have found that speed of response, being sensitive to workers' problems, active listening, understanding, sympathy, imbuing confidence and organising around issues are all vital to recruiting new members to the Union.

There is little doubt that the T&GWU, like most other UK unions, desperately needs to recruit more women, part-timers, young workers and ethnic minority workers in order to stem the tide of falling membership (for example less than a fifth of the T&GWU's 897 000 members are women). Recognising the 'revolution in the UK labour market with massive reductions in available full-time and permanent employment and an increase in the availability of part-time, often casual and irregular jobs', combined with the shift from manufacturing to services and the decline of public sector employment, the 1995 Biennial Delegate Conference of the T&GWU determined to 'Organise for Strength', and initiated 'a rolling programme of activities to enhance recruitment, organisation and ultimately the industrial and political strength of the T&G' (T&GWU, 1995b:15). The strategy is based on:

- identifying potential areas of membership growth.
- training programmes for both lay members and full-time officers (FTOs) designed to enable them to recruit and organise with confidence and professionalism.
- the development of regional recruitment teams, both lay and full-time, with clear objectives and local and regional accountability.
- the exploitation of information technology to improve membership records and develop a database of companies with recognition agreements as well as non-union employers.
- the regeneration of branches as campaigning centres throughout the Union.
- more positive coverage of recruitment and organising activities in Union publications.
- a programme of recruitment among temporary, fixed-term, casual, and contract workers.
- the provision of adequate resources to effect the strategy.

Of particular importance is the development of a new culture within the Union that prioritises the delivery of a strategy for recruitment and organisation, 'recognising the sometimes different needs of those workers who have not automatically seen the T&G as a natural home' (ibid:14). This, for one full-time union official at least, has been the root of the Union's membership crisis: 'We can talk about the new strategy, everyone can agree on the primacy of organising, and we've put the framework in place, but all we've really done is create an *atmosphere* in which people are now taking recruitment and organising seriously. This doesn't represent a *cultural* change' (interview notes). Previous T&G initiatives had foundered on the inability of the Union to effect an 'organising culture', a situation in which 'organisation and recruitment are second nature to us, a part of the day-to-day life of the Union' (T&GWU, 1996:2).

Failing to Link Up

The roots of the T&GWU's 'Organise for Strength' strategy go back to the Union's Link Up campaign, launched in February 1987, which was aimed specifically at hitherto unorganised groups. Initially the campaign was focused on a 'model agreement' and a 'charter of rights' for temporary and part-time workers, but as the campaign developed, 'Link Up aimed to present a positive image to the wider community, playing down the view of unions as representatives of a narrow sectional interest group, linking recruitment with the social aims of the union, and emphasising community as well as workplace involvement' (Snape, 1994a:231). Specific initiatives in the Link Up campaign included 'Recruit-a-Mate', joint schemes with the Citizens Advice Bureau aimed at offering the Union's advice facilities to members of the public, and participation in an anti-sectarianism campaign aimed at young people in Northern Ireland (ibid:225). Unlike previous recruitment initiatives, which were essentially reactive and *ad hoc*, Link Up was a nationally coordinated campaign that sought to develop a more strategic approach to targeting and monitoring. Recruitment was now emphasised throughout the Union, matching recruitment priorities and the collective bargaining agenda to the key employment growth areas and to groups that had previously been ineffectively or entirely unorganised (ibid:230).

Ultimately, however, Link Up foundered on the rocks of (dis)organisation, disillusion and opposition (from both employers and union officials). The problems that beset the Link Up campaign were manifold, not least the fact that it was a (top down) *campaign* rather than a *strategy*. The fact that it was a 'campaign' gave the impression, in the words of Ken Fuller (Regional Organiser, South East and East Anglia), that 'we expected Officers and lay activists to dash about with application forms in their hands for two or three months and then revert to "normality"' (T&GWU, 1996:2). 'Normality' for many FTOs was to do *no* recruitment or workplace organising, and their response to the Link Up campaign was at best 'patchy' (Snape, 1994a: 227). Even if they have the inclination, most FTOs rarely find the time to undertake sustained recruitment and organising initiatives, and the majority prioritise other work (see Kelly and Heery, 1989, 1994:103–4; Mason and Bain, 1991; and Snape, 1994b:57, 1995:562–5). Moreover for most FTOs, whose job revolves around negotiation and servicing the existing membership, targeting part-time or temporary workers was regarded as too difficult, excessively time-consuming, and ultimately cost-ineffective (Snape, 1994a:227). As no additional officers were recruited for the campaign, one of the main effects of Link Up was simply to increase the workload of FTOs, which many resented.

Anticipating some of these problems, the T&GWU used lay recruitment teams composed of rank-and-file activists as a low-cost resource to supplement hard-pressed FTOs, not only to recruit in their own workplace but beyond. However very little formal training was offered to lay activists and many grew disillusioned when recruitment proved difficult. The failure systematically to link activists and FTOs, and the regional and local activities of FTOs to the national campaign, proved to be an important flaw. Thus in the absence of effective monitoring and support structures, the Union was almost entirely dependent on the enthusiasm and initiative of individual officers and activists. As one FTO put it, 'there was no framework to support recruitment activities, it wasn't institutionalised in the Union. So when your best activists lose interest, or lose their job, there's nobody to replace them' (interview notes). Just as the FTOs' response to the campaign was at best patchy, the success of lay organising teams was equally mixed.

With FTOs leading the campaign and the vast bulk of the workload falling on their shoulders, attempts were made by the Union to improve its image with employers in order to secure recognition. For union officials schooled in the industrial relations of the 1970s, when the emphasis of trade unionism had been firmly rooted in collective bargaining, recognition became the lynch-pin to both recruiting and retaining members in the new target industries and workplaces. Formal recognition by employers allowed FTOs to 'service' the union members, providing them with an agreement and procedures that defined the role of the union (or more precisely the union official). This highlighted an inherent contradiction in the Link Up campaign between the employee and employer 'markets' for unionism (see Willman, 1989). On the one hand, when the Union appealed to the 'employee market' it emphasised health and safety issues, pay and conditions of work, training, equal opportunities, and the wider social aims of the Union. On the other hand, when appealing to the 'employer market' the Union sought to downplay its militant image and paraded, with other union beauties, in a contest to convince management that the Union could be, *inter alia*, reasonable, flexible, accommodating and cooperative (see Snape, 1994a:231). Thus, Link Up simultaneously represented both a rejection of the 'business unionism' associated with the EETPU at the time (see Blyton and Turnbull, 1994:96–103) and a campaign that ultimately pulled the Union in that very direction. In fact in 1989 the T&GWU followed the example of the EETPU and other moderate unions by producing 'A Prospectus for Growth: The Route to Effective Industrial Relations', a document that set out the advantages *to employers* of recognising the Union (Snape, 1994a:231; see also Fisher, 1995). The subsequent rejection of this approach, however, and the determination of the T&GWU not to enter any further 'beauty contests', left the Union's recruitment policy somewhat in limbo. All the practical problems remained, most notably the (over) reliance on FTOs to spearhead new recruitment activities. Moreover the most fundamental question remained unanswered: should the relationship between the union and its members be based on 'servicing' or 'organising'?

From servicing to organising

'Organising for Strength' represents an endorsement of the 'organising model' of trade unionism, a model that has now been embraced by several other unions and the Trades Union Congress (TUC) (see Turnbull, 1997). The organising model is essentially 'a new name for a back to basics grassroots organising, using the methods which built unions in the first place. It recognises that genuine organisation and collectivism are still the best ways of winning justice and dignity for workers' (Organising Works, 1995:3). The central tenet of this model is that rank-and-file members *are* the union, and as such they should be empowered to recruit other workers (on the basis that like recruits like), generate their own agenda and resolve as many of their own problems as practicable. The iron law of organising is: 'Never do for others what they can do for themselves'. In its *Organisers' Manual*, for example, the T&GWU warns that 'the workplace must never get into dependency mode. . . . Self-organisation shouts to members: "It's your Union, you are the Union, take control and get involved"' (T&GWU, 1995a:35).

Under the organising model the objective is no longer recognition but organisation (the former is simply one element of the latter). As one T&GWU lay organiser explained:

> We work around recognition. The priority is self-organisation, helping people to look after themselves. Tactically it can be fatal to go for recognition, especially if you lose. Much better to organise around an issue like health and safety, win an improvement, then go for the next issue. Success breeds success. More people join and the organisation gets stronger. If the workers are looking after themselves, if *they are* the Union, what does it matter if the T&G has formal recognition? (interview notes)

To achieve (self) organisation, an 'organising cycle' is set in motion where employees/members, with the assistance of lay organisers and/or full-time officials, identify an *issue* that affects and is of concern to most people in the workplace, and most importantly is winnable. *Organisation* is built on the back of this issue, setting in place structures or networks to communicate effectively on a one-to-one, face-to-face basis with every employee in the workplace. Organisation is used to *educate* each worker on the issue that concerns the workforce and what can be done, through *unity*, to redress the problem. When members understand the issues they can then be asked to become involved in collective *action* to win changes at work. Further issues are then identified, repeating the process to consolidate active trade unionism in the workplace. Thus, the organising cycle – issue → organisation → education → unity → action – is designed to build union consciousness, encourage membership participation and foster rank-and-file leadership.

The organising model, then, is not just about recruiting new members but rebuilding a new form of participative unionism. Through organisation the T&GWU is determined to re-establish both the industrial and political strength of the Union, as the latter depends ultimately on the former (T&GWU, 1995b:15). As one Union official put it,

> The Union was always large numerically but small ideologically. We didn't educate the members. All we had was a 'factory gate' culture, and because we've been 'institutionalised' industrially we've relied far too heavily on employers – you know, check-off [for the payment of union dues], union–management [closed shop] agreements, and facilities provided by the employer. Organising for Strength is about to change all that (interview notes).

Strength from organisation?

At a practical level, Organising for Strength has resolved, or at least alleviated, many of the weaknesses of the Link Up campaign. First and foremost it is a *strategy* that FTOs readily admit, on occasion somewhat wryly, 'isn't going away' (interview notes). Equally important, systematic training programmes have been implemented for both lay organisers and FTOs. The aim is to develop a network of three-member lay organiser teams throughout all eight Regions of the Union, led by FTOs whose job is to coordinate their activities and meet regularly with the teams to review progress, identify new targets and provide support. The advantage of such networks is that they are not overly dependent on the work of particular individuals – mutual support is provided and the introduction of new organisers facilitated in the event of turnover. In Region 1, where the strategy is most developed, more dedicated support is provided by two FTOs, who have been 'stood down' from their servicing responsibilities to work full time on recruitment and organisation, and by an Organising Support Unit which not only acts as a resource for officers but also deals with direct membership enquiries (cold calls), produces leaflets and other organising materials, and works with lay organising teams and FTOs in the field. Louise Chinnery and Karen Hannant complete the structure and further reinforce the strategy in the South-East and East Anglia.

Problems still remain, of course, most notably the difficulties lay organisers find in securing time off work to recruit beyond their own workplace and the failure of many FTOs to adequately support, and in some cases even to meet with, their lay organising teams, despite the introduction of a clearly articulated monitoring system (see Turnbull, 1997). The quantitative results, however, are encouraging if somewhat mixed. In T&GWU Region 1, for example, the Union lost 1117 dues-paying members between January and March 1996, but the number of new recruits was the highest since the third quarter of 1994.

More importantly, of the sixty-six branches with lay organising teams, the average net gain was 4.5 members per branch. If other branches in the Region had performed as well the net gain in membership would have been over 4200. Retention, of course, is the other half of the battle, and branches with lay organisers also display better retention. If just 10 per cent of the 'leavers' during the January–March 1996 quarter had been retained, the Region's overall net gain in membership would have been 160. By the end of 1996 the organising strategy appeared to have at least stemmed the Region's decline, with total membership increasing by 182 on the previous year.

Qualitative measures of success are inevitably more subjective, especially the development of an 'organising culture', which most senior officials in the Union regard as central to organising for strength. The comments of one national official perhaps sum up the task facing the Union: 'It's rather like changing the direction of a huge ship, like an oil tanker – you do it by degrees, and all the time you're still moving forward in essentially the same direction' (interview notes). For almost two decades that direction has been one of seemingly inexorable decline (from 1989–94 alone the T&GWU lost more than a quarter of its membership). It is therefore too early to pass any definitive judgement on the Organising for Strength strategy, which at best appears to have stabilised rather than reversed membership decline. Snape's (1994a:231) evaluation of the Link Up campaign was that the T&GWU's internal growth strategy was not only heavily constrained by economic and political factors but was very much a secondary and derivative determinant of aggregate union growth. For unions to accept that membership is 'received' rather than 'achieved' (Undy *et al.*, 1981), however, would surely seal their fate.

Unionism in the 1990s

The questions confronting the trade union movement in the mid 1990s are simple yet momentous. How seriously has the power base of the union movement been eroded since the 1970s? Has that former influence, as McIlroy (1988:42) and others (e.g. Coates, 1980:59) suggest, been exaggerated, such that any decline in power since 1979 has similarly been exaggerated? To what extent has any decline been due to cyclical or more deep-seated structural factors? If cyclical factors are diminishing trade union influence, how long are the cycles? Has there been a decline in 'collectivist' attitudes among the workforce, or conversely is there now greater 'individualism'? What policies have trade unions adopted in order to rectify their position? With what success? Can unions regain their former position of influence, or are they a spent force?

Overall, the future health of the union movement rests, as it always has done, on securing the twin (and closely interconnected) goals of, on the one hand, workers who are willing to sign up, participate in union activities and remain union members, and on the other hand, employers who are willing to recognise trade unions as bargaining or representative agents for their workforce. The key question, of course, is how unions might best secure these interrelated goals. What should be the basis of the relationship between the unions and their members, and the unions and employers? Should unions seek to improve services for existing members, in anticipation that non-union members will be attracted by such benefits, or alternatively seek to empower their members and encourage greater participation to make the union more relevant to both current and potential members? Should unions seek cooperation with employers via 'social partnership' or new-style agreements, or confront employers and define the interest of their members in opposition to those of management? The organising model embraced by the T&GWU, for example, is based on a 'participative' rather than a 'transactional' (servicing) relationship between the union and its members. Moreover, rather than the union being a 'third party' in the eyes of rank-and-file members, and especially management, the organising model seeks to establish that there are just two parties to the employment relationship: the employer and the workforce, who are united in their union.

In contrast to this approach, many unions have emphasised new union benefits, such as insurance schemes, credit cards, free legal advice and the like, and have even negotiated single-union agreements with 'no-strike' clauses giving primacy to consultative over collective bargaining arrangements (see Blyton and Turnbull, 1994:96–103). Part of the thinking behind such initiatives is that because the climate of employee relations is believed to have changed 'irreversibly' since the 1970s, with new management practices that seek to undermine any perceived need for collective representation combined with government hostility to collectivism, trade unions must in turn respond by offering new services to members and new procedural arrangements to employers. But is this in fact the case? Does this prognosis apply to all workers or just to those in 'high-tech' sectors of the economy? Put differently, why do workers join trade unions? Some unions, such as the T&GWU, clearly believe that both current and potential members' interests are basically unchanged: essentially the protection of employment rights and the improvement of pay and conditions, which can best be secured through membership participation (collective action). These different approaches – 'managerial unionism' versus 'participative unionism' (Heery and Kelly, 1994) – are a central focus of this chapter. Before considering these, however, it is necessary first to review the extent to which the position of trade unions really has changed since the 1970s, the factors contributing to that change and the scale of the task facing the union movement in securing a greater degree of influence at both local and national levels in the immediate future. In sum, what has happened to trade union power in recent years?

Batstone (1988) suggests that the power resources of labour include scarcity value in the labour market, disruptive capacity in the production process, and political influence within the political arena. The scarcity value of any worker's labour clearly depends on his or her skills and the availability of other (alternative) sources of labour. One means by which workers attempt to control the supply of labour and enhance their power is through union organisation. Thus union membership is an indicator (or more accurately a prerequisite) of trade union power. The disruptive power of labour within the production process depends on a range of factors including technology, interdependencies between processes, stock levels and the nature and extent of work-related changes being introduced, but also depends on union organisation within the workplace (including the extent of union recognition, the scope of joint regulation and the strength of shop organisation). Finally, the political power of trade unions depends, among other things, on the political party in power, the relationship with the government of the day, union involvement in national (and increasingly international) policy-making bodies and the content of labour-related legislation.

In order to establish a broad picture of trade union influence it is therefore useful to consider aggregate information relating to union membership as a whole, more localised information regarding union presence and activity at the workplace, and wider political activities. Some indicators such as the changing relationship between unions and the state and the nature of industrial action are dealt with separately in Chapters 6 and 10. The present chapter proceeds by reviewing the current state of trade unionism, the responses that have been made by the unions themselves, and the prospects for the future development of the union movement. Without pre-empting all the arguments, our assessment points to the propriety of more participative forms of trade unionism and the need for greater interunion cooperation, which in turn should enhance the role and influence of trade unions in the UK.

Union membership

Unlike other indicators of union power, union membership figures are readily accessible, though not always wholly accurate (see Kelly and Bailey, 1989), but the extent to which a change in membership size affects the degree of influence that a union can exert, or the way it may affect employer reactions to trade union claims, calls for much more localised and detailed enquiry. Nonetheless it is the aggregate level of trade union membership – or more specifically overall trade union density (that proportion of the potential membership who are actually trade union members) – that tends to be used as the main bellwether of overall trade union influence. In terms of the numbers belonging to trade unions in the UK, the recent picture has been one of persistent decline. In fact the fall in membership since 1979 is the longest continuous decline on record (Waddington and Whitston, 1995a:157). This contrasts sharply with the 1970s, which saw a major rise in unionism, primarily reflecting the increased unionisation of white-collar workers. Between 1968 and 1979 total union membership rose by three million and union density increased from 44 per cent to 55 per cent. During the years 1979–95, however, the number of trade union members in the UK fell by 39 per cent (Table 5.1), and the density of unionism dropped from over half to around a third of the workforce. The losses of the 1980s were broadly equivalent to the gains of the 1970s.

TABLE 5.1   Membership of trade unions in the UK, 1974–95

	Total membership at end of year (000s)	% change in membership since previous Year
1974	11 764	+2.7
1975	12 193	+3.6
1976	12 386	+3.0
1977	12 846	+3.7
1978	13 112	+2.1
1979	13 289	+1.3
1980	12 947	−2.6
1981	12 106	−6.5
1982	11 593	−4.2
1983	11 236	−3.1
1984	10 994	−3.2
1985	10 821	−1.6
1986	10 539	−2.6
1987	10 475	−0.6
1988	10 376	−0.9
1989	10 158	−2.1
1990	9947	−2.1
1991	9585	−3.6
1992	9048	−5.6
1993	8700	−3.8
1994	8278	−4.9
1995	8089	−2.3

Source: Certification Officer of Trade Unions and Employers' Associations.

The decline in membership was particularly sharp between 1979 and 1981, during which time total membership fell by 1.2 million, or 9 per cent. However a reduction in membership was recorded every year during the 1980s, leading some commentators to conclude that the high-water mark of trade unionism in the UK had been reached in 1979 and was unlikely ever to be eclipsed. This pattern of membership decline continued into the 1990s. In 1995 trade union membership stood at just 8.1 million, the lowest since the war. Union density levels, estimated from annual Labour Force Surveys (LFS) and based on workers in employment, showed a decline from 39 per cent of employees in 1989 (when such data were first collected) to just over 32 per cent in 1995 (Cully and Woodland, 1996:216).

Various arguments have been put forward to account for this decline. While some have noted the interaction of several factors, others have sought to identify primary influences, including changes in workforce composition, macroeconomic variables and the influence of labour legislation. Green (1992), for example, concentrates on the significance of structural shifts (specifically in regard to the industrial context and the composition of the workforce) in accounting for the decline in union density. According to Green's calculations, around 30 per cent of the decline in density in the later 1980s was due to compositional factors such as changes in industrial and occupational structures, establishment size and proportions of different groups in the labour force (see also Millward and Stevens, 1986; and Chapter 3 above). Sometimes referred to as the 'mountain gorilla hypothesis', as the unions' natural habitat, like that of the mountain gorilla, is seen to be gradually dying out, this argument points to the adverse structural conditions facing trade unions in the 1980s and 1990s, including a decline in employment in heavily unionised industries such as coalmining (where the overall union density level in 1990 was 90 per cent) and the growth in service sector employment, particularly in the private sector, where density levels are typically far lower. In real estate and business services, for example, overall union density in 1995 was 13 per cent compared with 9 per cent in the wholesale trade and only 8 per cent in hotels and restaurants (Cully and Woodland, 1996:221). Furthermore, as Green (1992) notes, union membership levels are higher overall for men than women, for full-timers than part-timers, and for those working in larger rather than smaller establishments (see also Chapter 9). The figures in Table 5.2 bear this picture out.

The problem with the compositional argument, however, is that it is a *description* of what has happened to union membership, not an *explanation* of trade union decline. As Kelly (1990:34–5) has pointed out, there is no reason why a decline in manufacturing or the growth of female employment should automatically signal a decline in union membership. After all, in the 1970s union density among females rose faster than among males. Similarly, during the 1980s the fall in density has been faster among males than females (Waddington, 1992:292–3). The net membership fall of 211 000 between 1980

TABLE 5.2   Distribution of union density in Britain, 1990 and 1996

| | Union density % | |
	1990	*1996*
Men	43	33
Women	32	29
Full time	43	35
Part time	22	20
Workplace Size		
fewer than 25 employees	20	16
25 or more employees	47	39
All	38	31

Note: Union membership statistics reported by the Certification Officer (Table 5.1) are consistently higher than LFS data as the former include union members who are retired or unemployed whereas LFS data are based only on those in employment.
Source: Labour Force Survey (LFS).

and 1990, for example, represented a net decline of 210 000 among male union members and just 1000 among females (Bird *et al.*, 1992:188). In the 1990s membership has fallen less slowly among female employees, part-timers, non-manual workers and service sector employees compared with male, full-time, manual, and production sector workers (Cully and Woodland, 1996:217). Moreover data from the Certification Officer indicates that the number of female trade unionists *increased* by 34 000 (or 1 per cent) in 1993–94 (Sweeney, 1996:52). More significant, perhaps, is the fact that *intra*-establishment union density declined in the 1980s (Andrews and Naylor, 1994). In other words, even where unions are recognised they have still lost members, which composition effects clearly cannot account for. As far as Kelly (1990:34) is concerned, the compositional argument 'is a perfect example of a plausible but specious correlation, which begs numerous questions but answers hardly any'. One such question is why unions managed to increase membership in the 1970s when the changing composition of the labour force was 'averse' to union growth, but conspicuously failed to do so in the 1980s?

A more convincing argument is the effect of cyclical changes that affect the *incentives* and *opportunities* for workers to join trade unions, and for employers to resist unionisation. Rising real wages, for example, reduce the incentive for workers to join, while high unemployment provides employers with an opportunity to resist unionisation. Equally, many unemployed union members believe that trade unions do not cater for those on the dole and so have little incentive to continue their membership (Gallie, 1996:169–70; and Lewis,

1989:274–5). These macroeconomic variables are highlighted by Disney (1990) in his account of membership decline in the 1980s (for longer-run analyses of business-cycle influences on union membership see Bain and Elsheikh, 1976; Booth, 1983; and Carruth and Disney, 1988). One of the most important incentives for management to resist unionisation has been government action (and example) in the public sector, where management have been able to secure the goodwill of their government paymaster by 'taking on' the unions (see Ferner, 1989; and Pendleton and Winterton, 1993), although union membership is still much higher in the public sector (61 per cent) than in the private sector (21 per cent) (Cully and Woodland, 1996:219–20). In addition, recent legislation has allowed employers to restrain trade union activities (see Chapter 6).

Freeman and Pelletier's (1990) analysis focuses directly on the importance of the legal environment for employee relations, and in particular on the decline in union density due to the labour laws passed in the Thatcher years. By analysing movements in union density between 1948 and 1986, controlling for macroeconomic and compositional variables and comparing movements in union density in the UK with that of Ireland, where different labour legislation has prevailed, the authors conclude that membership levels re-spond to the degree of favourable or unfavourable legislation towards trade unions. Among other impacts, legislation in the 1980s undermined union security based on the closed shop and weakened ACAS's role in supporting union recognition (see the Appendix to Chapter 6). But is legislation the *cause* of union decline, and membership losses the *effect*, or the other way around? After all Conservative governments adopted a step-by-step approach to legislative reform as the unions declined (see Chapter 6), and the decline of union density slowed after 1983 (see Table 5.1), whereas according to the legal argument it should have accelerated (see Andrews and Naylor, 1994:415; and Waddington, 1992:310–11). Research data from the Social Change and Eco-nomic Life Initiative (SCELI) suggest that the Conservative governments' privatisation programme may have constituted a greater threat to the unions' longer-term influence than their specific legislative programme for industrial relations reform (Gallie and Rose, 1996:64; see also Gallie, 1996:153–5).

The foregoing studies attempt to go beyond commentaries that simply list a range of influencing factors without assigning weights or priorities either to the different factors or to the various interactions between them. The lack of agreement on the relative importance of different factors, however, indicates the difficulty of achieving a satisfactory conclusion (for recent reviews see Mason and Bain, 1993; and Waddington, 1992). Not least this reflects the fact that the decision to join a union is influenced by several variables, including, most obviously, the presence of a union to join and the attitude of the employer towards union membership. Green (1990), for example, using data from the General Household Survey, found that on average less than 30 per cent of female part-timers were trade union members, but where a trade union was available to join the figure rose to over 60 per cent. In the SCELI study, Gallie (1996:166–7) discovered that the attitude of employers to union organisation was one of the most important predictors of union membership. Many authors have identified employers' attitude to trade unions, and in particular employers' willingness to recognise unions as the bargaining agent for a group of employees, as a crucial influence on actual membership decisions (e.g. Bain, 1970; see also Chapter 9 below). For Metcalf (1991:19), 'recognition is the fulcrum on which the health of the labour movement turns'. Fulcrums are points of balance, and in identifying the need for unions to balance their appeal to both employees and employers, Willman (1989:263) notes that 'unions operate as mediating organisations between employers who see some benefit either in the granting of recognition or its maintenance . . . and employees who seek various forms of insurance and representation. It follows that, to succeed, they must appeal to both sets of interests'. In many of the single factor arguments the role of the individual employer is omitted or underemphasised, whereas in practice the interaction between individual propensity to join, the presence of a suitable union and the employer's attitude are closely interlinked (the problem for trade unions, of course, especially in the private sector, is how to secure membership in the absence of statutory recognition procedures and in the face of overt employer hostility). The individual factors contribute to an understanding of this relationship but do not in themselves fully explain it.

Furthermore, single factor arguments can act to obscure the changing influence of different factors in different periods. Millward *et al.* (1992:101–2), for example, argue that in the first half of the 1980s the demise of large, highly unionised manufacturing plants played a key role in the decline in union membership. In the second half of the decade, however, weakened support for unionism among employees, various government measures constraining unionism and antipathy amongst a growing number of employers are judged to have played a greater role in the continuing decline of union membership. Beaumont (1986:33–4) in fact suggests that employer opposition to unions passes through several phases, starting with the reduced influence of existing joint structures (fewer regular meetings, meetings less well attended and so on), the development of new structures to by-pass trade unions, stronger opposition by management towards the possible unionisation of any uncovered groups (for example white-collar staff), and finally derecognition of existing unions. Comparing the UK with the United States, where union membership peaked at around a third of the workforce in the mid-1950s but is now less than one in six, Beaumont suggests that the UK may have only just set out on the road to deunionisation.

Returning to the more recent past rather than the prospects for the future, Metcalf (1991) argues that the emphasis on particular factors has served largely to exclude other influences. According to Metcalf (ibid:22), union membership and density are determined by the interaction of five factors:

the macroeconomic climate, the composition of jobs and the workforce, the policy of the state, the attitude and conduct of employers and the stance taken by unions themselves. Waddington (1992:311–14) suggests a similar cocktail. What is significant about parts of Metcalf's list and both the 'macroeconomic factors' and 'legislation' arguments, is their cyclical character (the cycles turning on economic and/or political change). Even Green's (1992) analysis of structural changes in industrial and workforce composition only 'accounts' for a minority of the decline in union density, and there are no *a priori* reasons why these compositional factors should be associated with falling membership. Successful periods of union organising (the 1890s, 1910–20, 1933–45 and 1968–79) are closely associated with 'long waves' (Kondratieff cycles) of capitalist economic development, when unions have been able to satisfy employee demands for protection and advancement at work (see Kelly and Waddington, 1995). As Boyer (1995:552–3) notes, 'waves of unionization are linked with general movements about social values which shift back and forth from individualistic to more holistic and solidaristic: trade unions prosper after dramatic episodes of economic collapse and build upon the high values attached to collective action'.

In the longer term, therefore, union density among currently low unionised sectors, occupations or groups could increase. Indeed this has been happening in some cases, such as among women, part-timers and those employed in instrument engineering or insurance. Thus one implication is clearly that the recent decline in union membership is potentially a temporary rather than a permanent feature of employee relations, albeit a decline heightened by the conjuncture of several different economic, political and industrial factors. However sufficient industrial, economic and political change has occurred to guarantee that any revival of union membership is unlikely to flow automatically from, for example, a fall in unemployment, a reduction in real wage increases or even the election of a pro-union government. In other words a single twist of the temporal spiral, to use the metaphor developed in Chapter 1, is unlikely to bring the union movement back to the position of the mid to late 1970s. If nothing else, the more favourable influences on union growth are unlikely to coincide. Between 1986 and 1989, for example, total employment in Britain rose by 1.4 million and official unemployment dropped by more than 1.3 million, but the failure of trade unions to recruit these workers in sufficient numbers (the majority of whom were employed on a part-time basis and/or in the service sector) resulted in a further net fall in union membership of more than a third of a million (Bird *et al.*, 1991:340).

More generally, the scale of structural change in the pattern of economic activity and workforce composition requires trade unions to develop different approaches to membership organisation and representation than were adopted in previous decades. Yet as various writers have pointed out, such adaptation is not a new phenomenon for the trade union movement (see for example Bain, 1986; and Kelly 1988, 1990). Indeed, despite the various images of the trade union movement as mountain gorilla faced with an ever-shrinking habitat or a lumbering carthorse unable to adapt to changed circumstances, at different points in their history trade unions have demonstrated considerable versatility, for example in gaining acceptance among the growing non-manual workforce in the postwar decades and particularly during the 1960s and 1970s (Bain and Price, 1983). Put differently, unions are not simply the *object* of 'external' factors, as economists typically assume (e.g. Disney *et al.*, 1995:417–18). They are also the *subject* of their own history, capable of determining, to a significant extent, their own fate (see Gallie *et al.*, 1996; Mason and Bain, 1993:333; and Waddington and Whitston, 1995a:186).

This fact is evident at present, as the actual pattern of union membership change is far more complex than the figures in Table 5.1 would suggest. These figures show net change but this summary statistic fails to reflect the degree of flow into and out of trade unions. For the picture since 1979 has not been simply one of union members 'flowing out' of trade unions. On the contrary, throughout the 1980s trade unions continued to be active recruiters (though some critics would argue they were not sufficiently active in the circumstances). Metcalf (1991:22) notes, for example, that the shopworkers' union USDAW recruits and loses roughly a quarter of its members each year, reflecting the lack of employment stability in much of the retail sector. In 1987 USDAW recruited 108 444 new members, but recorded an increase in membership of only 5223 (Waddington, 1992:313; see also Upchurch and Donnelly, 1992). Similarly, between 1985 and 1992 the T&GWU recruited almost 1.9 million new members and yet still recorded a net loss of 354 000 members (Snape, 1994a:229). Furthermore, while the majority of TUC unions lost members during the 1980s, in particular the larger unions listed in Table 5.3, some actually registered a net gain, and in several other cases the drop in membership was contained to less than 5 per cent of the total. Surveying the TUC-affiliated unions overall, Kelly (1990:32) notes that sixteen TUC unions in fact had a higher membership in 1988 than they did in 1979, while a further seven unions reported membership rises in at least four of those nine years. More recently, in 1996 several unions (including CWU, GPMU and USDAW) increased their membership. Spectacular growth has been recorded by several non-TUC-affiliated unions, most notably the Royal College of Nursing, which increased its membership by 6 per cent between 1989 and 1994. Excluding the Police Federation, non-TUC affiliated unions and associations increased their membership from 363 000 in 1978 to over a million by the early 1990s (Farnham and Giles, 1995:13). Thus while the net outcome has been an overall decline in membership, unions continue to attract new members. A picture depicting only dwindling membership, with employees unwilling to become union members, is in reality a gross oversimplification.

What is not yet clear is to what extent the 1970s and 1980s were unusual decades for trade unionism in the UK, the one decade characterised by

TABLE 5.3   **Membership of major TUC-affiliated unions, 1979 and 1996**

Union	1979	1996	% change 1979–96
Unison[1]	1 657 926	1 355 313	−18
T&GWU	2 086 281	896 550	−57
GMB	1 096 865	740 319	−33
AEEU[2]	1 661 381	725 743	−56
MSF[3]	701 000	446 000	−36
USDAW	470 017	283 255	−40
CWU[4]	334 453	275 055	−18
GPMU[5]	313 000	216 991	−31
NUT	290 740	175 127	−40
NAS/UWT	152 222	157 146	+3
PTC[6]	221 445	151 175	−32
BIFU	131 774	123 540	−6
CPSA	223 884	121 749	−46
UCATT	348 875	106 558	−69

Notes:
1. formerly NALGO, NUPE and COHSE.
2. formerly AEU and EETPU.
3. formerly ASTMS and TASS.
4. formerly NCU and UCW.
5. formerly SOGAT and NGA.
6. formerly SCPS, CSU and IRSF.
Source: TUC Annual Reports.

conditions that were particularly conducive to growth, the other by the conjunction of several factors that were anything but conducive to growth. By the mid 1990s membership levels had fallen significantly compared with 1979, but the loss of membership was in no way a rout of trade unionism from the UK workplace. Nonetheless, it is evident that the road to membership revival may be far harder for trade unions than in previous periods, not least because of the number of employers who appear to be more inclined to question both the need to locate trade unions at the heart of employee relations and the propriety of dealing with employees on a collective rather than an individual basis. It is to the presence of trade unions at the workplace that we now turn for a further view of the contemporary state of trade union influence.

Unionism in the workplace

Data from the last Workplace Industrial Relations Survey (WIRS) (Millward *et al.*, 1992) reveals the extent to which the overall fall in membership levels has been associated with both a decline in the number of workplaces with a union presence and in the number of establishments where unions are recognised by employers as bargaining agents. Between 1984 and 1990 the proportion of establishments with union members fell from 73 per cent to 64 per cent. All of this decline took place in the private sector – public sector workplaces, virtually without exception, continued to have union members. A similar decline is evident in relation to union density in the establishments taking part in the different WIRS studies. Between 1984 and 1990 overall union density in the sample organisations fell by ten percentage points, with continued marked variations in density levels between different sectors of the economy: in 1990 union density in the public sector stood at 72 per cent, compared with 48 per cent in private manufacturing and 27 per cent in private services (ibid:59).

Union recognition by employers for negotiating pay and conditions also fell during the later 1980s. In 1984 two thirds (66 per cent) of establishments in the WIRS sample recognised trade unions for some of their workforce; by 1990 this had fallen to just over one half (53 per cent). The fall in recognition was most pronounced in private manufacturing, where the proportion of establishments recognising trade unions fell from 65 per cent to 44 per cent in the six years to 1990 – one of the clearest indicators of a significant decline in trade union presence in the UK economy. This decline in recognition primarily occurred in smaller establishments with fewer than 200 employees (ibid:72), which are discussed in more detail in Chapter 9. Only a relatively small proportion of this reduction was due to explicit derecognition strategies by employers (ibid:74), which are estimated to have affected fewer than 200 000 employees between 1988 and 1994 (Gall and McKay, 1994: 436; and *Labour Research*, May 1996), although derecognition was a significant factor in specific industries such as provincial newspapers (Smith and Morton, 1990) and docks (Turnbull and Weston, 1993c:185–6). Moreover there is some evidence, in line with Beaumont's (1986:34) prediction (see above), that derecognition may be a growing trend, with more 'purposive' or strategic cases of derecognition (e.g. BP, Esso, Mobil, Pfizer, Shell, Tioxide UK and Scottish Agricultural Industries) as opposed to 'reactive' cases (e.g. small engineering companies post 1989) and 'complete' as opposed to 'partial' derecognition (Claydon, 1996:163–9; see also Claydon, 1989; Gall and McKay, 1994; Gregg and Yates, 1991:364–5; and *Labour Research*, April 1988 and May 1996).

In addition, Beaumont and Harris (1992) predict the growth of 'double-breasted' arrangements, a term borrowed from the US construction industry, where a multiplant company recognises a union in some (well-established) plants but refuses recognition in other (newer) plants. Non-union establishments in the UK are more likely to be foreign-owned, to have recently changed ownership, and to employ a relatively higher proportion of non-manual workers, all of which are on-going trends within the economy (ibid:281). At present, however, more significant than either derecognition or double-breasting are new (single site) employers refusing to accept union recognition and the ending of industry-wide bargaining (most notably in engineering) which is not being replaced by company or plant bargaining activities in many small companies (see Disney *et al.*, 1995; and Chapter 7 below). The Workplace Industrial Relations Survey also identifies a fall in union recognition in the public sector, from 99 per cent of workplaces in 1984 to 87 per cent in 1990. As Millward and his colleagues (1992:73) note, however, this fall is almost entirely accounted for by the government's unilateral withdrawal in 1987 of negotiating rights for teachers in state schools in England and Wales. Thus taken together, the decline in the number of establishments with union members, the drop in union density levels and the fall in the number of workplaces recognising unions for purposes of negotiation signal a significant weakening of the position of trade unions in the UK in recent years. Nevertheless, the point is worth underlining that the trade union movement in the UK still entered the 1990s with a majority of larger establishments recognising trade unions as the bargaining agents for at least part of their workforce.

Just as union membership and recognition levels fell in the second half of the 1980s, so too did the proportion of employees covered by collective bargaining. The WIRS study shows this proportion falling from 71 per cent of employees to 54 per cent between 1984 and 1990 (Millward *et al.*, 1992:93). This fall was felt equally in the private and the public sector. In the latter, where coverage fell from 95 per cent to 78 per cent of employees between 1984 and 1990, this was accounted for mainly by the loss of negotiating rights among teachers and nurses, together with the contracting-out of services by local government and the civil service, which has been accompanied by a reduction in the role of trade unions. These developments, however, could represent an *opportunity* for trade unions: 'Paradoxically, contracting may also provide exactly the stimulus to expanded forms of workplace unionism, and increasing levels of activity, that have been missing to date' (Colling, 1995b:137). Opportunities, of course, must be seized (via collective organisation), which in the context of previously neglected workplace structures in the public sector will not be an easy task (ibid:143; see also Fairbrother, 1996:110–11).

Notwithstanding the marked changes in union membership, recognition and the coverage of collective bargaining, further evidence of both the resilience of workplace organisation and the opportunities for union renewal abound. By 1990, for example, there had been little change in agreed time-off arrangements for union representatives, while union representatives' access to office facilities also remained broadly the same. Likewise little change had occurred to check-off arrangements (deduction of union subscriptions by employers). In both 1984 and 1990 just under three quarters of establishments with union members reported check-off arrangements (Millward *et al.*,

1992:124; see also Dunn and Wright, 1994:33–4), although anecdotal evidence from several unions suggests that recent legislation giving union members the right to reconfirm whether or not their union subscriptions are collected by automatic deductions from their pay has adversely affected membership levels (see the Appendix to Chapter 6; and *Labour Research*, August 1993, September 1994, July 1996). One further aspect of the union presence at the workplace that changed substantially in the 1980s relates to the closed shop. Millward and his colleagues estimate that in 1984 around three and a half million manual workers were covered by closed shop arrangements. By 1990, following the 1980s legislation making it progressively more difficult for closed shops to operate lawfully (see Chapter 6), official coverage had fallen dramatically to between a third and half a million (ibid:99), although informal arrangements remain in some workplaces, especially for manual and craft workers (Wright, 1996). More importantly, following the logic of Hyman's (1989a:179) argument that membership gains in the 1970s were often obtained *without* securing the ideological commitment of the workforce as membership was often a condition of employment (the closed shop) and involved limited interaction between the union and the membership (due to check-off arrange-ments), these developments might paradoxically foster a more committed, if numerically depleted, membership in the future.

If recognition is an indicator of the extent to which trade unions retain a place in the institutional structure of employee relations, their involvement across a range of decision making and the types of change being introduced into workplaces should provide additional insights into the influence that unions are able to exert within the organisation. Clearly such insights will only be tentative: not only will conditions vary markedly from one context to another, but also attempting to infer patterns of influence without detailed analysis of particular decision-making processes is hazardous. In terms of the more strategic-level decisions taken in organisations, it is apparent from the longitudinal research undertaken by Hickson and his colleagues (1985) that trade union involvement was minimal even during a period when their overall strength was seen to be higher than in the current period. At more parochial levels of decision making, however – for example in relation to aspects of internal work organisation – it is evident that union influence developed to a much greater extent, particularly in industries such as engineering (Terry and Edwards, 1988).

One of the most important characteristics of the UK trade union movement during the 1960s and 1970s was its reliance on shop stewards (elected representatives of trade union members at the place of work where they are themselves employees). In the full employment years of the postwar period, when employers faced relatively 'soft' (Commonwealth) product markets, informal bargaining with shop stewards proved a flexible and effective method of handling a whole range of employment issues at the workplace (see Chapter 7). For the unions, the reliance on shop stewards proved to be very cost-effective, but the growing influence of shop stewards arguably led to a loss of authority (and control) for the unions' district committees, executives and even branches (the basic units of organisation of virtually all trade unions). During the 1960s this presented relatively few problems for the union movement. In fact shop steward activity not only proved an effective method of securing improved pay and conditions at work, but played an important role in 'democratising' a number of highly autocratic unions (most notably the T&GWU). But shop steward organisation, an increasing number of whom were paid by management to work full time on union activities (see Terry, 1983, 1995:206–7), was in many respects 'fair weather' unionism. In the 1980s, when the chill wind of Thatcherism began to blow, many shop stewards found themselves isolated: members were fearful of losing their jobs and were unwilling to support shop stewards victimised by management, while the unions were unable to provide sufficient (full-time officer) support. Not surprisingly many managers took the opportunity to by-pass shop stewards (see for example Brown, 1983; and Chadwick, 1983), as reflected in the marked decline in workplace bargaining between 1980 and 1984 over issues ranging from physical working conditions, redeployment, staffing/ manning levels, and redundancy/redundancy payments (Millward and Stevens, 1986:248).

In the latter half of the decade, however, the situation appeared to stabilise, due in part, no doubt, to the general change of management policy in the middle part of the 1980s (see Edwards, 1987:150; and Chapter 4 above). Among those establishments in the WIRS samples where trade unions were recognised, in the latter half of the 1980s the proportion of establishments with union representatives declined from 54 per cent (1984) to 38 per cent (1990), although again much of the decline was concentrated in smaller workplaces with fewer than 100 employees (Millward *et al.*, 1992:110). But there was comparatively little overall change in the extent to which issues such as physical working conditions, redeployment, staffing levels, size of redundancy pay and recruitment were subject to joint regulation: among manual unions the extent of joint regulation of these issues fell slightly between 1984 and 1990, while among non-manual unions it increased slightly (ibid:251–2). In 1990 over three quarters of establishments jointly regulated physical working conditions with their manual and/or non-manual unions; half or more jointly regulated staffing levels, while around a third subjected recruitment decisions to joint regulation. Hence while the proportion of establishments recognising trade unions declined significantly during the 1980s, as did the level and density of union membership, in those establishments where unions continued to be recognised the degree of joint regulation over a range of issues appears to have remained fairly stable. More recent survey evidence (Godfrey and Marchington, 1996), as well as several case studies (e.g.

Darlington, 1994), reveal that in a great many workplaces the role and influence of shop stewards displays remarkable stability.

The comparatively unique dependence of UK trade unions on workplace organisation in general, and shop stewards in particular, is likely to continue through the remainder of the 1990s and beyond, given the decentralisation of collective bargaining (see Chapter 7) and extensive privatisation (see Chapter 6). In this context the propriety of participative forms of trade unionism is immediately apparent. As Fairbrother (1996:136) argues:

> No longer is it possible for unions to organise on the assumption of relatively remote and inactive memberships, involved in union activity at the behest of national leaders or regional officers. . . . Instead, a premium is now being placed on forms of collective organisation that are rooted in the workplace in ways that were not necessary in the past.

UK unions arguably have no alternative to the shop steward model (Terry, 1995:224–5), but if workplace unionism is to be effective, workplace representatives will have to be 'leaders' rather than 'populists' (Batstone *et al.*, 1977). The former display a much higher commitment to trade union principles and the union as a whole, act as representatives of rank-and-file members rather than simply as delegates, initiate workplace issues, and help create and perpetuate a strong trade union ideology among the workforce (ibid: 34–5). Not only are management more likely to develop a strong bargaining relationship with stewards who are both willing and able to lead the membership (ibid:176–7), 'leaders' display greater success in securing increased wage levels, in maintaining various forms of worker control, and in manipulating consciousness in favour of trade union principles (ibid:250; see also Darlington, 1994).

For unions to realise the potential of (participative) workplace organisation they must develop supportive relationships between shop stewards and the union bureaucracy on the one hand, and empower rank-and-file members on the other. In recent years, however, many unions have concentrated their efforts on developing a 'managerial servicing' relationship, where members are regarded as passive consumers of union benefits rather than active participants in union activities (see Bacon and Storey, 1996; and Heery and Kelly, 1994:7–10). A servicing relationship clearly sits more comfortably with management–union cooperation, and many unions have made overtures to employers in the form of new-style agreements or social partnerships. These initiatives merit critical scrutiny. First, however, the political influence of trade unions is considered. Many unions and many commentators (e.g. McCarthy, 1991:19) believe 'significant progress is dependent on an improved legal framework on recognition' (Waddington and Whitston, 1995a:192) which, if correct, will require the exertion of political as well as industrial influence.

Beyond the workplace: unions and politics

All trade unions are involved in political activity, by virtue of necessity (Crouch, 1982b). Trade unions in the UK have always maintained a clear and, some would argue, too rigid a separation between their industrial and political activities (Hyman, 1989a:167–9), but as Flanders (1975:30) argued, unions have been compelled, at a minimum, to seek to establish a legal and economic environment that allows them to flourish as industrial organisations. But unions' political activity extends well beyond sectional (or vested) interests, for they must take on broader social issues such as housing, transport, education and health care if they are to broaden their appeal (what Flanders described as the union's 'sword of justice'). Thus at the national level the trade union movement in general, and the TUC in particular, gradually extended their involvement with government bodies in the 1960s and 1970s. In part this reflected an increased tendency for governments to take soundings on economic and industrial policy from both employer and union organisations. This led to union membership of bodies such as NEDO (National Economic Development Office) which, together with the little 'neddies' concerned with particular sectors, were established to secure tripartite discussions on national and sectoral economic issues. Other bodies on which trade unions gained a presence were the Industrial Training Boards, the Manpower Services Commission, the Health and Safety Executive, the National Enterprise Board and the Council of ACAS.

By 1975 more than 2000 trade union nominees were sitting on tripartite bodies at national and local level (McIlroy, 1988:44). In addition the pact established between the unions and the 1974–9 Labour government (the Social Contract) increased the degree of union involvement in the government's economic management (see Chapter 6). However, although this period is regarded as the high point of union political influence, it must be recognised that the historical separation of politics from industrial relations left the union movement with no overall vision of the trade unions' role in society. In addition political involvement in the 1970s was based less on a corporatist ideology (discussed in Chapter 6) than on the pragmatic need of governments to come to terms with the industrial power of trade unions, which might disrupt (however unintentionally) national economic policy (Hyman, 1989a:169–73). Thus as McIlroy (1988) has pointed out, the amount of influence the trade unions had in the tripartite arrangements and under the Social Contract can easily be inflated (see also Coates, 1980). Many of the tripartite bodies, for example, were consultative rather than decision making in character, allowing the government to take soundings rather than committing them to joint decision making. Similarly the breadth of the Social Contract and the powers it gave to trade unions must not be exaggerated. In practice the Social Contract 'increasingly became simply an instrument for the control of wages. There was no open and formalised bargaining between the state, capital and labour, where broad social objectives were articulated, analysed and bargained over' (McIlroy, 1988:43).

The point here is that the degree of trade unions' influence on the state in the 1960s and 1970s can easily be overstated: greater involvement there certainly was, but the extent to which this translated into real influence is more questionable. Coates (1980:59) even goes so far as to argue that 'the visibility of trade union leaders in the process of policy making was less an index of their power than of their subordination'. One possible consequence of this tendency to overstate union influence is that any subsequent perceived decline in that influence is also likely to be exaggerated. It is true that during the 1980s the union presence on national bodies was reduced or removed altogether. Tripartitism lost favour in the Thatcher years. Yet it is probably more accurate to represent this as a reduction in access to national consultative arrangements with the state, than as a removal of unions from joint decision-making bodies. Moreover this decline in involvement was under way before the 1979 Conservative electoral victory: the Social Contract had effectively broken down well before the 1974–9 Labour government left office. What is more the subsequent success enjoyed by the Thatcher government in circumscribing union influence at the national level in the 1980s may be seen as attesting, in part, to the restricted nature of that union influence – and certainly its fragility – during the preceding decade.

There is no doubting, however, the political problems that afflicted the labour movement in the 1980s and early 1990s, and the consequent decline of political influence. In particular the relationship between the trade unions and the Labour Party, and the decline of electoral support for the Labour Party even among trade unionists, proved particularly problematic. Initially the Labour Party and the trade unions, through the TUC, were united in their opposition to the first Thatcher government (1979–83), with the TUC leading political campaigns and demonstrations against the new government. The unions actually increased their influence within the Labour Party at that time, as in addition to holding the majority of seats on the Party's National Executive Committee (either directly or indirectly), a new electoral college system for the election of leader and deputy leader of the Party gave the trade unions 40 per cent of the vote, the Parliamentary Labour Party (PLP) 30 per cent, and the constituencies 30 per cent (previously the PLP elected both leader and deputy leader). This change, however, along with the Conference block votes held by the larger unions, which no longer overwhelmingly supported the right of the Party, led to the breakaway of more than twenty Labour MPs to form the Social Democratic Party in March 1981, which effectively split the labour vote. This split, combined with the failure of past Labour governments' economic policies, the unattractive image of bureaucratic state socialism (inefficient public services and costly nationalised industries), and the growing influence of the militant left within the Labour

Party led to a second general election defeat in 1983 (see Hyman, 1989a:175–7). Of course the Falklands War also played a major part in the 1983 election, but less than 40 per cent of trade unionists voted for Labour in 1983, fewer than ever before.

Union policy then changed from political opposition and the hope of a return to 'the good old days' under a Labour government, to 'new realism'. The idea of collaboration with both employers and the Tory government had taken root (Kelly, 1990:58–9). The labour movement was now split on both the industrial and the political front. However members continued to support *their* union, even on politically contentious issues such as the closed shop (the unions won 82 per cent of the 111 ballots on the closed shop between 1982 and 1986) (ibid:44) and union political funds (see Leopold, 1986; and Chapter 6 below). Such limited support failed to prevent two subsequent general election defeats for Labour, which clearly exacerbated the political problems facing the labour movement. The 1987 defeat, however, focused the attention of a number of unions on recruitment activity as the prospect of a Labour government being returned seemed an ever more distant prospect, as proved to be the case in the 1992 election.

In 1997 the incoming Labour government promised the unions 'fairness, not favours' and continued to distance itself from the labour movement (for example, the principle of 'one member, one vote' had been passed at the 1993 Labour Party Conference, further eroding the unions' influence within the Party, and the 1995 Conference had abandoned Clause IV of the Labour Party's constitution, which committed Labour to public ownership). As one senior union official remarked, the relationship between the unions and New Labour is rather like that between parents and their teenage offspring: 'You can drive me to the disco, pay for my booze, but park round the corner so my mates can't see you' (*The Independent*, 6 September 1996). Given the new relationship, and the fact that Labour intends to retain many elements of Tory legislation passed during the 1980s and early 1990s (for example prestrike ballots and restrictions on secondary action and the closed shop), the unions' political demands have been moderated and their legislative demands targeted at key areas. For example the unions would like to restore their role as 'social partners' via a properly organised public forum (possibly along the lines of the NEDC, which was abolished by Mrs Thatcher), but they seem to have rejected the idea of corporatism (see Chapter 6). The call for 'social partnership' is part-and-parcel of the unions' commitment, and in particular that of the TUC, to European integration and the Social Chapter as a more promising route to the 'institutionalisation' of a more entrenched framework of legal rights for representation and consultation at both the workplace and societal levels (see Chapter 11).

A key legislative proposal by New Labour is the repeal of the 1993 law on check-off, which obliges union members to authorise the deduction of union subscriptions from their wages every three years (discussed further in

Chapter 6). This will greatly facilitate the retention of union membership (or at least end the current farce of unions having to 're-recruit' their existing members every three years). The 'biggest obstacle to a restoration of union membership' (Waddington and Whitston, 1995a:192), however, is the absence of a statutory recognition procedure that would compel employers to recognise and bargain in good faith with trade unions where the majority of the workforce vote for union representation. New Labour is committed to such a procedure, although legislation is unlikely before 1999. Even with a statutory recognition provision in place, however, and an (initial) endorsement of union membership, trade unions must still persuade workers to sign up and, more importantly, participate in union affairs. For many but not all workers, recognition may be a necessary condition for union organisation, but it is by no means sufficient. Put differently, membership, organisation and the exercise of collective strength must still be 'achieved'. Political influence may be inseparable from the industrial power of trade unions, but the former is invariably dependent on the latter, and the latter is ultimately in the hands of the unions themselves.

Trade union responses

Trade unions have not been passive victims of membership decline. It has already been noted how the overall net decline in membership masks significant (though insufficient) recruitment, to the point where a number of unions in fact recorded an increase in membership during the 1980s. Trade unions have various options to secure new members. For example they might simply decide to 'sit tight' and wait for the external environment to improve (unemployment to fall, manufacturing to recover, firms to grow in size and so on). Alternatively, they might undertake a series of initiatives to recruit new members, wherein leaders develop new strategies, recruitment drives are targeted at specific groups and the effectiveness of the organisation is improved. Many unions have sought to offer new services, both to employers and employees, while others have stuck with a more traditional approach, emphasising the role that trade unions can play in protecting employee rights, securing pay rises and improving conditions of work. Finally, there are choices, and constraints, facing both individual unions and the labour movement as a whole as a result of the structure of different unions, their respective job territories, and the authority of the TUC. Some unions, for example the old craft-based unions such as the NGA, have a closed membership base while others, most notably the two major general unions (the T&GWU and the GMB) and a number of ex-craft-based unions that now recruit more widely, such as the AEEU, are engaged in competition for members across broadly similar job territories. In recent years the TUC has attempted to regulate such competition more closely, as well as the signing of single union agreements, but Congress has very limited power over its affiliates (expulsion, for example, the TUC's ultimate sanction, can actually *increase* competition between unions as the excluded union is no longer bound to respect other unions' membership territories, and *vice versa*). Figure 5.1 summarises these possibilities.

On the more specific question of recruitment, unions face several options. They can seek more members in areas where they already have recognition; they can attempt to recruit in areas where no recognition agreement exists (in the hope that as membership grows, recognition will be afforded to them); they can merge with another body and thereby increase not only their membership but also their recruitment base; and they can try to secure single-union agreements with employers at a non-union or greenfield site, which will then act to 'deliver' a membership from among those employed at the site (William, 1989). While the first two options involve the recruitment of individual members, the last two involve the organisation of groups of members. As Willman (ibid) argues, this will typically make the options of merger or employer agreement much more cost-effective recruitment strategies than seeking individual members, particularly in areas where employers are hostile to unionism. Given the financial constraints facing many unions (ibid:266), which have not been reversed in recent years despite continued reform of financial management systems within trade unions (Willman and Morris, 1995), the more cost-effective means are likely to hold sway, even though this will tend to result in greater inter-union competition for members in certain areas (what Willman terms 'market share' unionism) rather than a more 'expansionary' recruitment drive into the virgin territory of the private services sector. These options, which for most unions are concurrent if not always complementary strategies, are explored in more detail below.

	OPTIONS		
Possibility to increase membership:	Environment	vs	Union initiatives
Union policy to attract new members:	Extended services	vs	Traditional unionism
Recruitment territories and job boundaries:	Inter-union competition	vs	Regulation

Source: Adapted from Mason and Bain (1991:36–7).

FIGURE 5.1   Trade union options for the 1990s

Union mergers

The move towards 'market share' unionism is clearly evident in the heightened merger activity that has characterised the recent period. By the early 1990s virtually all the biggest unions were involved in merger discussions or had recently completed a merger (see Kelly, 1990:59). This pattern is not new: there has been a steady fall in the number of unions since 1920 (Table 5.4). What is new, however, is the pace of decline in the number of unions, largely brought about by increased merger activity. The 1980s recorded the steepest decline of any decade with the number of unions falling by over one-third in the ten-year period. The increasing concentration of UK's unions is indicated by the fact that in 1995 the eight largest unions (each with 250 000 or more members) accounted for over 62 per cent of all union members. Less than 10 per cent of all unions now account for over 84 per cent of all union members.

Mergers can take various forms. In 1989–90, for example, there were three amalgamations (where two or more unions join together to form a new union) and thirteen transfers of engagements (where one union is subsumed by another and loses its legal status) (Bird *et al.*, 1992). One unique merger was that in February 1985 between the Civil and Public Services Association (Post and Telecom Group) and the Post Office Engineering Union to form the National Communications Union. The NCU was the first ever example of a major section of one trade union leaving to join with another to form an entirely new organisation. In 1995 the NCU merged with the UCW to create the Communication Workers Union. Other significant mergers over the past decade include the amalgamation of ASTMS and TASS in 1988 to form

TABLE 5.4   **Number of trade unions in the UK, 1900–95**

	Number of unions	% change over previous period
1900	1323	—
1910	1269	− 4.1
1920	1384	+ 9.1
1930	1133	−18.1
1940	1004	−11.4
1950	732	−27.1
1960	664	− 9.3
1970	543	−18.2
1980	438	−19.3
1990	287	−34.5
1995	238	−17.1

Source: Certification Officer and Department of Employment.

Manufacturing, Science and Finance (MSF), the amalgamations in 1990 of the National Union of Railwaymen and National Union of Seamen to form the National Union of Rail, Maritime and Transport Workers (RMT), the merger of the AEU and EETPU to create the Amalgamated Engineering and Electrical Union (AEEU), and the merger of the National Graphical Association and SOGAT to form the Graphical, Paper and Media Union. In July 1993 the UK's largest union was created by the merger of the white-collar local government union NALGO, the public sector manual union NUPE and the health service union COHSE to form Unison (see Table 5.3). Similarly, discussions are under way on the possible merger of the two largest general unions, the T&GWU and GMB, which if successful would then become the largest UK union with over 1.5 million members. In general, however, more unions seek merger than actually achieve it (Willman, 1996).

A significant feature of many of the more recent mergers was that, unlike the *defensive* mergers of the 1970s, where small unions sought the protection of bigger unions in order to avert serious financial problems or membership decline (see Undy *et al.*, 1981), a more *consolidatory* or *aggressive* approach to mergers was evident in the 1980s and early 1990s (see Buchanan, 1992). This typically involved two relatively strong unions in a given industry or occupation deciding to pool their resources for mutual advantage, for example the merger of the NGA and SOGAT to form the GPMU, and the ACTT and BETA to form BECTU. More aggressive mergers, designed to protect relative membership share and expand trade union job territories as the basis for further growth, included MSF, Unison and the AEEU. Merger activity, then, may be driven by the problems of membership decline, but it is not an entirely defensive act – indeed in some cases it may be just the opposite.

Whatever the 'urge to merge', however, the outcome has *not* been to simplify the historically complex structure of UK unions, or to reverse membership decline. Early unions were (closed) craft-based organisations that over time opened their membership to less skilled workers in order to survive (for example the AEU). These unions were joined in the late nineteenth century by the first mass organisations of unskilled workers, which recruited any and all workers, although they usually had a strong base in particular industries. The roots of the T&GWU, for example, formed from an amalgamation of more than a hundred separate organisations, were the docks and wharves, where strong local unions had developed (see Coates and Topham, 1991). Many unions can therefore lay historical claim to similar 'job territories'. If the present trend continues, the union movement could soon be dominated by just four or five 'super unions', but their membership base would be even more diverse and they would no doubt continue to compete for members (Waddington, 1995:214). Thus while centralised financial control could improve the administrative efficiency of these 'super unions', the problem of representative effectiveness could actually be exacerbated (Willman and Cave, 1994:405).

Two of the more innovative 'solutions' to such problems are 'single table' and 'single union' agreements, but these arrangements typically involve changing the relationship with *employers* in the first instance (although there are important implications for the relationship between the union and its members). The non-union sector, in contrast, is being 'attacked by several expansionist unions, apparently with limited success, whose efforts are competitive' (ibid:406). As Willman and Cave (ibid:407–10) demonstrate, inter-union cooperation (joint ventures) would probably be more effective than further mergers, and may be easier to coordinate between the 'super unions'. Returning to Figure 5.1, the conclusion is that regulation, whether by the TUC or joint ventures between major unions, is essential to reverse the current decline of union membership.

Recruitment through employer agreements

Just as mergers deliver whole groups into a union, albeit either from a staff association or another union, so too the signing of a single union agreement with an employer can ensure a substantial number of members for the union concerned. Hence despite the cost of making approaches and presentations to employers, the potential pay-offs are considerable – not only recognition but a 'captive' workforce from which to recruit. Furthermore, with employer recognition typically come other benefits for the union – in particular union subscriptions being collected at source via check-off arrangements, as well as facilities for trade union representatives such as office facilities and time off for union activities.

For trade unions the experience with single union agreements since the early 1980s displays some similarities to, but also a number of important differences from, what has gone before in terms of union recognition and member representation. Many other worksites, for example, are represented by a single union. In the most recent WIRS study more than a third (36 per cent) of establishments with recognised unions had only a single union (Millward *et al.*, 1992:81). If anything this will become more common in the future as a result of union mergers. But like anywhere else, trade unions who have signed single union agreements at greenfield or non-union sites must still convince the potential membership that it is worthwhile belonging to the union, rather than 'free ride' under the umbrella of the recognition agreement. Research on greenfield sites (Newell, 1993) suggests that employees still demonstrate a propensity to join a trade union, even where they benefit from company-specific training, single status, and extensive communications and consultation, all of which supposedly 'negate' the need for trade union membership. At the plants studied by Newell, workers displayed high levels of dissatisfaction with management, as do workers in the UK generally (ISR,

1996). But what are the benefits from union membership under a new-style, single-union agreement?

It is important, in the first instance, to distinguish single-*union* from single-*table* agreements. The latter, which are also on the increase, represent a 'coming together' (cooperation) of unions who together negotiate with the employer around the same table, thus saving time and resources for the company, increasing flexibility and precluding 'leap-frogging' pay claims (Gall, 1994). Like single-union agreements, single-table bargaining is often associated with single status, more integrated pay schemes (including performance-related pay), multiskilling and teamwork. The key difference is that single-table agreements are negotiated at 'brownfield' sites where unions are typically well established, whereas the distinctive feature of single-union agreements is that unions typically begin their recruitment of members *after* recognition has been granted, rather than secure recognition as a result of building up a strong and committed membership base. On greenfield sites in particular it is not uncommon for agreements to be signed even before any employees are engaged (IRRR, 1992, 1993). Thus, in a very real sense, in these cases trade unions in the first instance are recruiting *employers* rather than employees. In reality, however, it would be more accurate to say that the initial recruitment process works the other way round: employers choose the union they are prepared to recognise. This presents the union movement with the problem of interunion competition (what some have dubbed 'beauty contests') and individual members with inadequate representation and protection.

Although the incidence of single-union agreements remains small, and the number of workers covered by such agreements arguably insignificant (see Gall and McKay, 1994:446; and IRRR, 1993:10), the rise of single union agreements in the late 1980s and early 1990s posed a serious challenge to interunion cooperation. The explicit 'business unionism' of the EETPU in particular caused a serious rift within the union movement, leading to the expulsion of the electricians from the TUC in 1988 (see Blyton and Turnbull, 1994:101–3). Once a union 'breaks ranks', this acts to create a process of 'whipsawing', as the Americans call it, where unions compete to 'do business' (sign deals) with employers and in the process sign away employees' rights and union responsibilities. The EETPU's agreement with Hitachi in South Wales, for example, included a joint commitment to pendulum arbitration rather than industrial action to settle unresolved issues, complete job flexibility, single status, and discussion on pay and conditions routed initially and primarily via a consultative Company Members Board rather than through separate union–management negotiations (ibid). Different single-union agreements vary in their individual components. The Hitachi agreement, for example, refers to pendulum arbitration while the agreement at the nearby Pirelli plant in Aberdare commits the union and management to 'binding arbitration of a non-pendulum kind' (Yeandle and Clark, 1989:39; see also

Garrahan and Stewart, 1992; and IRRR, 1993). In each and every case, however, the trade union's influence is arguably much diminished. Not only do such agreements approximate to a new form of 'enterprise unionism', virtually excluding *external* trade union influences and any wider social, economic, political or legal agendas that the union, let alone the union movement, might be involved in, but the union also has a greatly reduced internal role. Management have effectively usurped many of the traditional functions of the union, and it should come as no surprise that union membership under some single union agreements is extremely low.

The typical response of the unions involved in such agreements is that the alternative would be non-unionism. What many unions have ended up with, however, may in fact be little better. This is one reason why the General Executive Council of the T&GWU decided in 1992 not to participate in any further union 'beauty contests' (Snape, 1994a:231). From the point of view of the union movement, and certainly the individual employee, would it not be better for a union to win the support of the workforce and then secure recognition from the employer, rather than the other way round? After all unions have had to do this in the past, and have done so with considerable success, especially at larger workplaces in the manufacturing sector, where most of the single union deals are to be found. The problem for the union movement, then, is not the apparent *need* for 'new realism', but the *opportunism* of individual unions caught up in a struggle to prevent the further decline of their membership base and their failure in many such instances to address the real needs of the workforce. As Kelly and Waddington (1995:424) argue, 'It is fallacious to suggest that unions must "satisfy" employers; a more rewarding approach, albeit more difficult to achieve, is to find ways of making employers tolerate a trade union presence'. The organising model adopted by the T&GWU, MSF and several other unions seeks to achieve both objectives: to meet the demands of employees and command a hearing from employers.

Recruiting new members

In recent years a great many unions have devoted resources to recruiting new members, albeit with limited success (see for example Kelly and Heery, 1989, 1994; Mason and Bain, 1991; Snape, 1994b, 1995; and Turnbull, 1997). For some unions, such as multi-occupational industry unions (e.g. the NUM and the ISTC) and single-occupation, single-industry unions with an already high union density (e.g. ASLEF), the potential to recruit new members is virtually non-existent. The greatest scope exists for the general unions (e.g. the T&GWU and the GMB) or those in areas of employment growth where union density is low (e.g. BIFU in finance and USDAW in retail distribution). As Kelly and Heery (1989) illustrate, recruitment targets vary significantly for different unions, depending on the proximity of the job territories of potential members to those already organised (to varying degrees) by the union, and the coverage of recognition agreements among the target groups. In some instances (close consolidation) the union might simply be involved in a 'mopping-up' exercise of non-union members within the union's existing job territories where collective agreements are in place. Much of the T&GWU's recent recruitment activity, for example, has been directed towards '100 per cent' or '100 per cent plus' campaigns (which include subcontractors such as cleaning, catering and security). In other situations (distant consolidation), the union might have a recognition agreement for the industry or specific companies, but organisation is poor and union density is low, perhaps because establishments are small and difficult to organise and/or labour turnover is high. Data from the Labour Force Survey suggest that around three million non-union employees are working in establishments with union recognition, which gives some indication of the massive potential for membership consolidation. Other potential membership groups are not covered by a recognition agreement (usually higher level or management grades) but do work in organisations where union density is already high (close expansion). Finally, the most difficult groups to recruit (distant expansion) are those in job territories where the union has neither recognition agreements nor (successful) experience of organisation to build on. It is among such groups (discussed in more detail in Chapter 9) that the potential for membership growth is greatest but union organisation is most difficult. Figure 5.2 provides a summary of these different recruitment targets.

Proximity of Target Territories

		Close	Distant
Coverage by Recognition Agreements	Yes, Consolidation	Non-members in organised establishments covered by recognition agreements, e.g. civil service.	Non-members covered by company/national recognition agreements but in weakly/non-organised establishments, e.g. retail distribution.
	No, Expansion	Non-members in organised establishments not covered by recognition agreements, e.g. white-collar staff in manufacturing.	Non-members in unorganised establishments without recognition agreements, e.g. insurance, hotels.

Source: Kelly and Heery (1989:198).

FIGURE 5.2 Typology of union recruitment

Identifying potential membership targets, or what unions often refer to as 'mapping' (building up a detailed profile of the workplace, workforce, company policies, existing terms and conditions and so on), is simply the first step of a recruitment and organisation strategy. The most important question a union must ask when recruiting new members is 'why should workers sign up?' Many unions, for example, have sought to attract new members by offering a wider range of services to the *individual*, based on the assumption that:

individualism now outweighs collectivism in what union members want, and if individualism is the clear direction being pursued by employers in their relations with their employees, trade unions need to examine their supply side . . . to meet the new individual demand (Bassett and Cave, 1993:8).

The new 'role models' for trade unions, according to Bassett and Cave (ibid:17), should be the Automobile Association or BUPA, reconstituting trade unions 'as businesses – private-sector organisations engaged in providing a range of services for people who wish to buy them'. This form of 'passive consumerism' is evident in the provision of union credit cards, insurance schemes, legal advice, trade discounts and a range of other private benefits.

The shortcomings of this approach, however, are legion. For example it overstates the extent of 'individualism' adopted by employers in their 'human resource management' policies (see for example Blyton and Turnbull, 1992; Gallie and Rose, 1996:63; Legge, 1995; and Chapter 4 above), and more importantly the extent to which employees have embraced individualism or, more specifically, now place individual benefits over and above collective protection in their reasons for joining a trade union. Given the extent of social injustice, inequality of income and opportunity, work intensification, and employment insecurity in the UK today (see Chapter 3), it is hardly surprising that new union members cite 'support if I had a problem at work' as the principal reason for joining, along with 'improved pay and conditions'. Very few new members cite non-work-related services such as trade discounts, financial packages and the like (Whitston and Waddington, 1994:37: see also Sapper, 1991). In short, 'Individualism was not central to union decline, and collective issues remain at the core of workers' demands of unions' (Waddington and Whitston, 1995a:197; see also Gallie, 1996).

The central problem for trade unions is not so much the assumed growth of individualism as a discernible shift in the balance of power in favour of employers, which makes it more difficult for unions to 'deliver' on day-to-day workplace issues (Kelly and Waddington, 1995:421; and McIlroy, 1995:399). Put differently, how do unions translate collective demands into concessions from employers? Kelly's (1996:79) assessment is that 'militancy is likely to prove a better guarantor of union survival and recovery'. Moderation, as Kelly (ibid:95–6) demonstrates, has brought unions only meagre returns and has subjected the union to greater dependence on the 'goodwill' of the employer (see also Turnbull, 1997). This is the inherent danger of a 'servicing model' of trade unionism which is contrasted with the 'organising model' in Figure 5.3. In the context of an 'organising cycle' (issue → organisation → education → unity → action), however, 'militancy' is a method rather than an aim, with the emphasis first and foremost on *solidarity* as opposed to *strike* action (the former might include wearing badges or T-shirts emblazoned with workers' demands, petitions, boycotts, sit-downs or phone-ins) (see Organising Works, 1996:118–20). While the servicing union expects its members to ask no more than 'What can the union do *for me*?', the organising union asks 'What can *we* achieve *with* the union?' The organising union depends upon membership being of value *in itself*: members should be able to identify their own issues, organise to solve their own problems and satisfy their aspirations on a collective basis. If all union members defined their own interests in isolation and then simply looked to 'the union' to service their needs, not only would the costs prove prohibitive, but the very basis of organisation and unity would be precarious and ultimately ephemeral. In short, there would be no union.

The organising model is clearly based on 'participative' forms of union organisation. Indeed the basis of 'self-organisation' is that workers recruit their fellow workers (like recruits like), set their own agenda and solve as many of their own problems as is practicable. In the present context of UK industrial relations the propriety of the organising model is readily demonstrated (see Turnbull, 1997). For example a recent survey revealed that 'made contact myself' and being contacted by shop stewards are the most prevalent forms of union recruitment (Whitston and Waddington, 1994:37). Very few members are recruited by FTOs (ibid), which suggests that a more appropriate role for officers would be to support and coordinate lay activists or full-time organisers rather than direct recruitment (which is precisely the structure established by the T&GWU). As Whitston and Waddington (1992:4) conclude: 'The real challenge to the survival and expansion of the union presence amongst British workers is not historical redundancy, but the process of reorienting bargaining agendas, and restructuring the relationship between workplace organisation and the wider union'.

Conclusion

The difficulties facing the trade union movement in the 1990s are considerable, but they are not insurmountable. Membership continues to decline, but unions continue to attract new members and their popularity (according to opinion polls) is now at its highest for twenty years (*The Independent*, 29 December 1992; see also Edwards and Bain, 1988). More importantly there are

A servicing union means . . .	An organising union means . . .
The union is seen as a third party. It enters the workplace to increase membership or solve problems.	Members own the campaign to unionise their workplace.
Unions tell members how they can solve their problems.	Members identify their own issues and organise to solve them together.
Relying on the employer to provide a list of the names of workers to the union official.	Mapping the workplace and staff attitudes are crucial – names and information are provided by workers.
Relying on workplace access and employer cooperation.	Initial organising can be done outside work – in workers' homes and other places.
Cold selling union membership by organisers.	Establishing initial contacts and finding natural leaders to help recruit.
Selling the union for services and insurance protection.	Workers empowered to act for themselves through education and support.
Relying on full-time officials to recruit and solve problems.	An internal organising committee formed and workers encouraged to build the union through one-to-one organising.
Recruiting is seen as a separate activity.	Recruitment and organising are integrated.
Results are achieved, but they are likely to be short term.	Results obtained through sustained efforts – more likely to be permanent.
The union is blamed when it can't get results.	Members share decisions and solve problems together with union leaders.
Members complain they pay fees and the union does nothing.	Members make a real contribution to union struggles and identify with the union. An attack on the union is an attack on themselves.
Organisers resent members for not coming to meetings or participating.	The image of the union is positive and active.
Management acts, while the union reacts and it is always on the defensive.	The union has its own agenda with members involved and it keeps management off balance.

Source: Organising Works (1995).

FIGURE 5.3   Servicing and organising models of trade unionism

clear indications that many more workers would join a union given the opportunity or the incentive. For workers to have the opportunity to join, unions must actively recruit and organise in the workplace. For workers to want to join they must be convinced that, through collective action, union membership can change their working lives and not simply enable them to buy cheap insurance or secure discounts on a range of (private) benefits. In both the workplace and beyond, however, trade unions have seen their industrial and political influence eroded. Again, however, there are not only important elements of continuity in trade union influence, but new opportunities. If it is borne in mind that, contrary to the popular accounts of the halcyon days of the 1960s and 1970s, the union movement has always been characterised by differentiation, division and disunity (Hyman, 1991b), then the present-day dilemmas facing trade unions are, in part at least, aspects of longer-running problems. Thus, as in the past, unions currently have a degree of choice in responding to the changes and challenges of the 1990s:

> There are opportunities for policies which appeal to new working-class constituencies (or often, old sections whose interests have hitherto been neglected); for initiatives which address members' interests outside the workplace, and thus provide a fertile basis for transcending particularistic employment identities; and for programmes which link workers' interests as producers and consumers (as, for example, in demands for the improvement of public health care) so as to enable the construction of new types of encompassing and solidaristic alliances (ibid:16).

Of course, given the changes to the composition of the workforce, economic policy and the political context, the future role of trade unions within the economy, while significant, will be very different from that of the past. More strategic union policies designed to reverse their fortunes, most notably the emphasis on recruitment, organisation and participation, is a case in point. Although not a perfect substitute for 'exogenous' changes more favourable to union organisation, the development of strategic union initiatives based on the organising model are at least less dependent on changes in labour market and trade union legislation, economic revival or a warmer political climate. Over the next decade, then, trade unions will continue to play an important part in employee relations, despite the best efforts of some employers to undermine trade union recognition and influence.

For almost two decades Conservative governments argued that unions should 'modernise' by improving the provision of services to employees, 'encouraging union members to adopt an individualistic (even consumerist) approach to union membership' (Martin *et al.*, 1995:148), and by offering single-union, no-strike deals to employers (Department of Employment, 1991:10). In their more direct dealings with labour, however, successive Conservative governments pursued a policy of 'decollectivisation': 'the *de facto* redistribution of power to employers within new institutions for the management of employee relations in order thereby to counter any resurgence in labour's collective power' (Smith and Morton, 1993:108). It is to the general role of the state in employee relations that we now turn.

CHAPTER 6

Employee relations and the state

Abolition of the National Dock Labour Scheme

A Statutory Solution

On Thursday 6 April 1989 Norman Fowler MP, then Secretary of State for Employment, made a surprise announcement in the House of Commons. To roars of approval from Conservative backbenchers, the government announced its intention to abolish the National Dock Labour Scheme (NDLS), first introduced in 1947 under the Dock Workers (Regulation of Employment) Act 1946. Predictably, the following day saw unofficial strikes across the country at eleven ports, but this action was quickly called off the following Monday after nervous union instructions to return to normal working. Not only had the spontaneous action by the dockers not been preceded by a ballot, but the leadership of the Transport & General Workers' Union (T&GWU) feared that any industrial action at this stage against the abolition of the Scheme might be deemed 'political' (and therefore unlawful) and eventually result in the sequestration of union funds. Thus began a protracted legal argument in the Courts to establish, first, whether there was a legitimate industrial dispute between the employers and the dockers, and secondly, at the Appeal Court, whether such a dispute was in breach of a statutory duty on the part of the dockers to work. The legal argument was eventually won by the Union, but not without considerable delay. While the courts debated the dockers' right to strike, the government rushed the Dock Work Bill through Parliament under a guillotine that severely limited debate. By the time the Union had established its right to strike, the Scheme had already been abolished.

As soon as the Dock Work Bill received Royal Assent (3 July 1989), the employers moved quickly to dismiss registered dockers using generous severance arrangements funded jointly by the government. By the time the Union could hold a strike in defence of the Scheme (10 July 1989) the employers had already dismissed 1200 dockers (13 per cent of the total). Redundancy pay was then used to break the strike itself, as employer after employer ordered their workers to return to work by a specified date, under new terms and conditions, or else face instant dismissal and the loss of all entitlement to severance pay. Behind the scenes the government signalled its own determination to defeat the dockers by offering to pay severance to *all* dockers made redundant by their employer, 'without any cash limits on these payments' (Sir Alan Bailey, Permanent Under Secretary at the Department of Transport, evidence to CPA, 1991:4). In short, the government decided on the abolition of the Scheme 'without cost being the primary consideration' (CPA, 1991:vii). As one of nineteen shop stewards (unfairly) dismissed by management at the port of Tilbury during the strike later reflected, 'we didn't lose the strike, the government bought it' (interview notes).

Of the 9300 registered dockers employed in the industry immediately before the strike, over 8000 (86 per cent of the total) were subsequently made redundant at a (one-off) cost of over £130 million to the British taxpayer (Turnbull and Wass, 1995:522–3). From being a stronghold of union organisation and an industry renowned for worker militancy and 'restrictive practices', two in five port employers no longer even recognise a trade union, there is no longer any national-level collective bargaining, and labour flexibility is now ubiquitous (Evans *et al.*, 1993; Saundry and Turnbull, 1996; Turnbull and Wass, 1994; Turnbull and Weston, 1993b, 1993c; and Turnbull *et al.*, 1992:175– 213). Through a single Act, the government had transformed employee relations in the industry literally overnight. Deregulation of employment was followed in 1991 by the privatisation of the remaining trust (quasi-public) ports, following the earlier sale of the nationalised ports in 1983, marking the complete reversal of state policy towards the port transport industry.

The state in the docks

The introduction of the NDLS in 1947 was a direct response to the problems of poverty and degradation in dockland areas caused by the irregularity of employment and the almost perpetual oversupply of labour. But it was also a response to the economic inefficiency of casual labour, which led not only to under- and unemployment but also to inappropriate allocation and the underutilisation of labour. Thus in the absence of regulation it was possible for some employers to experience a shortage of labour, especially on specialist cargoes, while men stood idle in other areas of the port. Statutory regulation of employment was therefore deemed appropriate to ensure that labour supply matched labour demand; to minimise daily frictional unemployment caused by the mismatch of men and jobs; to improve productivity and efficiency by ensuring the allocation of men to the work for which they were best suited (by skill, aptitude or preference); and to maintain a healthy and well-trained workforce through the provision of guaranteed income, amenities, welfare and training programmes (financed collectively by the employers).

These were the essential features of the NDLS, which was administered by a National and twenty-two Local Dock Labour Boards (the unions holding joint, 50:50, representation with the employers on these Boards). All employers and dockers had to be registered with the National Dock Labour Board, and only registered employers could hire registered dockers to perform 'dock work'. The latter was defined by statute, though the definition differed in each of the eighty-four ports originally covered by the Scheme, and any non-registered employer could be prosecuted for undertaking dock work, as could registered employers if they engaged non-registered dockers. As a result it was illegal for registered employers to employ 'scabs' (non-registered labour) during a strike (hence the importance of abolishing the Scheme *before* the T&GWU could call a strike), although troops were used as dock workers on several occasions during major disputes (Morris, 1986:100–3). Hiring was centralised and placed under the control of officers of the Local Dock Labour Board in each port, with some exceptions, most notably Glasgow and London, where a 'free call' was retained (Dash, 1969), and if no work was available then dockers would be paid attendance money. If at the end of a week their earnings plus any attendance money fell below the guaranteed weekly wage, negotiated nationally by the unions and the National Association of Port Employers (NAPE), then the dockers' wage would be made up to the minimum by the Dock Labour Board. Such payments were financed by a percentage levy on the employers' wage bill.

Despite the extensive legal regulation of employment in the docks, the majority of ports were not nationalised. Most ports enjoyed 'trust' status, which evolved from nineteenth-century Conservancy Boards set up to replace the ailing private dock companies that were financially unable to develop or maintain adequate port facilities (see Thomas, 1994:136; and Turnbull *et al.*, 1992:41–2). Trust ports operate under individual Acts of Parliament that lay down the constitution, responsibilities and composition of the controlling boards, and although these boards were not directly responsible to parliament they had to submit an annual statement of accounts. Trust port status was therefore a vehicle for ensuring a degree of administrative independence from the state and particular port interests (e.g. shipping lines, agents, forwarders, manufacturers and local authorities), although these interests were often represented on the authority or board of commissioners set up to administer the port.

Around 30 per cent of the UK's port capacity was brought under direct public ownership in 1947 with the nationalisation of the railways (the railway companies had built and owned a number of ports). But nationalisation was more by accident than design, and there was certainly no national planning of infrastructure investment nor any coordination of operations between ports (see Turnbull, 1993). Only the manual grades working in the nationalised ports, such as maintenance workers and lock-gate operators, were therefore part of the public sector (ibid:188–9). These workers inherited established negotiating machinery from the railway companies, which produced a pattern of industrial relations similar to that in many other areas of the public sector. Industrial peace and patterns of accommodation were secured through elaborate, formal negotiating machinery and through informal relationships and understandings between management and trade unions (Bonavia, 1987:133). The dockers, in contrast, were employed predominantly by small, private stevedoring (cargo handling) companies and warehouse operators. Moreover, under the 1947 Dock Labour Scheme they were still hired on a casual basis (for a minimum of four hours). In effect the Dock Labour Board was the 'holding employer' while the stevedoring and other companies were the 'operational employers', hiring men from the 'labour pool' on a twice daily basis.

It was anticipated that the provisions of the NDLS and the role of the unions in decision making would lead to industrial peace and greater efficiency in the ports. If anything, however, it had the opposite effect (Turnbull *et al.*, 1996; and Turnbull *et al.*, 1992:14–29). Indeed the docker became the UK's most strike-prone worker in the postwar period (ibid; and Turnbull, 1992). Official inquiry followed official inquiry, usually in response to the grave effects of major dock strikes on the economy. Finally, in 1967 the industry was decasualised following the recommendations of the Devlin Committee (1965). In other words all dockers were now assigned to individual employers on a permanent basis. Lord Devlin, a retired High Court judge and devout Roman Catholic, equated both casualism and striking with sin, leading to the inevitable conclusion that a permanent relationship between employer and employee, which was the *sine qua non* of labour control in almost all other industries, would excise conflict in the docks. As the Committee concluded, 'if the method of employing labour in the docks was the same as in industry generally, there would be no need for anything more' (Devlin, 1965:3). Thus it was widely anticipated that decasualisation would lead to industrial peace and economic efficiency through the improved management of employee relations. In the event the Devlin reforms delivered neither industrial peace (Turnbull and Sapsford, 1991; and Turnbull *et al.*, 1996) nor economic efficiency (Saundry and Turnbull, 1996; Turnbull and Weston, 1992).

Although the failure of reform in the docks was in many respects the result of industry-specific effects – most notably the devastating impact of new technology (containerisation) on jobs, the growth of ports not covered by the Scheme, such as Felixstowe and Dover, and the persistent problems of surplus labour – the shortcomings identified by the Devlin Committee were essentially a more extreme version of the more general 'malaise' of UK industrial relations identified by the Donovan Commission (1968) around the same time. This was particularly the case for the more strike-prone industries such as coal, shipbuilding and vehicles (see Turnbull and Sapsford, 1991; and Chapter 10 below). The subsequent failure of state regulation in the docks was therefore identified with a more general failure of 'traditional' industrial relations (the Donovan diagnosis), namely the inadequate development of a more rational and coherent structure of joint regulation between management and unions (see Chapter 7). The failure of the Donovan model in the 1970s paved the way for the Thatcherite strategy of the 1980s.

During Margaret Thatcher's first government the port employers pursued a policy of voluntary reform through negotiations with the T&GWU, but even minor changes to the administration of the Scheme were rejected out of hand by the Union, often backed up with the threat of national strike action (Turnbull *et al.*, 1992:84–8). Since any change to the Scheme, as far as the dockers were concerned, would involve a diminution of their terms and conditions of employment, the Union simply would not countenance any alteration. Each time a national strike was threatened the employers backed off. But after the national dock strikes of 1984, during Mrs Thatcher's second term in office, the employers were finally convinced of two things: first, that only the complete abolition of the Scheme would bring about the changes they desired; second, that they could defeat the dockers in a national dock strike (ibid:88–109). The employers, through NAPE, therefore decided to launch a concerted campaign to persuade the Thatcher government to abolish the NDLS.

Clear the Decks – Abolish the National Dock Labour Scheme

'Clear the Decks' was the title of a pamphlet produced in 1988 by David Davis MP, Conservative member of parliament for Boothferry and a leading campaigner for the abolition of the Scheme. According to Davis (1988:11):

> Each Scheme port stands as a fossil amidst an economic wasteland of its own creation . . . the Scheme encourages practices of unimaginable wastefulness; undermines effective management; destroys discipline; stultifies technological development and by a combination of high costs and low reliability, drives away business. . . . A Scheme designed to enhance efficiency has in fact destroyed competitiveness; a Scheme designed to guarantee supply of labour, has crippled capacity and created unemployment.

What Davis and many others could not understand was why the Scheme had survived untouched after ten years of Conservative government. As an angry editorial in *The Times* (9 March 1988) calling for the abolition of the Scheme exclaimed, 'The survival of the National Dock Labour Scheme into the era of Thatcherism is a blatant anachronism. While the labour market in other industries has been significantly deregulated the Scheme continues apparently immune to the Government's principles of industrial realism'. The government had itself argued that, 'the key contribution of Government in a free society is to do all it can to create a climate in which enterprise can flourish, above all by removing obstacles to the working of markets, especially the labour market' (Department of Employment, 1985:1). Why, then, had the Scheme survived unscathed?

The NDLS was perhaps the most glaring of all obstacles to the 'working' of any labour market in the UK economy, and as such a complete anathema to the free market philosophy of the Conservative government (Turnbull, 1991b). But while from an ideological, entrepreneurial and economic perspective the Scheme was deemed unacceptable, outdated, restrictive and expensive, from a political perspective 'abolition would seem to offer only small and nominal benefits, more than outweighed by the disruption and conflict it would provoke' (Phillips and Whiteside, 1985:268). Past governments had expressly avoided public sector or essential service disputes because of the political costs involved, but Mrs Thatcher's government determined not only to 'take on' the unions but to make a virtue out of doing so. The government's strategy was revealed in 1978 when a report of the Conservative Party's policy group on the nationalised industries was leaked to *The Economist* (27 May 1978). Issuing a 'call to battle' and outlining which possible strikes to fight, the document classified industries into three categories according to vulnerability (for the government), with water, electricity, gas and the health service in the most vulnerable group, coal, docks and rail in the intermediate group, and public transport, education, telephones and steel in the least vulnerable group. In order to counter the 'political threat' from 'the enemies of the next Tory government', the report set out a five-point plan to avert (at least initially) any strike in the most vulnerable group, and then to ensure victory 'on ground chosen by the Tories' (ibid). By the late 1980s the time was right for a dock strike (Turnbull *et al.*, 1992:103–9).

By the Conservatives' third term in office, if not earlier, the government was convinced of the employers' case for the abolition of the Scheme. In fact the arguments presented in a NAPE document produced in 1988 entitled 'The Case Against the Dock Labour Scheme' were repeated almost verbatim in the government's own White Paper *Employment in the Ports: The Dock Labour Scheme* (Department of Employment, 1989), which announced the abolition of the Scheme (Turnbull *et al.*, 1992:98–103). What had altered by 1988–9 was the conviction that the employers, backed by the government, could win a national dock strike. As David Davis (1988:46–7) pointed out, a national dock strike would be *incomplete*, since it was unlikely to include all Scheme ports (as had proved to be the case in 1984) or cover all Scheme port employees (for example non-registered maintenance staff); *ineffective*, as ports outside the Scheme already handled 30 per cent by weight (and 50 per cent by value) of all UK traffic, while supplies of key commodities could be met from stockpiles; *poorly supported*, as many (older) dockers would no doubt opt for severance payments (of up to £35 000 per man); and ultimately *short-lived*, as many of the smaller ports were unlikely to strike and even the more militant ports such as London, Liverpool, Hull and Tees would only be able to sustain a strike for up to six weeks. Legal restraints on the ability of the T&GWU to call a strike, and in particular to make the strike effective through picketing and secondary action, were also in the employers' favour, and the employers' gut feeling was that the dockers would 'not be able to match the NUM or even the NUS for the psychological support engendered by common action against a "joint enemy"' (ibid:40). This ultimately proved to be the case (Turnbull, 1992), but as Davis also pointed out, if all else failed, severance terms could be restricted to those who returned to work by a specified date nominated by the employer: 'This method, used to bring the coal strike to an end, would be very effective in "the all or nothing" strategy that might be followed if there is a national dock strike' (1988:40). In the event the 1989 dock strike was indeed incomplete, ineffective, poorly supported and short-lived (Turnbull, 1992; and Turnbull *et al.*, 1992), and severance pay was indeed instrumental in bringing the dockers to heel (Turnbull and Wass, 1994).

The docks under deregulation and privatisation

The employers greeted the abolition of the Scheme with euphoria: '*At last they became managers of their own destinies*' declared Iain Dale (1991:2, original emphasis), the former public relations director of NAPE. It also resulted in a marked improvement in profitability, at least for the major port authorities (Turnbull *et al.*, 1992:233). For employees still working in the industry, however, real (and even nominal) wages are generally much lower than under the Scheme, hours are longer, working patterns are more intense and the risks, in terms of accidents, sickness and even death, are now far greater (Turnbull and Wass, 1994). For the majority of ex-registered dockers the end of the Scheme signalled the end of a lifetime of employment in the industry, although at least 1500 of those made redundant returned to work in the industry, typically on a temporary or casual basis (ibid:500). The return of casual employment is contrary to the promises of the employers and the assurances the government had made prior to the abolition of the Scheme. Indeed a central argument of the government's White Paper was that employment regulation was no longer necessary: the Scheme was a 'damaging anachronism . . . [that] has now outlived the circumstances of its birth'

(Department of Employment, 1989:32). More specifically, 'modern cargo handling methods require the employment of properly trained *permanent* staff' (ibid:13, emphasis added).

The acid test of government reform must be whether or not deregulation made UK ports more efficient, given that the Conservative governments' economic policies extolled the virtues of competition and assumed that the performance of nationalised or state-regulated industries was inferior to that of the private sector (on average) and that relative performance was superior in the presence of competition between private and public sectors (Fine, 1990:13). However the return of casual labour indicates not only that many port employees are not properly trained, as reflected in the increase in accident rates and deaths in many ports, but also that many of UK ports were neither 'modern' nor 'efficient'. The repeal of the Scheme generated much greater competition in the industry, as the government desired and expected, but intense inter- and even intraport competition in an industry already burdened by overcapacity created a vicious spiral of cost-cutting. As labour accounts for around 60–70 per cent of port operating costs, even on highly capital-intensive container operations, employers are constantly re-evaluating working methods and terms and conditions of employment in order to achieve further (marginal) cost savings. Not only are there only limited (short-term) efficiency gains from such a policy, but the Conservative government recreated many of the problems that were identified with industrial conflict and economic inefficiency in the past, which in turn could have a detrimental effect on the long-term performance of UK ports. In short, deregulation and privatisation failed to deliver the anticipated boost to jobs, investment, productivity and traffic (see, *inter alia*, Evans *et al.*, 1993; Saundry and Turnbull, 1996, 1997; Turnbull and Wass, 1995; and Turnbull and Weston, 1993b, 1993c).

With hindsight it is now apparent that the abolition of the Scheme may have been a necessary condition for change in the industry, given the intransigence of the dockers and the T&GWU, but it was never sufficient to achieve the goals of international competitiveness set by the government. More importantly, it was the *form* and not the *fact* of (joint) regulation that was the problem, as comparisons with successful European ports clearly illustrate (Turnbull and Weston, 1992). In addition the comparison with our EU partners highlights the importance of a much wider role for state regulation through the direction of an integrated transport policy, the coordination and concentration of traffic, and the subsidisation of port investment and maintenance programmes. If nothing else the return of casual forms of employment, the deployment of untrained workers and rising accident rates suggest a *prima facie* case for some form of regulation in the docks. The Conservative governments' desire to defeat yet another big battalion of the labour movement, regardless of cost, eroded rather than enhanced the long-term competitiveness of the port transport industry.

The state and the employment relationship

Not only in the docks but throughout the economy, the influence of the modern state permeates every aspect of people's working and non-working lives. First and foremost, economic policy and the (in)efficient management of the economy have a major impact on the number and type of jobs available. If a worker is unemployed, the state provides unemployment benefit. To improve their chances of obtaining work, the unemployed can enrol on government training schemes. When actually seeking work, the employer cannot (by law) discriminate against applicants on grounds of sex or race. When in work, women who perform work of equal value to that of their male counterparts must (by law) be paid an equivalent wage. Health and safety standards in the workplace are at least in part determined by the state. Legislation governs possible breaches of employment contracts by employees, as during a strike, or the termination of such contracts by employers, as in the case of redundancy or dismissal. Workers' pay is in part settled by reference to the rate of inflation and the 'cost of living', which is a key outcome of government economic policy. More directly, about one in five of the nation's workforce is employed by the state, either in central government (for example the industrial and non-industrial civil service and the NHS), local authorities (including education, housing, social services, the police and fire service), or in the (ever shrinking) public corporations (for example the postal service, BBC, CAA and the Royal Mint). This illustrates the fact that 'the state' is not simply 'the government'. The latter is one element of the former (albeit a crucial one), which also includes the administrative agencies of the nation, the judiciary and the legitimate agencies of violence (the police and army). Thus,

> More than ever before men now live in the shadow of the state . . . It is for the state's attention, or for its control, that men compete; and it is against the state that beat the waves of social conflict (Miliband, 1969:1).

Given the pervasive influence of the state on all aspects of society, it is inevitable that any theory of the state is also a theory of society and the distribution of power within that society (ibid:2). Thus the state can be conceptualised as 'an institutional complex which is the political embodiment of the values and interests of the dominant class' (Parkin, 1971:27). As was demonstrated in Chapter 2, capitalist societies are characterised, above all else, by an asymmetry of power between capital and labour. In this context, state intervention in the economy in general, and the employment relationship in particular, is inseparable from the nature of capital-labour relations. Put simply, capitalist economies have a capitalist state, wherein the capitalist class might not govern but it certainly rules (Miliband, 1969:55). In general, then,

What the state protects and sanctions is a set of *rules* and *social relationships* which are presupposed by the class rule of the capitalist class. The state does not defend the interests of one class, but the *common* interests of all members of a *capitalist class society* (Offe and Ronge, 1982:250, original emphasis, quoted by Edwards, 1986:148–9).

This is not to suggest, however, that the state will always and everywhere act in the interests of the capitalist class. The latter is itself an extremely hetero-geneous group, and what may be in the interests of financial capital may be contrary to the interests of industrial capital, just as the interests of small-scale capital may not be best served by policies designed to improve the stability or profitability of large-scale capital. The dominance of financial interests over those of manufacturing, for example, is a major factor in the poor performance of the UK's industrial capital, as documented in Chapter 3 (see Coates, 1994; and Hutton, 1996). In the case of the docks, abolition of the NDLS led to a massive increase in the profits of the port authorities (the owners of UK ports), especially the former nationalised port group ABP. Small stevedoring compa-nies, on the other hand, now face intense competition, rates wars and profit margins that have been sliced to the bone. Given the divergence of capitalist interests, this introduces a degree of autonomy for state action. Moreover state action is not always unified by a common set of values and behaviour, and this results not only in contradictory tendencies within state policies but also in state action that is not directly beneficial to capital (at least not in the short term). A common perspective on the mid to late 1970s, for example, is that the interests of labour prevailed over those of capital. Not only were trade unions believed by many people to be 'above the law', enjoying an 'unrivalled position in the courts with the sole exception of the Crown itself' (Minford, 1985:109), but unions appeared to have virtually unlimited access to political power: industrial disputes were settled over 'beer and sandwiches' at Number 10, union representatives sat on a variety of tripartite bodies (discussed in the previous chapter), and Jack Jones (then General Secretary of the T&GWU) was thought by many people to be the most powerful man in the country. Ultimately, however, labour and the unions did not seriously challenge the hegemony of the capitalist class. As Crouch (1979:19) argued at the time, the greater role afforded to trade unions 'is best regarded as a strategy pursued by capitalism when it cannot adequately subordinate labour by preventing its combination and allowing market processes to work'.

From 1974 to 1979 the unions had a Social Contract with the Labour government, which represented a major departure from earlier post-war arrangements based on 'voluntarism', or what in a legal context Kahn-Freund (1959:224) described as 'collective *laissez-faire*'. The three key features of voluntarism were a preference for collective bargaining rather than state regulation as a method of settling wages and other terms of employment, a preference for a non-legalistic form of collective bargaining, and a desire among the parties for complete autonomy in their relations (Flanders,

1975:174). In short there was a preference for *industrial self-government* rather than statutory regulation or state intervention. The 1970s, in contrast, were characterised as a period of 'corporatism', which Panitch (1981:42) describes as 'a system of state-structured class collaboration'. During the period of the Social Contract the trade unions offered wage restraint under the Labour government's incomes policies, in return for a protective code of individual employee rights and an extension of trade union immunities from the common law consequences of collective organisation and industrial action. Thus for many the state was perceived to be acting in the interests of labour rather than capital.

The term 'immunities', according to Lord Wedderburn (1989:5), is a rather unhappy one, or more poignantly for the trade union movement a rather unfortunate one, as it implies that strikers are in some way 'privileged' or 'above the law' (Welch, 1991). This could not be further from the truth, 'rather as if an Act that gives slaves an immunity against recapture were interpreted as necessarily granting them a "privilege"' (Wedderburn, 1989:5). During the period from 1871 to 1906, trade unions secured the 'liberty of', rather than a 'right to', collective organisation and industrial action: statutory protection provided only minimum *social* rights to organise and act collectively, and took the *legal* form of 'privileges' (the immunities UK unions enjoyed from the law were the equivalent of what in other countries took the form of positive rights to organise and to strike, as guaranteed by legislation or by the constitution) (Wedderburn, 1972:272–3). Thus the immunities granted to UK unions did *not* place them above the law, in fact quite the reverse as 'the law retained a restrictive function: the freedom to take industrial action was always qualified by the possibility of legal remedies to restrain the unlawful consequences of such action' (Lewis, 1983:363). This was not how the situation was portrayed, however, either by the media or the Conservative Party, both in opposition (1974–9) and government (1979–97).

In 1979 Keith Joseph MP, arguably the architect behind much of the 'New Right' thinking on trade unions and the Thatcherite programme of the 1980s, suggested that unions were 'uniquely privileged' and that Labour had enacted a 'militants charter', which he derided as 'a charter for the systematic destruction of law-abiding, job-creating, free enterprise, in the name of socialism' (1986:103). Even in the 1990s this view was continually reiterated and reinforced. In the 1991 Green Paper on *Proposals for the Further Reform of Industrial Relations and Trade Union Law*, the government argued that,

> It *was a widely held view* in the 1960s and 1970s that the severity and damaging consequences of Britain's industrial relations problems were exceeded only by their intractability. . . . The balance of bargaining power *appeared* to have moved decisively and permanently in favour of trade unions. In many cases union leaders *were seen* to be both irresponsible and undemocratic in exercising their industrial power (Department of Employment, 1991:1, emphasis added).

It is then but a short step from the rhetoric of popular opinion to the assertion that 'the law gave trade unions virtually unlimited protection to organise strikes and other forms of industrial action' (ibid). The importance of such rhetoric should not be overlooked, since a key function of the state, in addition to assisting the process of capital accumulation, is to legitimise the system of dominance that characterises the capitalist mode of production (Edwards, 1986:147). Thus Thatcherism was not just a political project to create a new 'enterprise culture', but was, 'fundamentally, an ideological project intended to realize a new moral, organizational and social order' (Keenoy and Noon, 1992:561). As with other political projects, Thatcherism tried to rewrite the past in order to redefine the future, while all the time responding to the pressures and events of the present.

In order to understand the role of the state in employee relations it is essential to evaluate different political projects – specifically voluntarism, corporatism and Thatcherism – in the context of the central spheres of state activity, namely the state's role as economic manager, legislator and employer. As in other chapters, our primary interest lies with contemporary developments in employee relations, but these are set within a very clear historical context. The 'social Darwinism' of the Thatcher project, for example, represented complete rejection of the postwar 'settlement' or 'consensus' built around full employment, the involvement of trade unions in government decision-making bodies, an acceptance by all major political parties of the separation of industrial relations and political controversy (keeping politics out of the workplace and collective bargaining), and a similar commitment to the welfare state (Crouch, 1982a:19). The politics of Thatcher's economic programme can only be understood in relation to the abandonment of the postwar settlement, which the New Right condemned as being too *dirigiste*.

Above all, then, Thatcherism sought to 'roll back the frontiers of the state', to give the market free reign, to deregulate the labour market and to promote a new individualist order. As Hutton (1996:15) laments, 'Altruism and the civilising values of an inclusive society have been sacrificed on the alter of self-interest, of choice, of opting out and of individualism'. Such was the emphasis on individualism that Mrs Thatcher even announced that 'there is no such thing as society' (*Financial Times*, 19 November 1986). But in reviewing the consequences of almost two decades of Conservative government, a period that witnessed root-and-branch changes to the very fabric of our society, one of the most striking features is that not only did many state policies fail to live up to expectations, but there were also many unanticipated outcomes. In the economic sphere, the most important outcomes were the failure of the state to transform the performance of the economy, which remained locked into a (self-reinforcing) cycle of relatively low wages, low productivity and low investment, an economy beset by periodic crises, balance of payments constraints and consequently 'stop–go' economic management. In this respect the experience of the port transport industry, where the pulse of boom and bust is often magnified by the ebbs and flows of foreign trade, is not untypical.

In their legislative role, the policies of the Conservative governments were out of step with both previous philosophies of statutory employment regulation and those currently prevailing elsewhere in the European Union. Individual UK workers came to have far fewer rights as employees than they do as citizens. For trade unions, the law sought to circumscribe their activities to an extent not witnessed since the nineteenth century. During the 1989 dock strike, for example, at the Appeal Court ruling in June 1989 the judges declared that the original High Court judgement, at which the employers failed to secure an injunction, did not give sufficient consideration to the 'grave effect' that a dockers' strike might have on the 'public interest'. It was no exaggeration to suggest that, until the ruling was reversed by the House of Lords, it was difficult to see how organised labour in any industry could take legitimate industrial action: the very legality of any strike action was in the balance (Turnbull *et al.*, 1992:127; see also Simpson, 1989). Even after the House of Lords ruling, the law still favoured the employer at every turn. As Ron Todd, then General Secretary of the T&GWU later reflected, 'The days must go when employers can wake up a judge at dead of night, give him a drop of brandy, show him a headline from the *Sun* and get him to sign an injunction' (*The Guardian*, 5 October 1989).

Finally, as an employer the state has massively reduced its involvement in the public sector through a process of commercialisation and rationalisation and its programme of privatisation. Privatisation of the nationalised ports, for example, allowed Associated British Ports to diversify into property development and led to a steady reduction in employment, which declined markedly after 1989. But intervention in other areas has greatly increased the role of the state, for example through the policy of setting cash limits in the public sector. Paradoxically, deregulation required not only a strong and more centralised state but also a highly interventionist state. More pertinent to the study of employee relations was the Conservative governments' attempt to 'stiffen the sinews of managements to make sure they assert their "right to manage", regardless of union and workforce opposition and any resulting disruption to public services' (Ferner and Colling, 1991:393–4). Thus the state still sought to set an example to private sector employers, but it was no longer concerned to be the 'good employer', as defined in the past. Management through confrontation (Ferner, 1989) became the order of the day. To be sure the government refused to be drawn directly into the many public sector disputes of the 1980s (see Chapter 10), but nonetheless wholeheartedly supported management. The estimated £240 million it cost the government to defeat the dockers was nothing compared with the £5 billion spent during the miners' strike of 1984–5 (Adeney and Lloyd, 1986). And yet despite – some would argue *because of* – these policies, by the mid 1990s there was still a crisis of public sector finance, low morale among the workforce and poor service quality.

The state as economic manager

The postwar settlement constructed by the Labour government of Clement Attlee was an inclusive programme based on need rather than ability to pay, and was underwritten by Keynesian demand management policies. The state would 'pump prime' the economy to set in motion a multiplier effect – one employee's wages, initially paid for by the state, would become another employee's source of income, as wages were spent on consumer or other goods, creating further spending and income, and so on – and this would ensure full employment. Beyond this, however, the state played a relatively limited role in the affairs of industry. Even in the nationalised industries any planning was unambiguously *indicative* rather than *dirigiste* in character. Instead the state supported the philosophy of industrial self-government. But this 'liberalist' system contained inherent weaknesses, not least the problem of maintaining the magic triangle of Keynesian demand management: full employment, price stability and a balance of payments surplus. Deficits on the foreign account, for example, put pressure on sterling and forced the government to damp down domestic demand. But this led to rising unemployment and pressure from labour and the unions to restore full employment. The latter, when combined with a system of free collective bargaining (that is, without state regulation), led to rising wage demands and wage drift (discussed in Chapter 7) and put pressure on costs and therefore prices. If prices rise, UK goods become more uncompetitive on world markets, leading to balance of payment problems, *et cetera*. Debate raged about the source of this instability in the UK economy (see Coates and Hillard, 1986), but while the state equivocated, the magic triangle became ever more elusive. The result was a continual cycle of stop–go economic management.

The most expedient solution to the UK's economic ills, for each successive postwar government, appeared to be wage restraint. Initially, incomes policies, if they could be called that, were informal, largely *ad hoc* arrangements, such as the February 1948 *Statement on Personal Income, Costs and Prices* and Harold Macmillan's call for a 'price plateau' in May 1954 to promote price and pay stability. Selwyn Lloyd introduced a temporary 'pay pause' in 1961–2, but the Conservative government's subsequent incomes policy recommendation of 2.0–2.5 per cent was ignored by unions and employers. In effect, these policies were the prelude to formal restraint under the Labour governments of 1964–70 (see Davies, 1983), which marked a significant change in the government's role in employee relations – direct intervention, if only on an inter-mittent basis, signalled the end of free collective bargaining. But incomes policies ran aground on the rocks of rank-and-file militancy, with trade union leaders unable to control membership demands for higher wages in the face of rising prices. Moreover in the public sector – where the government could enforce pay norms more effectively and where there was limited scope for self-financing pay increases above the norm as a result of productivity improvements – incomes policies not only upset established pay comparisons with private sector employees but also destroyed the façade of government neutrality in management–employee relations. This 'politicisation' of public sector employee relations was a key factor in the growing unrest of the 1970s (see Chapter 10).

The 'quasi-corporatist' project of the 1960s gave way to a 'bargained corporatism' in the mid to late 1970s, when trade union leaderships again promised wage restraint in exchange for a 'share' in economic policy making. But they failed to secure the latter or deliver the former, with rank-and-file rejection of then Prime Minister Callaghan's 5 per cent maximum under Phase IV of the government's incomes policy playing a major role in the explosion of industrial conflict during the so-called Winter of Discontent (1978–9). But what stands out during the entire period from 1945 to 1979 is the 'extra-ordinary passivity and incapacity of the state in the face of growing economic difficulties' (Rowthorn, 1986:264). The state

> has never seriously pursued a concerted modernising strategy. . . . The hesitant and ineffectual character of government policy since the war is the outcome of a particular balance of class forces in Britain during the period. Capital has in general been opposed to a policy of vigorous planning and detailed state intervention in industry, whilst the working class has lacked the consciousness or unity of purpose to impose such a policy (ibid).

In other words each of the three major actors in employee relations – management, labour and the state – 'found it easier to guard their own mutual autonomy' than to press home radical reform (MacInnes, 1987:16), such that the power of each party over the other was of a negative rather than a positive order (see Fine and Harris, 1985:17; and Harris, 1986:261–3). 'Employers, unions, and the state were all strong enough to maintain defensive positions while too weak to organize radical departures from the tradition of compromise and muddling through' (Edwards *et al.*, 1992:6). In short, nothing united the different parties in a way that might make possible a national economic and industrial strategy, 'since the only thing that really brought them together was their incapacity for strategy' (Crouch, 1995:236).

Margaret Thatcher sought to change all this. Of course the New Right did not define the root cause of the 'British disease' to be the deadlock of social relations and institutional arrangements between capital, labour and the state, but the inordinate power of labour and the excessive intervention of the state itself in all aspects of social and economic life. As Crouch (1982a:118) argues, the new liberal philosophy of the Conservative government had strong antecedents in the nineteenth century and a long tradition within the Tory Party itself. But the idea of rolling back the welfare state, reducing government intervention in industry, abandoning any kind of (formal) incomes policy, breaking off all relations between ministers and trade unions, allowing unemployment to rise to contain inflation and union power, and ultimately letting the market reign, had been shunned within a Conservative Party committed to compromise and accommodation (at least from 1945 to 1979). Under Mrs Thatcher, however, such ideas were now government policies, while 'the kind of relationship between a Conservative government and trade unions of which Churchill and Monckton boasted was seen as an object of shame by her' (ibid). As Figure 6.1 illustrates, the 'neo *laissez-faire*' policy of Mrs Thatcher's Conservative Party was grounded in the liberal tradition of the past, but was predicated on a weak trade union movement.

The objective of government policy in the 1980s can be simply stated: namely to encourage enterprise through the deregulation of markets, especially the labour market. Thus the economic foundations of Thatcherism can be found in the writings of free market economists such as Milton Friedman and in particular Friedrich Hayek. Indeed Lord Wedderburn (1989:15) has argued that the 'mixture of market forces and strong government' of the Thatcher years, 'displaying a determination to put down those who might disrupt the "spontaneous order", is quintessentially Hayek'. Of the UK economists in this genre, the work of Patrick Minford (1985) is illustrative. Minford argues that trade unions use their 'monopoly power' (derived from their legal 'privileges') to raise wages above the market rate. As a result, employers hire fewer union workers, which swells the ranks of the unemployed. According to neoclassical economics, therefore, unions not only increase (wage) costs and thereby inflation, but cause unemployment and a more unequal distribution of income within society, and in the process reduce the efficiency of both individual firms and the economy as a whole through

		Position of trade unions	
		Strong	Weak
Nature of system	Liberal	Free collective bargaining	Neo-*laissez-faire*
	Corporatist	Bargained corporatism	Corporatism

Source: Crouch (1982a:201).

FIGURE 6.1 Typology of state–union interaction

the imposition of restrictive practices, demarcations and the like. In short, unions are a 'public bad' (IEA, 1978).

According to this argument, therefore, one way to reduce unemployment, and in the process improve efficiency and equality, 'is to reduce the power of unions to raise wages. As union wages fall, the demand for union labour rises, people are withdrawn from the non-union sector, non-union wages rise and more people are prepared to work in it' (Minford, 1985:104). This became, of course, a primary focus of government policy throughout the 1980s and into the 1990s. The main method used to reduce union power was the law, withdrawing the immunities of trade unions in relation to strike action and undermining union influence within the workplace by, for example, out-lawing the closed shop. These developments are discussed in more detail in the following section. At this point it should be noted that along with legislation to weaken union bargaining power the Conservative governments sought to deregulate the non-union sector of the economy, effectively forcing the (voluntarily) unemployed (as Minford defines them) back into work through such measures as raising the disqualification period for unemploy-ment benefits from thirteen weeks to six months for those who 'voluntarily' quit their job; specifying that all claimants (*viz.* Jobseekers) should not only be available for but also actively seeking work (and provide proof to that effect); stipulating that claimants could lose their entitlement to benefits if they rejected a job on the ground of inadequate remuneration; reducing the real level of benefits (which became the lowest in Europe when calculated as a percentage of the average weekly wage); undermining (and ultimately abol-ishing) the powers of wages councils; and eroding the protection afforded to individuals with regard to unfair dismissal, redundancy, maternity leave and the like. Qualification for unfair dismissal protection, for example, was raised from six months to one year's employment in 1979 and then two years in 1985, and it is not uncommon for employers routinely to dismiss staff (with no obligation to pay redundancy) weeks or even days before they complete their two years' service. Not surprisingly, most of those employers do not recognise trade unions (NACAB, 1993; and see Chapter 9 below). Minford (1985:129) advocated the removal of *all* restrictions on the 'free' working of the labour market, including equal pay for women.

In the docks (Turnbull, 1991b), construction (Evans, 1990) and indeed the economy as a whole, labour market deregulation, and the attack on union bargaining power, failed to transform economic performance (Coates, 1994; Evans *et al.*, 1992; Hutton, 1996; Neale, 1992; and Nolan, 1989). The Con-servatives claimed their policies had secured an 'economic miracle' in the 1980s, but as the economy sank into an even more prolonged recession in the early 1990s than that of the early 1980s, the economic miracle appeared more like a mirage. Despite the best efforts of a succession of Conservative governments, earnings growth outstripped inflation in all years from 1982 to 1989, a trend that continued (overall) even in the more austere 1990s, indicating not so much the continued power of the trade union movement as the flawed assumptions of neoclassical economics. One very clear illustration of this is that while union membership continued to *fall*, income inequality continued to *widen*. This is one particular area where the unions' 'sword of justice' role appears to have outweighed any 'vested interest', contrary to the assumptions of the New Right, as unions have traditionally organised lower-paid workers, promoted equal pay and sought to standardise pay for given job classifications (see Gosling and Machin, 1992). Thus as union power eroded, the inclusive programme of the postwar settlement gave way to a policy based on exclusion, what Hutton (1996:106–8) calls the 30/30/40 society, where 30 per cent are 'disadvantaged' (the unemployed and economically inactive), 30 per cent are 'marginalised' (poorly paid and insecure workers in casual, fixed-term, part-time and even some full-time jobs), and 40 per cent are 'privileged' (those who enjoy well-paid, full-time work or secure self-employed status). For the New Right, however, the extremes of penury and opulence are to be celebrated, not criticised, as the free market philosophy of the new economics assumes that inequality and insecurity drives efficiency.

Contrary to the competitive neoclassical model of the labour market, however, the presence of non-competing groups (labour market segmentation) and chronic skill shortages at a time of mass unemployment prevented the downward pressure on wages that Conservative governments desired, illustrating that the market can be a very blunt instrument when attempting to improve economic performance. More importantly, the deregulation of the labour market through the erosion of individual workers' rights served only to facilitate greater exploitation of the more vulnerable groups of society (NACAB, 1993). In 1992, for example, ACAS dealt with an enquiry every 15 seconds, including more than 72 000 individual conciliation cases (up 12 000 on the 1991 figure) relating to claims that statutory employment rights and protection had been infringed. In 1996 the figure was over 100 000. The number of successful unfair dismissal cases more than doubled between 1989 and 1994, while the total industrial tribunal caseload tripled. In 1994 Citizens Advice Bureaux dealt with 882 257 requests for help with employment-related problems. As Chapter 9 illustrates, non-union workers in particular are in need of *greater* trade union and statutory protection, not less. The result has been to reinforce the pattern of low wages, low productivity and low investment, both in physical and human assets, that characterises the UK economy. In fact, by enabling employers to exploit the growing pool of low-paid workers (the 'marginalised' and 'disadvantaged' segments of the labour market), and at the same time intensify the labour process (even the 'privileged' feel more insecure), this has not only destroyed the 'psychological contract' between management and labour (what economists call X-efficiency) but inhibited the introduction of more efficient production systems by extending the life of a particular (outdated) stock of machines. Short-term efficiency gains have been encouraged at the expense of longer-term dynamic efficiency (Neale, 1992:283; and Nolan, 1989:87). Thus, contrary to the analysis of the New Right, it can be argued that, 'if trade unions had been *more* militant industrial capital would have been forced to be more competitive . . . a militant trade union movement struggling effectively for high wages would have made labour costly and forced capital to modernise' (Harris, 1986:261, original emphasis).

In sum, the problem of the UK economy lies not in the power of organised labour and the extent of state intervention, rather the *weakness* of the former and the *character* of the latter. Successive governments reinforced rather than transformed the sclerosis of social and institutional relations between capital, labour and the state. This was especially true of the Conservative governments of the 1980s and 1990s, where the principal outcomes of macroeconomic policy failure were record levels of unemployment, redundancy and bankruptcy. These were precisely the outcomes that the enterprise culture was supposed to resolve, creating a new cycle of boom-and-bust economic management. Ironically the failure of economic policy proved more effective than legislation in achieving the government's primary objective of undermining the power of organised labour. As in the economic sphere, however, in its role as legislator the state encountered a string of unanticipated and unintended outcomes.

The state as legislator

Just as the elusive goals of Keynesian demand management slipped further and further out of reach in the late 1960s, so too did the consensus that supported legal abstention in employee relations. The tradition of non-intervention was based on the principle that 'the peaceful exercise of collective economic sanctions in the field of industrial conflict should be completely lawful' (Auerbach, 1990:12). As Lord Wright put it in the case of *Crofter Hand Woven Harris Tweed v. Veitch* (1942), the right to strike was 'an essential element in the principle of collective bargaining' (quoted by Lewis, 1991:61). Hence, there was perceived to be 'no incompatibility between the public interest and a *degree* of trade union power, whether economic, social or political' (ibid:62, emphasis added). But this benign view of trade union power was severely damaged by rising strike rates in the 1960s (see Chapter 10).

Despite calls for greater statutory intervention in employee relations, the Donovan Commission (1968) proposed a voluntary programme of reform, although its Report did recommend removing the legal immunity of unofficial strikes in some situations. The major political parties were less patient, however, and while Labour's proposals in the White Paper *In Place Of Strife* (1969) were withdrawn in the face of trade union opposition, the Conservative Party's proposals in *A Fair Deal at Work* (1968) were effectively implemented as the Industrial Relations Act 1971 under the new government of Edward Heath. This Act transformed the legal regulation of employee relations in the UK by introducing a comprehensive, restrictive legal code to curb the activities of trade unions (including legal penalties for strikes, the creation of several 'unfair industrial practices', and outlawing the closed shop). More importantly, its introduction demonstrated yet again that legal abstention in the UK was always *conditional*:

> The basis of positive statutory control of industrial relations rested – as with the more general ideology of *laisser-faire* to which it was obviously linked – on an essentially practical basis: that the state recognised no need to intervene directly in the sphere of production, and that capital recognised no need to call on state support in its day-to-day handling of labour. This meant in turn that trade unions should lack either the power or the will to interfere excessively with managerial objectives (Hyman, 1981:131).

Thus when labour and the unions challenged the interests of capital, the state (either the government or the judiciary) intervened. For example, having been granted immunity from criminal law conspiracy in the 1870s, and following the emergence of militant 'new unionism' among the semi- and unskilled workforce in the 1880s, the judiciary used the civil wrong (or tort) of conspiracy to restrict union organisation and industrial action. This was reversed by the Trade Disputes Act 1906, which protected unions aganst action for civil conspiracy if acting 'in contemplation or furtherance of a trade dispute' (the so-called 'golden formula' of trade union immunity), but the state imposed direct controls on strike action during both world wars, when disruption to production could not be tolerated, and again after the general strike of 1926 (the Trade Disputes and Trade Union Act 1927). Judicial bias against the unions was again in evidence in the 1960s and late 1970s in a number of cases (see Griffith, 1981:72–84). In *Duport Steels Ltd v. Sirs* (1980), Lord Diplock even went so far as to declare that union immunities were 'intrinsically repugnant to anyone who has spent his life in the practice of the law', openly affirming that their effects 'tended to stick in judicial gorges' (quoted by Wedderburn, 1989:7).

The Industrial Relations Act, therefore, was not a temporary aberration but the explicit emergence of an underlying tension that ran right through the voluntarist tradition. But the most notable thing about the Act was that it was a spectacular failure. It was very unwieldy (with 170 Clauses and nine schedules) and was poorly drafted, including both 'reformist' and 'restrictive' elements. The former included 'regulatory' elements to provide individuals with a 'floor of rights' (such as the right not to be unfairly dismissed, longer periods of notice and more information about the contract of employment) and 'auxiliary' elements to assist the processes of employee relations (such as a code of 'good industrial relations practice' and a union recognition procedure). The restrictive elements, however, sought to turn the unions into an industrial police force, requiring trade unions to register, have their rule books subject to legal scrutiny, conduct ballots before strikes and be responsible for the enforcement of *legally binding* collective agreements (breaking the tradition of voluntarism under which such agreements were 'gentlemen's agreements' and not legal documents). More importantly these restrictive elements ran counter to the reformist elements. As Lewis and Simpson (1981:21–2) asked, 'How could the law encourage trade unions to control workplace activity while at the same time undermining their security?'

Ultimately, the Act 'foundered on the rocks of union opposition and employer indifference' (ibid; and Weekes *et al.*, 1975). The latter was particularly important, as 'the draconian strategy of the Heath government did not match the perspectives of important sectors of British capital, whose aim was to enlist the "voluntary" co-operation of union representatives in imposing greater shopfloor discipline' (Hyman, 1981:133). In this instance, then, the relative autonomy of the state was clearly at odds with the interests of capital. Moreover, the government was itself humiliated when it ordered a ballot of railway workers who then voted massively in favour of strike action, and when a group of London dockers (the 'Pentonville Five') gaoled for refusing to call off strike action were hurriedly released without action being taken against them (the government's retraction in this instance being prompted by the TUC's threat to call a general strike).

The Industrial Relations Act was repealed by the incoming Labour government in 1974, save for the provisions on unfair dismissal, returning the legal *status quo* to the position first established in 1906. Individual employee rights were strengthened and extended by a number of parliamentary Acts, as were the collective immunities of the trade unions. Significantly, however, the intentions behind the legislative programme of the corporatist Social Contract 'were at the time a far more accurate reflection of the role that the parties wanted the law to play in industrial disputes than the policy underlying the Industrial Relations Act' (Elgar and Simpson, 1993:71–2). Regulatory or reformist law that grants workers, as a collective, the 'right' to strike and, as individuals, a 'floor of rights', is not necessarily anticapitalist as the New Right suggest. In fact, such laws can promote more effective and professional management. Even on the docks, where the power given to the unions in jointly regulating recruitment, dismissal and discipline was unique in being sanctioned by statute (Wilson, 1972:99) and where 'employers' "prerogatives" were circumscribed to an extent unique in English law' (Collis-Squires, 1977:23), the objective was always to improve the efficiency of management (see Devlin, 1965; and Turnbull and Weston, 1992). Communications might improve, for example, and employers would no longer be able to victimise employees or rely on an arbitrary and unjust system of 'hire and fire'. Equally, in many respects, the Social Contract laws were in the interests of capital (although not necessarily in the interests of all capital*ists*). In any event, they 'were characterised by a gap between aspiration and reality. They were supposed to be a great extension of worker and trade union rights. . . . In practice, these rights secured workers and unions only limited benefits' (Lewis, 1986:34–5). The overriding concern was to modernise employee relations, not to effect a redistribution of power between capital and labour, as evidenced by the fact that only weak sanctions were attached to the new rights (which predictably were interpreted in a narrow and legalistic manner by the judiciary) (ibid).

The key question was always, and still is, how to strike a balance between the interests of capital and the rights of labour. Within the Conservative Party there have always been two schools of thought on this issue. James Prior MP, shadow employment spokesman from 1974 to 1979 and Employment Secretary from 1979 to 1981, argued in the House of Commons debate on the Employment Bill (1979) that

> The law should always give full recognition to the inherent weakness of the individual worker *vis-à-vis* his employer, to the need for him to be organised in a union and to the need for his union to have such exceptional liberties as may be necessary to redress the balance (quoted by Wedderburn, 1989:3).

For Prior and other Tory 'wets', as they were dismissively labelled by the Thatcherites, the major lessons from the experience of the Heath government (1970–4) were the need for legislative reform to be limited and specific, to respond to the mood of 'public opinion' and, above all, to be subject to full consultation, even with the unions (see Auerbach, 1990:19–20). This was reflected in the content and objectives of the Employment Act 1980 (details of this Act and other labour laws passed during the 1980s and 1990s are given in the Appendix to this chapter).

Others in the Conservative Party, however, saw the failure of the Industrial Relations Act as a strategic and tactical lesson – there was nothing wrong, in principle, with the content and objectives of the Act. Heath was judged to have simply gone about things the wrong way, injecting a massive dose of legalism overnight, and then backing down ignominiously when the going got tough. The 'Iron Lady', in contrast, was 'not for turning'. Moreover, Mrs Thatcher favoured the idea of 'freedom of contract' between employer and employee, drawing on the ideas of Hayek (1979) who has argued that 'the unions are destroying the free market through their legalised use of coercion. . . . There can be no salvation for Britain until the special privileges granted to the trade unions three-quarters of a century ago are revoked' (Hayek, 1984:55–8; see also Hanson and Mather, 1988:89–90). The reality, of course, is that freedom of contract is 'a legal fiction to legitimise the superior strategic strength of the employer who could dictate the terms to the individual employee' (Lewis and Simpson, 1981:7).

Legislative reform accelerated in 1982 following the arrival of Norman Tebbit at the Department of Employment. His appointment

> signalled a clear and deliberate shift in the Government's rhetoric with regard to trade-union immunities. The regulation of industrial conflict was not to be seen as simply a matter of striking an equitable balance between the strength of employers and employees, and of tackling the worst and most destructive abuses of trade-union power. It was also to be presented as an important arm of the Government's economic, and in particular, labour market, policy at a much wider level (Auerbach, 1990:75).

In short, legislative reform was now integrated with, and was a major instrument of, the economic policy outlined in the previous section. The most significant elements of Tebbit's Employment Act 1982 were, first, the redefinition of industrial disputes, where such action had to 'relate wholly or mainly' to industrial (and certainly not political) matters, thus abandoning the 'golden formula' of legality if such action was 'connected with' action 'taken in contemplation or furtherance of a trade dispute'. The Employment Act 1982 thereby 'denies legitimacy to many disputes which are clearly about industrial relations issues' (Simpson, 1986:192). Second, trade unions were given a 'legal personality' through the removal of their immunity from civil court action, meaning that unions could now be sued for a wide range of unlawful activities. Given that a union with over 100 000 members could be required to pay £250 000 in damages for unlawful action, it would only take a few court cases to bankrupt even the most financially secure trade unions. Significantly, the substitution of union liability for the liability of union officials (as under the Industrial Relations Act 1971) allowed for 'sanctions without martyrs' (Wedderburn, 1989:30–2). In the docks strike of 1989, for example, there was never any possibility of a repeat of 1972 and the Pentonville Five fiasco.

The restrictions on strike activity were just one, albeit the most draconian, constraint on union activity designed to weaken the influence of trade unions *vis-à-vis* the employer and the state. Although the right to strike is still seen by many as a fundamental human liberty,

> Today, we find that industrial action is liable to be unlawful if it is secondary or sympathetic, concerns a union membership or recognition issue, involves persons picketing away from their place of work, lacks the support of a majority of those involved in a ballot, or possibly one of a set of ballots, is regarded as politically inspired, or otherwise falls outside a narrow range of legitimate topics for dispute (Auerbach, 1990:2).

Furthermore, the position of the British striker is one of 'extreme vulnerability' (Ewing, 1991:vii):

The legal position of the British worker engaged in a labour dispute is quite remarkable. A strike, for whatever reason, is a breach of contract; any form of industrial action short of a strike can lead to the total loss of pay; those engaged in industrial action may be dismissed with impunity (regardless of the reason for the industrial action); there is no right to unemployment benefit; and strikers and their families are penalized by social welfare legislation, even when the dispute is the singular fault of the employer (ibid:141).

'The short point', according to Elgar and Simpson (1993:106), 'is that English law does not recognise an individual right to strike'.

Other measures designed to weaken the bargaining power of trade unions included the progressive restriction, and ultimately the illegality, of the closed shop; the removal of all measures designed to support collective bargaining (such as commercial contracts that specify the employment of unionised labour and the abolition of the statutory procedure for union recognition); and the requirement to hold ballots on the establishment of funds to finance political (as opposed to industrial) activities (for example to provide financial support to the Labour Party). As an illustration of the effects of the law, during the 1989 national dock strike, in addition to the stalling tactics used by the employers to delay the strike itself, management at the Port of Tilbury selectively dismissed over 100 dockers, including all the shop stewards and former union activists, derecognised the T&GWU, and forced the remaining dockers back to work on new terms and conditions of employment dictated by management (under the threat of dismissal and loss of all entitlement to severance pay). The Union subsequently held a ballot outside the dock gates in which over 70 per cent of the workforce voted by an overwhelming majority (over 90 per cent) in favour of union representation. But the port is still non-union. As the Conservatives made clear in their *Proposals for Reform of Industrial Relations and Trade Union Law*, 'Employers are now free to decide whether or not to recognise trade unions' (Department of Employment, 1991:9). Employees have no such right. As for the Tilbury shop stewards, despite an Industrial Tribunal ruling that they were unfairly dismissed and should be reinstated, management refused to reemploy them.

Liverpool dockers employed by the Mersey Docks & Harbour Company (MDHC) befell a similar fate in September 1995 when they refused to cross a picket line set up by workers dismissed *en masse* by Torside, a local stevedoring company that supplied labour to MDHC. In one of the most remarkable disputes in recent history, MDHC issued new *individual* contracts of employment, delivered by dispatch riders, to around 200 of the 329 dockers, accompanied by an ultimatum to sign the contracts and return to work. The majority refused to sign and at the time of writing (summer 1997) were still in dispute, picketing the gates of the Royal Seaforth Container Terminal every morning and organising international solidarity action from Sydney to Stockholm, Auckland to Arhus, Los Angeles to Le Havre, New York to Rotterdam, Montreal to Piraeus and Tokyo to Bremerhaven, causing delays to vessels calling at the port of Liverpool. Secondary action of this sort in the UK would, of course, be illegal (for a discussion of the dispute, see Lavalette and Kennedy, 1996; and Saundry and Turnbull, 1996). To the local clergy, MPs and the people of Liverpool, MDHC's action may seem abhorrent, but it is perfectly legal under the letter of the law. Indeed while it may be illegal to pay women less than men, or black people less than whites, employers can not only dismiss strikers with impunity for breach of contract but can legally pay trade unionists less than non-union employees. This provision (TUERA 1993) is just one of many elements of UK employment law that falls below ILO standards.

The biennial attack on trade union immunities through the 1980s and early 1990s also sought to restructure the internal relationship between trade unions and their members. The emphasis was on giving precedence to the rights of the individual *over* the collective, or in the Conservative government's rhetoric, 'giving the unions back to their members' (see Martin *et al.*, 1995). For example, as well as unions no longer being allowed 'unjustifiably' to discipline a member, including those refusing to take part in a lawful strike (that is, disputes sanctioned by the majority in a ballot) or encouraging others to 'scab', union membership complaints against trade unions now warrant special legal support and can be taken to a new Commissioner for the Rights of Trade Union Members (the Commissioner, who cost UK taxpayers a total of £336 646 in the year to April 1996, was able to offer concrete assistance to just eight applicants). Complaints by an employee against an employer for unfair dismissal and the like, in contrast, do not warrant similar support despite being far more prevalent (the Tilbury case, for example, cost the T&GWU around £1.5 million to fight). Underlying the legal regulation of unions' internal affairs is the assumption that union officials are more militant than their rank-and-file, which was reflected in the Conservative governments' preference for individual, secret and fully postal ballots.

What the Tory government of the time envisaged was that individual decisions reached through postal ballot would be more *moderate* – there would be fewer strikes, more moderate union leaders elected, and political activities rejected (see Fairbrother, 1983; and Hyman, 1987b). In all these areas, however, the legislation backfired. More than 80 per cent of trade union members now belong to a union with a political fund, for example, and over twenty unions have established a political fund for the first time (see Blackwell and Terry, 1987; and Leopold, 1986, 1997). In union leadership elections, to date, only two sitting general secretaries have failed to secure reelection, in both cases due to specific issues within the unions concerned and not due to any general swing from 'left' to 'right' (in NATFHE, in fact, the leftist candidate was elected). As Smith *et al.* (1993:380) conclude, 'the legislation has singularly failed to initiate a transformation in the political complexion of union leadership or a reorientation of union policy in a "moderate" direction' (see also Martin *et al.*, 1995:150). One adverse effect of the new balloting system, however, for both government and the unions, is that participation in union elections has been *reduced*, which is hardly indicative of democratising the unions or 'giving them back to their members' (ibid; *Labour Research*, May 1990; and Leopold, 1997:296).

The failure of the legislation on balloting was the result of an inadequate conception of democratic practice in contemporary UK trade unionism and the capacity of trade unions to negotiate the context of their constitutional processes and the resulting political outcomes, regardless of formal statutory requirements (Smith *et al.*, 1993). Of particular importance was the fact that the Trade Union Act 1984 allowed workplace ballots, which gave union officials the opportunity to address members *within a collective context*, which if anything strengthened the relationship between union representatives and the rank and file. Moreover ballots have had the effect of legitimating, in the eyes of many members, the process of union decision making without effectively changing its character. Thus, 'far from undermining collective consciousness, ballots have been adopted in ways which largely reinforce it' (Martin *et al.*, 1991:198), which no doubt accounts for the latest legislative reforms, which now require fully postal ballots (see Appendix). Union success in strike ballots (see Chapter 10), for example, indicates that union members may now be *more* willing to strike, and that solidarity may actually be enhanced as 'No' voters 'have no means of knowing who their fellow opponents are – it would be an unusual trade unionist indeed who would defy a majority vote and cross a picket line alone' (ibid:206; see also Brown and Wadhwani, 1990; and Dunn and Metcalf, 1996:84).

Conservative support for 'minority dissidents, even single voices' (ibid:73) within trade unions has not been matched by support for non-unionists. In fact quite the opposite. A third of the workforce, for example, now lack protection for unfair dismissal from unscrupulous employers (McIlroy, 1995:401), while more than 70 per cent of young workers (aged less than 24 years) are without such protection (TUC, 1996b:6). In its 'index' of employment rights based on the legal regulation of working hours, fixed-term contracts, minimum wage legislation and the legal right to representation in the workplace, the OECD placed the UK second last among the industrialised nations of the world (the United States came last) (OECD, 1994a). Under the legal fiction of 'freedom of contract',

> The legislative assault on collective organization and collective bargaining created a space filled less by statutory determination of terms and conditions of employment than by unilateral employer decision. The legal principles promulgated since 1979 have been compatible with, and encouraging of, increased scope for the exercise of managerial prerogative (Dickens and Hall, 1995:296).

In sum, then, the Conservative laws have had an adverse effect on the rights of individuals at work, and in many respects a perverse effect on trade union organisation and representation in specific situations. To be sure, the law was put to good effect by employers in a number of disputes during the 1980s (see Auerbach, 1988; Elgar and Simpson, 1993; Evans, 1985, 1987; Ewing, 1991; and Ewing and Napier, 1986), not least the dockers' strike of 1989 (Simpson, 1989; and Turnbull *et al.*, 1992), and there is some, albeit limited, evidence of an increasing (and certainly strategic) use of injunctions, or the threat of injunctions, during industrial disputes (Dickens and Hall, 1995:283–5; Dunn and Metcalf, 1996:85; Gall and McKay, 1994; and *Labour Research*, September 1990). But the Conservative assertion (for example Department of Employment, 1991:3–4) that the law has been instrumental in democratising unions or reducing strike activity is too simplistic (see Brown and Wadhwani, 1990; and Elgar and Simpson, 1993). Even the Conservatives' 'health warning' now printed on all ballot papers informing employees that striking is a breach of contract, is unlikely to affect the decision to strike. As Mesher and Sutcliffe (1986:267) argue, employees do not see strikes as a permanent break in their contract, and therefore do not consider the legal consequences. More generally, as Elgar and Simpson (1993:107) point out, 'legal prohibition cannot guarantee the ending of practices which do not owe their existence to the law'. Legislation *registered* the decline of trade union power and strike activity in the 1980s and 1990s, rather than *precipitated* it. In short, Conservatives' economic policies have been more instrumental in weakening unions than their programme of legislative reform (see Dunn and Metcalf, 1996:92–3; Edwards, 1992:377; Mayhew, 1985:66; and Chapters 5 and 10 of this volume). In the public sector, where the state is itself the employer, government policy over the past twenty years has actually exacerbated industrial conflict.

The state as employer

In his biography of Margaret Thatcher, Hugo Young (1989:35) wrote:

> Mrs Thatcher had always said, when asked to crystallise the essence of the British Disease, that the nationalised industries were the seat of it: where monopoly unions conspired with monopoly suppliers to produce an inadequate service to the customer at massive cost to the tax-payer. They were, she thought, two sides of the same debased coinage. The nationalised industries, which should have virtue on their side, were hopelessly distorted and confined by state control and the absence of market competition. The unions, who were beneficiaries of these monopolies were accomplices to the most scandalous inefficiencies, and had to be stripped of power.

The public sector, in short, was portrayed as the very antithesis of the enterprise culture that the Conservative government had sought to foster: bureaucratic, inefficient, ineffective, inflexible, unresponsive to customer needs, and highly unionised. In economic terms, the Tories argued, the public sector was too big, not only for the state to finance but for the economy to sustain. As Bacon and Eltis (1978) put it, the UK had too few producers of marketed goods and services due to the expansion of the public sector, in particular public services. Private enterprise was being 'crowded out' by the rise of public expenditure, which in the mid 1970s accounted for almost half the nation's GDP, and this was putting an ever increasing strain on an only slowly growing industrial base. As the Conservative Party's pre–1979 election manifesto declared, 'The state takes too much of the nation's income: its share must be steadily reduced. The reduction of waste, bureaucracy and over-government will yield substantial savings' (quoted by Beaumont, 1992b:19). Public sector policies in the 1980s and first half of the 1990s therefore focused on rationalisation, commercialisation, deregulation, decentralisation and ultimately denationalisation. Consequently the postwar consensus in the public sector was jettisoned.

Although there is great diversity across the public sector in respect of the nature of work, occupational structure, composition of the workforce, and so on, a number of common characteristics can be identified, many of which help to differentiate public from private sector employee relations. Pendleton and Winterton (1993), for example, identify the following features (see also Beaumont, 1992b; and Winchester, 1983a):

- formal separation of political and operational control, with industry boards responsible for day-to-day management, operations and administration, while government ministers are empowered to give general direction to the board.
- an 'obligation' to be a 'model employer', setting a 'good example' to the private sector with respect to health, safety and welfare, and in encouraging trade union organisation, and supporting collective bargaining (which under the Nationalisation Acts was a statutory obligation) and offering a high degree of job security.
- formalised and (largely) centralised collective bargaining procedures, with explicit provision for arbitration.
- high levels of union membership (and invariably a multi-union structure) with well-developed systems of workplace representation.
- hierarchical, and bureaucratic, management structures with internal promotion, a uniform approach to employee relations and an emphasis on keeping services running.

During the 1950s and 1960s the most notable consequence of these structures and procedures was a relatively low level of industrial conflict (although the coalmining industry was a notable exception, as demonstrated in Chapter 10, illustrating again the problem of generalising across the public sector). Industrial peace was secured through the institutionalisation of conflict, as disputes and grievances were resolved through well-developed procedures and a commitment by all parties to maintain consensus and keep the trains running, the lights on, the water flowing and so on.

In addition, consensus rested on the relative absence of market pressures, allowing the development of greater stability in employee relations (see Chapter 4). That consensus was certainly not attributable to industrial democracy or industrial planning. In the postwar reconstruction and nationalisation of many sectors of UK industry, the 1945 Labour government flinched from conceding any more than nominal worker involvement in the running of industry. The docks, in this regard, stand out from the rest of industry as the National Dock Labour Scheme 'was the only radical attempt to institutionalise a high degree of genuine participation' (Wilson, 1972:99). Such participation was doomed to failure, however, in the absence of industrial planning or the wider coordination of transport policy (Turnbull, 1993; and Turnbull and Weston, 1992). This was symptomatic of state policy in the nationalised industries as a whole:

> the nationalised industries have been used as a mechanism for regulating the private economy rather than providing the basis upon which the economy as a whole can be planned. . . . The development of individual nationalised industries, as well as coordinated planning amongst them and the rest of the economy, has been subordinated to macroeconomic objectives such as the reduction of inflation or reducing public expenditure (Fine and O'Donnell, 1985:157).

As voluntarism gave way to corporatism and legal abstention gave way to statutory regulation, industrial peace in the public sector gave way to rising levels of conflict. Indeed during the time of the most intense conflict of the postwar period (1970–74), the public sector accounted for over 40 per cent of the 70 million working days lost (Winchester, 1983a:167). Industrial militancy was a direct result of incomes policies, or as Fine and O'Donnell (1985:157) put it, the subordination of public sector management and employee relations to the macroeconomic objective of reducing inflation. As already noted, incomes policies invariably have a more direct, and often arbitrary and unjust effect on public as opposed to private sector workers, which upsets the established practice of pay comparability between the two sectors. It is hardly surprising, therefore, that 'virtually all episodes of incomes policies in Britain have been broken, at least formally, by public sector strikes, with groups of public sector employees spearheading the resulting "pay explosion"' (Beaumont, 1992b:125). Small wonder, then, that the Conservative Party castigated public sector unions as the 'enemy within', especially after the electoral defeat of Edward Heath in 1974 on the back of the miners' strike (and Heath's question to the nation – 'who runs the country?') and of course the débâcle of the so-called Winter of Discontent.

The scale of rationalisation in the public sector during the 1980s is indicated by the decline of both employment and public expenditure as a proportion of GDP. Employment in the public sector has declined from around 30 per cent of the total working population in the late 1970s to around a quarter by the late 1980s and just one fifth by the mid 1990s. As Table 6.1 illustrates, employment increased by 27 per cent between 1961 and 1979, but declined by 30 per cent between 1979 and 1995. Likewise public sector expenditure as a percentage of GDP had fallen to less than 40 per cent by the late 1980s (the lowest level since the mid 1960s), compared with over 48 per cent in the mid 1970s. Reduced employment was predominantly caused by privatisation, as the decline of employment in public corporations clearly illustrates (excluding NHS trusts, employment in the public corporations stood at just 442 000 in 1995, a fall of 79 per cent since 1979), while cash limits (External Financing Limits) played an important role in reducing public expenditure. However, despite falling numbers and ever more stringent controls on public expenditure, by 1993–4 the PSBR had reached £45.9 billion, the second highest figure as a proportion of national output since the Second World War, largely as a result of social security spending (which increased from 9.5 per cent of GDP in 1979 to 12.2 per cent in 1992) and the long-term loss of revenue (estimated to be around £3.5 billion per annum), after a short-term windfall, from the sale of nationalised industries.

Although privatisation was a key component of Conservative government economic policy, it was the culmination of a much broader policy of commercialisation within the public sector. In fact, it was not a prominent issue on the agenda of the new government in 1979. Instead attention focused on cash

TABLE 6.1   Changes in public sector employment (thousands)

	Central government[1]	Local authorities[2]	Public corporations[3]	Total
1961	1790	1869	2200	5859
1966	1842	2259	1962	6063
1971	1966	2652	2009	6627
1975	2301	2917	2035	7253
1979	2387	2997	2065	7449
1983	2384	2906	1662	6952
1986	2337	3010	1199	6546
1989	2303	2934	844	6081
1993	1641	2680	1158	5479
1995	1054	2644	1531	5229

Notes:
1. Includes HM Forces and NHS.
2. Includes education, social services, police and construction.
3. Figures for 1993 and 1995 include NHS trusts.
Source: *Labour Market Trends*.

limits to control public sector spending (a policy in fact inherited from the previous Labour government, introduced in 1976) and of course pay. As such, cash limits operate as an incomes policy 'by the back door', but they are far more flexible in that they allow for variability around the 'norm', such that the 'norm' is no longer the 'expected', and selective discrimination can be built into the policy in order to avoid confrontation with more vulnerable (for the government) groups. The miners, for example, were 'paid off' on several occasions in the early 1980s, while cash limits in the steel industry made the 1980 strike almost inevitable (see Docherty, 1983; and Chapter 7 below), as planned in the infamous Ridley Report (*The Economist*, 27 May 1978). In addition to cash limits, ministers repeatedly called for 'responsible' wage behaviour in the public sector, and from 1981 to 1986 announced a pay provision figure for central government services in an attempt to limit pay increases (see Beaumont, 1992b:172). During the 1981 civil service strike Margaret Thatcher even threatened to resign in order to ensure that her divided Cabinet would remain opposed to the unions' pay claim (ibid). At the operating level within the civil service, the introduction of the Financial Management Initiative saw the reorganisation of departments around cost centres to shift the emphasis towards 'ability to pay' (defined by the government's own cash limits) rather than comparability. The *Next Steps* report (Ibbs, 1988) recommended the creation of 'executive agencies' in the civil service to create a closer synergy between policy and the efficient management of services. By 1993 these agencies employed around 60 per cent of all non-industrial civil servants, the largest being the Social Security Benefits Office (with 62 000 staff), and HMSO was the first to pull out of national collective bargaining and adopt its own pay and grading system (in 1990). John Major's government maintained the downward pressure on public sector pay by imposing a 1.5 per cent 'ceiling' on the wage bill in 1993 and then 'freezing' the pay bill in subsequent years by only allowing increases financed by 'efficiency savings', cuts in services and job losses (see Bailey, 1994:119–31, 1996; and Goodman, 1996:155–6).

While the emphasis of government policy was very clearly focused on decentralisation and directing management attention towards labour costs, which was both consistent with broader Conservative government economic policy and the very high proportion of operating costs accounted for by labour costs in the public sector (Ferner and Colling, 1991:397), there was also a very clear attempt to change public sector management and set a very different example as the 'model employer'. For management, the emphasis shifted to a more professional approach with clearer assignment of accountability; attention to outputs rather than procedures, with explicit standards of performance; the promotion of internal competition; decentralisation of decision-making authority; a shift in financial responsibility from the centre to individual operating units; and greater flexibility, and efficiency, in the management of human resources (Ferner, 1991:3; and Winchester and Bach,

1995:316–17). In addition, management policy, and certainly that of the Conservative governments, towards employee relations became confrontational rather than cooperative and was implicitly, if not explicitly, anti-union. For example managements were encouraged to withdraw from unilateral arbitration procedures, to move away from national pay bargaining, and not to encourage trade union membership (in August 1990, for example, the Treasury issued notice to this effect to government departments when recruiting new staff). Union recognition was withdrawn from senior management staff in BR, and collective bargaining for teachers in England and Wales was abolished by the government in 1987 (to be replaced, from 1987–91, by an Interim Advisory Committee on pay and subsequently a statutory pay review body). In addition, the government denied trade union membership to 8000 civil servants at GCHQ in 1984 (a decision reversed by the incoming Labour government in May 1997). In effect, then, the relationship between public and private sector employee relations was turned on its head: rather than set a 'good example' (as defined above) to the private sector, the Conservatives gave a different lead through a more confrontational approach in the public sector. As Fredman and Morris (1989:29) conclude, 'For those who support the promotion of employment protection and collective rights, the abandonment of the traditional good employer model is highly regrettable.'

Some of the problems that this reversal has created have been highlighted in the NHS, where 'the dumping of bad private sector practice as preached by too many consultancy firms on to workable public sector traditions will result in a massive loss of efficiency and trust' (Seifert, 1990:57). The same applies in teaching, where the crude application of private sector practices 'will bring years of resentment, inefficiency and muddle' (ibid; see also Winchester and Bach, 1995:331). The penchant for flexibility in the public sector, as practised in the private sector, especially on a numerical and temporal basis, has led to a massive growth in subcontracting, ranging from office cleaning, land and building maintenance and laundry work in central government, to Compulsory Competitive Tendering (CCT) imposed on local authorities under the Local Government Act 1988 (for example for refuse collection, street cleaning, school catering, the maintenance of grounds and vehicles, and more recently leisure services and sports-field upkeep). The effect of such policies has not only been a decline in pay and conditions, and of course union membership (Beaumont, 1992b:63; and Ferner, 1991:15), but a deterioration of service (Ascher, 1987). However unions have had some success in resisting contracting-out and prevented a deterioration in employees' terms and conditions of employment in many cases (see Colling, 1995b). The extension of Transfer of Undertakings (Protection of Employment) legislation to the public sector, such that under CCT the successful bidder must hire public sector employees on their existing terms and conditions, will further strengthen labour's position. In fact many contracts have already been secured by in-house bids (Beaumont, 1992b:67), illustrating yet again the continuity of employee relations in the face of, and contrary to, Conservative government policy and intentions. This applies across many areas of the public sector (see for example Fry, 1988:18; Martinez Lucio, 1993:43; Pendleton, 1991a:425, 1991b:220; and Winchester and Bach, 1995:329–30).

Of course this is not to deny that change has taken place, only to suggest that, within an extremely diverse area of employment such as the public sector, elements of traditional employee relations survive – in some areas with remarkable tenacity. Specific indicators, such as reduced employment and major improvements in productivity (Beaumont, 1992b:177; and Pendleton and Winterton, 1993), indicate substantial change, but caution is again warranted:

> the various measures of output change do not appear to be widely underpinned by significant attitudinal and institutional change. In this sense many instances of change appear to be relatively self-contained in nature, which raise doubts about whether they can be sustained through time (Beaumont, 1992b:177).

This leads Beaumont to conclude that the Conservative governments failed to transform public sector employee relations to anything like the extent they sought:

> the public sector industrial relations scene is currently an awkward mixture of relatively long-established procedural arrangements, a more assertive management strategy and a great deal of political and public questioning about the appropriate balance between efficiency and social considerations in public sector decision-making – and indeed about the appropriate boundary between the public and private sectors (ibid:184).

This boundary between the public and private sectors has been significantly redrawn over the past decade or so, as more than thirty organisations and industries have been returned to the private sector, as Table 6.2 illustrates.

Once a nationalised industry or corporation is privatised the government obviously loses direct political control over its objectives and behaviour, as the privatised company is now expected to satisfy shareholders and financial markets rather than political paymasters (Ferner and Colling, 1991:393, 1995:493–5). Privatisation of the British Transport Docks Board in 1983, for example, and the subsequent deregulation of the industry in 1989, elevated the interests of financial shareholders above those of employee stakeholders. ABP, the new owners, dismissed former registered dockers *en masse* (of 1700 employed prior to the 1989 strike less than twenty remained by the early 1990s), the majority of whom were themselves shareholders, in order to boost profits (see Turnbull, 1993:204). Like many other privatised industries, the ports now have their own collection of 'fat cats' who have become millionaires at the expense of their workforce and the taxpayer. Peter Vincent, for example, who led a management–employee buyout (MEBO) of the trust port

TABLE 6.2 Privatisations

Year	Organisation/industry	Year	Organisation/industry
1981	Cable & Wireless	1990	National Girobank
1982	Britoil	1990	Electricity distribution
1982	National Freight Company	1990	Liverpool Airport
1983	Associated British Ports	1991	Electricity generation
1984	British Telecom	1991	Trust ports
1984	British Shipbuilders	1992	British Technology Group
1984	Jaguar	1993	East Midlands Airport
1986	British Gas	1993	Northern Ireland Electricity Service
1986–8	National Bus subsidiaries	1994	British Coal
1987	British Airports Authority	1994	London Regional Transport
1987	British Airways	1995	Bournemouth Airport
1987	Rolls-Royce	1995	Cardiff Wales Airport
1987	Royal Ordinance	1996	British Rail
1987	TSB	1996	British Energy
1988	British Steel	1996	HMSO
1989	Water		

of Medway, purchased for just £29.7m in March 1992, made £12 million in cash and shares when the port was sold to the Mersey Docks & Harbour Company (MDHC) for £103.7 million just six months later. The port was a more attractive proposition after Mr Vincent had sacked the entire dock labour force during an industrial dispute over a cut in their salaries and an increase in working hours. The dockers were forced to sell back their shares to the MEBO for £2.50 per share, just six weeks before MDHC paid £38 per share (see Saundry and Turnbull, 1997). Cutting labour costs is of course an easy way to 'satisfy' shareholders and boost the 'performance-related' pay of directors, as the rationalisation of British Airways (described in Chapter 4), British Steel (described in Chapter 7) and other recently privatised companies clearly illustrates. Such rationalisation is in fact a *precondition* of privatisation, to make nationalised companies profitable and therefore attractive to shareholders.

Even in the private sector, however, the government is able indirectly to influence management policy, as regulatory agencies for industries such as gas, electricity and telecommunications use pricing formulae that hold price increases below the retail price index by an amount that takes into account the potential for efficiency gains. This creates continued pressure on management to cut costs, including labour costs (see Ferner, 1991:13–14). In the water industry, for example, where a natural (regional) monopoly exists based on the river basins of each of the ten privatised water companies in England and Wales, competition is 'engineered' through a price formula based on the retail price index plus 'k', where the 'k factor' is assessed separately for each water company on the basis of investment requirements, operating costs, revenues and efficiency targets. Crucially, Ofwat, the industry regulator, makes comparisons *between* water companies to determine k and inject 'yardstick competition' into the industry (see Ogden, 1994:69–70, 1995:209). This has introduced strong cost competition between operators, which invariably falls on labour, one of the largest and more easily varied operational costs.

Subcontracting has been one of the water companies' favoured strategies to cut costs, reducing the business to its 'core' activities – a process that Yorkshire Water has described as 'onion management' (on the premise that management can peel off successive layers and still be left with an onion in the middle). Cutting the labour force by half was one reason why Yorkshire Water was unable to meet its target of reducing leakage to 18 per cent by 1992 (water loss increased to 26 per cent in 1994 and is currently around one-third) and one reason, no doubt, why Trevor Newton, the Managing Director, felt obliged to abstain from bathing during the drought of 1995. Other invaluable water saving tips from Yorkshire Water included sending letters to local firms advising them to limit production, extend staff holidays, fit time controls on works showers, or even relocate outside the county! After making profits of £150 million in 1995, despite the drought, and spending just £11 million on remedying leakages but paying £50 million to shareholders, Yorkshire Water advised its customers that they would have to pay higher bills if supply was to be guaranteed in the future (in 1995 some parts of Yorkshire came perilously close to rota cuts of 24 hours on, 24 hours off). The people of Yorkshire, whom the company described as 'culturally ignorant' about the value of water, were not impressed. Complaints flooded in, and the company was forced to hire an additional seventy staff to cope with the deluge. Graffiti on a wall in Halifax read: 'Get your own back – turn the taps on'.

The net effect of stock market pressures, and the process of privatisation itself, has been to erode the spirit of public service upon which such organisations are still reliant and seriously to damage staff morale (Ferner, 1991:18–19; Ferner and Colling, 1991:400; Nichols and O'Connell Davidson, 1991; and Ogden, 1993). As the UK entered the 1990s there was growing public concern about the quality of public services (and growing hostility to further privatisation), and not just the water industry, where 'responsibilities to citizens are now conceptualized in terms of "dealing with the regulators" and meeting minimum legally required standards' (Ogden and Anderson, 1995:555). British Gas, for example, was forced to recruit 700 new staff in 1996 to deal with a torrent of customer complaints, after previously sacking 25 000 employees (including 3000 in customer service and support operations). The Office of Electricity Regulation (Offer) was perturbed to discover that electricity companies had signed 'interruptable' gas supply contracts for their gas-fired stations, which, as the nomenclature implies, allows gas supplies to be halted under some circumstances (specifically when demand is greatest). The capacity of the national grid fell from 61 693 megawatts at privatisation to 57 200 megawatts in February 1996, while peak demand continues to rise. The priority of private electricity companies, as John Baker of the CEGB pointed out in the run-up to denationalisation, is 'not to keep the lights on at all costs. It will probably pay us to overstress our plant' (*Independent on Sunday*, 4 February 1996). Although plant is now 'overstressed', the number of maintenance staff in the electricity industry has been cut by 40 per cent since privatisation.

Throughout the 1980s and 1990s then, change in the public sector has been managed more through confrontation than consensus and cooperation, resulting in a series of set-piece industrial disputes that invariably ended in defeat for the unions and an aftertaste of resentment among the workforce. The Conservatives, of course, pointed to improved productivity and other indices of efficiency to vindicate its approach, and as Ferner (1991:19) argues, we should not lose sight of the need to improve efficiency given the squeeze on public resources. But at the same time the ability of public sector and recently privatised company managements to deliver such efficiency improvements in the absence of employee commitment, rather than mere compliance, must be open to doubt (especially when directors award themselves massive pay increases unrelated, or at best only weakly related, to company performance) (see Conyon, 1995; and Ogden and Watson, 1996). More importantly, evidence suggests that many of the significant improvements in productivity in the public sector, and especially the monopoly utilities, took place *before* privatisation (Bishop *et al.*, 1994:13). Certainly in the ports, the most significant improvements in productivity were registered prior to privatisation, and even deregulation. The cost savings attributable to deregulation (abolition of the NDLS) were estimated by consultants commissioned by the Conservative government to be just over £140 million per annum (Evans *et al.*, 1993:63), but these 'benefits' accrue principally to the major (privately owned) port authorities and the international shipping lines, rather than directly to the customer, and are in any event exceeded by the £148 million per annum cost to the taxpayer (arising from redundancy and reorganisation costs, lost tax revenue and social security payments) (see Turnbull and Wass, 1995). Privatisation itself has had little if any effect on customer service, and both the financial and economic (productivity and traffic) performance of the privatised ports has failed to match that of the public sector ports (both historically and contemporarily) (Saundry and Turnbull, 1997). Given that the state has effectively abandoned control over large sectors of UK industry that, had they been in the public sector, might have been used as the basis upon which to build a long-term economic strategy, the privatisation programme of successive Conservative governments, 'instead of being a sharp break with the past, marking the success of a new political force, Thatcherism, was the culmination of the British state's long abdication from the real planning of production and accumulation even in the nationalised industries' (Fine and Harris, 1985:18).

Conclusion

The fundamental importance of the state's role in employee relations has been demonstrated over the past two decades, but primarily in a very negative fashion. Successive Conservative governments failed to secure low levels of unemployment, the manufacturing base of the economy has been devastated by two recessions, legal protection for both individuals and trade unions has been seriously eroded, and the government fostered a new, confrontational style of management in the public sector and abandoned any lingering prospect, even possibility, of state intervention through the nationalised industries to engineer an economic recovery or a more coordinated programme of accumulation and investment. Inequality and unemployment have been used as instruments of economic management, the former to create entrepreneurial spirit and individual ambition and the latter to keep down inflation (the Conservatives' primary economic objective) and hold the trade unions in check. Yet contrary to the analysis and predictions of the New Right, the labour market 'still refuses to conform to Professor Hayek's model of the world. Most workers, and almost all managers, never seem to have read the works of Patrick Minford' (McCarthy, 1987:17–18). More appropriate analysis, and certainly a more positive labour market policy, is much needed, especially in respect of training and the problems created by unemployment. It is many years since the UK was the 'workshop of the world', but the economy is in danger of sinking to third world status, at least in relation to other EU countries.

Similarly, on the question of legislation and employee rights and protection, the UK formerly led the world in setting international standards, but now violates those standards on a regular basis (Ewing, 1989). Above all the UK has been out of step with Europe and the Social Charter (see Chapter 11). If the legitimacy of trade unionism in the UK was more widely accepted and the rights of individuals at work more adequately protected, this would provide the basis for more stability and higher trust in employee relations. The state can play a positive role in this regard by affirming and underwriting such relations through the establishment of a protective structure of labour law that confers positive rights to both individuals and trade unions, not, as has been the case under recent Tory governments, one that seeks to construct economic recovery on their removal. Surely it is fallacious for the state to abandon its role as a 'good employer' and infuse market relations into *all* aspects of society, promoting a 'contract culture' in employee relations where avarice is deemed the most laudable form of behaviour, and then expect individuals to behave as 'concerned citizens' outside the workplace. The state not only has the capacity to express the 'common good', but is also 'the exemplar of the relationship between the individual and the wider society. The extent to which the state embodies trust, partnership and inclusion is the extent to which these values are diffused through society at large' (Hutton, 1996:25). Equally, the positive role that the state can play in raising investment levels and in the direction and coordination of capital accumulation in the port transport industry and many other sectors of the economy, and the need for greater planning of public services, energy provision, health care, education, *inter alia*, must be acknowledged and not simply derided as the source of our present economic and social ills.

Appendix: Conservative legislation in the 1980s and 1990s

Employment Act 1980

- significant reduction of employee rights under the unfair dismissal provisions
- maternity rights to reinstatement reduced
- restrictions on the closed shop (non-membership allowed on grounds of strongly held personal convictions)
- any new closed shop requires the support of over 80 per cent of the workforce (or 85 per cent of those voting)
- repeal of trade union recognition procedure
- new restrictions on picketing (and a new code of practice)
- 'secondary' picketing outlawed
- new limitations on 'secondary' and sympathetic strikes
- extension of grounds for refusal to join a trade union

Employment Act 1982

- reinforcement of restrictions on the closed shop (protection and compensation for non-membership)
- ballots on closed shops extended to all existing arrangements
- 'union labour only' commercial contracts illegal
- selective dismissal of strikers now legal
- new definition of a trade dispute
- 'political' strikes now illegal
- removal of trade union immunities from the civil courts

Trade Union Act 1984

- ballots to be held every five years to elect (voting) officials to the unions' National Executive Committees
- secret ballots before industrial action (not more than four weeks before the action is to take place)

- ballots to establish political funds (to be reaffirmed every ten years)
- redefinition of 'political objects' on which political funds can be spent

Wages Act 1986

- wages councils are only allowed to specify a single minimum rate of pay and a single overtime rate
- workers under the age of 21 years are no longer covered by minimum wage protection

Sex Discrimination Act 1986

- removal of exception for small firms (five employees or fewer) from complying with the Sex Discrimination Act 1975
- restrictions on women's working hours and other conditions removed
- discriminatory clauses in collective agreements void

Employment Act 1988

- unions must hold separate ballots for industrial action if those who are likely to take part in such action have different places of work
- ballot papers must ask whether the member is prepared to take part in a strike or action short of a strike
- members have a right not to be 'unjustifiably disciplined' by their union
- ballots for union officials extended to all National Executive Committee members (whether or not they have the power to vote on the NEC)
- new Commissioner for the Rights of Trade Union Members
- post-entry closed shop 'illegal' (unenforceable)

Employment Act 1989

- right to time off for trade union duties narrowed
- equal access for men and women to employment, vocational training, promotion and working conditions

Employment Act 1990

- pre-entry closed shop illegal
- union vicariously liable if any of its officials (including shop stewards) call for industrial action
- restrictions on unofficial strike action

- employers given greater freedom to dismiss any employee taking unofficial industrial action
- further restrictions on secondary action

Trade Union Reform and Employment Rights Act 1993

- union members to be given the right to decide which union to join
- fully postal ballots before any strike
- unions must provide employers with at least seven days' notice of official industrial action
- union members to authorise (and reconfirm every three years) the collection of union subscription by automatic deduction ('check-off') from their pay packets
- abolition of the 26 wages councils
- removal of ACAS's requirement to encourage collective bargaining

PART 3

INTERACTIONS AND OUTCOMES IN EMPLOYEE RELATIONS

CHAPTER 7

Developments in the process and outcomes of collective bargaining

Re-casting employee relations in British Steel

An industry transformed

In 1978 annual crude steel production in the UK stood at just under 21 million tonnes. Most of the 165 000 employees involved in producing that steel worked for the nationalised British Steel Corporation (BSC). In that year it took BSC 15.3 man hours to produce each tonne of liquid steel. A decade later, in 1988, the output of the UK steel industry was just over 19 million tonnes, 8 per cent lower than the 1978 level. Employment in the industry, however, had been cut by a massive 67 per cent to a little over 55 000. BSC's productivity levels had correspondingly risen dramatically (to 5 man hours per tonne) and as a result BSC had gone from being a comparatively high-cost producer of bulk steel to one of the world's lowest-cost producers. Since 1988, the year BSC was privatised and renamed British Steel plc (BS), rationalisation has continued as management have made further cuts and concentrated activity at the most efficient works. By 1992 the BS workforce had fallen to below 45 000, partly reflecting the closure of the Ravenscraig works early in that year.

These trends have continued during the mid 1990s. In 1995 the company's output of crude steel was just under 16 million tonnes and its overall productivity levels had improved further to 3.7 man hours per tonne. Employment costs, which had been 30 per cent or more of total costs in the late 1970s, had fallen to under 22 per cent by 1996. This fall in labour costs, coupled with other factors such as investment in newer and larger-scale technology, was increasingly reflected in the company's profits, which rose to over £1 billion in 1995–6. In 1997, with its UK workforce down to 43 000, BS announced another major workforce restructuring programme over the coming five years as part of a strategy to maintain its position as a low-cost producer. Reports of this programme indicate that it could entail the loss of a further 8000 to 10 000 jobs by the year 2002.

Behind these bare statistics lies the story of an industry transformed (and continuing to transform), not to mention the severe impact wrought on numerous steel communities and tens of thousands of people formerly dependent on the industry for their livelihood. Inside the industry, the process of steel making, little altered for over half a century, has undergone radical changes in scale and technology. What is particularly notable, though, is the way the process of transformation has been inextricably linked with major changes in the structure and process of collective bargaining. Given the stability of employee relations structures in steel up to 1980, the extent and pace of developments thereafter beg a series of questions. What factors were central in the change process? What were the major aspects of employee relations change? Why did the changes occur so rapidly compared with what had gone before? And what have been the main implications of the changes for the different parties involved?

The critical period of change came in 1979–80. By that time the economic problems facing BSC were clear: principally, large-scale obsolescence due to inadequate investment and a failure to modernise over several decades, and enormous overcapacity due to the stagnant world market for steel and declining competitiveness in the domestic market. It is true that in response to these problems some rationalisation of the corporation had already taken place during the 1970s. BSC had closed entire plants (such as the East Moors works in Cardiff in 1976) as well as shutting down parts of plants (for example steel making at Ebbw Vale) in order to concentrate bulk steel-making activity and other processes on fewer sites. In the face of mounting economic crisis and financial losses, however, the extent and pace of this rationalisation programme was seen as seriously inadequate. The upshot was a new rationalisation programme announced in 1979 – known as 'Slimline' – and moves to fundamentally alter the character of employee relations. In large part, the latter was to be achieved through the recasting of collective bargaining arrangements in the industry.

As with the rationalisation of plant and production processes, some attempts at reforming the character of employee relations had been made in the 1960s and 1970s, principally through forms of productivity bargaining (see Blyton, 1993; and Owen Smith, 1971). Negotiations in BSC at that time were characterised by a substantial degree of centralisation, supplemented by local bargaining. Thus pay rates in the industry were negotiated nationally and separately with each union, while other terms and conditions (for example hours and holidays, shift and overtime premia) were negotiated nationally between BSC and a combined union committee comprising the main production union (the Iron and Steel Trades Confederation, ISTC) and the various craft and general unions with members in the industry (BSC established separate negotiating arrangements with the management union, the Steel Industry Management Association). With this structure in place, the additional role of local bargaining was to supplement national agreements in such aspects as tonnage bonuses and 'abnormal conditions' payments connected to working in conditions that were, for example, unduly hot or dusty.

The attempts at employee relations reform before 1980 sought to create the conditions for increased labour productivity via agreed redundancies and locally agreed changes in manning arrangements and working practices involving increased flexibility among and between production and craft tasks. The overall outcome, however, was little change. Inter-union differences, rigid demarcations, a lack of monitoring of change and the varied nature of craft work proved significant obstacles to the development of new work practices. Given the pace at which rationalisation had been proceeding before the late 1970s, and the degree to which the structure of negotiations and pattern of work organisation were resilient to change, the twelve months from late 1979 were thus all the more remarkable for the developments that occurred and the ways these laid the basis for a refashioning of employment relations in steel on a scale hitherto unknown in the history of the industry.

'Slimline' and the national strike

In 1979 BSC published its emergency 'Slimline' plan against the background of mounting economic crisis and the newly elected Conservative government's instruction to stem losses and reach breakeven point by 1980–1. The plan was based on a 25 per cent cut in output, to be achieved by total and partial plant closures, and concentrating activity at more efficient works (see Blyton, 1992c and 1993 for more details). The most visible outcome over the next three years was a scale of redundancies unprecedented in the European steel industry (Harris, 1988; and Houseman, 1991).

At the same time BSC announced its intention to reduce the prominence of national pay bargaining and increase the degree to which earnings were tied more directly to local performance. This was consistent with the Thatcher government's economic policy, an important part of which was based on cash limits to the public sector and the requirement that pay awards be self-financing. The first outcome of this was the BSC management's 1980 pay offer, which was based on local performance bonuses with no provision for a national, across-the-board increase. This refusal to make a national offer, coupled with the job insecurity arising from possible further plant closures, culminated in a protracted national strike in 1980, the first official national strike in the industry since 1926 (for accounts of the strike itself, see Docherty, 1983; and Hartley *et al.*, 1983).

The various outcomes of the thirteen week strike, involving almost 100 000 workers, are far from easy to quantify, not least because the effects on management and worker attitudes continued to be felt in the industry long after the dispute was over. In several ways the strike acted as a watershed. As one manager put it, 'while the strike was on, we [the managers] sat down and said what we are not going to stand for when it was over' (interview notes). The strike failed either to shift government policy on the funding of the industry, or to bring about any reconsideration by BSC of its closure programme. In terms of the wage settlement, a Committee of Inquiry (the Lever Committee), set up under the auspices of ACAS, recommended an improved pay offer, which was accepted. A significant part of this increase, however, was to be made up of local bonus payments negotiated at district level.

The move to local negotiations

In the aftermath of the strike the centre of gravity of employee relations shifted down to the local level. While national negotiations continued to exist, their role and significance were increasingly circumscribed. Rather than negotiating basic pay rises, the national bargaining machinery came predominantly to function as a mechanism for reaching framework agreements for local negotiations and for consolidating elements of previous local bonuses into basic rates.

Central to the development of local union–management relations was the introduction of a works lump sum bonus (LSB) scheme in 1980 which tied a significant element of potential earnings (initially up to 18 per cent) to the achievement not only of plant performance targets (including output and quality levels) but also to the acceptance of change by the workforce, including manpower reductions, the introduction of subcontractors, alterations to work practices, and technical change. By putting a monetary value on cooperation, this LSB scheme, based on multi-union committees at works level, was to play a crucial role in assisting management to fulfil its rationalisation programme in the coming years. Worker cooperation took three main forms. First, by making job cuts one of the LSB targets, management were able to define job losses as essentially local issues, outside the remit of the national industrial relations machinery. The offer of comparatively good severance terms for those made redundant, coupled with tying reduced manning levels to bonus payments for those remaining, combined to diffuse much local union opposition to the redundancy programme. At the same time national unions were effectively excluded by what they saw as this 'divide and rule' policy by BSC, executed through local employee relations. This exclusion also reflected the unions' diminished power due to membership losses and the difficulty of remounting anticlosure campaigns so soon after the national strike.

Second, the financial incentive of the LSB payments reduced opposition to other changes that in the past had been resisted by trade unions both locally and nationally. The most significant of these changes was the increased use of subcontract labour to undertake a wider range of activities within the steelworks (see Fevre, 1987). There were also specific agreements on technological change and job enlargement involving not only craft and production workers but also non-manual staff. Through job enlargement and increased subcontracting, coupled with increased automation of various parts of the steelmaking process, BSC management sought to cover the huge reductions in manpower that occurred at sites continuing in production: reductions of more than two thirds of total employment were implemented at major plants such as Teesside in the North-East and Port Talbot and Llanwern in South Wales.

Third, by tying bonus payments partly to achieved performance, this acted to stifle any oppositional activity that might affect output. With high levels of inflation prevailing in the early 1980s, securing increases in income was a high priority for those remaining in work. With the LSB potentially worth almost one fifth of earnings, this was an important source of income for those still employed in the industry. Moreover the significance of the LSB was further strengthened from 1984 onwards when BSC management made the payment of any national increases conditional on the successful conclusion of local LSB negotiations within a six-week 'window' from the signing of a national agreement (Avis, 1990). Thus both local and national pay improvements were made to hinge on the acceptance of manpower change and performance improvements at the local level.

Throughout the 1980s and 1990s, LSB negotiations have remained a crucial element of the company's relations with its workforce. Over that time the constituent elements of the bonus package have undergone shifts in emphasis, but the overall effect has remained unchanged. By 1983 the main redundancies had been achieved and the components of the LSB came more to reflect the concerns of output and quality. Significant quality improvements were achieved throughout the 1980s, due to such factors as increased use of continuous casting technology, improved chemistry, finer rolling tolerances and more sophisticated monitoring techniques, including the widespread use of statistical process control (SPC) techniques by the workforce.

Since the latter part of the 1980s working practices have become an increasingly important area for local negotiation. Prominent in this have been the issues of craft restructuring and teamworking (see Blyton and Bacon, 1997; and Morris *et al.*, 1992). Under craft restructuring, the former complex craft structure was simplified into two general craft disciplines (broadly covering the mechanical and electrical areas) with training programmes to permit greater flexibility within the disciplines and some (albeit relatively small) degree of cross-discipline competence. Just as craft restructuring challenges many of the traditional demarcations surrounding particular skills, team-working represents an equivalent challenge to the traditional occupational hierarchies among production workers. Under teamworking the seniority-based production crews are replaced by flatter work teams that often incorporate both production and maintenance functions and in which the position of team leader is dependent on competence and performance appraisal rather than length of service.

To date, local agreements on craft restructuring are far more widespread than agreements on teamworking, not least because of continued union opposition to teamworking in a number of plants (see Bacon *et al.*, 1996). While much of the detail of craft restructuring was negotiated outside the LSB machinery, the latter nevertheless played two important roles for local managements. First, 'in principle' acceptance of craft restructuring was first secured in LSB agreements. Second, craft union representatives were faced with the prospect that failure to agree the details of restructuring would result in those details becoming incorporated into LSB negotiations. The threat of craft issues being made the subject of a wider bargaining forum – and particularly one involving not only the numerically greater production grades, but also one where bonus payments would hinge on a settlement – exerted a strong influence on craft unions to reach a local settlement with management.

Privatisation of BSC in 1988 exerted further pressure on the decentralisation of employee relations. The establishment of four separate business divisions within the privatised British Steel (General Steels, Strip Products, Stainless and Diversified) led to the termination of any remaining national bargaining and the introduction of business-level negotiation machinery. Thus privatisation involved the creation of strategic business units, devolution of financial responsibility to the individual businesses and devolution of employee rela-tions machinery. According to BS management, this would enable each business to pursue separate negotiating positions, depending on their indivi-dual performance (Avis, 1990). In practice, however, business-level agree-ments have continued virtually to mirror one another, while the key focus of employee relations has remained firmly at the local rather than business level.

The new managerial attitude towards employee relations after the 1980 strike also brought to a close BSC's worker director scheme. This scheme had involved six trade union members forming one third of the Corporation's Main Board, with a further twenty-one worker directors sitting on the various group boards (for more details see Brannen *et al.*, 1976). These Main Board positions were terminated after the strike and the number of worker directors on the group boards was allowed to run down by non-renewal. Abandonment of the worker director scheme further underlined the managerial objective of reducing the degree of centralised influence held by the trade unions. In more recent years the local focus of employee relations in British Steel has been further underlined by the introduction of such initiatives as Total Quality Performance. One effect of this has been to increase the amount of direct (though largely downward) communication within individual works, as management have sought to secure greater commitment to product quality.

An apparent, albeit partial, reversal of this pattern of development occurred in 1996 with British Steel's establishment of a European Works Council (EWC). During the 1990s BS became increasingly international in character, with around 10 000 employees working outside the UK, both in production facilities (notably in Sweden, Germany and the United States) and distribution activities in twelve European countries. The EWC draws representatives from these various European countries, together with six national trade union officials. However the consultative role of the Council, rather than any negotiating function, has been strongly emphasised by the company. In their initial announcement of the EWC, for example, BS management made clear that 'under no circumstances [will the council become involved or discuss] any issues relating to collective bargaining or negotiations within group undertakings' (quoted in the *Financial Times*, 1 August, 1996). Rather the Council's agenda will include broad strategy, manpower and employment, business reorganisation and areas such as health and safety and environment, where these issues have a 'transnational impact' (for further discussion of EWCs, see Chapters 8 and 11). Thus the establishment of a European Works Council does not significantly challenge the company's emphasis on decentralised industrial relations developed over the period since 1980.

The outcomes of decentralised bargaining

The decentralisation of collective bargaining in British Steel illustrates a marked shift in emphasis in the conduct of employee relations during the past two decades. While elements of change were visible earlier, the conjunction of several key factors in 1979 and after fuelled both the depth and pace of change. Market pressures, government policies and the outcome of the national strike combined to create a context in which management were not only forced to make substantial changes to the industry's operations, but were also provided with the conditions conducive to a refashioning of employee relations – specifically involving a diminution of centralised bargaining machinery and national trade union influence, and an increase in the significance of local agreements. The upshot was the creation of a system that has proved highly amenable to the pursuit of a managerially defined agenda for change. Unlike experiments in the 1960s with productivity bargaining, the LSB scheme has allowed management to reassert its control over labour in a context in which the latter has been generally weakened by the broader labour market conditions prevailing after 1979, and specifically weakened by the market conditions for steel and the failure of the national strike to bring about any reversal of state or employer policy towards employment in the industry.

From management's point of view, the reassertion of control has been successfully pursued by decentralising employee relations and tying pay awards to fundamental changes in work organisation. The result has been the general acceptance of change with little organised resistance and a closer linking of earnings to local performance.

The pattern of collective bargaining

In British Steel and many other sectors of industry, collective bargaining remains a central feature of contemporary employee relations. Historically, it has been the principal mechanism for the determination of pay rates and other basic terms and conditions for the majority of the workforce, and more generally represents a key arena for the conduct of collective relations between managers and managed. By the early 1970s collective agreements covered over 80 per cent of all male and over 70 per cent of all female manual workers in British industry, and over 60 per cent of the non-manual labour force (both male and female).

In the mid 1980s, seven out of ten employees were covered by collective bargaining arrangements, almost twice as high a proportion as the current density of union membership. Right up the late 1980s collective bargaining represented the principal means of determining pay and other conditions of employment for the majority of British workers. The results of the third Workplace Industrial Relations Survey (WIRS), however, indicated that the coverage of bargaining arrangements had diminished significantly by 1990 and now applied to a much lower proportion of the workforce (Millward *et al.*, 1992). Over the WIRS sample as a whole, 54 per cent of employees were covered by collective bargaining in 1990, compared with 71 per cent in 1984. This decline represents one of the most dramatic changes in the character of industrial relations during the 1980s. In the private sector as a whole, coverage dropped from a majority of employees (52 per cent) in 1984 to a minority (41 per cent) in 1990, while in the public sector the decline was from 95 per cent to 78 per cent (ibid:90–6). At the same time, across the sample as a whole, collective bargaining still applied to the majority of establishments (as opposed to employees), and remained by far the most important method of determining pay and conditions in the public sector, as Table 7.1 illustrates. Subsequent Labour Force Survey data suggests that the coverage of collective bargaining has fallen further during the 1990s with as few as 37 per cent of employees being covered by collective bargaining by 1996 (Cully and Wood-land, 1997:238; see also Beatson, 1993, and Heery, 1997:94). Differences between the WIRS and LFS samples, however, make precise comparisons difficult (see also Brown, 1993; and Milner, 1995).

TABLE 7.1   Coverage of collective bargaining, 1990

Proportion of establishments with % of employees covered in the specified range	All establishments	Private manufacturing	Private services	Public sector
None	47	56	64	13
1–19	4	3	3	5
20–49	7	8	4	10
50–79	11	13	7	16
80–99	13	14	10	19
100	18	6	13	37
Overall % covered	54	51	33	78

Source: Millward *et al.* (1992:91).

Although collective bargaining is evidently of major importance in many industries and services, suggesting an underlying continuity of employee relations, Millward *et al.* (1992:350) argue that so great were the changes in the latter half of the 1980s 'that it is not unreasonable to conclude that the traditional, distinctive "system" of British industrial relations no longer characterizes the economy as a whole' (see also Beaumont, 1995; and Purcell, 1993). In this context it is not just the coverage of collective bargaining that has changed but also its structure and content, with consequent effects on the outcome of bargaining relationships (Dunn and Wright, 1994). Just as was evidenced in the British Steel case, where changes in bargaining arrangements (in conjunction with other factors) proved critical for management in securing other objectives, so too it is possible on a wider scale both to map the main dimensions of change in bargaining structures and to identify some of the implications of those changes for the content, process and outcomes of bargaining relations. In addition, it is possible to identify the continuing problems and shortcomings of collective bargaining as a means of pay determination for certain work groups and for the regulation of certain kinds of issue.

John Goodman (1984:145) succinctly describes collective bargaining as 'a process through which representatives of employers and employee organisations act as the joint creators of the substantive and procedural rules regulating employment'. 'Substantive' rules relate to aspects of the *substance* of the employment relationship, such as the wage rate, the length of the working day or week, holiday entitlement, sick pay and the like. 'Procedural' rules, on the other hand, establish the procedure by which, or *how*, substantive agreements are to be reached (how negotiations are to be conducted, by whom, how any disputes that may arise should be handled and so on). In other words collective bargaining is not only a *market* process affecting the sale of labour power, but also a *political* process which, as a rule-making activity that involves power relations between the parties, serves to define rights, duties and obligations (Flanders, 1975:220). In the words of Slichter (1941:1), collective bargaining is a system of 'industrial jurisprudence', or as Flanders (1975:236) put it, 'an institution for regulating labour management as well as labour markets'. In this respect collective bargaining can be regarded as a form of 'industrial government' and a means to 'industrial democracy' (ibid).

Others have argued that the outcomes of collective bargaining can be usefully seen as not just a set of substantive and procedural agreements, but more generally as a means of management control (that is, a managerial process). At first sight this argument may seem curious, since one of the defining features of collective bargaining is that it is a process in which issues are subject to *joint* control. So how can it act to augment management's control? The argument here relates both to the consequences of trade unions participating in collective bargaining activity, and to the possible repercussions of the absence of bargaining relations. With regard to the former, the joint establishment of the basic terms on which labour is sold will conceivably vest those terms with greater legitimacy in the eyes of the workforce (and are thus less likely to be challenged by the workforce) than where the terms are set unilaterally by the employer:

> There are numerous ways in which a positive acceptance of the union, an effort to integrate it into the administrative structure of the enterprise instead of treating it as a thing apart, can contribute to efficient management. . . . This sort of relationship, in which union and management officials not only accept each other's existence but support each other's objectives, is frequently referred to as 'mature collective bargaining' (Reynolds, 1956:176–7).

The establishment of legitimacy is part of a broader issue, however. As Sisson (1987) argues, by entering into a collective bargaining relationship with employers over some aspects of the employment relationship, employee representatives not only demonstrate their willingness to reach a compromise with employers over those aspects, but by implication also signal their broad acceptance of managerial rights in other areas and, more generally, the respective roles of management and labour within the *status quo*. Thus in the historical development of the rule-making process that constitutes collective bargaining,

> relatively few of these rules were (or have become) the subject of joint regulation; in most cases only a framework of minimum pay and conditions was involved. In fact much more important was the legitimacy that trade union involvement in the rule-making process gave to the employers' right to manage. For collective bargaining involves *mutual* recognition. In agreeing to make some rules subject to joint regulation, employers were requiring that trade unions should recognize the employers' right to make other rules unilaterally. In a number of cases . . . this trade-off was explicit . . . the exercise of managerial prerogative [was] the *quid pro quo* for the employers' willingness to negotiate over pay and other conditions of employment (ibid:12, original emphasis).

No wonder Harbison (1954, quoted by Jackson, 1991:162) has called collective bargaining 'one of the major bulwarks of the capitalist system'. By entering bargaining relations with trade unions, employers simultaneously 'gained an additional source of supervision over worker behaviour and an institutionalised means of pay settlement' (Ursell and Blyton, 1988:94). In addition there are areas of workplace activity where, if anything, control rests with the work group rather than with management. Hence, for management, collective bargaining may represent an attempt to establish a degree of joint control where formerly they did not even have that. This strategy underpins much of the development of productivity bargaining in the 1960s, in which management sought to gain a greater degree of influence over 'job control' issues such as demarcation, the organisation of work and overtime working.

As well as according legitimacy both to the specific areas of joint agreement and, following the argument above, to wider areas of managerial action, collective bargaining also represents a potential source of managerial control in the way in which it institutionalises conflict by channelling the power of organised labour into a mechanism that, while acknowledging that power, at the same time circumscribes it and gives it greater predictability. 'By collective bargaining,' wrote Dahrendorf (1956:260), 'the frozen fronts of industrial conflict are thawed'. Thus while collective bargaining clearly does not lead to a *cessation* of industrial conflict, the existence of negotiating machinery tends to act to *temper* that conflict and reduce the chances of it fundamentally threatening the basic existence of the enterprise. Thus in the case of BSC prior to 1980, for example, the extensive national bargaining structures acted as an important contributor to the absence of large-scale strikes in the industry.

This is not to suggest that employers welcome collective bargaining with open arms or (as we discuss below) have not sought to diminish its role when given the opportunity to do so. Recent evidence suggests that it is now harder than ever before for unions to gain recognition in new companies, new sites, or in those industries where recognition has always been difficult to achieve (Beaumont, 1987; Brown *et al.*, 1995:140–1; and Kessler and Bayliss, 1992:97–8). There are strong historical precedents for such resistance. The early period of trade unionism in the UK and elsewhere is replete with examples of embryonic unions fighting for recognition with employers who were highly averse to conceding *any* part of their prerogative to joint control. Faced with growing craft union organisation within the workplace, however, together with increased militancy among the newer unions of semi- and unskilled workers, employers found themselves in a position where to yield to collective bargaining over basic pay and conditions was the lesser of two evils. In so doing, employers ensured that much of the conflict between capital and labour became institutionalised, the basic legitimacy of the system was tacitly acknowledged and union power became accommodated within the broad *status quo*.

Sisson (1987) and others have pointed to specific historical incidents, such as the industrial unrest in the iron and steel industry in the 1860s and the 1897–8 strike and lockout over a shorter working day in the engineering industry, as critical events in the formation of particular bargaining arrangements. It is also important, however, to avoid treating these events in isolation. Part of the broader explanation of why UK employers did not demonstrate more concerted opposition to the growth of trade unionism, for example, and why they accorded recognition rights relatively early, may lie in the apparent complacency that gripped many UK employers in the late nineteenth century (see Gospel, 1992). Easy access to colonial materials and markets lowered competitive pressures that might otherwise have fuelled a stronger employer zeal to minimise labour costs by destroying union organisations (Ursell and Blyton, 1988:94). Moreover the nature of early trade union growth in Britain among the 'labour aristocracy' of craft workers – a unionisation designed to maintain a separateness from, rather than a solidarity with, the growing class of semiskilled and unskilled workers – meant that employers were 'anxious to avoid giving succour to a more militant unionism by rejecting the extant version' (ibid:94). Thus in extending recognition and joint regulation to a union movement initially dominated by skilled workers, employers were seeking to accommodate a brand of unionism that shared many of the individualist values of *laissez-faire* capitalism. As we discuss below, the state also came to share this view that the institutionalisation of conflict within collective bargaining accorded a greater degree of stability. As a result, for more than half a century the state both directly and indirectly supported the development of collective bargaining arrangements.

Though often discussed as if it were a homogeneous and comparatively simple entity, in practice collective bargaining is both a complex and diverse process. Walton and McKersie (1965) have observed that bargaining encapsulates negotiations occurring within, as well as between, the major parties, and incorporates attempts to structure attitudes as well as to establish agreements over the terms of the employment relationship. In addition, collective bargaining exhibits considerable variation in the *level(s)* at which bargaining activity takes place and the linkages between different levels; the *coverage* of bargaining across different work groups, usually referred to as the bargaining *unit*, which may be few or many, wide or narrow; the range or *scope* of topics subject to joint regulation; the *processes* that constitute collective bargaining; the extent or *depth* of union influence within bargaining activity, and the degree to which union representatives and managers become involved in the interpretation and application of rules and practices; and the *forms* that bargained agreements take, whether they are written or unwritten, formal or informal, precise or flexible (see for example Clegg, 1979a:115; and McCarthy *et al.*, 1971:3–5). It is clear that in the recent period significant changes have occurred along several of these dimensions. It is to a consideration of these changes, and the consequences for the parties involved, that we now turn, for it is evident that the type of changes evidenced in the British Steel case are far from unique. And as the steel example illustrates, changes in the level of bargaining and the nature of representation can have a significant bearing on the kinds of issue included in (and excluded from) collective bargaining, and the resulting outcomes stemming from that bargaining activity.

To this end the remainder of the chapter examines changes occurring in patterns of bargaining and assesses the extent of change in levels of union influence in those bargaining relations. Following an historical review, the significance of the period since 1979 is emphasised. Of particular note is the fact that despite the tradition of free collective bargaining in the UK, the outcome of the bargaining process has been foreclosed on numerous occasions in the past as a result of incomes policies (see Chapter 6). In contrast the 1980s and 1990s represent one of the longest sustained periods of 'free' collective bargaining in the postwar years. This period has witnessed many significant changes in the structure and content of collective relations between employer and employees, not least the decline of multi-employer collective bargaining and the historically unprecedented withdrawal from collective agreements by many companies.

The development of collective bargaining structures

Early collective bargaining activity tended to be local in character, as individual or neighbouring groups of employers struck bargains with the representatives of local work groups. In the UK, early trade unions and employer bodies organised on the basis of individual localities or districts: for both parties national organisation came later, and in some industries much later. To continue our iron and steel example, employers' associations in the industry maintained their regional organisation until comparatively recently: in 1925, twenty-five separate employers' associations were functioning, and by the time of the 1967 nationalisation ten iron and steel employers' associations remained in existence (Owen Smith, 1971:39). In such industries as engineering and shipbuilding, the localised character of collective bargaining was reinforced by the early development of shop steward organisation before and after the First World War (Hinton, 1973).

In the early decades of the twentieth century, however, local arrangements for collective bargaining became increasingly overlaid by national, industry-wide collective bargaining arrangements involving (the by now nationally organised) trade union organisations and national industry associations of large numbers of employers. The upshot was the growth of industry-wide agreements on pay and other basic terms and conditions (covering issues such as hours, holidays and overtime rates). Where industries comprised many employers, pay agreements tended to establish *minimum* or 'standard' pay rates, while in the public sector, national pay determination involved the setting of *actual* rates and scales.

Various factors contributed to the growth of industry-wide bargaining. First, in different ways it served the interests of all parties to concentrate their bargaining activity at the national level. For employers this meant a more concerted response to growing trade union organisation, particularly as unions began to expand significantly among semi- and unskilled workers, became more militant (for example strike waves in 1912 and 1921) and developed as national organisations. Within national bargaining arrangements, employers in particular districts and localities were less vulnerable to trade union pressure. National bargaining also allowed small employers to reduce the amount of time and resources they devoted to negotiating with trade unions. More significantly, perhaps, it kept unions out of the workplace, or at least neutralised their impact (Sisson, 1987:188).

For the expanding trade unions, national bargaining arrangements allowed them to rationalise their bargaining activity and marshal their meagre finances to service more effectively a small cadre of negotiators. National bargaining also underlined the role of trade unions within an industry, improving their prospects of membership growth. National bargaining arrangements also increased the extent of union recognition by individual employers – a factor that has since been identified as a key influence on union membership growth (Bain, 1970; Bain and Elsheikh, 1980). Even today, as Table 7.1 illustrates, once union recognition is achieved the tendency is for coverage to be high if not complete. In the Workplace Industrial Relations Survey for 1990, in 60 per cent of workplaces with union recognition, 80 per cent or more employees were covered (Millward *et al.*, 1992:92).

Finally, for the state the extension of collective bargaining represented an important institutionalisation of conflict, as well as an important counter to bouts of industrial unrest and a mechanism for promoting industrial coopera-tion during wartime and other crises. In fact the state supported the expansion of national bargaining arrangements in several ways. During the First World War, for example, the introduction of industry arbitration under the terms of a Treasury Agreement (subsequently incorporated into the 1915 Munitions of War Act), coupled with the taking of certain industries directly under state control for the duration of the war, encouraged a centralisation of employee relations.

In combination these factors resulted in national bargaining covering at least a third of the employed labour force and over half the total trade union membership by 1917 (Clegg, 1985:168). In that year the government estab-lished a Committee of Inquiry (under the chairmanship of the deputy speaker, J. H. Whitley), and in five reports issued over the next two years the Whitley Committee recommended the establishment of industry-wide collective machinery for all industries, centred on national Joint Standing Industrial Councils (JICs) supported by joint committees at district and works levels. National committees were rapidly established in many industries and the public sector: by 1921 seventy-four JICs had been set up (Ursell and Blyton, 1988:115). Though many fell into decay during the recessionary years of the 1930s, there was a revival of interest in industry-wide collective bargaining during the Second World War, again stimulated by the government taking direct control of some industries and looking to secure peaceful industrial relations and cooperation with wartime production requirements in others. The upshot was that by the end of the war 15.5 million employees out of a total workforce of 17.5 million were covered by some form of national bargaining machinery (Jackson, 1991). This proportion rose further as the nationalisation Acts of the late 1940s brought hitherto unorganised groups (particularly non-manual workers) within the scope of national collective agreements.

From throughout that period a degree of local bargaining activity continued, in some industries more than others, concerned with the application of national agreements, the supplementing of those agreements in particular areas and the establishment of local work rules. The Whitley model also advocated the establishment of works committees to discuss local issues. While these always remained less prominent than the national JICs, they became well established in certain industries, particularly in the growing public sector. Furthermore, during the Second World War the government promoted the establishment of factory-wide Joint Production Committees: by mid 1943 there were over 4000 of these in the engineering industry alone, dealing with a range of issues from technical matters to levels of absenteeism and the application of 'dilution' agreements (the introduction of workers into skilled jobs who had not completed the normal apprenticeship) (Clegg and Chester, 1954:338; and Currie, 1979:156). Similar committees were established in shipbuilding, mining and construction. While the emphasis was on consultation rather than negotiation, these and similar committees nevertheless contributed to the maintenance of local collective relations at a time when most attention was being given to the development of joint machinery at the national level (see Chapter 8 for a discussion of joint consultation).

From the mid 1950s onwards, however, there was a reassertion of local bargaining activity in the private sector, which gained further momentum during the 1960s. Industry-wide agreements remained in place but were increasingly subject to elaboration and extension at the local level. Following Sisson (1987), local bargaining in large parts of manufacturing moved from 'supplementing' national agreements to 'supplanting' them. The shop steward movement grew from an estimated 90 000 in 1961 to between 250 000 and 300 000 by the late 1970s (see Terry, 1983), as did the degree of job control that work groups exerted over aspects of work pace and effort. Explanations for this growth in workplace bargaining have been sought mainly in labour market and economic conditions. The general argument is that labour shortages, coupled with improved union organisation within the workplace, provided both a power base and a means for unions and work groups to mobilise that power to force wage concessions. The spread of piecework and bonus schemes is seen to have provided increased opportunities for bargaining to take place over rate fixing for particular jobs. The general conditions of economic growth are further seen to have encouraged employers to secure local settlements in order to avoid disruptions to production and retain scarce skilled labour.

Sisson (1987) has also noted the significance of the relative weakness of most industry agreements in the UK, compared with their counterparts elsewhere in Western Europe. In Europe, the broader range of substantive issues covered by national agreements resulted in local bargaining activity remaining an essentially administrative activity *vis-à-vis* the national agreements. In the UK, however, the narrower range of coverage of industry agreements meant that local collective bargaining developed a more substantial and independent role, filling larger gaps left by the national settlements. While national minimum rates were agreed at industry level, local level negotiations (often informal) increasingly took place over issues such as piecework rates and bonuses, as well as demarcation issues and other working practices such as manning levels (Cliff, 1970). Thus the relative weakness of national industry agreements in the UK gave trade unions significant room for bargaining at the local level, and left individual employers faced with the need to establish rules and agreements in those areas insufficiently covered by the industry agreement. As Ogden (1982:170) notes, the variety and complexity of collective bargaining arrangements at that time were 'generally seen to be unsatisfactory not least because they are highly fragmented, encourage the pursuit of comparisons, breed competitive bargaining, are a major source of disputes, and produce dissatisfaction which fuels inflationary wage claims'.

The overall outcome was that by the time of the review of industrial relations by the Royal Commission on Trade Unions and Employers' Associations in the mid 1960s, it was not only judged that those relations were operating with a considerable degree of, or more precisely too much, informal workplace bargaining activity, despite the widespread retention of national industry agreements, but also, and of greater importance, that this bargaining was 'ineffective' (Donovan, 1968). The existence of this dual system, and in particular the informality, autonomy and fragmentation displayed by the workplace activity, was blamed not only for the increased number of strikes (see Chapter 10), well over 90 per cent of which were 'unofficial' (Durcan *et al.*, 1983:109–10), but also the relative decline in productivity and increase in wage drift (that is, earnings substantially exceeding nationally negotiated base rates). The significance of local bargaining on earnings levels by the late 1960s is illustrated by Cliff (1970:39). For example, while the nationally agreed standard rate for engineering fitters in 1968 was under £13 per week, in practice average earnings for fitters at that time, excluding overtime but including local agreements, was almost £23 per week, more than 75 per cent higher than the national minimum rate (see also Donovan, 1968:9).

Essentially it was the *form* of collective bargaining in the UK that was identified as the problem. Collective agreements were basically 'gentlemen's agreements', and as such were not legally enforceable. This is in stark contrast to other countries such as the United States where there is a substantive agreement on all matters currently subject to joint regulation, the agreement runs for a fixed term, and is legally enforceable. During the period of the contract there is a procedure in operation to settle disputes arising over the interpretation of the agreement, but disputes outside the agreement must await termination of the contract itself, when amendments or extensions may be negotiated. Industrial action is only permitted at the end of the contract as a means of reaching a new agreement. Clegg (1979a:116–17) classifies this as the 'statute law' model of collective bargaining, which he contrasts with the 'common law' model that is more reflective of (some areas of) UK industry. Under this model there is again a disputes procedure, but *any* dispute can be referred to the procedure. In other words no distinction is drawn between disputes of right under the existing agreement, and disputes of interest concerning the terms of a new agreement. Industrial action is allowed whenever a procedure has failed to resolve a dispute. Substantive issues can be regulated by as many agreements as the parties choose to make (rather than a single 'contract book' agreement as in the United States).

Clegg (ibid:117) suggests that the common law model fits the public sector reasonably well, but points out that in the private sector in particular, negotiation and administration associated with collective bargaining is often more notable by its absence. Moreover in some key areas, such as disciplinary codes and redundancy arrangements, there is often no direct trade union involvement, while formal agreements are often rare. More characteristic are *ad hoc* arrangements, custom and practice and unwritten *status quo* agreements. This 'primitive' or 'basic' model of collective bargaining, as Clegg (ibid:123) labels it, is underpinned by a tacit agreement to disagree and an acceptance that there are areas where joint regulation is unwelcome. Both parties have the right to make rules and take industrial action to impose them on the other side, although agreed rules are made wherever possible to avoid anarchy and disruption. Under such arrangements the action/reaction of one party will be shaped by expectations about the other party's likely response, leading to what Walton and McKersie (1965) describe as 'attitudinal structuring' and a continuous state of flux in employer–employee relations.

By the end of the 1960s both major political parties favoured legal reform of industrial relations via the adoption of something akin to the statute law model. For Donovan (1968), however, the solution to the shortcomings of the dual system lay in the extension and formalisation of local bargaining arrangements around more comprehensive agreements, drawn up and administered by an enhanced industrial relations management function. In other words the *form* of collective bargaining should be changed and its *scope* extended. Thus formal bargaining at the plant or company level was envisaged as expanding beyond its traditional subject areas to encapsulate a wide range of job control issues, such as manning levels, demarcation and work rates, which had hitherto been determined by 'custom and practice'. In addition, payment by results (PBR) should be replaced by measured day work (MDW) or other payment schemes to reduce wage drift, the introduction of job evaluation would reduce the problems of fragmented bargaining and comparability claims, and new dispute procedures would help to reduce strikes. Underlying these recommendations was the criticism that negotiations had traditionally been 'a one-sided affair' (Donovan, 1968:85) with employers failing even to secure concessions on working practices in return for wage increases. Under the expanded version of collective bargaining, however, wage rises would be *exchanged* for agreements on job control issues.

An influential model informing these recommendations, and much quoted in the Donovan Report itself, was the productivity agreement reached earlier at Esso's Fawley refinery (Flanders, 1964). In this highly detailed, book-length agreement, Esso management sought to regain control over labour costs and secure productivity improvements by entering into an agreement with local trade unions, which exchanged a (substantial) pay increase for detailed changes in working arrangements involving, among other things, reduced overtime, greater job flexibility and a simplification of the pay structure. For members of the Royal Commission and others, Esso's 'Blue Book' agreement, and productivity bargaining more generally, became a model of how collective bargaining might be better organised.

By the end of the 1960s, initial enthusiasm for productivity agreements was waning, not least because most failed to deliver significant increases in productivity, due in part to many being used more as a way to by-pass the incomes policies in operation. However, workplace bargaining continued to develop in importance during the 1970s, with shop steward organisation spreading among non-manual groups and beyond manufacturing into public service settings such as local authorities (Nicholson *et al.*, 1980). In the decade after the Donovan Report some formalisation of local bargaining did occur (see for example Marsh, 1982), partly as management responded to growing shop steward organisation and an increased number of strikes (see Turner *et al.*, 1977). But on the shopfloor, control over working practices by individual work groups if anything increased, although the extent to which this hindered managerial control has been hotly debated (see for example Hyman and Elger, 1981; and Kilpatrick and Lawson, 1980). The growing influence of shopfloor groups may in part have been due to employers' lack of investment in newer technologies at that time, which allowed work groups to retain and reinforce the informal rules devised around older, non-automated equipment (see for example Belanger, 1987). More generally, it must be acknowledged that the managerially led reform of collective bargaining proposed by Donovan not only discounted trade union resistance, but assumed that the 'formalisation of the informal' was in the best interests of *both* parties. As Ogden (1981, 1982) and others have demonstrated, this was simply not the case. As a result,

> Even though trade unions may not positively challenge managerially determined arrangements regarding the levels at which bargaining takes place, trade union power acts as a significant constraint on what choices management may make. Consequently, decisions about bargaining structure may represent defensive responses by management as well as offensive initiative (Ogden, 1982:182).

Of equal importance, however, were the shortcomings of UK management. Under the Donovan proposals the onus was placed upon management to implement change, albeit by consent and through the process of joint regulation. The prescription, as Ogden (1981:31) notes, was that 'if management accepted their responsibility, embraced the opportunities collective bargaining offered, and took advantage of the techniques available such as job evaluation . . . they could regain control where they had lost it and improve efficiency and productivity'. But management failed to carry through the Donovan programme for at least three reasons (in addition to the problems of union or work group opposition). First, managers valued the informality and flexibility of the existing system, such that while there were considerable changes in the nature and conduct of bargaining over *market* relations, there was little change as far as *managerial* relations were concerned (Sisson and Brown, 1983:137). Thus by the end of the 1970s the UK had developed a dual structure of pay bargaining, with multi-employer, industry-wide agreements still prevalent in industries with a large number of small firms, relatively low capital requirements and ease of entry, while elsewhere there was a move towards a formal, single-employer pay bargaining system (ibid:147–8). As for managerial relations, however, the scope of collective bargaining 'appears as hazy as it ever was. It is massively variable from industry to industry and from workplace to workplace, heavily dependent upon the form of management controls and the relative power of the protagonists' (ibid:149–50).

The second factor accounting for the failure of reform was the inability of many managers to carry through the Donovan proposals. Many had neither the capacity nor the expertise to exercise sufficient (formal) control over industrial relations at the plant or company level (Ogden, 1981:39, 1982:181). As Michael Edwardes, former Chairman of British Leyland (now Rover) makes clear in his autobiography *Back From the Brink*, ten years of vacillation by plant management in employee relations had left them with little credibility or authority (1983:78). But as Nichols (1986:165–6) illustrates, this was not so much a case of workers gaining control as of managers losing it. When combined with the failure of many firms to organise productive activity effectively, this undermined workers' respect for management and led to a deterioration in employee relations (see Chapter 4 above; and Batstone, 1986:41).

Finally, in following Allan Flanders' famous dictum that management should 'regain control by sharing it', Donovan not only assumed that management were prepared to share control, but that they would be willing to change their attitude towards trade unions in general and shop stewards in particular. As Ogden (1981:36) notes, however, 'the idea of giving them [shop stewards] more by sharing power was complete anathema to them [management]'. Despite Fox's (1966) critique, most managers still hold a unitarist perspective on employee relations (Poole *et al.*, 1981; and Poole and Mansfield, 1993). Not surprisingly, 'The effort to "educate" management of the need for change in attitudes – from unitary to pluralist frames of reference, from management by prerogatives to joint regulation – deemed essential in the programme of reform has generally met, with some exceptions, little success' (Ogden, 1981:37). In short, management did not seek to share power, but to restore their prerogative.

Thus by the end of the 1970s there was still a very complex and varied pattern of collective bargaining in the UK, in terms of each of the various dimensions identified (level, form, scope, depth and so on). According to Hugh Clegg, draftsman of the most influential chapter in the Donovan Report, that on collective bargaining

> the true disciples of the Royal Commission have been those managers of British companies who have carried through a reconstruction of their industrial relations at workplace level along much the same lines as the Commission's report had recommended, with considerable increases in productivity and a substantial decline in strike activity (1990:6).

But the more widely accepted view, and certainly that of the incoming Thatcher government, was that the Donovan prescription had failed, certainly in its intentions to deliver a higher rate of productivity growth that would reverse the relative economic decline of the UK economy (for an exposition of this view see Metcalf, 1989). Not surprisingly, then, the 1980s was to witness more dramatic change, as the experience of British Steel and many other organisations clearly illustrates.

Decentralised bargaining

The 1980s and early 1990s witnessed a number of developments in the pattern of collective bargaining, several of them interrelated. Two aspects of structural change were most prominent: first, a further decline in the prominence of national, multi-employer agreements, coupled with a corresponding rise in single-employer bargaining; and second, a tendency within larger companies for bargaining activity to be devolved to the level of individual divisions, units, establishments and/or profit centres. In some respects this latter development represented a *reassertion* of locally based bargaining relations. Indeed the tendency for some authors to discuss this latter development simply in terms of a 'decentralisation' of bargaining activity is misleading given the prior development in several industries of highly decentralised workplace and workshop bargaining arrangements. In positioning collective bargaining more clearly at the establishment level, what the more recent developments simultaneously involved was decentralisation of bargaining activity from the corporate level and an attempt to diminish the role of informal shopfloor bargaining by shifting the focus of local joint regulation from the individual section and department up to more formal activity at establishment level. Yet while important distinctions exist between the conduct of bargaining relations in the 1990s and the 1960s, as we discuss below, it is equally important to identify the various underlying continuities that are also evident, despite developments in forms and terminology.

The continued move away from multi-employer to single-employer bargaining both in manufacturing and some service activity is now well documented (Millward *et al.*, 1992:219), though the particular reasons behind the apparent acceleration in this trend (and why it has not occurred in all industries) are somewhat less clear. In general, changes have been driven by product markets rather than labour markets, reflecting the fact that: 'The overwhelming desire by managers has been to get employees to work harder and more efficiently in return for pay increases. . . . Decentralized bargaining has allowed bargaining over market relations to be linked to bargaining over managerial relations' (Jackson *et al.*, 1993:161–2).

Thus the major surveys of industrial relations activity conducted in the mid 1980s (CBI, 1988; Marginson *et al.*, 1988; and Millward and Stevens, 1986) point to the declining importance of multi-employer agreements in pay determination in both manufacturing and services, and the growing tendency for pay to be determined at a single level rather than national industry settlements supplemented by local agreements (Brown, 1993:194–5). Summarising the information collected in the second Workplace Industrial Relations Survey (conducted in 1984), Brown and Walsh (1991:48) note that by that date multi-employer bargaining was the principal means of fixing pay for only about one fifth of employees in the private sector. The shift away from multi-employer bargaining continued in the latter half of the 1980s and the 1990s, (Gregg and Yates, 1991; and Millward *et al.*, 1992). Brown and Walsh (1991:49), for example, note that at least sixteen major national bargaining groups were terminated during the latter part of the 1980s, covering more than one million employees in industries such as banking, shipping, television, roadstone quarrying, cement, airports, food retailing and newspapers. The most significant of these terminations was the withdrawal from collective bargaining by the Engineering Employers' Federation (EEF) in 1989 during a protracted dispute with the Confederation of Shipbuilding and Engineering Unions

(CSEU) over a shorter working week. The EEF had already become less important as a bargaining agent, not least due to the tensions arising from its seeking to represent both very large companies, such as British Aerospace, and hundreds of small engineering concerns. The timing of its formal withdrawal from collective bargaining, however, was prompted by the CSEU's strategy of pursuing selective strike action in a small number of companies in order to secure settlements at 'key' sites, thereby undermining the official EEF's final offer and establishing precedent agreements that the CSEU anticipated would 'cascade' down to other companies (see Blyton, 1992a; and Pickard, 1990).

Elsewhere, one outcome of the abolition of the National Dock Labour Scheme (discussed in Chapter 6) was that the National Association of Port Employers wound itself up at the end of 1989, so that there was no longer a national employer body for the T&GWU to negotiate with (the T&GWU wanted a comprehensive national agreement to replace the statutory Dock Labour Scheme). Local (port and company based) agreements had already assumed greater prominence during the 1980s (Finney, 1990:12; and Turnbull *et al.*, 1992:106), but many of the major operators took further steps to subdivide their port operations into separate companies or divisions, each with its own distinct set of terms and conditions (Turnbull and Weston, 1993c:185–6). Associated British Ports, the former nationalised ports group and the industry's biggest operator, went a stage further, derecognising trade unions for collective bargaining purposes and placing all its employees on individual contracts. The extension of these arrangements to manual workers following the abolition of the Scheme in 1989 represented the culmination of a process started in 1988–9 among management grades (Turnbull *et al.*, 1992:183).

A more widespread decline in the importance of employers' associations was evident by the late 1980s. Historically, the advantage to employers of forming an association to deal with trade unions was not only to economise on the costs of collective bargaining, but more importantly to take labour costs out of competition (by all employers in the industry paying basically the same rate) and to lessen the impact of trade unionism at the workplace level, thereby preserving managerial prerogative (Sisson, 1983:132). However, just as the number of trade unions declined in the postwar period, with greater concentration in fewer, larger organisations, a similar process occurred among employers' associations. The membership of employers' associations held up very well, despite the declining number of associations, largely because the functions of such associations extended far beyond the negotiation of pay and conditions of work and included the operation of disputes procedures, as well as advisory and consultancy services on issues such as incomes policies and labour law. In the early 1980s, membership of employers' associations was maintained largely because of these non-bargaining functions, but by 1990 membership had fallen by a half (Millward *et al.*, 1992:45–6). In part this may reflect the increasing complexity of employment law, and employers increasingly turning to lawyers rather than employers' associations for advice (ibid:47–8).

This overall trend away from national industry agreements negotiated by employers' associations should not, however, be allowed to mask the continued importance of national bargaining in certain contexts. In some industries multi-employer bargaining arrangements remained important. Marginson *et al.* (1988:141), for example, found that multi-employer bargaining was the principal means of pay determination in the textiles, clothing and footwear sector; while industry-wide agreements also remained prominent in the construction sector. As Sisson (1987) noted, where the proportion of employers in an industry are small and competition between firms intense, employers are more likely to support a common coordination of pay determination (see also Booth, 1989; and Deaton and Beaumont, 1980). In relative terms, multi-employer bargaining was in fact still the dominant form of collective bargaining for the economy as a whole in 1990, as Table 7.2 illustrates, although the future picture of national multi-employer bargaining in the private sector at present appears to be one of terminal decline as more firms move collective bargaining to within the firm.

In the public sector, national bargaining arrangements remain the cornerstone of pay settlements (Bach and Winchester, 1994), though changes in the determination of pay and conditions are increasingly evident. In his analysis of industrial relations in local authorities, for example, Kessler (1991) points out that by the late 1980s, while only a dozen or so local authorities in the UK had withdrawn from national machinery altogether, it had become much more common (in around half of local authorities, according to one survey

TABLE 7.2 **The bargaining basis for pay increases, 1980–90 (percentage of establishments, all sectors)**

| | *Manual employees* | | | *Non-manual employees* | | |
	1980	*1984*	*1990*	*1980*	*1984*	*1990*
Multi-employer	32	40	26	29	36	24
Single employer (multi-plant)	12	13	13	11	13	15
Plant/establishment	9	7	6	4	4	3
Other	1	1	2	2	1	1
No collective bargaining	44	38	52	53	46	57

Note: columns may not sum to 100 due to rounding.
Source: Millward *et al.* (1992:219).

quoted by Kessler) for national conditions to be modified by local variations (see also Beadle, 1995:138, on pay devolution in the civil service). Pressure to introduce local variations stemmed in different cases from employers and/or unions in response to local financial and labour market circumstances. Similar pressure to increase the significance of local agreements also became evident in parts of the civil service with the advent of executive agencies (HMSO, for example, prior to privatisation in 1996, had introduced local bargaining) (see Chapter 6), and in the National Health Service with the advent of trust hospitals, greater financial decentralisation and other health service reforms (Bach and Winchester, 1994; and Seifert, 1992). Overall it is likely that national bargaining arrangements in the public sector will come under further pressure, with many settlements increasingly elaborated by local agreements in much the same way as former national agreements in engineering and elsewhere were supplemented: a pattern that in engineering, for example, acted to undermine the national agreements and contributed to their demise. The demise of many national agreements in the public sector, of course, was occasioned by privatisation. The sale of the ten regional water authorities in England and Wales in 1989, for example, spelled the end of national bargaining, although company-level bargaining had been on the agenda for much of the 1980s and Thames Water actually issued twelve months' notice of its withdrawal from national agreements in December 1987 (see Ogden, 1993, 1994). The more recent sale of British Rail put paid to national bargaining on the railways.

Related to the growth of single-employer bargaining is the question of where, within individual companies, collective bargaining is located. Much of the discussion of this question (see, for example, Marginson *et al.*, 1988; and Purcell 1991) has centred on the extent to which large organisations are positioning their collective bargaining arrangements to correspond with the decentralisation of financial accountability to individual profit centres. The majority of large UK organisations (around four in five) operate with some form of multidivisional structure (also termed 'M-form') rather than as loose holding companies ('H-form'), or with a non-divisionalised, functionally organised, highly centralised structure (Hill and Pickering, 1986). In multidivisional firms a common pattern is for strategic management to be separated from operating management. Top management at the apex of the organisation holds exclusive responsibility for strategy formulation and determining the budgets of individual operating divisions and units. Operational decisions, on the other hand, are taken by managers in the different operating divisions; these managers are responsible for the day-to-day running of the different businesses, though the financial performance of these designated 'profit centres' is closely scrutinised by corporate management and used as the basis for future planning and capital allocation.

As operating divisions and units are made increasingly accountable for their financial performance, this can stimulate a demand for greater control over labour costs, not least by relocating collective bargaining activity within the individual profit centre, thereby giving managers, among other things, greater scope to respond to local labour market conditions. Purcell (1991; see also Purcell, 1989; and Purcell and Ahlstrand, 1989) has argued that these changes in business strategy, and particularly the devolution of financial accountability to smaller profit centres, has been the main reason for decentralisation of bargaining arrangements within companies away from the corporate level and down to division or establishment levels. He cites examples such as British Airports Authority, Cadbury, Lucas, Metal Box, Racal, United Biscuits, Pilkington's and Massey Ferguson-Perkins Engines, where corporate bargaining has been replaced by more decentralised arrangements (Purcell, 1991:37). British Steel is a further example of this repositioning of bargaining activity to reflect greater local accountability for performance, costs and profit. Survey evidence from the 1980s supports the general picture of a preference, in some industries at least, for bargaining to be located away from the corporate level. Marginson and his colleagues, for example, found that among those companies that negotiated with trade unions over pay (almost nine out of ten in their sample of large companies), the majority relied on bargaining at single or joint establishment level, rather than at company or industry level (Marginson *et al.*, 1988:141). This pattern was particularly evident in the engineering and food, drink and tobacco sectors. On the other hand industry bargaining was mainly concentrated in clothing and textiles, while corporate bargaining was most evident in financial services.

As observed above, while in many cases this process has been generally described in terms of decentralisation of bargaining from multi-employer and corporate levels down to operating divisions and establishments, in practice such a process may also simultaneously entail an important centralisation of bargaining relations up from individual sections, workshops and departments to the establishment or divisional level. Full devolution to profit centres, whilst it might focus managers' attention more keenly on the cost implications of pay bargaining, might conversely establish (more costly) local precedents that are then replicated elsewhere. As a result, 'To put it bluntly, much of the decentralization that has taken place is an "illusion". Things may "happen" at local level, but they are not "decided" there' (Storey and Sisson, 1993:212; see also Sisson and Marginson, 1995:105–6). As management retain greater (centralised) control of decentralised bargaining, the resulting bargaining activity at the establishment level is generally of a more formal nature than that criticised by the Donovan Commission in the 1960s.

Our steel industry case is an example of this simultaneous decentralisation and centralisation of bargaining around plant and business levels. On the one hand decentralisation is clearly evident: from national company-wide negotiations down to the four businesses, as well as to the plant level lump sum bonus (LSB) negotiations. However the LSB arrangements were introduced in combination with important 'moratorium' clauses. Essentially these clauses circumscribed individual shop stewards' scope to bargain over the details of new work systems, and in particular they severely restricted local unions from making claims for regradings based on changes made to the nature of workers' jobs. In practice this has meant that the existence of the multi-union LSB committee at works level, coupled with the moratorium on regrading and related issues, has effectively removed much of the bargaining opportunity at sub-establishment level and thereby reduced the bargaining role of the departmental shop stewards. The outcome in steel has been that employee relations are principally located at works level, with a greater degree of formalisation, structural simplification (involving a joint union committee, rather than separate negotiations with the various unions) and the diminution of bargaining activity at sub-works level. To a greater or lesser degree, the evidence indicates a similar pattern in a growing number of organisations.

Effects of changes in bargaining structure

Tracking and accounting for the changes in bargaining levels reveals several important issues that are relevant to the understanding of employee relations. In the recent period, for example, the extent to which shifts in the focus of collective bargaining activity have mirrored changes in financial accountability reinforces the need to look beyond employee relations itself to understand how aspects of those relations are structured and function. In the case of recent changes in the structure of collective bargaining, these appear to have been driven to an important degree by changes in organisational structure. Yet in itself, identifying changes in structure is only of limited utility in understanding the dynamics of employee relations. More significant is the question of what impact such changes have on the issues and outcomes of those relations. Are the processes and outcomes significantly different depending on what level collective bargaining is primarily focused? Examining these issues also begs the question of how much influence trade unions exert in their bargaining relations with employers.

Before looking at the possible impact that changes in bargaining levels have on issues and outcomes, however, a word of caution is needed. Changes in bargaining levels in the UK have not occurred in a vacuum. On the contrary, the last twenty years or so have witnessed substantial changes in the context of those relations. We have drawn attention to many of these in earlier chapters: changes in the nature of economic activity, and in the ownership, structure and functioning of work organisations; developments in the composition of the labour force and the coverage and influence of collective organisations representing the labour force; and shifts in the legal context of employee relations and the broader political climate. With so many factors changing in the same period, obtaining a precise measure of the impact of any single factor is impossible: not only are several variables in a state of flux at any one time, but the overall impact of many of these variables is heightened by their interaction with one another. This is evident in relation to the decentralisation in bargaining levels, for example. The fact that these developments have been taking place against a background of weakened union influence – indeed in some cases may have been taking place precisely because of this weakened unionism – indicates that any evaluation of structural changes must also take account of other coterminous developments.

Yet despite these problems of assigning weights of significance to particular factors and trends, the British Steel case, like many others, points to one overriding effect of decentralisation in the current context: the ability of management to focus collective relations more sharply on plant-specific and performance-related issues. In the steel industry, the introduction of business-level collective bargaining, coupled with the greater role vested in plant-based employee relations helped establish a basis for tying collective bargaining much more closely to the fortunes of the business in general, and the achievement of specific performance targets and labour efficiencies in particular. One LSB agreement, for example, included an appendix of over ninety job-related items, many specifying greater flexibility, particularly in the form of broader job boundaries (Blyton *et al.*, 1993). More generally, the combination of more formal plant-based collective bargaining and weakened trade unionism has provided the context for management to shift the focus of employee relations more squarely on to labour utilisation and production issues. The localised nature of the joint machinery allows for a more detailed discussion on such issues as working patterns, manning levels, the content of individual jobs and the use of subcontract labour. The determinants of the wage–effort bargain have therefore shifted in line with changes in the overall structure of collective bargaining, reflecting to a far greater extent the 'needs' of the organisation. This is evident with respect to both pay determination and flexibility.

With the decline of multi-employer bargaining and the decentralisation of pay bargaining to the company, division, plant or profit centre level, the process of wage determination is now largely, and increasingly, shaped by influences that are *specific* to the firm. Gregg and Yates (1991:372) – in a survey of 558 UK companies, asked to compare the period 1985–9 with the earlier period of 1980–4 – found that increased importance was being attached to the financial performance of the company, and they suggested that such pressure was increasingly being transmitted to the workforce. Furthermore, 'the notion of a single "going rate", a prevailing percentage increase representing a target for employee wage demands, has been replaced by a greater diversity of company wage decision making' (Ingram, 1991b:98). Data from the CBI's annual survey of around 1000 to 1400 manufacturing establishments over the period since 1979 confirms the importance of company-specific circumstances, with pay rises awarded increasingly on the basis of the individual company's 'ability to pay' (ibid:104). Clearly such a policy is only possible, or at least advisable, in the absence of strong trade union organisation, which might otherwise press for the most favourable pay awards to be 'standardised' across all other employers in the industry. In Gregg and Yates' (1991:372) survey, only 14 per cent of employers indicated that a specific external settlement was an important determinant of the 1990 pay increase. As with many other changes in employee relations, however, this particular trend should not be overstated. In fact almost as many respondents (79 per cent) mentioned the importance of 'going rates in industry' as mentioned 'financial position of the company' (88 per cent) in the Gregg and Yates survey (ibid), while a substantial number of respondents to the CBI surveys (around 40 per cent) continued to cite external comparability as a significant pressure on wage settlements (Ingram, 1991b:102). Not surprisingly, detailed company-based research casts doubt as to whether decentralised bargaining necessarily increases the responsiveness of pay to business performance (Walsh, 1993:416–17).

The development of flexibility agreements has also been attuned to the 'needs' of the organisation. Marsden and Thompson's (1990) study, for example, shows a strong tendency for flexibility agreements to be negotiated at the local level. Of the 116 private sector agreements studied, ninety-one (that is, almost four out of five) were negotiated at the single establishment level, compared to nineteen at the single employer/multi-establishment level and six at industry level. The main emphasis in the agreements related to job demarcation and labour deployment within the plant. The same study reinforces the view of establishment bargaining becoming more formalised and less *ad hoc* than much of the earlier localised bargaining. 'Many agreements', conclude Marsden and Thompson (1990:91), 'sought a more systematic approach to changing working practices than had been adopted previously.' Like attempts at productivity bargaining before them, flexibility agreements have illustrated the possibility for management to use collective bargaining as a means to secure greater control over labour deployment and utilisation (see also Ingram, 1991a; and Dunn and Wright, 1994).

Another example of plant bargaining being used to bring labour efficiency to the fore are settlements over the shorter working week in the engineering industry. A common feature of many of the agreements reached in the late 1980s and early 1990s was the way the plant agreements tied the reduction in working time to changes in working arrangements designed to increase the utilisation of that time: for example, by the introduction of 'bell-to-bell' working, the reduction or elimination of informal breaks and time allowances, the introduction of new shift-work patterns and the staggering of meal-breaks to ensure continuity of production (Blyton, 1992a, 1992b; and Richardson and Rubin, 1992).

In all these examples a related effect of the decentralisation of employee relations is the potential it provides management to define issues as essentially *local* in character and seek to handle them internally, rather than involving full-time union officials. As such it clearly complements the legal reforms discussed in Chapter 6, which Wedderburn (1989) describes as a process of 'enterprise confinement'. For many national unions this is understandably perceived as a 'divide and rule' policy towards the trade unions, designed to marginalise the national union organisation and prevent a coordinated, collective response. In our steel case the classic example of this was the issue of mass redundancies in the industry. By tying specific manpower reductions at particular plants into the local bargaining machinery and making the (comparatively large) severance terms dependent on local agreements on the job cuts, any mounting of a broader union campaign against the redundancies was undermined (for a discussion of redundancies in the 1980s and 1990s see Turnbull, 1988a; and Turnbull and Wass, 1997). Thus decentralising the principal focus of employee relations, particularly in the context of diminished trade union power, can act not only to increase management's ability to pursue particular issues within the employee relations machinery, but also to exclude others. Just as a generation ago productivity agreements underlined the necessity of a localised collective bargaining relationship to agree changes in the detail of working practices, so too in recent years the decline of multi-employer bargaining and the increased location of employee relations within profit centre divisions or establishments has further underlined the way bargaining level can influence both content and conduct of those relations. But what of the pattern of collective bargaining relations more generally, and the particular question of what aspects of the employment relationship are subject to collective bargaining? What about the *scope* of collective bargaining, and the degree of influence that trade unions exert in their relations with management? It is to these questions that we now turn.

Union influence in collective bargaining

In terms of formal relations with management, both surveys and case studies have been employed to examine the patterns of, and changes in, union involvement and influence over decision making. Surveys however, have inevitably been limited in their sensitivity to such intangible variables as 'the exercise of influence': managers may report that they no longer negotiate with union representatives over various issues, but informal control might persist. For example even the abolition of the National Dock Labour Scheme, the rout of the T&GWU in the 1989 national dock strike and the end of all national and in many cases port level negotiations failed to eradicate worker control of the production process in several ports (Turnbull, 1991b; and Saundry and Turnbull, 1996). Nevertheless large-scale surveys do provide some idea of the breadth and depth of union involvement and the pattern of aggregate change over time. They indicate too the unevenness of change and the consequent dangers of over-generalising in this area. For example in the early years of the 1980s there was an overall increase in the proportion of workplaces where pay rates were determined by collective bargaining, though this aggregate figure masked certain differences between sectors. In contrast the same study indicates a sharp decline in the extent to which management negotiated over non-pay issues (such as physical working conditions, redeployment and redundancies) during the same period, especially at the workplace level, although again this was more evident in some sectors than others (Millward and Stevens, 1986:248). Contrary to expectations, this decline did *not* continue in the latter half of the 1980s. In fact more establishments reported that *new* issues were being added to the bargaining agenda than reported that issues were no longer subject to negotiation (Millward *et al.*, 1992:253–5; see also Chapter 5 above).

A somewhat different picture emerges, however, from Marginson *et al.*'s study of large organisations in the first half of the 1980s. For example, in terms of the range of negotiated issues, more than three quarters of managers identified little or no change. Of the minority who did perceive a change, more than four fifths identified the union's role to have increased rather than decreased (Marginson *et al.*, 1988:139). A similar picture emerges from the responses of divisional and establishment managers. As the authors conclude, at the very least the pattern of response 'helps to dispose of simple arguments to the effect that firms have been directly attacking union organizations' (ibid:139–40). Even when recognition did decline in the latter half of the 1980s, this was largely due to the decline of more 'traditional' workplaces: 'the structures of collective bargaining remained in many respects similar in character to those at the start of the 1980s, but they were present in fewer workplaces and affected fewer employees' (Millward *et al.*, 1992:352).

There is some indication, however, that survey methods fail to pick up more subtle changes in trade union influence. For example in a more detailed case-study approach Morris and Wood (1991) found greater evidence of reduction in the trade unions' bargaining role during the 1980s, while in a longitudinal case study conducted over a ten-year period Kinnie (1992) identified a significant reduction in trade union influence, with various issues becoming increasingly subject to consultation with trade unions rather than joint regulation. This accords with our own research in a variety of work contexts, including steel, docks, engineering, electronics, airlines and the automotive industry over the past fifteen years: unions maintain a bargaining role on certain issues but this is being increasingly undermined by management handling work-related changes outside the bargaining framework. The growth of joint consultation committees is often cited in this context as a threat to union influence, but yet again there is no simple or straightforward correlation between either the presence or growth of joint consultation and declining trade union influence. While these and related developments are discussed in more detail in Chapter 8, it is worthwhile noting at this juncture that collective bargaining and joint consultation are not always competing structures (Marchington, 1989:391–2); that the growth of such committees may be somewhat illusory due to an equally high though less visible death rate (MacInnes, 1985:106); and that the results from WIRS 1990 show a *fall* in the proportion of workplaces with joint consultation committees (although the decline was due to the changing composition of workplaces rather than a tendency to abandon such committees) (Millward *et al.*, 1992:180).

Of more significance might be other forms of employee involvement, such as quality circles and team briefings (also discussed in Chapter 8), and new management policies such as human resource management (HRM). Storey's (1992) extensive case-study analysis of firms introducing HRM-style techniques (such as increased use of direct communication and task-related participation groups) attests to trade unions, in some contexts at least, becoming increasingly marginalised (see also, Martinez Lucio and Weston, 1992). Typically, managers in the organisations studied were found to be developing new HRM initiatives alongside traditional collective bargaining machinery. While Storey identified little change in the periodic pay bargaining structure, the overall result of the parallel developments in other employee-related initiatives was seen 'to downplay the status and significance of trade unions and industrial relations' (Storey, 1992:258). Indeed the author's impression in these cases was that 'the general tendency was to maintain the previous machinery in a ticking-over mode while experimenting rather more enthusiastically with policies and approaches which signalled a departure towards new priorities' (ibid:257; see also Sisson, 1993). Despite this, the tensions and contradictions inherent in the HRM approach may yet serve to undermine, rather than augment, management control of employee relations (see the contributions to Blyton and Turnbull, 1992).

A further challenge to union organisation is the rise of single-table bargaining, where management sit down with all the unions recognised by the company to conduct annual negotiations, rather than negotiate with each union separately. Whereas only thirty-five cases of single-table bargaining were reported in the 1980s, covering just 29 000 employees, between 1990 and 1994 alone there were eighty-five reported cases covering an estimated 380 000 workers (Gall, 1994:62–3). British Steel is one of the more prominent examples of single-table bargaining, along with Rover Cars and Customs & Excise. In general, management aim to reduce the time spent negotiating with many different unions, seek to preclude 'leap-frogging' pay claims, ensure that payment for different jobs reflect equity and equal value considerations, and facilitate the introduction of new technology, more flexible working arrangements, performance-related pay, and single status (the harmonisation of terms and conditions of employment for blue-collar and white-collar staff) (ibid:66–7). Although single-table bargaining has been encouraged by the TUC, both to encourage inter-union cooperation and to prevent the kind of divisive 'beauty contests' in which unions found themselves embroiled in the 1980s (see Blyton and Turnbull, 1994:96–103), in many cases single-table bargaining has been driven by management attempts to cut costs, and thereby terms and conditions of employment, and to dictate both the structure of employee representation and the agenda of collective bargaining.

Thus looking across the quantitative and qualitative studies as a whole, the picture is a far from simple one. On the one hand, decentralising collective bargaining has enabled management to link bargaining to work-related issues such as performance levels, workforce flexibility and manning levels, although the extent to which they were able to establish a systematic link, such that pay genuinely reflects organisational performance, is more questionable (Walsh, 1993). In terms of pay determination, the general indication is that the extent to which pay was determined by collective bargaining remained broadly unchanged in the early 1980s, and in some areas was extended, but declined significantly in the late 1980s and early 1990s. In terms of non-pay issues, however, the picture (based on WIRS) is one of declining union influence between 1980 and 1984 (though the decline appears to have been uneven and variable from sector to sector), followed by the stabilisation of such bargaining during the latter half of the decade. Evidence from a survey of large companies conducted in 1992, in contrast, suggests a further contraction of the range of issues subject to negotiation (Marginson *et al.*, 1993). Case-study evidence indicates an equally complex picture. For example, many studies point to the marginalisation of trade unions in non-pay issues and management pursuing changes to work and employee relations without subjecting them to joint regulation. Overall, then, as noted in other areas of employee relations, union influence in bargaining relations displays elements of both continuity and change: continued union presence and therefore the potential for collective influence, but one that in some contexts has become restricted to a narrower range of issues in general and to an increased focus on production and workforce efficiency issues in particular.

Conclusion

Historically, collective bargaining has served management well, and it is therefore not surprising that there has been no concerted rush in recent years to dismantle it. It has provided a means not only for institutionalising conflict, but also for regulating key aspects of the employment relationship. As a result, bargaining remains the cornerstone of employee relations in many establishments and companies. The foregoing discussion has shown that while changes have been occurring in the structure of bargaining, and while union influence appears to have diminished in many bargaining arenas, both management and unions have sought to retain it as a mechanism for joint regulation.

At the same time collective bargaining is not without its obvious short-comings as a mechanism of employee relations. As regards pay determination, for example, collective bargaining works tolerably well where employee representatives are not only reasonably strong but also have the freedom to exert their influence in the bargaining setting – if necessary by threatening strike action. In a number of contexts, however, for example where employees are located in essential services, the strike weapon is judged by many to be an inappropriate basis of bargaining power. That is, bargaining power based on the union's ability to call a strike is not necessarily the best model for seeking to resolve pay issues of groups such as the police, fire-fighters, nurses and – as we discuss in Chapter 10 – ambulance drivers. What may be appropriate in, say, a private sector car plant should not necessarily be seen as appropriate in every other work context. In terms of poorly organised, low-paid work groups, for example, it may be argued that collective bargaining acts to reproduce and reinforce pay inequalities, with the more powerful, highly unionised groups doing better out of collective bargaining than the less powerful and less well organised. In other areas, such as nursing and teaching, the response has been to set up pay review bodies to replace collective bargaining. This system has considerable merit, though it is also open to abuse by both sides. To work effectively pay review bodies need to be independent and supported by all groups, who consent to abide by agreed review procedures. Otherwise the review's recommendations simply become the starting point for a process of pay determination by other means, rather than its culmination.

There are other situations where collective bargaining is not necessarily the most appropriate form of employee relations arrangement, such as over the introduction of new technology (e.g. Davies, 1986), though given the extent of worker and trade union support for technical change this does not appear to have been a significant constraint on management action – if anything, quite the opposite (see Daniel, 1987:113, 183). Furthermore, as a control mechanism collective bargaining over non-pay issues has proved problematic for management in the face of worker resistance or the absence of a coherent approach on the part of management themselves. Since most UK firms adopt a distinctly *ad hoc*, pragmatic approach to employee relations (see Chapter 4) it is hardly surprising that the coverage, content and form of collective bargaining has changed over time, and more specifically declined in influence during what has been a period of recession, intensified competition and falling trade union membership. Indeed on current trends there is the possibility that, as the number of industries that have traditionally relied on collective bargaining continues to decline, collective bargaining may become still less prominent as a means of regulating both pay and non-pay issues. But to reiterate what has been a persistent theme throughout this chapter, in many contexts collective bargaining is, and remains, an effective *managerial* process. If bargaining activity does continue to decline, it is a concern for the future that no effective alternative has yet been found for bargaining and the traditional system of collective interest representation (Beaumont, 1995; Brown, 1993; Millward, 1994; Millward *et al.*, 1992:350; and Sisson, 1993). Thirty years after the Donovan Report, management may have 'regained control', but in many cases not by sharing it. In the process the protection of employees' rights, the representation of their collective interests and the fair remuneration of their labour have, in many industries and firms, been severely eroded.

CHAPTER 8

Employee involvement and participation

Employee involvement at Nissan

The five-minute meeting

It is 8 a.m. and the start of another shift in the press shop at the Nissan car plant in Sunderland, Tyne and Wear. The supervisor and the twenty men (comprising two teams, each with a team leader) leave the meeting room where they have been chatting and reading newspapers prior to the shift commencing, and go out onto the shopfloor. They congregate in a circle by the presses while the supervisor discusses a problem they had encountered the previous day with some faulty pressings, which had got through as far as the paint shop. The upshot of this discussion is that one of the group is detailed to go down to the paint shop and go through the stack of parts waiting to be painted, in order to find the faulty ones (Popham, 1992).

Nothing very remarkable about all this one might suppose, except in one or two respects. First, it is a scene that is being replicated simultaneously throughout the plant, and one that is repeated at the beginning of each shift. Employees are required to be at their work area no later than the shift start time in order that the first few minutes of the shift can be used to discuss issues such as work schedule changes, work redistribution, process changes, training, social events or the introduction of a new member. The principal subjects of the discussion, however, tend to be quality-related (Wickens, 1985b:19, 1987:85–6). For the former Personnel Director at Nissan, this sort of shift meeting is of central importance to the functioning of the work teams:

217

> In Nissan, if there is one aspect to be singled out as important in team building and commitment it is the five minute meeting at the start of the day . . . its importance in NMUK [Nissan Motor Manufacturing UK Ltd] cannot be overestimated (Wickens, 1987:85).

The former Personnel Director also emphasised the importance of the *routineness* of this activity and its contrast with more formal ways of structuring communication:

> There is no grand concept of 'briefing groups' . . . where everyone once a month waits for the production lines to stop and for the great message to come down 'from upon high' . . . for five minutes before the start of each shift we have groups of people just talking together without any real hassle (Wickens 1985a:7–8).

The Nissan plant was opened by Margaret Thatcher in 1986 and was subsequently described as her 'favourite factory' (*Guardian*, 18 June 1987), following a visit in 1987 when she took the opportunity to castigate the UK's 'moaning Minnies': the Japanese, now firmly established on UK soil, would finally show UK management and workers alike how to run a successful company (see Turnbull, 1988c:18). Employee involvement is a key component of success and forms part of a well-articulated company philosophy which also emphasises teamworking and flexibility as contributors to high-quality output and a highly committed workforce. The role of employee involvement in this is encapsulated in the 'philosophy statement' developed by Nissan managers, which includes the following (extracts from Wickens, 1987:82):

> We seek to delegate and involve staff in discussion and decision-making, particularly in those areas in which they can effectively contribute so that all may participate in the efficient running of NMUK.

> Within the bounds of commercial confidentiality we would like everyone to know what is happening in our company, how we are performing and what we plan.

> We want information and views to flow freely upward, downward and across the company.

The result, according to the company, has been the creation of a 'harmonious and productive working environment' (*Guardian*, 8 September 1987).

Teamwork: involvement or control?

Building commitment begins with recruitment, as the easiest way to get a compliant workforce is to recruit one. At Nissan the most important shopfloor workers are supervisors and team leaders (Smith, 1990:10), and Nissan management worked particularly hard to secure a supervisory team who could successfully carry out the task of eliciting productive and high-quality work from those under them. In response to its advertisement the company received 3500 applications for the first twenty-two supervisor jobs. A similar degree of choice was available to the management for the team leaders and manufacturing staff (as assembly-line workers are termed). One thousand people applied for the initial forty team leader positions, while 11 500 applied for the first 300 manufacturing staff jobs (Wickens, 1987:171). Supervisors play a primary role in the selection of subordinates (ibid:91), which is part of a strategy based on a recognition that 'a return to forms of "personal" and informal control over subordinates is likely to be more flexible and more rapidly enforced by line management (supervisors) compared to systems which largely rely on bureaucratic/procedural forms of control' (Lowe, 1992a:155).

With extensive attitude and aptitude testing to ensure that the most 'suitable' people secured the posts, management had considerable scope to establish a workforce whose outlook was wholly consistent with the company's own philosophy.

> In industry there are lots of people who do not want to be involved . . . all they want to do from 8am to 5pm is to get the job over. There are a lot of people like that who do not want to be flexible, who do not want to move around from one job to another. . . . At Nissan we hope that our selection process will be able to let us have individuals that do not have that attitude (Wickens, 1985a:30).

Once recruited, a process of intensive induction then follows, intended to develop loyal employees with a sense of the company's history and purpose. Work itself is organised around teams (each with about ten employees) which are the foci of employee interaction with team leaders. Team members are encouraged to identify with their teams and take greater responsibility for their work area, including supporting one another, being flexible between jobs, monitoring their own quality and keeping the work area clean and tidy. Employee 'involvement' is further encouraged through *kaizen* (continuous improvement) activities. Within *kaizen* teams and *kaizen* workshops, employees are encouraged to participate in improving the way their own jobs are performed. In other organisations such activity typically takes the form of a suggestion scheme, often with financial rewards associated with ideas that are adopted. At Nissan, however, the notions of involvement and improvement are portrayed as part of the job, rather than as a separate 'suggestion scheme' activity. Thus, in addition to the daily work-area meetings, Nissan encourages *kaizen* teams to seek improvements in quality, productivity, ease of working or the working environment. Oliver and Wilkinson (1992:217) note that 90 per cent of all changes in the body shop are claimed to have been suggested by employees, and in the manufacturing area up to fifty *kaizen* teams may be working at any one time.

To facilitate such teams, the company has provided meeting areas, one for each supervisor, equipped with tables, benches and so on, together with facilities for making tea and coffee. For the company, *kaizen* is central to a strategy that asserts 'managers and supervisors should have as a prime objective the bringing out of new ideas and concepts from their staff' (Wickens, 1987:88). Put another way, *kaizen* activities are the vehicle through which management appropriates employees' mental skills and knowledge of the production process. The rhetoric may be one of 'worker empowerment', 'employee participation' and 'involvement', but the prime objective remains the more efficient production of cars and more effective management control. Employees are charged with greater responsibility, but this does not imply worker control or autonomous teamworking, still less industrial democracy.

The Company Council

Away from the shopfloor, employee involvement at Nissan centres on the Company Council. This Council was established under the terms of the single union agreement signed by Nissan with the AEU (now the AEEU). The Company Council is the sole body at Nissan where representatives of the workforce meet with management. Under its terms of reference, the Company Council is charged with the aim of 'promoting effective communication and harmonious relations between the Company, its employees and the Union'. These terms of reference also state that the Council should be a 'forum in which elected members can discuss with representatives of the Company those matters which directly affect them', and significantly that 'it is recognised that all concerned have a mutual interest in ensuring the prosperity of the Company'. The Council comprises a mixture of elected and nominated members. Ten elected members cover manufacturing staff in the main areas of activity (for example body and press shops, trim lines and assembly, chassis and engine, paint shop, material handling, training centre, and administration), together with maintenance technician and supervisor grades. In addition a number of members (including the chair and secretary) are nominated by management, and include the managing director, the director of personnel and the production director.

The Company Council performs three main functions. First, at quarterly meetings the Council discusses different aspects of the business, including production levels, quality issues, market share, profitability and investment. In these matters it acts as a consultative forum. However, whereas in most other unionised plants it is usual for consultation machinery to be separate from grievance and bargaining arrangements, at Nissan the Company Council performs all of these roles. For in addition to its consultative function, the council has a second function as the final decision-making body in the in-house grievance procedure, and a third as the sole forum for the negotiation of salaries and terms and conditions of employment. These negotiations are held at specially convened meetings of the Company Council and can include the local AEEU full-time official, who ratifies the agreement. Only in what are seen as 'exceptional circumstances', where the Council fails to resolve a pay or conditions issue, is reference made to ACAS for conciliation and, if necessary, pendulum arbitration.

The implications of this structure are far-reaching. It is the Company Council and not the AEEU that acts as the basis of employee representation in determining pay and conditions. The elected members of the Council may be union representatives or union members, but equally – with union density at around only three in ten and with eligibility to stand for election to the Council open to anyone with two years' service – may not be. Moreover, as its terms of reference detail, the Council requires all members – elected and nominated alike – to act in the company's best interest. The key point here is that the union has no formal collective bargaining rights. The Company Council's areas of responsibility act therefore to marginalise the union. According to McFadden and Towler, this structure 'has the effect of portraying the trade union as trouble-makers when they raise valid and legitimate issues with the company' (quoted by Oliver and Wilkinson, 1992:221). Furthermore, for Garrahan and Stewart (1992:69), 'The Company Council delivers participation without power, whilst the union achieves recognition but is marginalised from any participation in procedures'.

This acceptance of a diluted form of recognition is the price the AEEU has been prepared to pay for the opportunity to recruit the Nissan workforce. However the relatively low density of union membership suggests that the pay-off has not been particularly good. Indeed writers such as Garrahan and Stewart (1992) argue that it is precisely this preparedness to compromise its independence that has undermined employees' propensity to join, viewing the union as effectively made powerless by the terms it has agreed with the Nissan management. In effect, what the Company Council structure allows – and notwithstanding the fact that discussions on pay and conditions are held at separate meetings of the Council – is for management to locate all its dealings with the workforce within an essentially *consultative* relationship. Paradoxically this presents something of a dilemma for management: if union organisation and representation is emasculated, and the company's own consultative procedures perceived as a sham, then employee discontent could lead to autonomous shopfloor organisation. Not surprisingly, then, management have actively encouraged employees to join the AEEU. Thus where management draws the line between consultation and negotiation, and the extent to which such activities are complementary or competing processes of regulation, will be key determinants of both management control and employee resistance.

Participation and employee relations

At different points in the development of employee relations, the question of to what extent employees and/or their representatives should take part in decision making has been a recurring issue. The pattern of work group meetings and joint consultation at Nissan is part of the latest wave of interest in forms of employee involvement and participation. Yet while it remains true that examples of different participatory arrangements stretch back a century or more, in unionised workplaces at least, until recent times participation has occupied more of a marginal than a central role within employee relations policies and practices, compared with collective bargaining structures (a notable exception being those companies, discussed in Chapter 4, that have adopted a 'sophisticated modern' approach to employee relations that is characterised by the use of extensive joint consultation aimed at minimising the role of collective bargaining, especially that of a 'distributive' character). A traditional view in the past, exemplified in a much-quoted passage from the Donovan Report (1968:54), has been that, 'properly conducted, collective bargaining is the most effective means of giving workers the right to representation in decisions affecting their working lives, a right which is or should be the prerogative of every worker in a democratic society'.

There are those, however, who maintain that this pattern is now changing as a result of several factors combining to project (diluted forms of) participation, rather than collective bargaining, more centrally into employee management policy and practice. Thus as the coverage of collective bargaining has diminished in recent years (see Chapter 7), non-bargaining forms of management–employee relations have taken on an added significance (Millward *et al.*, 1992:151). At the same time it is arguable that pre-existing obstacles to the effective development of participation remain: not least general management opposition to relinquishing their decision-making prerogative, reinforced by a widespread trade union ambivalence, both towards accepting greater responsibility within organisational decision making, and towards the extension of participatory forms that provide not only very limited influence but also entail the direct involvement of individual employees rather than their trade union representatives.

It is this issue of the contemporary significance of participation or 'involvement' initiatives that gives rise to the core questions of this chapter. To what extent is the current interest in 'employee involvement' significantly different from previous interest in 'workers' participation' and 'industrial democracy'? To what degree do forms of involvement represent any real sharing of decision-making power? What are management's objectives in introducing different forms of involvement? Are there continuing obstacles to the development of effective participation? What is the significance of forms of employee involvement for other methods of management–workforce interaction, notably bargaining relations? More generally, what implications does the current interest in employee involvement have for the broader fashioning of employee relations in coming years?

To address these questions, we must begin first by briefly situating the current developments within a broader conceptual and empirical framework. This entails reviewing the nature of participation, the different forms it can take, the attitude of the different employee relations parties towards participation, and the historical pattern of development of participation prior to the latest wave of interest. This will help clarify the extent to which the recent developments both share similarities with and are distinct from previous periods of interest in participation. Having examined the arguments and evidence we will also be in a better position to assess the depth and robustness of the latest changes. Our overall view is that despite the outwardly convincing language of human resource management, employee involvement, total quality management and so on towards the importance of building commitment through more open styles of decision making, we remain somewhat sceptical that the latest period marks a sea change in the trajectory of participation. Not only is there an unwillingness, as in the past, to tackle issues that have inhibited the development of participation and industrial democracy, but many of the changes of the past decade or so owe more to the attempts of management (and the state) to exert control over labour than they do to involve or empower employees.

The nature of participation

At one level the notion of employee participation is straightforward. For Wall and Lischeron (1977:38), for example, participation refers to 'influence in decision-making exerted through a process of interaction between workers and managers'. As soon as we begin to investigate such a definition, however, complexities begin to appear. Marked variations are possible, for example in the degree or *depth* of participation, the range or *scope* of decisions subject to participation, the *form* that participation structures might take, the organisational *level(s)* at which participation occurs, and the *purpose* and *outcomes* of such activity. In combination these various sources of diversity give rise to a concept and a range of activity that is heterogeneous rather than unified – indeed so heterogeneous that the validity of the concept itself is brought into doubt. Furthermore, conceptual confusion is increased by the many expressions used to denote aspects of the activity – for example 'industrial democracy', 'participation', 'involvement' and 'empowerment' – and the tendency for these to be used interchangeably, despite the very evident gap in the power-sharing implications of what formerly went under the heading 'industrial democracy' and what now travels under the banner of 'employee involvement'.

Depth of participation refers to the degree to which employees or their representatives influence the final decision (Marchington *et al.*, 1992:8). Participatory activity may be seen as forming a continuum rather than as an absolute, with points on the continuum signifying different levels of employee involvement and influence. At one end of the continuum, illustrated in Figure 8.1, the minimum level of involvement is represented by the receipt of information from management, with no active involvement in any decision-making process. Further along the continuum (moving from left to right in Figure 8.1), employees and/or their representatives have the opportunity to exert advisory power, based on joint consultation. Studies of joint consultation indicate that, in practice, various activities take place under the guise of consultation (see for example Blyton 1981; and Marchington, 1989, 1994). In general, however, consultation primarily involves management discussing production and other issues with representatives of the workforce, seeking comments and suggestions, while retaining authority over the final decision-making process.

The main distinction along the continuum lies between consultation and joint decision making, for under the latter, employees (or their representatives) are formally entitled to exert *influence* rather than simply be *involved* in the decision-making process. For some observers, it is only at this point that true participation occurs, with everything to the left of this point representing 'pseudo' or 'phantom' participation (Ramsay, 1980). Finally, at the right-hand edge of the continuum, employees themselves enjoy full control over decisions. Where this exists in traditional enterprises, it is likely to be confined to areas of task arrangement, for example craftsmen controlling the way their craft is practised. In terms of higher levels of decision making, employee control is largely confined to workers' cooperatives, although even here workers may control the immediate labour process but little else (Mellor *et al.*, 1988:81–2; and Turnbull and Weston, 1993a).

Clearly the implications for management of participatory forms from the left-hand side of the continuum (information and consultation) are markedly different from those reflecting the principles of the right-hand side (joint decision making and employee control). This diversity has allowed *all* parties in employee relations – employers, employees, trade unions and the state – to express support for participation, though in practice this has entailed giving

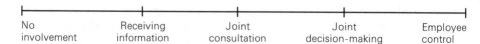

| No involvement | Receiving information | Joint consultation | Joint decision-making | Employee control |

FIGURE 8.1   A continuum of employee participation

support to quite different principles and practices and with distinct – and to a degree, opposing – objectives in mind. As discussed below, the recent managerial (and state) interest in involving employees has been focused squarely on those forms located on the left-hand side of the participation continuum: management have been more concerned to 'tell and sell' than to promote industrial democracy.

The diversity arising from variation in the depth of participation is also reflected in the multitude of *forms* that participatory activity can take. These cover a broad spectrum, from suggestion schemes to worker cooperatives, from briefing groups to board-level representation. As well as the different degrees of involvement and influence they bestow upon employees and their representatives, these different forms can also be classified in terms of the degree to which they are *formal* or *informal* activities, and whether they entail employees participating *directly* in decision making, or whether participation is achieved *indirectly* via the election of representatives. Typically much of the participatory activity that occurs at the lowest levels of the company – involving, for example, the organisation of individual tasks and discussion of production schedules – takes place directly (as in the five-minute meetings at Nissan). Involvement in higher-level decision making, on the other hand, typically takes place via representative forms of participation (such as Nissan's Company Council).

Variation also exists in the different *levels* at which participation can occur. As we shall see below, recently attention has been concentrated on extending the degree of involvement at the lowest levels within the organisation. This contrasts with the situation in the 1970s, when the emphasis was more on the extension of participation at higher levels through board-level representation. In a more general analysis, Clegg (1976) examined the pattern of development of participation and industrial democracy in six countries, identifying the structure of collective bargaining as a major influence on the level and form of participation typical in a country. Where bargaining structures were identified as being strong at workplace level – as in the UK – much of the need for local-level participation is seen to be met by the presence of local union-management machinery. The result is a low degree of participation at that level other than as secondary to the bargaining machinery. However, where collective bargaining is focused away from the workplace at industry or national level – which has been the case in Sweden for example – this is seen to leave a vacuum of employee voice at the local level, which stimulates greater participatory activity at the local level. For Clegg this was an important factor, accounting, for example, for the greater interest in direct forms of participation in Sweden in the 1960s and 1970s, such as job enrichment schemes, compared with the UK, where participation was primarily confined to limited indirect participation via joint consultation.

A further source of variation is the *scope* of different participation machinery, that is the range of decisions that employees or their representatives participate in. This scope may vary between 'immediate' level decisions such as work distribution, 'medium' level decisions such as process changes, and more 'distant' level decisions such as major technological change, product changes, investment plans and so on. The growth of financial forms of involvement since the mid 1980s – through, for example, employee share-ownership schemes – has further added to the possible scope of participatory activity.

Overall the range or scope of issues subjected to participation will depend on a variety of factors. These include the attitude of the parties involved (particularly management's predisposition to make issues available for participation); the degree of experience (and competence) that employees and their representatives have in participation; the degree of stability in product markets, which influences the time for participatory activity to occur; the nature of ownership and organisational characteristics, including the size of organisations and the degree to which decision making is a centralised or decentralised activity; and the extent to which participation is based on a statutory requirement (as is the case, for example, in Germany and Scandinavia) or voluntary agreement. In a twelve-country study in the 1970s, the Industrial Democracy in Europe research group highlighted the central importance of statutory support and managerial attitudes in explaining variations in the level of industrial democracy between countries (IDE, 1981). Participation tended to be higher in those countries where it was underpinned by legislation (such as the German and Swedish Co-determination Acts), and where managerial attitudes were more supportive of cooperation and openness in decision making. However the overall low level of participation identified by this study, and the variations between different enterprises within a single country, is understandable only if account is taken of the many other variables that can influence the depth and scope of participation.

Perspectives on participation

Variations in perspective on the *purpose* and *outcomes* of participation are evident in the way various groups have supported participation at particular points in history. We have already referred to the tendency for different actors to use different terminology when discussing participation. This contrast in language is significant; it reflects fundamentally divergent views about the nature and purpose of participation. For managers, support for participation stems largely from the principles of 'human relations' management, which draws attention to the importance of the social aspects of organisation in general, and the connection between, on the one hand, communication and consultation between management and workforce, and on the other, increased worker commitment, higher job satisfaction and motivation, and reduced resistance to change (McGregor, 1960; and Mayo, 1933). Greater involvement of employees in the planning and particularly the implementation of change is viewed as a means of breaking down resistance and improving the overall level of worker integration into the production process. Improved communication also affords management a greater opportunity to dispel rumours, correct 'misunderstandings' and 'get its message across', a factor that has been particularly emphasised in the latest period of interest in employee involvement. Participatory mechanisms have also been viewed as a means used by management at different points to 'head off' calls by organised labour for a greater redistribution of power and reward in industry (Ramsay, 1977). For Ramsay and others, this explains why managerial interest in participation tends to move in cycles, growing at times of increased labour power and labour unrest, only to diminish when labour power subsequently weakens. We shall return to this issue below.

The human relations view is consistent with a managerial orientation that is strongly unitarist in perspective. More than this, however, management's advocacy of certain types of participation represents an acknowledgement that employee commitment needs to be actively *secured* rather than passively assumed, and that involving employees in decision making is a means of achieving this. Management's support for (some forms of) participation is also an acknowledgement of the potential contribution of employee knowledge to the management of the organisation – in particular, tapping valuable worker experience of the way work tasks are organised and performed. More generally, this management orientation is an acknowledgement that many employees seek not only financial recompense from work but also a more extensive engagement with the institution in which they spend a large proportion of their waking hours.

Many of these aspects of management's orientation to participation show up in attitude surveys. Overall, these demonstrate a considerable positive disposition among managers towards certain forms of participation, specifically the forms that Clegg *et al.* (1978:5) characterise as being 'soft on power' – that is, those which focus on day-to-day operational issues and involve no significant transfer of decision-making power from management to work group, and thus no disruption of the hierarchical structure of managerial authority. These 'soft' forms contrast with 'harder' or more 'power-oriented' forms of participation, which focus on major organisational decisions and involve joint decision making rather than retention of managerial prerogative. The five-minute meeting at Nissan, for example, is clearly of the former rather than the latter type.

This pattern of support for unitary forms of worker involvement, extending, at most, consultative rather than joint decision-making powers to employees, is similarly evidenced in the two studies of managerial attitudes conducted by Poole and his colleagues at the beginning and end of the 1980s (Poole *et al.*, 1981; and Poole and Mansfield, 1992). In both the 1980 and 1990 surveys of UK managers, general support is shown for greater participation in the respondent's own organisation. In the 1990 survey, for example, only just over a quarter (26 per cent) of the managers disagreed with the view that there was a need for greater employee participation in their organisation (Poole and Mansfield, 1992:203). Specific support was also in evidence for such forms of participation as regular meetings between work groups and their supervisors, joint consultation and financial participation through employee shareholding (ibid:203, 205). In contrast managers in both the 1980 and 1990 studies were much less willing to endorse more power-oriented forms of participation based, for example, on extending collective bargaining or worker directors (ibid:204). This pattern was repeated in a 1994 survey of managers' attitudes towards HRM (Poole and Jenkins, 1996:35–6). As Poole and Mansfield (1992:207) comment, 'Managers appear to support most employee involvement practices so long as these do not radically affect their control function within the firm. In other words they tend to prefer a unitary rather than a pluralist approach to employee participation in decision-making'.

The general orientation of trade unions towards participation is different from that of most managers. First, trade unions in the UK have been distinctly wary of forms of participation that imply any integration of employees and their representatives into the management of the enterprise; forms that extend only very limited (advisory) powers to employees and/or their representatives; and forms that establish alternative (and competing) lines of communication between workforce and management to that represented by the trade union organisation (Hyman and Mason, 1995:151–5). These views have manifested themselves historically in such ways as (1) a critical, or at best lukewarm, reaction to those forms of participation that are 'soft on power', viewing these as fettering employees with responsibilities but without any commensurate power; (2) a preference for increasing participation via the extension of collective bargaining, thereby securing participation based on joint decision-making activity, executed via the trade union channel and undertaken using a mechanism in which union negotiators have a recognised competence; and (3) an equivocal response to certain other forms (such as worker directors) that, while more power-oriented, are nevertheless seen as potentially compromising the union's independent negotiating position (Ursell *et al.*, 1980; and Ursell, 1983). The lack of unity over worker directors was evidenced in the different union responses to the recommendations of the Bullock Report (1977) on worker directors in larger corporations. While the TUC supported worker directors and the Bullock Majority Report (which advocated worker directors on a single company board), many individual trade unions were far less enthusiastic, fearing that their negotiating position would be compromised if union representatives sitting as members of a board of directors were party to decisions that subsequently became the focus of negotiations (Elliott, 1978).

In (partial) contrast to trade union views, studies of employee attitudes towards participation point to a predisposition for greater participation, particularly in decisions with a direct bearing on their own jobs and working environment (see for example Wall and Lischeron, 1977). While more direct participation is generally desired in these immediate-level decisions, attitude surveys reveal a weaker desire to participate in higher-level decision making (such as on planning and investment) and a greater preference that any participation at this level should be effected through representatives rather than involving employees directly (ibid). Other studies of worker response to direct and indirect forms of participation indicate that while involvement in direct forms of participation can have a measurable impact on employee attitudes and behaviour (for example being associated with higher job satisfaction and lower levels of absenteeism), the existence of indirect forms of participation tends to elicit no equivalent response among employees (see for example Rubenowitz *et al.*, 1983). Over time, however, there is a tendency for the appeal of direct forms of participation to diminish as they become more of a routine and less of a novel activity (Wall and Lischeron, 1977). Positive attitudes are also likely to diminish if participation is not perceived to be achieving results: in particular if management are seen to be failing to act on ideas raised by employees in the participation forum (see Collard and Dale, 1989; Hill, 1991; and Hyman and Mason, 1995:160–1).

Several studies on both sides of the Atlantic have also pointed to a tendency for higher-grade workers to favour consultation activity and the development of joint cooperative programmes with management, to a greater extent than their lower-level counterparts (Cook *et al.*, 1975; Dyer *et al.*, 1977; and Ponak and Fraser, 1979). In part this may reflect the existence of a greater 'participatory competence' among higher-level employees. Pateman (1970), for example, argues that participation is a learned capacity: only by experience do employees gain the necessary skills, and thus a greater predisposition towards participation. These include the social skills of learning to function in group settings, including the ability to overcome inhibitions stemming from members holding very different statuses outside the group, for example manager and shopfloor worker (Blyton, 1980; and Blyton *et al.*, 1981). More senior-grade employees are not only likely to be better educated (and therefore able to articulate their ideas more easily), but many may also have more experience of working in small groups as part of their work roles. We shall return to this issue of participatory competence below.

At various junctures the state too has advocated forms of employee participation. At times the explicit motive for this has been to win workforce cooperation and reduce conflict. This has been particularly evident during wartime. In the First World War the introduction of increased consultation in the munitions industry was reinforced towards the end of the war by the recommendations of the Whitley Committee. This committee had been established to devise ways of dissipating growing labour militancy, reflected in an increased number of strikes, support for workers' control and the growth of shop steward organisation (Ursell and Blyton, 1988:111; see also Chapter 7 above). The principles of Whitleyism – embodied in its recommendations for joint committees at national, district and local levels in each industry – included not only support for collective bargaining but also that relations between employers and employees should be based on joint cooperation and collaboration. Increased consultation was viewed as resulting in

> the better utilisation of the practical knowledge and experience of the workpeople . . . [a] means of securing to the workpeople a greater share in and responsibility for the determination and observance of the conditions under which their work is carried on . . . [and] co-operation in carrying new ideas into effect and full consideration of the workpeople's point of view in relation to them (para. 16, Interim Report, quoted by Charles, 1973:104–5).

As noted in the previous chapter, the upshot of the Whitley recommendations was a rapid take-up of the Joint Industrial Council (JIC) model, with over seventy established between 1918 and 1921, covering 3.5 million workers. As with many later forms of joint committee, however, the initial enthusiasm for JICs subsequently waned and many fell into disuse during the interwar period, together with much of the local Whitley structure (Charles, 1973; and Cole, 1923). A significant revival did occur during the Second World War: forty-six new JICs were established during the war, together with additional consultation in the form of factory-wide Joint Production Committees, which were introduced with government approval. This support for consultation also became a statutory feature in the nationalisation Acts in the latter half of the 1940s, while the Whitley model of joint committees became prominent in the Civil Service and local government as well as in the newly formed National Health Service (Ursell and Blyton, 1988:144).

More recently, the pattern of state support for participation has reflected the markedly divergent attitudes of different governments towards trade unions and employee relations. In the 1970s, for example, individual government ministers not only supported the establishment of worker cooperatives (Coates, 1976) but also established a Committee of Inquiry (the Bullock Committee) to examine ways to introduce worker directors into larger companies. This committee formed part of the government's commitment to the TUC under the terms of the Social Contract, and also represented a response to EU membership and the debate (which still continues) on the representation of workers' rights within organisations in Europe (Elliott, 1978). Disagreement within the Bullock Committee was evident right from the outset, for while the government set terms of reference to address *how* a worker director system could be introduced, the employer representatives on the Committee wanted it to examine the question of *whether* or not worker directors were an appropriate means of extending participation. Thus it was no surprise when the Committee was divided in its recommendations, issuing Majority and Minority Reports reflecting disagreement, among other things, on the nature and extent of worker representation at board level, and whether this representation should take place within a single-tier or two-tier board structure. In the face of considerable employer opposition, a diluted version of the Majority Report's recommendations was translated into a government White Paper in 1978, but action on this was dropped following the change of government in 1979.

In the 1980s and 1990s, Conservative government support for participation was markedly different. Specifically, support came in the form of legislation to provide tax relief for approved employee share-ownership and profit-related pay schemes. In the WIRS studies, the proportion of trading sector establishments with employee ownership schemes rose from 23 per cent in 1984 to 32 per cent in 1990 (Millward *et al.*, 1992). A study of employee involvement carried out in 1993 found that of those working in private sector firms that operated an employee share ownership scheme, almost half indicated that they participated in their firm's scheme (Tillsley, 1994:214).

The growth of such schemes, on what has been termed financial participation, reflected the Conservative governments' emphasis on the *individual's* involvement with the company (having a financial stake). In this way the government sought to promote material rather than participative-democratic forms of employee involvement. Individualism was also echoed in the Conservative governments' broader attack on collectivism and collective aspects of employee relations during the 1980s and 1990s through, for example, a reduction in union involvement in national policy-making bodies, and restrictions on the closed shop and the taking of industrial action (see Chapters 5 and 6). As well as supporting financial participation, the government (in Section 1 of the 1982 Employment Act) also made it a requirement for companies with more than 250 employees to report annually on its developments in employee involvement (see Hibbett, 1991, for a study of stated employee involvement practices in companies' annual reports; see also Hyman and Mason, 1995:70–3). While the overall impact of this measure appears to have been limited, Marchington *et al.* (1992:53) argue that it raised awareness of employee involvement issues and reinforced the notion of employee involvement as 'good management practice'.

The extent of consultation and communication

In the 1970s and early 1980s there was considerable debate on whether or not joint consultation was undergoing a revival (MacInnes, 1985; and Marchington, 1987). In part this reflected the difficulty of comparing different samples undertaken at different times, using different surveys and with different degrees of methodological shortcoming. The weight of evidence appears to suggest, however, that there was an increase in workplace joint consultation in the latter half of the 1970s. By 1980 workplace consultation committees were reported in one third of the establishments that took part in the first Workplace Industrial Relations Survey (Daniel and Millward, 1983). This overall level changed relatively little during the early 1980s: some decline in incidence in the private sector was offset by an increase in consultation committees in public sector establishments (Millward and Stevens, 1986:138–41).

By 1990, however, more marked changes in the incidence of consultation were evident. While the extent of committees was fairly stable in the public sector (operating in almost one half of establishments), in the private sector a significant fall was registered, particularly in manufacturing. While in 1980 over one third (36 per cent) of private sector manufacturing establishments operated joint consultation committees, by 1990 this had fallen to below one quarter (23 per cent) (Millward *et al.*, 1992:153). As Millward and his colleagues point out, however, this fall can largely be explained in terms of the changing composition of manufacturing workplaces, in particular a decline in larger workplaces, where consultation committees were more common than in smaller establishments.

In respect of the activities of consultation committees, just under one third (31 per cent) of managers in the 1990 WIRS sample indicated that their consultation committee was also involved in negotiations, indicating that in practice there is a significant overlap between consultation and bargaining activity. In terms of subjects discussed by consultative committees, the most frequent were (in order) production issues, employment, government legislation/regulations, pay, health and safety and working practices (the last three figured equally in discussions). Overall, at least two thirds of managers and union representatives covered by WIRS thought that the joint consultation committee had some influence on managerial decision making (ibid:159). As well as consultation committees dealing with health and safety, just under one quarter of establishments had committees specifically for health and safety issues (ibid:162). The proportion of establishments where management did *not* consult with the workforce about health and safety matters, however, increased from 26.5 per cent in 1984 to 36.1 per cent in 1990. Significantly, establishments that had moved away from consultation over this period reported the highest injury rates (Beaumont, 1995:42).

In addition to consultative committees, WIRS sought information on the incidence of seven other methods of direct communication and involvement. As Table 8.1 below shows, there was considerable variation in the frequency of different forms of communication. Overall, nine out of ten establishments used at least one of the methods listed in Table 8.1. While this proportion

TABLE 8.1   Methods used by management to communicate with or consult employees, 1990

	% of establishments
Regular meeting among work-groups or teams at least once a month to discuss aspects of performance	35
Regular meetings (at least once a month) between junior managers/supervisors and all the workers for whom they were responsible	48
Regular meeting (at least once a year) between senior managers and all sections of the workforce	41
Systematic use of the management chain for communication with all employees	60
Suggestion schemes	28
Regular newsletters distributed to all levels of employee	41
Surveys or ballots of employees' views or opinions	17
Other methods	13

Source: Millward *et al.* (1992:167).

appears to have changed little over the latter 1980s, the average number of methods used in each establishment increased over this period from 2.0 in 1984 to 2.4 in 1990 (Millward *et al.*: 1992, 168). A more recent study (conducted in 1993) similarly found a high incidence of (at least a minimum level of) employee involvement: 85 per cent of the national sample of employees questioned reported at least one method of employee involvement at their workplace, with employees located in larger and unionised workplaces most likely to cite the presence of employee involvement practices (Tillsley, 1994).

The WIRS studies reveal substantial growth in the latter half of the 1980s in the overall reporting of new initiatives for employee involvement. Newly introduced arrangements (in the three years prior to the survey) for employee involvement were reported in 45 per cent of establishments in 1990; the comparable figure in 1984 was under 35 per cent. A significant degree of the employee involvement taking place appears to be focused on organisational change. Tillsley (1994:214–15), for example, reports that among the large number of workers in her sample who had experienced some form of organisational change in the recent past, four fifths said they had been consulted prior to the changes being made. In unionised establishments the proportion that had been consulted prior to the changes being introduced rose to 85 per cent, compared with 78 per cent in non-unionised settings. In the latest WIRS survey, new initiatives were more commonly reported in the public than the private sector, and in services more than manufacturing. The most common initiatives involved 'more two way communication' and 'new joint meetings' (Millward *et al.*, 1992:178–9). Not surprisingly such initiatives are often described as a threat to trade union organisation and representation as they can compete with established procedures of union–management relations based on joint negotiation. The variety of such practices, however, should caution against assuming any simplistic inverse relationship between the presence of consultation and participation on the one hand, and joint negotiation on the other.

On the more specific issue of joint consultation, for example, Marchington (1989:386–92, 1994:672–83) distinguishes four different models, described as (1) an alternative to collective bargaining, (2) marginal to collective bargaining, (3) competing with collective bargaining and (4) an adjunct to collective bargaining. In the last case, collective bargaining and joint consultation are kept separate, with consultation used to 'fill the gaps' left by collective bargaining, but these activities are viewed as being complementary. At Nissan, in contrast, joint consultation clearly competes with, or more accurately replaces and excludes, any independent forms of joint negotiation. But as Marchington (1989:389–91) argues, the logic of this strategy rests upon the maintenance of a representative (shop steward) structure for the workforce, rather than its destruction, since the objective is to involve workforce representatives and thereby achieve a better understanding of the problems and challenges facing the firm. In doing so, it is hoped that representatives and employees will come to accept the 'inevitability' of management policy. This appears to be particularly important, at Nissan and elsewhere, during the current period of intense international competition and massive restructuring of the domestic economy.

Cycles or waves of participation?

Debate surrounding the history of participation epitomises the broader issue in employee relations as to whether its development is best characterised by a line or a circle: has there been a development of participation over time or is it characterised by a series of cycles, with no overall forward movement? Or alternatively, can the notion of a spiral (see Chapter 1) be profitably employed here, with the development trajectory of participation demonstrating both linear and cyclical characteristics? Some authors have argued that there is a recognisable growth of participation over time, engendered by factors such as increased levels of education or the growth in technological sophistication. As regards the latter, for example, one argument runs that as technology increases, workers using that technology gain a particular competence that acts to undermine the extant authority structure. Specialist knowledge is held more and more by those away from the top of managerial hierarchies. 'Little by little,' argues Goldman, 'technological progress demands that hierarchy be replaced by co-operation' (quoted by Brannen *et al.*, 1976:259).

In contrast Ramsay (1977, 1983) has persuasively argued that the history of participation can be viewed as a series of cycles, with periods of development followed by periods of decay with little or no overall change in the extent to which decisions in industry are subject to joint influence and control. In the current century, periods of heightened interest in participation include the two world wars (see above) and the 1970s, which witnessed both increased interest in worker directors and an apparent resurgence of interest in joint consultation (Marchington, 1987, 1992:20). According to Ramsay, these periods of interest in participation reflected particular conditions: labour shortages, industrial unrest, a desire by employers to accommodate labour power and – in two of the periods – the wartime needs of the state to secure cooperation. Once these conditions abated, however, either as a result of labour power weakening or wars ending, the participation structures fell into decay. Ramsay cites this as evidence that they were merely temporary means of accommodating potentially disruptive labour power, rather than a manifestation of employer or state commitment to greater worker participation in decision-making.

For at least one group studying the more diluted forms of participation in the recent period, however, this 'cycles of control' argument about how, why and when interest in participation develops, does not seem to fit. In seeking to account for the level of interest in employee involvement in the 1980s, Ackers *et al.* (1992) point to the absence of pressure during that decade to accommodate labour power. In the 1980s most managers transparently had little need to incorporate union representatives, and if the cycles of control argument were valid, the weakening of organised labour after 1979 'should have seen participation fade from the scene' during the ensuing decade (ibid:272–3). The fact that this did not happen as far as employee involvement initiatives were concerned is used as the basis for rejecting the 'cycles' analysis of participation after the 1970s, and replacing it instead with an argument based on 'waves of interest' in participation. While recognising that interest in participation 'ebbs and flows', in using the notion of waves rather than cycles the authors seek to avoid both the assumption that a common set of circumstances has given rise to interest in participation at different points in time, and also that there is an all-embracing theory that applies in the same way in all workplaces. In practice, argue Marchington *et al.* (1992:26), waves come in different shapes and sizes, and last for different lengths of time in different organisations. Some may endure for long periods while others fail to gather momentum or break soon after formation. Further, although waves may appear to be losing strength, they may increase in intensity again due to an extra push or drive from managers.

In this latest wave of interest a variety of forms of employee involvement have come (or returned) to prominence. Ramsay (1992:214) categorises these into four broad types:

- Task and work group involvement (e.g. job redesign, quality circles, teamwork and total quality management programmes).
- Communication and briefing systems (e.g. team briefings and two-way communication initiatives).
- Consultative arrangements (e.g. joint consultation committees).
- Financial participation (e.g. employee share ownership and profit sharing).

Marchington (1992), on the other hand, employs a sixfold categorisation, distinguishing between written and audiovisual communications, face-to-face communications, involvement in problem-solving, job redesign, joint consultation, and financial involvement. Elsewhere, Marchington *et al.* (1992) have adopted a simplified categorisation, distinguishing between downward communication systems (such as briefing groups), upward problem-solving mechanisms (for example quality circles) and financial participation (see also Tillsley, 1994). The various forms of employee involvement and the different possibilities for their classification notwithstanding, however, the different types in this latest wave share a number of common characteristics. First, they have not only been 'championed by management often without any great pressure from employees or trade unions', but have also been 'directed at securing greater employee commitment to and identification with the organisation and its success' (Marchington *et al.*, 1992:6). The majority are individual-centred in nature, that is, directly involving employees rather than working through representative structures. Most are also – and in some cases extremely – soft on power, designed principally to integrate employees into the organisation, secure organisational change, improve communications and employee contribution and 'get the company's message across'. They are not designed to challenge the basic authority structure of the enterprise. On the contrary, according to many observers these mechanisms act to reinforce that authority structure (e.g. Edwards and Whitston, 1993:238–9; and Waddington and Whitston, 1995b:440). Garrahan and Stewart (1992) have argued that in the case of Nissan, group discussions led by supervisors potentially undermine the communicator role of the shop steward, while activity in *kaizen* groups and 'total quality management' programmes helps bring about the self-subordination of the individual employee.

While for Marchington *et al.* (1992) the circumstances giving rise to this latest interest in employee involvement are distinct from earlier periods (which Ramsay identified as characterised by increased labour power and unrest), our own view draws somewhat closer links between the present and earlier waves of interest in participation. We concur that the 'participation as control' argument places too much emphasis on management's need to secure *control* and gives insufficient consideration to participation as a means of securing active labour *cooperation*. For as discussed in Chapters 2 and 4 above, managers rely not only on achieving a controlled workforce, but also one that actively engages with the labour process in order to increase the efficiency of that process. It is this desire to secure the workforce's active cooperation that represents an abiding theme in the managerial interest shown in participation – particularly those forms of participation that provide employees with a significant degree of involvement but comparatively little real influence.

That this need for active cooperation is not something attaching only to recent initiatives in employee involvement is evidenced in the extract quoted earlier from the Whitley Reports, with its references to securing 'the better utilisation of the practical knowledge and experience of the workpeople' and 'co-operation in carrying new ideas into effect'. For a state embattled by war, the Joint Industrial Councils were more than a means to reassert control, they were also a vehicle to gain the active involvement of employees in improving the production process and a means of bolstering collaboration in the war effort and its aftermath. It is in this respect, of participation as a vehicle for securing the active cooperation of the workforce, that the latest period has similarities with the past. What is different from, say, the development of participation in the 1970s, however, is that in the more recent period the influence of strong labour power has been absent. This has enabled management to shift the focus of participation completely away from any power-oriented forms of participation towards forms that are both soft on power and match most closely managers' own attitudes and orientations. The difference between 1970s-style industrial democracy and 1990s-style employee involvement, according to Marchington (1995:282), is that 'Employee involvement starts from the assumption that managers might see the advantages of *allowing* employees to become involved, whereas industrial democracy has its source in the *right* of the governed to exercise some control over those in authority' (original emphasis).

While diminished labour power may explain the particular direction that participation has taken, the factor that appears to have driven much of the interest in participation *per se* is the intensified level of competition since the 1980s, and in particular new managerial approaches (such as the 'excellence' movement and human resource management, HRM) together with Japanese-style production techniques (such as just-in-time, JIT and total quality management, TQM) that greater competition has occasioned. In most versions of HRM, for example, emphasis is placed on the importance of achieving greater employee commitment (Blyton and Turnbull, 1992), not least via the use of employee involvement 'as an important component of an organization's attempts to create a positive employee relations policy' (Marchington, 1992:176). Beyond HRM however – which has only been adopted by a small number of organisations (Sisson, 1993), though elements have been adopted more widely – the production pressures created by JIT and TQM, and more generally by lower staffing levels and more intensive work systems, have increased the need for active workforce cooperation. The absence of buffer stocks under JIT systems, for example, and the need to secure continuous improvements under TQM, have resulted in management *dependency* on labour cooperation in a way that was less apparent when, for example, banks of stocks and higher levels of work-in-progress provided management (and workforce) with a greater degree of insulation from short-term disruptions to production. Part of this dependence involves management securing an active labour contribution: that is, not simply management's need to 'get the message across' but also to harness employee knowledge in the task of continuously improving the production process (Delbridge and Turnbull, 1992; and Delbridge *et al.*, 1992).

Thus in the latest period, while labour market pressures have diminished, product market pressures have brought about a managerial reassessment both of the potential contribution of employees to quality improvement and of the significance of employee commitment in terms of overall productivity. The result has been a variety of initiatives – including employee involvement schemes – designed to secure workforce cooperation. This is not to argue that product market pressures were absent during former waves of interest in participation, nor that questions of controlling labour power are irrelevant to understanding current developments in employee involvement (in fact quite the opposite). Rather the balance between the two is different in the 1990s than it was in the 1970s.

Future prospects for participation

A continuing management need to secure active cooperation and employee contribution, together with the proven ability of joint consultation machinery to endure, and the recent extension of employee involvement through financial participation and various forms of downward communication and upward problem-solving machinery, all point to the likelihood that employee involvement and participation will remain a significant feature of employee relations in coming years. Two additional developments may be seen to reinforce this prospect. First, the increased attention being paid to total quality management (TQM) has been identified as significantly enhancing the prospects for employee participation (Hill, 1991). TQM is an approach to managing that gives primacy to quality, continuous improvement and customer satisfaction as the central tenets of the organisation. For the leading exponents of TQM (Deming, 1982, 1986; Juran, 1979, 1988; and Oakland, 1989), its adoption requires a fundamental cultural change within organisations in order to support the changes in attitudes and behaviour necessary to realise the goal of continuous quality improvement and the primacy of customer satisfaction. More importantly, exponents talk of 'worker empowerment' and 'mutual dependency' between management and labour. For Hill (1991:555), key aspects of the cultural change in TQM involve more open communication, more extensive involvement of a wider range of people in decision-making, and the creation of high-trust relations. Among those companies adopting TQM, he argues that

> decentralization and participation represent a major change in the style of managing for most companies, a shift from individual decision-taking and authoritative, top-down communication towards a more collective style with greater two-way communication and less emphasis on giving and receiving commands (ibid:561).

According to Hill, the cultural change encapsulated in TQM means that senior and middle management are more committed to the change, to greater shared involvement in decisions and to the creation of more space for devolved decision-making. However he rightly cautions against assuming too much from the participation activity: most participation is limited to work task and work organisation issues. This is in fact a key feature of such activities, widely used at Nissan and other Japanese transplants in the UK. Real autonomy for the workforce is largely cosmetic, as production decisions and all quality targets are dictated either by management-decreed goals and regulations or 'customer needs' (Delbridge *et al.*, 1992:102). External customers (the consumer on the street) determine the quantity of output and demand ever improved quality, while customers inside the organisation (fellow workers 'on the line') dictate the pace of work and monitor the quality of other employees' work. At Nissan a Vehicle Evaluation System is used for tracing quality defects to specific teams and individuals, and a Neighbour Watch Scheme ensures a system of peer surveillance (ibid:100). Not surprisingly, therefore, workers tend to experience TQM as a 'low trust' activity (Klein, 1989:64), and as a system of 'information and control' rather than genuine participation (Taylor *et al.*, 1991; see also Dawson and Webb, 1989:236; Legge, 1995:208–46; Sewell and Wilkinson, 1992; and contributions to Wilkinson and Willmott, 1995). Essentially,

> *Responsibility* is devolved to the shopfloor *but not control*, which remains highly centralized in the hands of management. Employees are only required to participate in incremental improvements to product quality and process efficiency, which

simply incorporates workers in the projects of capital without extending any real control or collective autonomy to the workforce (Delbridge and Turnbull, 1992:65–6, original emphasis).

A more likely stimulus to greater employee participation is the social agenda within the overall development of European integration. Extending employees' right to be informed and consulted over issues directly affecting their work is a key element of the Community Charter of Fundamental Social Rights (the 'Social Charter'). One aspect of this is the 1994 Directive (number 94/45/EC), which requires companies with more than 1000 employees and more than 150 employees in two or more EU member states to establish a European Works Council (EWC) or procedure for purposes of informing and consulting employees. The role of these councils and procedures is to supplement national structures to secure information and consultation rights for employee representatives with regard to transnational business and employment issues, including the probable development of the business, investments, substantial organisational changes, the introduction of new working methods or production processes, production transfers, mergers, cutbacks or closures, and collective redundancies (see Carley, 1995:27; Hall *et al.*, 1995; and Thomson, 1996).

Under the previous Conservative government's 'opt-out' from the social chapter of the Treaty on European Union (the Maastricht Treaty), UK firms only had to comply with the Directive in respect of workers based outside the UK. The Conservative government was less than enthusiastic about the Directive; for example, a former government minister commented that European Works Councils were an 'expensive irrelevance' (Michael Portillo, quoted in *People Management*, 31 May 1995). However in the event, and prior to the election of the Labour Government in 1997, a significant number of UK firms opted for the establishment of EWCs to cover all their employees, including those based in the UK. A particular stimulus for this, however, was that by voluntarily establishing such structures prior to the Directive's implementation date of September 1996, companies would avoid being compelled to follow the more tightly defined requirements of the Directive in the future. This was because companies with a pre-existing agreement for transnational information and consultation would be exempt from the terms of the Directive for as long as the agreement applied (Hall *et al.*, 1995:1).

UK companies that have already established EWCs or similar forums include BP Oil Europe, Coats Viyella, United Biscuits, GKN, ICI, NatWest, Pilkington's and BT, as well as a number of our case companies, including British Airways (Chapter 4), Marks and Spencer (Chapter 9), and British Steel (for more details of BS's European Works Council, see Chapter 7). The extent to which European Works Councils will be an effective vehicle for employee participation, however, remains uncertain. Previous EU initiatives on employee rights to information and consultation, and the representation of employee interests on company boards have, to date, made little headway. Hall (1992) attributes this in part to the lack of a single direction, with previous initiatives coming from two sources within the EU. On the one hand the section of the European Commission dealing with company law (DG 15) introduced a draft Directive in 1972 that proposed a structure for public limited companies involving two-tier boards, with employee representation on the higher, supervisory board (a proposal strongly influenced by the German model of worker directors). While this 'fifth' Directive was modified in 1983, it has yet to make significant progress, not least because of strong resistance from some employer quarters. On the other hand the branch of the Commission responsible for employment, industrial relations and social affairs (DG 5) has pursued proposals to extend workers' rights to be informed and consulted by employers. As Hall (ibid:555) notes, this has been successful in the areas of collective redundancies and transfers of undertakings, but more general proposals for informing and consulting employees in multinational enterprises (the so-called 'Vredling' proposals; see Vandamme, 1986) have also been more or less halted by resistance among employers and some governments (particularly the UK under the Conservative governments of the 1980s and 1990s). To a degree, this latter initiative has now been given new form in the European Works Councils (see also Thomson, 1996:39).

While many companies have established EWCs, and more will be required to do so under the terms of the Directive (including other UK firms following any cancellation of the opt-out by a Labour Government), it can be expected that many employers will seek heavily to circumscribe the agenda and role of their EWC, in line with the previous widespread reluctance to extend rights of information and consultation to employees in Europe, and the clear resistance of most large companies to develop collective bargaining at the European level (see the British Steel case in Chapter 7). Thus the effectiveness of EWCs as joint employer–employee representative bodies remains to be seen, though in the meantime they may act as a useful additional source of information on company developments for employee representatives, and facilitate greater interaction between worker representatives from different European countries. We shall return to the question of labour legislation, Europe and European Works Councils in the final chapter.

Notwithstanding these developments at the organisational and international levels, suggesting prospects for an extension of employee involvement and participation, a number of significant obstacles remain to the general development of participation. Above all, in the vast majority of cases organisations remain rigidly hierarchical, with an overriding emphasis on individual responsibility and accountability, top-down decisions and strict adherence to a hierarchically ordered chain of command. Such contexts are far from conducive to encouraging real and effective employee participation. They do not lend themselves to responding to bottom-up ideas: the result is that information made available to participation groups is almost inevitably inadequate, and insufficient attention is paid to ideas and suggestions emanating from these groups. The consequence is very likely to be a gradual disillusionment with the participation mechanism among those involved. The experience of different participation initiatives is replete with the waning of initial enthusiasm and the decay of particular mechanisms. This disillusionment is all the more likely where the organisation's decision-making processes are ill-equipped to incorporate participatory activity. Where management operate a 'fire-fighting' approach to decision-making, perhaps justifying this on the basis of product market volatility, little time is made available for participation to occur (Marchington, 1980). More generally, if senior and middle management are not fully supportive of participatory activity, insufficient space is likely to be incorporated into decision-making processes to allow effective consultation and participation to occur. The result in many cases is that consultation takes place *after* decisions have been made, the exercise then becoming one of management *selling* decisions rather than *consulting* over them. In the past, too much participatory activity has been simply 'bolted-on' to existing decision-making structures without due regard to the need to adapt structures to allow decisions to be influenced from below. This unwillingness to modify organisational structures is an additional factor encouraging the development of consultative rather than joint-decision-making forms of participation: the former can be accommodated into existing decision-making processes far more easily than the latter (Blyton, 1981).

Furthermore, as we have seen, much of what has been offered by employers in the 1980s and 1990s has been *involvement* rather than full participation based on a sharing of *influence*. Hence one obstacle to the development of participation is the limited nature of its current manifestations, and the inability of employees to secure more joint decision-making rights. There is no automatic movement along the participation continuum over time (Bate and Murphy, 1981). On the contrary, one effect of the current developments in involvement may be to stifle rather than (re)kindle demands for more extensive participation. As noted above, one way this may occur is by extensive management communication with employees which serves to marginalise the role of the trade union and the shop steward. In addition, as Pateman (1970) has pointed out, the gaining of a participatory competence acts as a vital ingredient in the extension of effective participation and democracy. It could be argued, however, that employees in the 1990s have gained merely an 'involvement competence' that does not adequately prepare them for a greater role in decision-making.

Finally, it remains to be seen to what extent recent developments in employee involvement form part of a concerted effort by management to move out of the low-trust dynamic that has been recognised as characterising much of UK employee relations (Fox, 1974). As Crouch (1982a:216) notes,

It is usually employers' representatives who bemoan the idea of 'two sides of industry' and who call upon workers to co-operate in the common good. But it was not workers who instituted the rigorous distinction between those who make decisions and those who receive instructions. Or, to put it another way, how can responsibility be demanded from those to whom responsibility is not given?

Participation is, by definition, a higher-trust and potentially positive-sum activity, where emphasis is placed on the shared resolution of issues to the mutual benefit and gain of those involved. However over the longer term such activity can only be sustained if it is nourished by other indications of higher-trust relations. Just as participation mechanisms cannot be satisfactorily bolted on to existing organisational decision-making structures, so too the values of positive-sum, high-trust relationships cannot be bolted on to an organisational climate otherwise characterised by low-trust relations. The latter, as illustrated in Chapter 4, is a pervasive characteristic of UK firms. In such a context, employee involvement and diluted forms of participation appear to trade unions, and indeed to many workers, as forms of management control rather than opportunities to influence management policy and decisions.

Conclusion

Employee participation has traditionally represented the Cinderella of employee relations in the UK. In part this probably reflects the extent of development of workplace trade union organisation and bargaining activity since the 1950s, as well as a more widespread failure to secure commitment towards participation among the parties involved. For McCarthy (1967), a secondary role for joint consultation was the inevitable outcome of the development of shop steward organisation and workplace bargaining. Once these aspects grew in significance, unions would understandably seek to shift as many important issues as possible from the consultative to the bargaining forum, in order to exercise joint decision-making influence rather than merely advisory power.

The recent period, in contrast, has been characterised by management-led interest in forms of employee involvement designed to enhance worker integration, cooperation and contribution. The weakened state of the trade union movement, Conservative governments that actively promoted indivi-dualised forms of involvement, and managerial philosophies emphasising the significance of employee commitment and contribution have all acted to support the development of individualised, employee-centred (rather than trade-union-centred) forms of involvement. Closer European integration may act to bring collective aspects of participation into closer consideration, but unions and employees would be unwise to pin too much hope on Europe.

Many of the underlying obstacles to participation remain, not least the unwillingness of management to relinquish hierarchical control and decision-making power, the low-trust relations obtaining between many managements and workforces, the lack of opportunity for many employees to gain the participatory competence necessary to mount a significant challenge to existing decision-making structures and processes, and more generally the underlying conflict of interests between employers and employees. It may indeed be true that the current context of weakened unions and decline in bargaining coverage is one in which non-bargaining forms of employee management interaction thrive. However for participation to attain its full potential in employee relations, these obstacles to its development need to be more satisfactorily addressed than has hitherto been the case. Put differently, if collective bargaining can no longer ensure the effective right of representation for employees in decisions that affect their working lives, but society still values participation as a democratic right of all workers, then urgent action by the state, employers and trade unions is called for.

CHAPTER 9

Managing without unions

Marks & Spencer: a manufacturer without factories?

Good jobs and bad jobs

In an industrial town on the outskirts of the Greater Manchester conurbation, Marks & Spencer has a well-placed and invariably busy store. In this respect the town is like many others, as virtually every desirable high street in the country plays host to the UK's most profitable retailer. Every week 14 million customers pass through the doors of M&S stores, buying the *St Michael* branded goods that have a deserved reputation for quality and value for money. Inside the stores the company's 42 000 employees (two thirds of whom work part time) are well looked after. The proverb 'Do as you would be done by' (Sieff, 1990:84) is the golden rule of the company's *human* relations policy – so-called because, as the former Chairman Lord Sieff (1984:28) explained, 'we are human beings at work not industrial beings'. Any policy derived from the 'law and the prophets' carries with it a strong moral obligation, as Lord Sieff makes clear (ibid:55, 118). Indeed the extensive provision of welfare and medical benefits such as subsidised meals, hairdressing, chiropody and dental check-ups, 'is an act of faith. When asked why the company spends so lavishly on the health of its employees managers reply that it "feels right" to do so' (*Financial Times*, 30 April 1991). Lord Sieff was always less speculative: 'Good human relations at work pay off; they are of great importance if a business is to be efficiently run' (1990:56). The latter is certainly true of Marks & Spencer, a company hailed by Peter Drucker (1974:98) as one of the most efficient in the world, and recently voted Britain's 'best managed company' for the third year in succession by a panel of institutional investors, captains of industry and business journalists (*Financial Times*, 19 March 1997).

    Less than two miles away from the M&S store is a family-run business, Sew & Son (a pseudonym), making ladies' underwear and nightwear for M&S.

Like many of M&S's 600 or more suppliers, the company has 'sold its soul to St Michael', as *The Sunday Times* (6 June 1983) once put it, on the basis of no more than a batch-by-batch contract (see Rainnie, 1984:149). The same could be said of Sew & Son's employees. Although they enjoy a subsidised canteen, their conditions of work are almost the opposite of those enjoyed by M&S staff. Lines of sewing machines buzz with continuous activity. Conversation is difficult above the noise, and costly. Payment is by the piece, so the pace of work has to be intense if the women are to earn a decent wage. On the M&S lines in particular, 'Everything is all speed' (interview notes). As the supervisor elaborated,

> On the M&S work, women either stick it or leave. They're always coming and going. The M&S work can make you ill, it's so fast. It has to be. You only get a few pence for every dozen . . . Marks & Spencer tell you how to organise the work. A man from their technical division came in and sorted it all out. And the quality has to be just right. If M&S find even one or two that are not right they send the whole lot back – could be as many as 200 dozen. They turn up any time to check quality. They're like ghosts in the factory – they don't own us, but they're always there (interview notes).

As another woman commented somewhat ruefully, 'I'd much rather work for Marks & Spencer than make the work for them' (interview notes).

Not surprisingly, Marks & Spencer has been described as a 'manufacturer without factories' (Tse, 1985:4). As such the relationship between M&S and its factories (suppliers) is of critical importance, not only to the reputation and financial success of M&S but to the continuation of small, low-technology firms in the clothing (and other) industries. Marks & Spencer pays for the welfare benefits of its own employees out of such dependency. In contrast, small textile firms often pay little heed to employee needs or their employment rights.

Who needs a union anyway?

Ever since the late 1960s, the non-union 'Marksist' approach to human relations (Tse, 1985:173–4) (not to be confused with Marxist!) has been popularised as an alternative to the collectivist, institutionalised approach based on the Whitley and later the Donovan model, as Lord Sieff (1986:182) points out in his memoirs. When employees are recruited to Marks & Spencer they receive a 'Welcome Pack' which gives information on the company and its principles. It is here they first encounter the company's commitment to fostering good human relations. For M&S, 'the newest recruit is in a sense the most important person in the company at any given time since by definition he or she is the least educated and experienced and therefore the most likely to fall below the company's standards' (Sieff, 1990:123). Thus 'A good firm will make its philosophy of good human relations clear to its employees from the moment they join the company' (ibid:81). A second booklet, 'Facts for New Staff', gives details of employees' conditions of employment. These include competitive rates of pay, non-contributory pensions, profit sharing and extensive medical care. Female employees, for example, are offered breast and cervical screening, while male employees can view a video and read a company leaflet on testicular self-examination. Everyday health and safety is covered in another booklet, 'The Right Move' (which advises on such matters as the lifting of heavy boxes), while 'Personal Safety' offers employees advice on going to and from work (see ibid:81–3).

According to Lord Sieff (1984:28), good human relations is not just about wages and conditions but also moral fortitude and a deeper understanding of employee needs. For this reason Tse (1985:118) argues that it is a misrepresentation simply to label the 'Marksist' approach to human relations as paternalism (*pace* Turnbull and Wass, 1998). The company's human relations policy, according to Tse (1985:119), also includes respect for the individual, attention to the problems of individuals at work, full and frank communications, the recognition of people's effort and contribution, and continuous training and development. In other words attention is paid not only to those factors that, according to Herzberg (1966), (dis)satisfy employees (wages, amenities, physical working conditions) but also those that motivate employees (achievement, recognition, responsibility, advancement). In the words of Lord Sieff (1990:121, 176),

> good human relations have a most beneficial effect on the morale of the employees and their performance. . . . The key fact about a policy of good human relations at work is that it is not *primarily* concerned with the nature of the work which the employee does but with the state of mind, the spirit in which he or she does it. A policy of good human relations at work is not about jobs, it is about people (original emphasis).

Of course policy statements and 'good intentions' are one thing, implementation is another. In all organisations there is invariably a gap between aspirations and outcomes, between the espoused management style and the reality of personnel practice (see Purcell and Ahlstrand, 1994:177). An important litmus test of actual policy would of course be employee perceptions, attitudes and experiences of work, but there is a dearth of such information for non-union workers. Management (e.g. Sieff, 1984, 1986, 1990) and managerialist (e.g. Howells, 1981) accounts of M&S, however, claim that the rhetoric of 'good human relations' is matched by the 'reality' of employees' experience:

> the company not only looks after the staff well, but, more importantly, the staff feel they are being treated as individuals; that they are given opportunities continuously to train and develop themselves; that management is on their side, not against and

above them; and that they see very little gap between what top management preaches and what is being practised (Tse, 1985:118).

Effective implementation is proclaimed to be the result of top management commitment, the importance attached to the personnel function and the unremitting zeal with which the policy is effected on a day-to-day, day-after-day basis. To quote Lord Sieff again,

> Good human relations cannot be legislated for. . . . Good human relations develop only if top management believes in and is committed to their implementation and has a genuine respect for the individual. This is not something tackled from time to time but demands continuous action (1984:29).

In short, 'good human relations owe more to example than precept' (Sieff, 1990:82). The example starts with the personnel function, which is heavily staffed and strongly represented on the board of directors. The strategic importance attached to personnel is a key feature of M&S (Tse, 1985:130), but the emphasis is very much on an organic relationship with line management (see Turnbull and Wass, 1997b). In fact the company's philosophy is that 'good human relations is not something that can be left to the personnel department' (Sieff, 1984:29). Rather, 'personnel work – in the broadest sense of the term – is conceived of not so much as a "function" but as a way of life, and as such it permeates the entire organization, from the board room to the sales floor' (Tse, 1985:141). Responsibility is therefore delegated to line and store management, who deal directly, and at times generously, with all personnel issues (Sieff, 1986:159). All local managers are told, 'if you are going to make a mistake, err on the side of generosity' (Sieff, 1984:30). Issues that cannot be resolved at this level are taken to the Welfare Committee, first established in the early 1930s, which meets and attempts to resolve issues on a weekly basis. Speed is of the essence.

As far as trade unions are concerned, Marks & Spencer's approach can best be described as 'pre-emptive' (Tse, 1985:122), straightforwardly *non*-union rather than explicitly *anti*-union. Put differently, the approach is one of substitution rather than suppression of union activity (Beaumont, 1987:130). Anybody who works for M&S can join a trade union, but the company 'cannot guarantee an audience' (Sieff, 1990:84). According to the company's Director of Personnel, M&S 'appreciate that in companies that are unwilling or unable to provide more than the basic terms and conditions for their employees, trade unions do have a valuable role to play in negotiating for their members' (Salsbury, 1993:569), but with such care and attention lavished on the promotion of good human relations, 'unionism simply finds it difficult to flourish in St Michael soil' (Tse, 1985:122). As a union official from the building industry commented to an audience of employers after a speech by Lord Sieff at the 1983 annual meeting of the National Federation of Building Trades Employers, 'If you all followed a policy similar to that about which Lord Sieff has spoken I would be out of a job' (quoted by Sieff, 1986:223). As Lord Sieff himself put it, 'I suppose that so few [M&S employees] join because they feel the management provide them with as much and perhaps more than an active trade union would' (1990:84). The same cannot be said, however, for the management of many of the suppliers who manufacture for Marks & Spencer.

You can't have a union!

At Sew & Son, not all the factory's output was earmarked for *St Michael*. While the majority of the women worked on the underwear section for M&S, a group of sixteen women in the ladies outerwear section produced skirts, jackets, trousers and suits for mail-order catalogue companies. This work was 'make-through', with payment based on ten complete items, and was therefore much more highly skilled. However, 'The boss didn't like outerwear, the make-through section', recalled one woman, 'there was no hum, no buzz. The women liked it. It was well paid and it was interesting work, there was some involvement' (interview notes). But work in this section declined and the women were transferred to M&S work, at first making T-shirts (until this work was transferred to a factory in Cheshire), and then on women's night-dresses. For the women, events had taken a turn for the worse. Under the work system designed by Marks & Spencer for the nightdresses the garment was broken down into twenty-one separate sections/operations. Not only was the work deskilled, but the women who had been transferred from outerwear were now earning a third less. At first they were paid an average wage (based on their earnings on the outerwear section) until they had become accustomed to the work, but as the supervisor recalled,

> When they were transferred to the nightdresses they'd already lost heart. When they went on to piece rates it was too much. Fifteen of them left in the end, all top machinists. So we took on young kids. We'd start ten on Monday morning and there'd only be four left by Friday. But it didn't seem to matter. You didn't have to be skilled, just fast. And young. They wouldn't start any older women. They still had to be trained, but only how to do the job fast. It wasn't a skilled job (interview notes).

Prior to the transfer onto the M&S work there had been some union recruitment activity in the factory. The women in the outerwear section had been receptive to the idea and nominated one of their number to act as their representative. The response from management, however, was distinctly hostile. The women were called into the owner-manager's office and told outright: 'We don't want a union in here. They only cause trouble' (interview notes). Instead he suggested promoting the women's representative to the position of supervisor over the outerwear section. This proved to be accep-table to the women, especially as the supervisor kept a close check on the distribution of work (to ensure equality) and the price of every item. As she later recalled, 'I always kept the price tickets. With it being catalogue work you got a lot of variety, so I always kept the tickets. When new work came in, management would try to set a lower price, but we wouldn't have any of it. We had the tickets, and they had to pay us' (interview notes). The cut in wages on the M&S work, alongside the deskilling of the work, therefore proved to be a particularly bitter pill to swallow. Even then, 'If they'd given us a few coppers more we might have got the girls moving, but the money was just too tight' (interview notes). Several women took their case to an Industrial Tribunal, but lost. Shortly after the supervisor left as well, as did her sister. As for the nightdresses, three months later the section was closed and the work transferred to another factory.

Harmony on the shopfloor?

The constraints imposed on the small textile manufacturer, Sew & Son, by the much larger retail company clearly generated instability in the former's employee relations. Conflict, in this instance, was manifest in the very high levels of labour turnover. Even at Marks & Spencer, however, where the dependency of small firms is used to pay for and protect the conditions of M&S staff, everything is not always 'sweetness and light'. In 1989, for example, the company introduced a telephone 'hotline' to management to enable employees to inform on colleagues suspected of shoplifting. The scheme was widely criticised for being open to abuse by the unscrupulous, and received a negligible response from staff. Both John Lewis and Tesco rejected similar schemes (Hamil, 1993:43). Later, in April 1991, M&S announced 850 redundancies, which in some quarters was seen to herald 'the end of Marks & Spencer's unofficial commitment to its staff of a job for life' (ibid:41). As Lord Sieff (1990:64–5) makes clear, any such commitment on the part of M&S was always implicit rather than explicit, but the effect on the staff concerned was nonetheless traumatic. 'The Baker Street headquarters in London was gripped by gloom and confusion', wrote the *Financial Times* (30 April 1991), while city analysts predicted 'the transition from a safe, job-for-life type organisation into a meritocracy. To a certain extent, M&S has always been carrying a lot of fat and it is the first time that it has gone on a diet' (ibid).

Marks & Spencer has been keen to quash any rumours that the company plans to cut welfare, adopt a less caring approach or change its culture (*Financial Times*, 11 May and 18 May 1991), but in July 1996 the company stopped providing free breakfasts (on the grounds that not all staff enjoyed this 'perk') and the very notion of a full-time employee was abolished (staff are now paid for hours worked rather than a set monthly salary). It must be recognised that M&S has always demonstrated 'a ruthlessness, manifested in a relentless pursuit of corporate objectives, which some commentators have characterised as authoritarian, albeit benevolently so' (Hamil, 1993:43). In other words benevolence and authoritarian management have never been alternatives but rather part and parcel of the company's human relations policy. The contradictions between these two characteristics, however, only became apparent in the face of very severe external pressures, most notably the economic recession of the early 1990s, which hit the retail sector particularly hard, and the consequent intensification of customer and competitive pressures (all the major retailers, for example, now offer longer opening hours, Sunday trading and customer loyalty cards, while some even provide a free car breakdown service at stores, baby changing facilities and 'runners', often on roller skates, to fetch goods from the shelves that customers at the checkout have forgotten) (see Turnbull and Wass, 1998). Alternatively the change of top-level management might signal a new approach. The current Chairman of Marks & Spencer, Sir Richard Greenbury, has been described as 'a very hard and very commercial man who is quite prepared to take the tough decisions' (*Financial Times*, 30 April 1991). While Sir Richard has claimed that he has no intention of changing the M&S culture (*Financial Times*, 18 May 1991), it seems that the company will no longer err so heavily on the side of generosity.

Non-unionism's growing ranks

Even using the most flattering (for trade unions) measure of union density (based on civilian employees in employment), only a third of the UK workforce now belong to a trade union (see Chapter 5). With non-unionism now dominant in the UK, numerically at least, the former labour editor of the *Financial Times* expressed some surprise that this had been all but ignored in texts on industrial relations, although he did suggest a reason why: 'you know how to find the TGWU: it's there, it's tangible. By contrast, non-unionism is amorphous, de-centralised, inaccessible' (Bassett, 1988:45; see also McLoughlin, 1996:301; and Scase, 1995:569). While this may be true of the vast majority of (small) non-union companies, it is certainly not true of all of them. Indeed as Bassett (1988:47) and others (e.g. Legge, 1995:36–7) note, the new role models for UK employee relations are no longer Ford or ICI, but IBM, Hewlett Packard and other large multinationals such as Black & Decker, Gillette, Mars, Polaroid, Texas Instruments, Nestlé, and of course Marks & Spencer. Such large, non-union manufacturing companies are the exception rather than the rule: as Nissan's former Personnel Director noted, of the 2000 UK manufacturing companies with more than 500 employees, only around twenty are non-union in the sense that the company does not formally bargain with a union (Wickens, 1987:127). Nevertheless the employment and other policies of these companies are increasingly well-known and more widely publicised. Many of these companies are strongly associated with the US 'excellence' literature, for example (Peters and Waterman, 1982). At the risk of overgeneralisation, the generic characteristics of these non-union companies tend to be a sense of caring combined with carefully chosen plant locations and working environments, market leadership, high growth and healthy profits, employment security, single status, promotion from within, an influential personnel department (and a high ratio of personnel staff to employees), competitive pay and benefit packages, profit sharing, open communications, and the meticulous selection and training of management, particularly at the supervisory level (see for example Beaumont, 1987:117–19; and Foulkes, 1981). As with Marks & Spencer, the inevitable question that trade unions confront from employees in such organisations is 'why should I join a union?'

Of course not all large non-union companies are benevolent, and for those which are benevolence is an act of business (to make a profit), not an act of charity. Some large non-union companies, such as McDonald's, are distinctly *anti*-union. Margaret Thatcher once said that 'we must expect that a lot more of our jobs will come from the service sector – from the McDonald's and the Wimpeys', but the neon lights of the hamburger economy 'hides a reality that is more like the slum industries of yesteryear' (Lamb and Percy, 1987:15). Labour costs at McDonald's outlets must not rise above 15 per cent of sales, such that if sales decline then staff numbers are cut back and work intensified. The company employs those with few other opportunities, typically women, ethnic minorities and youths (65 per cent of staff are less than 21 years old), and although annual labour turnover is 196 per cent, labour is cheap and flexible (76 per cent are part time) and tasks can be learnt in a day. In fact workers' skills have effectively been eliminated (there are no chefs), and computerised machines do all the cooking. The more important ingredients are tight labour control and a team grading system that keeps workers smiling for the customers, but at each other's throats (ibid:15–17; see also Goffee and Scase, 1995:123–4).

Clearly, then, not all large non-union companies are alike. Moreover small non-union companies are different again. More importantly there is a major discrepancy between the popular image and the reality of working in small firms. The popular image was articulated by a Committee of Enquiry on Small Firms in the early 1970s:

> In many respects the small firm provides a better environment for the employee than is possible in most large firms. Although physical working conditions may sometimes be inferior in small firms, most people prefer to work in a small group where communications present fewer problems: the employees in the small firm can easily see the relation between what they are doing and the objectives and performance of the firm as a whole. Where management is more direct and flexible, working rules can be varied to suit the individual (Bolton, 1971:23).

According to this account, employees choose small firms because of the non-economic rewards they offer. Not surprisingly the predicted outcomes are greater moral involvement, organisational attachment, and of course industrial harmony. As the Conservative Party document *Moving Forward* (1983) claimed,

> One of the advantages that small businesses do, in fact, enjoy is the generally good state of relations between the owners and managers and their employees. There is a sense of partnership based on the willingness to work for a clearly perceived common purpose from which everyone benefits (quoted by Goss, 1991:154).

Thus the 1980s became the decade of 'small business revivalism' and the 'enterprise culture' (Burrows and Curran, 1989:527). Under Mrs Thatcher 'the small firm has been taken up as the articulating principle of right-wing reaction to economic crisis' (Curran and Burrows, 1986:274), and the entrepreneur cast in the role of 'dynamic saviour of a moribund economy' (Rainnie, 1989:1). 'No longer reviled as a tax dodger or exploiter of cheap labour, small business exemplifies most of the current Government's ideals, whether small shop (thrift, independence) or fast expanding Thames Valley electronics concern (risk taking, ambitious, profit orientated)' (*Financial Times*, 12 June 1984, quoted by Rainnie, 1985b:141–2). In short, 'Small is supposed to be not only beautiful, but also dynamic, efficient, competitive and perhaps most important, a source of new jobs' (Rainnie, 1989:1).

For Conservative governments, then, the promotion of small firms in the 1980s and early 1990s was not only a key element of economic policy but also employee relations policy. The apparent industrial harmony of small firms was attributed to the absence of trade unions, minimum state intervention and, as a result, a more direct employer–employee relationship uncontaminated by 'outside' interference (Goss, 1991:152). For the Conservative Party, 'This combination of factors is claimed to reveal the employment relationship as it should be: a relationship between equals in the market (one the buyer and one the seller of labour) with a mutual interest in the success of the enterprise' (ibid). The reality, on *all* counts, both economic and industrial is, however, very different. For example, although the number of small firms has increased in recent years, and although small firms have increased their share of total employment (Bannock and Daly, 1990; and Dale and Kerr, 1995) and created a great many new jobs (Gallagher *et al.*, 1990), they also contribute more than their fair share to the ranks of the unemployed (Daniel, 1985; and Rainnie, 1989:2, 23). The death rate of small firms is almost as high as the birth rate (Daly, 1990), with record business failures in 1992 (more than 170 companies, partnerships and one-man businesses went bust every day in 1992) (*The Independent*, 31 December 1992). Almost half of all new businesses fail within the first three years, and only a third survive for six or more years. Much of the net increase in new businesses is concentrated in 'other services' (such as contract cleaning and hairdressing), hardly renowned for massive job creation (Daly, 1990:555–7). Moreover, while employment growth in the mid to late 1980s was mainly attributable to the very smallest companies (those with fewer than 20 employees), the 20–49 employees cohort performed particularly badly (Gallagher *et al.*, 1990:95–6), suggesting that most small businesses are likely to remain small (Hakim, 1989a, 1989b) and that such companies find it difficult to change from an informal to a more formal management structure. Hardly the acorns of future oaks.

The more important deficiency of the popular account of small firms, however, is that size *per se* is not a *necessary* characteristic of an organisation but a *contingent* one (Burrows and Curran, 1989:530). Size is an important variable in employee relations because of the very clear correlation between size and a number of key industrial relations indicators: as establishment size increases, organisations display more elaborate management structures (differentiated hierarchically and functionally), they devote more resources to personnel matters, and they are more likely to have formal management procedures for issues such as discipline and dismissal; bigger establishments are also more likely to recognise a trade union, have shop stewards present and experience strikes (see for example Brown, 1981; Millward and Stevens, 1986; and Millward *et al.*, 1992). But size plays a role in the functioning of an organisation *only* in relation to other factors (Curran, 1990:129). As Rainnie (1991:177) notes, 'to say that smallness *per se* is a characteristic that, alone, will determine the internal operation and external relations of this unit is bizarre'. The more important variables to consider *in relation to size* are industrial sector, technology, locality, labour and product markets. In their study of 397 small firms, for example, Scott and his colleagues (1989) found it more useful to subdivide the sample into four broad industrial groups, namely traditional manufacturing, high-tech manufacturing, traditional services and high-tech services. Size in itself could not account for the differences between firms.

Thus 'what constitutes "smallness" will be very much contextual – dependent upon economic sector, market size and the like' (Burrows and Curran, 1989:530). As the small firm sector extends from the corner shop to the high-tech firms of the M4 corridor and Silicon Glen in Scotland, such a heterogeneous collection of organisations demands, first, a *relational* conceptualisation of their activities, and second, identification of those factors which, in general and in combination, determine why a great many firms, and the majority of small firms, are non-union. As in the case of Sew & Son and many other small clothing manufacturers producing *St Michael* branded goods, the (dependent) relationship with its major customer, Marks & Spencer, plays a crucial role in shaping employer–employee relations (see also Rainnie, 1984, 1985a). Equally, the structural characteristics of the workplace and the composition of the workforce, the informal nature of employee relations and the (unitarist) attitude of the owner/manager can combine to produce an environment unconducive to trade union membership. Each of these variables is analysed in turn. Finally, the problems of trade union recruitment, organisation and representation are analysed in more detail. Is it realistic to anticipate that trade unions may halt or even reverse the decline in membership (described in Chapter 5) by successful organisation of non-unionism's growing ranks?

Small firms, big firms

The nature of employee relations in any organisation can only be fully understood in the context of, and in relation to, wider socioeconomic, political and legal structures (see Chapter 2). Interorganisational relations play an important part (Chapter 3), especially in the case of small firms where their relationship with much bigger firms can have a major bearing on their own labour process characteristics (Rainnie, 1991). Simply put, 'large capital determines not only the field of play, but also the rules of the game that small firms are engaged in' (Rainnie, 1985b:165). For this reason 'Size *qua* size . . . is secondary to the relationship with the wider economy and it is these which determine the organisational and social frameworks of the enterprise' (Curran, 1990:130). In the case of Marks & Spencer, for example, the highly competitive nature of the retail sector, and the uncertainty of market trends and changing fashions, has led to a relationship with suppliers that has been described as 'benevolent dictatorship' (Salmans, 1980:68). Retailers such as M&S did not create the highly competitive, small-scale clothing sector, but they have certainly taken advantage of it. And in doing so they ensured that this situation would continue (Rainnie, 1984:153). In other words a major reason why the clothing sector is characterised by low technology, ease of entry (and exit), and therefore small, predominantly non-union firms employing cheap female labour is because a dependent small-firm sector is necessary to the continuation of large-scale enterprise in retailing (Curran and Burrows, 1986:274).

> Briefly, the advantages to companies like Marks and Spencer of formally independent, but in reality utterly dependent small suppliers, are enormous and can be summed up as cheap flexibility, crucial at a time of increased competition. The existence of the *individual* small firm is not important, the continued existence of a *number* of them is vital (Rainnie, 1985b:157, original emphasis).

As early as the mid 1920s M&S pioneered a relationship with suppliers that allowed the company to decide *what it wanted to sell*, rather than simply buy what the manufacturers had produced. As Tse (1985:75) notes, 'Marks & Spencer has *dictated* a new type of relationship between the manufacturer and the retailer' (emphasis added). This account is somewhat at odds, however, with the more popular accounts of the harmonious, collaborative relationship that M&S enjoys with its suppliers. Tse (ibid:76–7), for example, talks of the relationship as a 'marriage', while Lord Sieff himself provides details of the technical support that M&S provides and the long-term partnership the company has enjoyed with many suppliers, adding that M&S encourages all its suppliers (who are required to sign a 'code of conduct') to offer similar terms and conditions of employment for their own workers (Sieff, 1986:161). Of particular concern to Lord Sieff was the condition of the supplier's toilets, which he appeared to regard as a barometer of the state of employee relations at supplier companies (ibid). But the companies discussed by 'Dan, Dan the lavatory man', as he was sometimes called (ibid), are all larger companies with whom Marks & Spencer would have more of a *mutually dependent*, rather than dominant relationship (see for example Sieff, 1990:93–111). With smaller companies, such as Sew & Son, M&S displays much less compunction about switching contracts or playing one supplier off against another (see Rainnie, 1984, 1985b).

Although the strategies of large firms play a crucial role in the restructuring of economic relations in general and those with, and within, small firms in particular (e.g. Shutt and Whittington, 1987), this should not divert attention away from the small-firm sector. What is often suggested, for example, is that the relationship between small and large firms is simply one of *dependence*, with consequent implications for employee relations. The general argument, as Goss (1991:160) points out, is that 'small firms – directly or indirectly – are generally in a dependent position, a dependence which is frequently reflected in patterns of industrial relations as employers seek to maintain a competitive edge through rigorous exploitation of labour'. In many respects this is undeniably true: the appalling conditions of many (sweat shop) firms bears testament to this (e.g. Byrne, 1986; Hoel, 1982; Phizacklea, 1987; and Pond, 1983). But as Rainnie (1991:187) points out, it is important to consider the relationship between small and large firms more directly and in more detail, since there are at least four very different relationships which can be identified:

- *Dependent* small firms complement and service the activities of larger firms (for example subcontracting). Labour costs must be minimised and flexibility is essential.
- *Dominated* small firms compete with large firms through the more intense exploitation of machinery and especially labour. Hyper-exploitation of labour is not uncommon.
- *Isolated* small firms operate in specialised and/or geographically discrete markets, the niches of demand that are unlikely to be touched by large capital. Living off the crumbs from the large firms' table, however, entails a hand-to-mouth existence and invariably sweat shop conditions for the workforce.

- *Innovative* small firms compete in (or even develop) specialised markets, but are always open to the potentially fatal attractions of large firms. Flexibility and innovation are essential, and attractive pay and conditions may be necessary to attract highly skilled workers (see Rainnie, 1989:85, 1991:188).

In the clothing sector, small firms generally find themselves in a *dependent* relationship with their larger customers, with obvious implications for employee relations. Tight supervision, authoritarian management and payment systems that tie the workers to their machines are just some of the outcomes cited by Rainnie (1985a:218). These are not universal or inevitable features of the clothing industry *per se*, but rather reflect *the relationship with the customer*. As Ram (1991:607–11, 1994) demonstrates in a study of clothing firms in the West Midlands, where output went to intermediaries rather than direct to the retailers, supervision was not so tight, the workers tended to work at their own pace and controlled effort levels, and there was extensive negotiation, and renegotiation, over the rate for the job. The difference between the outerwear section and the M&S work at Sew & Son bears out a similar point. At the same time, however, in either case there appears in practice to be very little room for manoeuvre: the field of play is determined by the customer, and while the *precise* rules of the game may be subject to interpretation (negotiation), the large firm can always move the goalposts or take the ball elsewhere to play.

Among the *dominated* and *isolated* groups of small firms are to be found those which depend largely on second-hand machinery and cheap labour (Rainnie, 1991:188), the 'chaff' of today's harvest rather than the 'green shoots' of future growth. These small firms operate in established markets (for example general printing) and/or those now populated by a large number of self-employed people. At a time of high unemployment the growth of self-employment (from just over two million to 3.3 million between 1981 and 1996, see Chapter 3), is as much an indicator of desperation and decline as opportunity and growth. Two-thirds of the self-employed work in distribution, hotels, repairs, construction and 'other services' (Dale and Kerr, 1995:462–5; and Daly, 1991:109–20). The greatest concentration of self-employed men is to be found in construction (ibid:119–21), where the growth of labour-only subcontractors (most of whom are self-employed) is a direct consequence of government and employer policies to deregulate and deunionise the industry (Evans, 1990). Work has been intensified, but the individualisation of the employment relationship and the removal of all trade union immunities has failed to transform the economic performance of the industry (ibid).

Lastly, among the *innovative* small firms we finally encounter those businesses that perhaps epitomise the 'enterprise culture' of the 1980s, the high-tech firms of the electronics, computer and related sectors (Rainnie, 1991:191–4). Contrary to popular belief, however, many, if not the majority, of these companies are in fact unionised. In a survey of Scottish electronics plants, for example, 70 per cent of employees worked in establishments where trade unions were recognised (Sproull and MacInnes, 1987:335). In a more comprehensive study using data from the second Workplace Industrial Relations Survey (1984), Beaumont and Harris (1988a:833–4) found that the extent of union recognition was actually *higher* in 'high tech' than 'non-high tech' industries for domestically owned establishments (both for manual and non-manual employees). In the case of foreign-owned companies, however, the reverse was true, especially in relation to manual employees (ibid). Given that many small, innovative (non-union) companies are subject to predatory takeover by larger (unionised) companies, the effect of small-firm/large-firm relationships, over time, is perhaps more likely to result in unionisation among the innovative small-firm sector, rather than a perpetuation of non-union status (as in the previous three groups identified).

While Rainnie's fourfold categorisation allows us to distinguish a greater variety of relationships that small firms experience, Curran (1990:130) argues that there is still an overall tendency for observers to suggest a subordinate or subservient role. Put differently, autonomy may in practice be greater than is often assumed among the small-firm sector (see also Ram, 1991, 1994). This can be illustrated by juxtaposing Atkinson's (1984) model of the 'flexible firm' and Piore and Sabel's (1984) model of 'flexible specialisation'. In the former, small firms are seen as part of the periphery, involved in a dependent relationship with large firms for whom they provide numerical flexibility or lower costs as a result of 'distancing' (the replacement of an employment contract with a commercial contract, possibly via self-employment and labour-only subcontracting). In the 'flexible specialisation' model, in contrast, small, craft-based firms are presented as an *alternative to* rather than an appendage of large firms, able to compete with the mass production techniques of large firms through the use of new technology (which lowers minimum efficient scale) and cooperative (network) relations with other small firms in the locality. Although there are both conceptual and empirical problems with both models (see Pollert, 1988), the contrast between the subordinate, peripheral firm (more likely to be non-union) and the craft-based firm (more likely to be unionised) serves to highlight still further the possible roles and relationships that can influence employee relations in small firms. The skills of the workforce, for example, is just one of the characteristics that plays a key role in non-union employee relations.

The structural characteristics of non-union firms and the composition of the workforce

Although 'single shot' pictures taken from cross-sectional surveys are in many respects unsatisfactory for the analysis of dynamic and diachronic processes of employee relations, they nevertheless provide a rich source of data on the *general* characteristics of non-union firms. This enables us to say whether, on the whole, non-union firms are more likely to be, for example, large or small and employ predominantly manual or non-manual workers, men or women, full-time or part-time staff. Data from the third Workplace Industrial Relations Survey (1990) confirms the results of previous surveys that indicate that, *ceteris paribus*, non-union establishments are more likely to be small, single-plant rather than multi-establishment undertakings, and located in the private sector (and especially private services) rather than the public sector. Among private sector establishments, for example, only 19 per cent of those employing 25–49 workers recognise trade unions, whereas over 50 per cent recognise a union once the 500 employee threshold is passed (Millward *et al.*, 1992:64; see also Cully and Woodland, 1996:223; and Scott *et al.*, 1989:17). It is hardly surprising, then, that union membership is extremely low in industries such as clothing, where over 50 per cent of firms employ fewer than twenty-five workers and nearly 90 per cent of all firms employ fewer than 125 workers (Rainnie, 1989:89–9). In textiles, clothing and footwear companies (SIC 17–19) with fewer than twenty-five employees, union density is just 13 per cent (Cully and Woodland, 1996:221). Data from all three WIRSs are presented in Table 9.1. A particularly interesting finding of the 1990 survey was that, as expected, older workplaces had a higher union density (independent of size) but the newest workplaces had higher density levels than those in the five to nine years age range. In other words, there appears to be something distinctive about workplaces that were established in the early part of the 1980s, as these were less likely to be unionised than those established later in the decade (Millward *et al.*, 1992:63–4). It is not unreasonable to suggest that this may well be connected to the broad changes taking place in management style in recent years, as discussed in Chapter 4.

Locality also plays an important part in union or non-union status. Non-union establishments, for example, are more likely to be located in areas of high unemployment (Millward *et al.*, 1992:63–4). Geographical subsystems are generally overlooked in the study of industrial and employee relations, although it is often suggested that the decline of major conurbations – the heartland of union organisation and industrial militancy – and the growth of industry in new towns or semi-rural areas (Mason, 1991:74–6) can have a significant impact on employee relations (e.g. Handy, 1984:85; Lane, 1982; and Massey, 1984). Bassett (1988:46), for example, notes that in Milton Keynes, Britain's fastest growing town in the mid to late 1980s, two thirds of local companies employed fewer than ten workers, two thirds of all jobs were in the service sector and around 80 per cent of all companies were non-union, a fact boldly advertised by the town's development corporation. Similarly, in a study of 411 companies in three new towns in Scotland (Glenrothes, Irvine and Livingston), over 86 per cent were non-union, a figure much higher than manufacturing in general (Beaumont and Cairns, 1987:14–15). On a regional

TABLE 9.1　Non-unionism by sector and size

(a) Sector (percentage of establishments that do not recognise a trade union)

	1980	*1984*	*1990*
All establishments	36	34	47
Private manufacturing	35	44	56
Private services	59	56	64
Public sector	6	1	13

(b) Size: non-unionism in private sector establishments (percentage of workforce not members of a union, by size of establishment)

Year	25–49	50–99	*(number of employees)* 100–199	200–499	500–999	≥1000
1984	74	70	61	53	40	28
1990	81	75	67	51	46	47

Source: Calculated from Millward *et al.* (1992:64, 71).

basis, there is essentially a North–South divide when it comes to union recognition, which is higher in the North and lower in the South, although this is qualified by above-average non-recognition in the North-West and an above-average number of plants in Scotland with *no* union members (Beaumont and Harris, 1988b, 1989). It is important to note that the North–South divide is *not* attributable to the industrial make-up of the different regions (for example more service sector companies in the South) (ibid), although the fact that the highest rates of new firm formation (from 1980–6) were in the South-East, South-West and East Anglia (Mason, 1991:74) is no doubt of some significance. In a study of 115 high-tech companies in the South-East, for example, McLoughlin and Gourlay (1992:675) found that 80 per cent were non-union.

Workforce characteristics are also notably different between union and non-union firms. The latter are more likely, *ceteris paribus*, to employ relatively fewer manual workers, more women, and a higher proportion of part-time staff (Millward *et al.*, 1992:63–4). In the clothing industry, for example, almost 88 per cent of the workforce is female (Rainnie, 1989:90). Many non-union companies also rely on family or kin, who are often placed in key positions in the company (e.g. Ram, 1991:609). In the small firms studied by Scott *et al.* (1989:47), sometimes as many as ten out of twenty employees were tied by bonds of kinship, thereby constituting a 'core' workforce that the owner/

manager could rely on. Family pressures are often brought to bear on the workers of small firms in a different way:

> Management in the clothing industry feels the necessity, but also the freedom, to impose discipline in their workers, particularly married women, from the word go. Taking advantage of the pressures on women brought to bear in trying to reconcile the dual roles of wife/mother and worker, management rely on this situation making women less likely to leave in response to poor wages and conditions (Rainnie, 1989:119).

Poor wages and conditions are a principal characteristic of small, non-union firms. The owner/managers of small firms take a *deliberate* decision to pay lower wages (Craig *et al.*, 1985; and Phizacklea, 1987), recognising that there is a trade-off between lower pay and higher labour turnover but reconciling this trade-off through the employment of disadvantaged groups such as married women (e.g. Rainnie, 1989:119), ethnic minorities (Ram, 1991:605, 1994:158–9) or young workers (Curran and Stanworth, 1981b:144), who are more stable, in employment terms, at lower levels of pay (due to their limited opportunities elsewhere). Goss (1988, 1991), for example, draws a contrast between non-union instant print shops that employ low-skilled, low-paid, predominantly younger workers, and unionised colour printing where skills are vital and the workforce older. Likewise Ram (1991:613–16) notes that ethnicity can be an important resource for management (invoking subservience, servility and passivity between husband and wife or mother-in-law and daughter-in-law), although such relations do not necessarily always work in management's favour.

The idea, then, that workers deliberately choose to work for non-union companies because 'convenience of location, and generally the non-material satisfactions of working in them, more than outweigh any financial sacrifice involved' (Bolton, 1971:21), begins to appear somewhat suspect. As Curran and Stanworth (1981b:145) note, 'small firm workers did not so much self-select themselves into jobs as a result of possessing certain stable motivational patterns but rather developed a market situation in which their job choices were often highly circumscribed'. Many employees in non-union firms, for example, are unable to develop stable employment patterns when they are forced to work on a casual or seasonal basis, as in the hotel and catering industry (e.g. Macaulay and Wood, 1992:21), or even work 'off the cards' so that the employer can avoid statutory employment laws and national insurance contributions (e.g. Ram, 1991:605–6; and Scott *et al.*, 1989:24–5, 92). Self-employment may be the only option available to many seeking employment, and it comes as no surprise that ethnic minorities, married people and women with dependent children are more likely to be self-employed, or that many of the self-employed have a second job as an employee, and vice versa (see Daly, 1991).

All these characteristics of non-union firms and non-union workers are invariably set within a highly informal working environment. Informality begins with recruitment and extends right through the organisation, from communications and grievance handling to the highly personalised, day-to-day relations between management and labour (Scott *et al.*, 1989). For management, and of course the advocates of small non-union firms, the absence of bureaucracy is seen as a positive advantage, not least as reflected in very low levels of strike activity. The key advantage lies, however, not in the extent to which informality allows for more direct and flexible arrangements to suit the individual, but in the extent to which such arrangements serve to obscure the conflicts of interest inherent in the employment relationship – not least those prevailing in the small non-union firm. In fact, as Curran (1990:137–8) notes, employer–employee relations in small firms are based on a contradiction that is likely to lead to *permanent* instability: small firms find themselves in largely dependent relations with big firms and are therefore more susceptible (less able to control) the external, competitive environment, yet within the firm relations tend to be highly personalised, such that when change and conflict cannot be contained or handled through such informal relations, 'it erupts with an intensity that is absent in more formal, procedurally regulated relationships' (Scott *et al.*, 1989:61). Is the absence of strike activity, then, an indication of industrial harmony or employee powerlessness in small, non-union firms?

Informality and industrial harmony in the non-union sector

According to Lord Sieff (1990:84), Marks & Spencer has never had a strike. Nor, for that matter, has IBM (Bassett, 1986:161) or many other large, non-union companies. Just as there is little incentive for workers in these companies to join a trade union, there is little incentive to strike. But the idea of industrial harmony in non-union firms is associated more directly with smaller firms, where it is assumed that better communications, easier working relations, personal ties, job satisfaction, employee involvement and a greater awareness of individual needs serve to overcome any inherent tension between capital and labour. The combination of low levels of union membership and very few strikes suggest that 'small is beautiful'. As far as small-firm employee relations are concerned, however, this would seem to be a 'modern myth' (Rainnie 1985a:213–16, 1989) that arises from a confusion of image and reality. The image presented by the Conservative Party, for example, in their pamphlet *Small Firm, Big Future*, is that 'Working relationships are easier and happier in small companies. Many of the problems that arise in large enterprises are unknown in firms where the owner is known to all his employees' (quoted by Rainnie, 1985b:148).

However there is virtually no empirical evidence to support such claims (Goss, 1988:115; and Scase, 1995), and that which does exist (e.g. Ingham, 1970) is methodologically suspect (Curran and Burrows, 1986; Curran and Stanworth, 1981a; and Rainnie, 1989:156–70). Invariably, the suggestion that the firm is 'one big happy family' is derived from the opinions of owners/managers rather than the workforce (Curran and Stanworth, 1981a:14–15; and Goss, 1988:115, 1991:158). In reality, quiescence need not imply individual deference, nor does the absence of strike activity imply the eradication of industrial conflict (see Chapter 10). It is therefore essential to delve further into the social relations of production within small, non-union firms, and in particular to elicit the opinions of the workforce.

One of the most striking features of small, non-union firms, as already intimated, is the informality of employee relations. In their study of 397 small firms, for example, Scott *et al.* (1989:16) found that 61 per cent had no regular meetings with workforce representatives, and 44 per cent had no arrangements for informing or consulting employees through informal meetings or internal memos (see also Millward *et al.*, 1992:364–5). As Gunnigle and Brady (1984:23) conclude from their study of twenty-five small manufacturing firms, 'there seems to be a dangerous perception of complacency about communications and consultation in small firms. Owner/managers place emphasis on the frequency of employer/employee contact rather than on the quality of such contacts'. If problems arise, these too are settled informally: less than a third of the firms studied by Scott *et al.* (1989:16), for example, had a formal, written grievance procedure (see also Millward *et al.*, 1992:364). As expected, larger firms were more likely to have formal procedures, as were those that were unionised (Scott *et al.*, 1989:16–17). In sum, procedural informality characterises the small, non-union sector to a much greater extent than either the unionised or large, non-union sector. Figure 9.1 summarises the principal differences between union and non-union, large and small firms (see also Millward *et al.*, 1992:236–9).

The notion of small firms being 'one big happy family' is, of course, a cliché, 'and yet as with all clichés it contains a grain of truth' (Scott *et al.*, 1989:51). The significant presence of family members within small firms has already been noted. More generally, personal relations tend to become employee or industrial relations in small firms. In the building industry, for example, where market conditions are highly unstable, employers frequently adopt a fraternal strategy with few overtly hierarchical relations. Instead the employer displays an 'all workers together' attitude, for example working alongside his employees on the job (see Goffee and Scase, 1982; and Scase, 1995:587–8). Thus it is the *particularistic* relations that develop between employer and employee that demand attention. Like family relations, feelings of 'good' and 'ill' tend to

264

	UNION		NON-UNION	
	Large	Small	Large	Small
Pay system	Formalised system	Industry agreement	Formalised system	Informal
Differentials	Continuous and extensive pay hierarchy, few on industry minimum	Relatively continuous	Wide differentials, many paid industry minimum	Discontinuous, narrow differentials, minimum rate often below industry minimum
Sick Pay/Pensions	Common, non-discretionary	Pensions uncommon, sick pay mainly for key staff	Common, but often restricted to specific groups	Pensions uncommon, sick pay for key staff
Holidays	Industry standard or better	Industry standard	Industry standard or low minimum entitlement increasing with grade/service	Low entitlement for all grades, often below industry standard
Job Guarantees	Collective agreement at industry or local level	Industry agreement/statutory measures	None (statutory measures only)	None (statutory measures only)
Manning Agreements	Formal/informal deals	Industry agreement/informal bargaining	Determined by management prerogative	Determined by management prerogative
Training Systems	Formal (linked to state schemes)	Recruit skilled workers externally or formal (linked to state schemes)	Formal (linked to state schemes)	Recruit externally trained or informal/firm-specific training

FIGURE 9.1 Pay, benefits and working arrangements in union vs non-union firms

Source: Adapted from Rubery (1987:62–3).

be more intensely held in small firms (Scott *et al.*, 1989:42, 51), as Rainnie (1989:127–8) illustrates:

Management stress on the 'family' nature of their own firm and relationships within it, not only points to the way in which a particular social formation is used to legitimate power structures (manager-as-father allowed to discipline the children/ workers), but also the way that disagreement can be termed pathological. The ideological power of the family is such that attacking this sacred institution is almost unthinkable within the ruling consensus. Likewise, anybody breaking the manage-rially defined boundaries of decent behaviour in a family firm, by definition steps out of the bounds of acceptable action.

The appearance of industrial harmony thus begins to appear somewhat suspect once the reality of (authority) relations between employer and employee within small, non-union firms is analysed more closely. When workers in small firms are questioned about relations with their employer, for example, they invariably report 'socially distant' relations (Curran and Stanworth, 1981b:148; see also Goss, 1988, 1991). Relations are often not overtly hostile, but 'it would be wrong to see such relations as necessarily tokening deep and strong affective relations between workers and bosses' (Curran and Stanworth, 1981b:149). Rather, 'friendship' and easy-going rela-tions are simply the easiest way to deal with others in a closed environment. Conflict may therefore be 'submerged' in small firms due to the need to manage intergroup conflicts on a personal basis (Stephenson *et al.*, 1983:33). But herein lies the source of instability: such relations may achieve a degree of integration and a veneer of industrial harmony, but 'if the basis of legitimacy is relationships other than those stemming purely from the employment relationship, their continuance is threatened by change. Change of many types can pull back the veil of obscurity and reveal the unmediated effect of the employment relationship' (Scott *et al.*, 1989:48–9).

Even 'happy family' owners/managers can change their tune when con-fronted by external pressures or internal dissent. Scott *et al.* (ibid:50), for example, refer to one manager who boasted of his caring, paternalistic approach, which he illustrated by reference to two older workers who had been allowed to stay on at the firm beyond their retirement age. At a subsequent interview, however, these two workers were referred to in less affectionate terms. In the interim period, profits had fallen and the company had gone into the red for the first time. The result had been redundancies, including the two older workers, who were now referred to in terms of 'getting rid of the shit'. As this and other examples cited by Scott *et al.* (ibid:50) illustrate, it is not uncommon for the advantages of family and affective ties to turn into their opposites, into feelings that border upon enmity (ibid:52). If an employee is not performing satisfactorily, for example, as a first step the owner/manager is just as likely to have a word with the employee's friend or a family member in order to put pressure on the offending party. Scott and his colleagues even cite the case of one employer who had a quiet word with an employee's husband at the local pub! If this approach fails, however, the owner/manager may not apply disciplinary action; instead problems are often left to fester until critical rather than corrective action is taken (that is, dismissal rather than discipline) (ibid:92). Dismissal is in fact twice as common in the non-union than the unionised sector of the economy (Millward *et al.*, 1992:364), and in many cases employees are dismissed without statutory notice or even fair grounds (see Dickens *et al.*, 1985). The majority of the 882 257 work-related complaints reported to the Citizens Advice Bureaux in 1993 (almost double the number reported in 1983) came from non-unionists, mainly those employed in small workplaces.

For this reason, and of course the generally poorer conditions of work and pay in small, non-union firms, there is a good deal of 'churning' among the workforce (Scott *et al.*, 1989:30). Overall numbers may be fairly stable, but there is a high rate of entry and exit. In the clothing industry, for example, labour turnover is high where firms deliberately adopt a 'like it or leave' approach (Rainnie, 1985a). As at Sew & Son, many decide, or are forced, to leave. Many more have little alternative but to stay. Exit and/or silence, then, rather than voice, is the most likely scenario. Most employees in small, non-union firms lack the articulateness and self-confidence to challenge or even question the self-assured and often highly opinionated owner/manager (Goss, 1991:165), and even if they do, managers either fail to listen or do nothing about it (Scott *et al.*, 1989:45). Knowing this, many employees see it as pointless to complain. This powerlessness is often combined with enforced compliance, which in some companies 'is made an explicit condition of continued employment, and the threat of dismissal kept ever-present' (Goss, 1991:161). As Scott *et al.* (1989:39) note, 'those who did not support management aims and policy were seen not only to be unreasonable, but also as being in some way treacherous'. The language may be strong (non-compliance as treachery), but such views are deeply held by many owners/managers of small businesses.

As a result, conflict is usually manifested in individual, invariably unorganised forms, such as absenteeism or high labour turnover. Edwards and Scullion's (1982:107, 1984:561–2) account of two clothing firms is a case in point (see also Chapter 10 below). In the absence of collective (trade union) support, individuals are understandably reluctant to challenge management directly (see for example Goss, 1991:165; and Rainnie, 1985a:219), especially as they will inevitably be labelled as 'troublemakers'. Owners/managers blame so-called 'troublemakers' for virtually all their labour ills, ranging from high turnover (unsettling staff), provoking unfair dismissal cases and encouraging absenteeism (Gunnigle and Brady, 1984:22; and Scott *et al.*, 1989:42). More generally, 'The notion of the "trouble maker" appears far too often to be dismissed merely as an interesting but insignificant feature of management accounts of the nature of their workforce. Rather, the importance of this notion is that it serves as an element within a *conflict neutralisation* technique' (Scott *et al.*, 1989:42, original emphasis).

In other words, the unitary perspective adopted by management serves to *personalise* conflict within the organisation (problems are attributed to individuals, not to inherent antagonisms that exist between management and labour in *all* organisations). While most managers are unitarist in outlook (see Chapter 4), such views appear to be more deeply held by the owner/ managers of small firms. Since they fail to recognise or accept *any* conflicts of interest as being legitimate, such attitudes play an important role in both the determination of management style in non-union firms and the inability of trade unions to organise such companies.

Management style in non-union firms

One of the problems which tends to beset any discussion of non-union firms and workers is that they tend to be studied predominantly from the perspective of the propensity of workers to unionise and/or the differences in management practice *vis-à-vis* unionised firms. Consequently 'the very term "non-unionism" becomes a limiting definition of workplaces' (Guest and Hoque, 1994:2), which tend to 'fall' into one of two principal 'types': 'traditionalists', who display outright hostility towards trade unions, or 'sophisticated paternalists', whose management policies effectively 'substitute' for union presence (see Turnbull and Wass, 1998; and Chapter 4 above). Sew & Son would be counted among the former, Marks & Spencer among the latter. The distinction between *anti*-union (suppression) and *non*-union (substitution) firms, however, is a somewhat false dichotomy. Sophisticated paternalists display an apparent indifference towards trade unions because, first, they can afford to, and second, because they rarely face any challenge from organised labour. If they are challenged, however, management are always quick to act and remain firm in their resolution to stay non-union.

In the IBM union recognition vote in Britain in 1977, for example, which Bassett (1986:162–4) cites as an example of both employee indifference towards trade unions and the effectiveness of the company's employee relations policies, IBM spent £10 000 on an advertising campaign to secure a 'No' vote (Beaumont, 1987:121; see also Oliver and Wilkinson, 1992:125–6), a fact that Bassett fails to acknowledge, or perhaps conveniently overlooked. According to Dickson *et al.* (1988), even IBM employees may not be permanently lost to the trade union movement, a point perhaps reinforced by the company's recent troubles. In the early 1990s, M&S faced an organising campaign by USDAW among warehouse staff following the imposition of a three-year pay freeze. This was to bring the salaries of (predominantly female) sales staff into line with those of (predominantly male) warehouse staff (by increasing the former by 26.5 per cent and freezing the latter), following an 'equal pay for work of equal value' case at Sainsbury's in November 1989. M&S accepted the right of warehouse staff to join a union but would not grant recognition, and certainly would not countenance the workers' claim to have their pay freeze cancelled. USDAW has accused M&S of victimising union members in one of its Glasgow depots by introducing 'unworkable shifts', with start times too early for employees to use public transport, an allegation M&S vigorously disputed (Hamil, 1993:43). M&S do recognise trade unions in their European stores, however, which the company attributes to employment legislation and industrial relations practices in these countries that require M&S to deal with trade unions (Salsbury, 1993:569). Industrial action at the company's stores in Dublin over pay, shift patterns and consultation proce- dures, however, suggests that 'internal' rather than purely 'external' factors are at work, illustrating yet again the highly *contingent* nature of management style discussed in Chapter 4.

If faced with a challenge, then, sophisticated paternalists can display vehement opposition to union organisation. It is at such times that the asymmetry of the employment relationship is revealed. As Hamil (1993:43) notes, few other companies would have the power to impose the kind of deal implemented at M&S in response to the equal value case, at least not without significant employee opposition. Management policy is clearly directed at the maintenance of an employee relations system that does not include trade unions, which is one thing that the sophisticated paternalists have in common with the traditionalists. In the case of M&S and other 'sophisticated patern- alists', however, management thinking is effectively pluralist to the extent that management recognises the need to manage employee relations *as if* the workforce has divergent interests. In this way management is able to identify concerns, allay fears, satisfy workers' aspirations *and stay non-union*. Actual policies, of course, are to all intents and purposes unitary in both composition and purpose, but are founded on a deeper management understanding of the employment relationship. At companies such as Sew & Son, in contrast, management thinking is unashamedly unitarist, but employee relations policies are often imposed *against* the express wishes of the workforce. Given that actual policies are often implemented through coercion, it is more appropriate to label the management style as 'authoritarian': if all the organisation's members are on the 'same side' and part of a team, as the unitary perspective holds, then surely management would only need to *inform* employees of its policies, not enforce them.

Such characteristics of management style among small, non-union firms in the clothing industry are not uncommon (Rainnie, 1985a, 1989:168). Likewise in hotels and restaurants management style tends to be highly autocratic and strongly anti-union (Macaulay and Wood, 1992:21; and Macfarlane,

1982:33–4). Variation obviously exists across different hotels, and in particular between the large chains, but there is a common framework within which different management styles function, namely 'a framework which is reluctant to accept the legitimacy of employees taking any meaningful part in the influence or control of their working conditions or environment' (Macfarlane, 1982:34; see also Millward *et al.*, 1992:365). More general studies of non-union firms confirm management attitudes to be a mixture of unitarism, paternalism and authoritarianism (Gunnigle and Brady, 1984:21–2; and Scott *et al.*, 1989). The former has already been discussed at some length in Chapters 2 and 4. Paternalism, as the nomenclature suggests, was traditionally based on a transfer of family/domestic relations into the workplace, with face-to-face relations between management and labour characterised by deference and indulgency (workers were treated as children to be looked after, rewarded and disciplined by their employer as a parent would a child) (Wray, 1996:702). This benevolent form of despotism is typical of many small firms (see Scase, 1995:285; and Wray, 1996:702). To sustain paternalistic relations as firms grow in size, formal consultation and communication procedures are adopted and indulgency is maintained by corporate largesse through profit-sharing schemes and other benefits (at M&S, for example, benefits include subsidised meals, medical care, hairdressing, store discount cards and the like). Sophisticated paternalism thereby remains loyal to the familial culture of traditional paternalism, but only in an attempt to maintain employee subordination (Wray, 1996:703–4). At the heart of all forms of paternalism, in other words, is a over-riding desire to perpetuate managerial authority.

The principal reason for unitarist attitudes and paternalistic and/or autocratic management practices in small firms appears to be possessiveness. Owner/managers in particular regard *their* company as unique and regard themselves as benign, fair, even-handed and reasonable (Scott *et al.*, 1989:36). 'Typically the business is seen as his possession to do as he wishes – and especially where the owner/manager is also the founder. It is important to realise that for many owner/managers the business is essentially an extension of their ego' (ibid:91). Many members of the British 'petty bourgeoisie' (broadly defined as those who own small-scale capital that is used for productive purposes in conjunction with the proprietors' and, often, others' labour) (Scase, 1982:148) 'show strong psychological inclinations towards notions of autonomy and independence, and this is often translated into an organisational form to ensure their maximisation' (Curran and Burrows, 1986:270; see also Ford, 1982:45–6). Consequently owners/managers not only believe in, but often impose their primacy over the labour process (Scott *et al.*, 1989:93). The implications for employee relations are immediately apparent. Not only does the personality of the owner/manager have a major impact on management style, but the owner's/manager's desire for independence and autonomy 'often result in ill-defined organisational structures with poorly defined roles, a high level of centralised decision-making and little forward planning. For employees the result may be feelings of lack of security and involvement' (Curran, 1990:138).

Generally, management policy in small firms is not formulated in a self-conscious way, relying instead on informal routinisation. This is especially true of labour relations policies, where there is little evidence of pre-planning: 'The dominant approach is one that stresses that as long as the workers are working there is no problem' (Scott *et al.*, 1989:34). In this respect the 'traditionalists' display a remarkable similarity with the unionised 'standard moderns' discussed at some length in Chapter 4.

Of course there are inevitable differences between small, non-union firms. Guest and Hoque (1994), for example, differentiate (newly established) non-union firms according to whether or not they have a human resource strategy on the one hand, and the nature of their human resource policies and practices, on the other. This gives rise to a fourfold classification of (1) 'good' non-union employers that have a clear human resource strategy and positive human resource management policies; (2) 'lucky' non-union companies that have opportunistically followed the latest 'fads and fashions' of human resource management; (3) 'bad' non-union companies that have no strategy and a low uptake of human resource policies; and (4) the 'ugly' face of non-unionism represented by employers who (strategically) deprive workers of their rights and exploit their labour. In a sample of 122 non-union firms studied by Guest and Hoque, only eight could be described as 'ugly' whereas fifty-six were 'good' employers. The comparatively high number of 'good' employers, in marked contrast to the picture suggested by WIRS 1990, is no doubt partly attributable to the 'self-selecting' rather than representative nature of the sample. One might expect 'good' non-union firms with more sophisticated employee relations policies to be small 'high tech' firms in the 'innovative' group identified by Rainnie (1989:85, 1991:188), but in fact most tended to be in the non-financial service sector rather than manufacturing (Guest and Hoque, 1994:6–7). A major deficiency of this study, however, is that employees were not asked whether their employer was good, bad or ugly.

In a specific study of high tech companies, McLoughlin and Gourlay (1992:673–4) consider management style along two different dimensions, namely individualism/collectivism (as discussed in Chapter 4) and the extent of 'strategic integration' (essentially the extent to which company policies achieve a 'tight coupling' between strategic intent, management attitudes and actual behaviour or, at the other extreme, are largely informal, idiosyncratic, uncoordinated or even contradictory). McLoughlin and Gourlay were concerned to establish the extent to which a sophisticated human resource management (HRM) strategy, such as that which is deemed to characterise companies such as IBM and Hewlett Packard, was pursued by non-union companies in this sector. The picture that emerged from a detailed study that included twenty-three non-union companies, illustrated in Figure 9.2, was that the companies most closely approximating to such an approach (Type I) all employed fewer than 500 workers, employed predominantly non-manual labour (less than 20 per cent were manuals in eight of the ten companies in this group), half had been established since 1979, and the majority were non-assembly/manufacturing plants (ibid:679).

Overall, the conclusion was that 'non-union status was likely to be the result of straightforward avoidance or opportunism as any HRM-derived sophisticated "substitution" strategy designed to obviate a perceived need for union representation on the part of employees' (ibid:685). Put differently, companies such as M&S and IBM are very much the exception rather than the rule among non-union firms: most non-union firms do not *need*, nor could the majority *afford*, to adopt a substitution strategy. Given the market position of most sophisticated paternalists, these companies are improbable 'role models' for most managers. Equally, for trade unions companies such as M&S and IBM remain an attractive but unlikely prize. The reality that trade unions must confront, and the problems they must overcome if they want to organise the growing ranks of non-union employees, are those that characterise the more traditional firms such as Sew & Son. Whether such companies are non-union as a result of deliberate avoidance or simply pragmatic opportunism (or indeed lack of attention by union recruiters), the question that remains to be answered is whether employees in such companies would be receptive to unionisation.

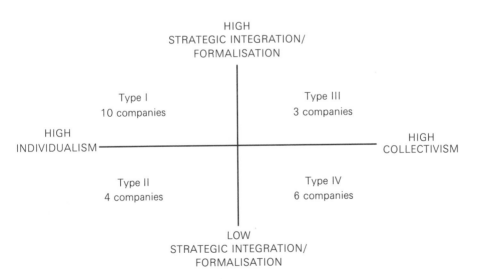

Source: McLoughlin and Gourlay (1992:675).

FIGURE 9.2   Dimensions of management style in non-union firms

Organising the unorganised

As the debate on trade unionism in the 1990s shifts from analysis of decline to prognosis for growth, attention has focused on the prospects for new union strategies to organise in the expanding service sector of the economy (see Chapter 5). During the 1980s, the structure of British trade unionism was exposed as seemingly inappropriate or incapable of dealing with many of the changes thrown up by economic restructuring and recession, government legislation and employer hostility. This was especially so in the service sector, the new towns and the small-firm sector where union organising attempts were often duplicated (and diluted) such that unions were often unable to present potential members with a single, clearly identifiable 'appropriate' union (Winchester, 1988:509). In hotels and catering, for example, the T&GWU and the Hotel and Catering Workers' Union (HCU) (a specialist union spawned by the GMB in 1980) compete for members. But within the T&GWU, hotels come under the Food, Drink and Tobacco division and officials simply do not know enough about the industry to recruit effectively. The HCU, on the other hand, adopts a 'softly, softly', non-confrontational approach, trying to build up membership by persuasion and establishing some confidence in the union among the management of larger hotel chains (Macaulay and Wood, 1992:22–3; and Macfarlane, 1982:35). Inappropriate structures and an ineffective approach to recruitment have led to the unions' role being characterised as one of 'studied invisibility', and it comes as no surprise that very few employees (only 15 per cent in one study) could even name the appropriate unions involved in the industry (Macaulay and Wood, 1992:23–5).

To recruit non-union members in the vast majority of non-union firms will require what Kelly and Heery (1989:198–9) classify as a 'distant expansion' recruitment strategy (see Chapter 5 for a more detailed review). Such firms are not covered by recognition agreements (unlike distribution, for example, where union membership is low but at least union recognition is in place, either on a company or a national basis) and are outside most unions' traditional areas of recruitment (unlike non-union white-collar staff in manufacturing). This presents a much wider, and more difficult, range of problems that unions must overcome if they are to attract new members. Obstacles to expanding membership in new job territories include high rates of labour turnover, the small size of many establishments, their geographical dispersion, and in particular employer opposition (ibid:199; see also Green, 1992:456; Macaulay and Wood, 1992:27; Millward *et al.*, 1992:77; and Turnbull, 1997). In hotels and restaurants, for example, employer antipathy puts trade unions 'in a "Catch 22" situation where, in order to appear a credible source of representation to employees, they must demonstrate an ability to participate meaningfully in the process of job regulation, but this can only be achieved where the employer has conceded sufficient recognition rights' (Macfarlane, 1982:30).

Without recognition from the employer, union effectiveness is more difficult (though not impossible) to establish and certainly more costly to maintain. As Willman (1989:263) argues, prerecognition representation is more expensive as the union is at best only allowed individual representation rights (e.g. in discipline or dismissal cases). Recognition allows some of the representation costs to be shifted on to the employer, which means that unions typically seek to operate in *two* markets, one for members and one for employers. In small firms the market for employers is particularly important since access to employees is more difficult to secure and the union must establish independent workplace organisation (participative self-organisation) if it operates only in the membership market (see Chapter 5). Invariably, therefore, 'unions will not seek to organise employees where they see no prospect of gaining bargaining rights, since they must deal only with individual issues which are costly' (ibid). Thus unions seek to offer something to the employer as well as the employee, as Figure 9.3 demonstrates.

Willman's (1989) analysis suggests that 'market share unionism', where unions compete for a declining membership base in already organised sectors rather than expand their membership in areas such as the private services sector (distant recruitment), is inevitable, given the hostility of employers, the costly nature of such recruitment, the financial weakness of most UK unions and the absence of legal recognition procedures that unions could use to force recognition on recalcitrant employers. However the presumed 'logic' of market-share trade unionism, which of course is inherently illogical for the labour movement as a whole, rests on two preconditions. The first is an absence of structures, procedures, or a central body with sufficient authority to effect coordination and cooperation between individual unions. A good illustration of these problems was the Special Review Body (SRB) set up by the TUC in 1987. Under the auspices of the SRB, Congress conducted six pilot studies of local labour markets in order to facilitate new membership recruitment. These studies revealed striking deficiencies in the internal information systems of many unions, limited knowledge of the key organisational and workforce characteristics of non-union firms, and strictly limited attempts to recruit many non-union workers (see Beaumont and Harris, 1990:276). But while the diagnosis of the problem was accepted by the major unions, they were not prepared to accept a more 'intrusive' (proactive or coordinating) role on the part of the TUC.

If anything the authority of the TUC has declined in recent years (Ackers *et al.*, 1996:27), although under the 'New Unionism' initiative launched in 1996 a new 'organising academy' has been established by the TUC to train union organisers in the techniques of the organising model discussed in Chapter 5.

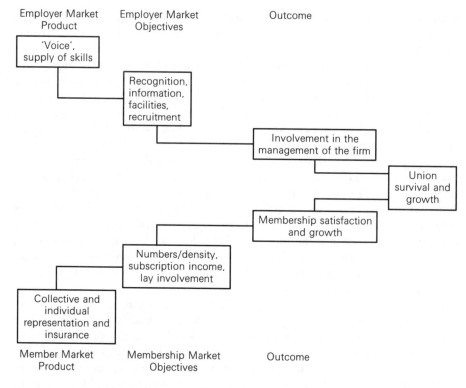

Source: Willman (1989:264).

FIGURE 9.3   The market for trade unionism

Dedicated organisers will target non-union workplaces and non-union work-ers, particularly women, young workers and ethnic minorities, disseminate 'best practice', and above all promote an 'organising culture' where recruit-ment and organising are regarded by everyone in the labour movement as a key priority. A 'facilitating' rather than a (centralised) coordinating role might actually prove more effective for the TUC, encouraging greater cooperation between unions by creating a network of union organisers equipped with a common 'core' of recruitment and organising skills. Of course there will still be competition for membership among a handful of conglomerate unions, given the overlap of recruitment territories (see Winchester, 1988:509), but there is considerable potential for union cooperation (joint venture), which might be easier to effect between the new 'super unions'. This might include:

- *rapprochement*: unions that compete simply agree not to do so on specific issues, thereby eliminating unnecessary expenditure.

- *information sharing*: unions exchange information and expertise to combat common problems (for example deregulation and privatisation).
- *resource swaps*: unions exchange people and assets – on a temporary or permanent basis – to provide expertise or support for specific campaigns, to disseminate 'best practice' and create centres of excellence.
- *selective integration*: unions merge service provisions, allow joint membership or create single representative structures (Willman and Cave, 1994:407–9).

The second precondition for the logic of market-share trade unionism to prevail is a dependence on employers. One of the dilemmas facing all trade unions is that, over time, organisational survival is increasingly separated from, and is largely independent of, the motivation, mobilisation, solidarity and 'willingness to act' of the rank-and-file membership. In effect the union substitutes external guarantees of survival – employer recognition and check-off arrangements, statutory recognition procedures and strong political ties to social democratic parties – for internal dependence on its members. As Offe and Wiesenthal (1980:107) point out, unions invariably develop bureaucratic structures in order to maximise the independence of the union officials and their control over internal decision making on the one hand, and a more 'individualistic' relationship with rank-and-file members on the other, emphasising individual incentives to join (for a review of these developments in the UK, see Heery and Kelly, 1994). The problem that then arises, of course, is that once the relative independence of the organisation from its members' 'willingness to act' has been achieved, 'the organization *no longer has any capacity to resist attempts to withdraw external support* and the externally provided legal and institutional status' (Offe and Wiesenthal, 1980:108, original emphasis). Many unions, as the T&GWU case in Chapter 5 clearly demonstrates, are now trying to work around employer dependence in general and union recognition in particular, despite the costs, because they recognise that ultimately unions must 'organise or die'.

Likewise, in its *Manual for Fulltime Officials and Organisers*, MSF is adamant that:

Organising to recruit and retain members is the most important issue facing us today. It fundamentally affects the future – and survival – of MSF. No one should purport to say that s/he believes in MSF unless they see organising to recruit as their number one priority. . . . The choice is stark. Either we seize the challenge of revitalising our union by recruiting, organising and mobilising members or we service an ever declining membership (MSF, 1996:1).

Even the AEEU has allocated £1 million specifically to recruitment, representing a move away from organising employ*ers* (via single-union agreements) to organising employ*ees*, in particular young workers, women and minority ethnic workers. More importantly, whereas union recruitment in the late 1980s and early 1990s was largely conservative and/or *ad hoc* (Beaumont and Harris, 1990:28; Kelly and Heery, 1989, 1994; Mason and Bain, 1991; and Snape, 1995), there is now growing evidence of more *strategic* recruitment based on a more participative form of (self-sustaining) union organisation (see Chapter 5). Even if unions are more proactive, however, two important questions remain: will non-union workers want to join, and will non-union employers surrender their autonomy and authority?

It must be recognised that many workers are indifferent towards trade union membership (e.g. Abbott, 1993:312), although unions would no doubt argue that they are simply yet to be persuaded. Ironically, some of the lowest-paid workers are not interested in union membership because, in one respect at least, they are better off *without* a union:

> Through the tipping system and control of the communal 'tronc' (the pooled tips which are shared out), a head waiter with flair can, for instance, negotiate the level of his own rewards. The chef (with *shamon*-like knowledge of how much food must be ordered, and control of information over how much actually is ordered) can negotiate his own perks. . . . Such workers stand only to lose by collective wage determination (Mars, 1982:45–6).

Scott *et al.* (1989:75), however, found that workers generally expressed a positive attitude towards trade unions, as did the hotel and catering workers studied by Macaulay and Wood (1992:26; see also Gallie, 1996). Further evidence suggests that many part-timers would like to join a union, but 'What is needed is an environment which encourages part-time workers to participate fully in union structures; which provides equal access to union education; and which welcomes the involvement of part-timers as representatives and activists' (Labour Research Department, 1996:17; see also Sinclair, 1996). With regard to young people, among whom union membership is extremely low (only 6 per cent of those aged below 20 years belong to a union and one-in-five of 20–29 year olds), a nationally representative survey conducted by MORI for the TUC revealed that four times as many 16–24 year olds had positive views about unions compared with those who expressed negative views. In general, however, there is a profound lack of awareness of trade unions among young people (TUC, 1996b; see also Cregan and Johnston, 1990; Payne, 1989; and Spilsbury *et al.*, 1987). In sum, 'The problem is not that young people are hostile to unions. On the contrary, it is simply that many young people have never had the chance to find out what unions can do for them' (TUC, 1996b:12). More than a third of the young people interviewed by MORI said they would join a union if asked, which is hardly surprising as a similar number in the sample earned less than £100 per week; half cited instances of unfair treatment at work, and yet over 70 per cent failed to meet the two-year qualification period for legal protection against unfair dismissal (ibid). A further independent study commissioned by the TUC (1996a) found that, all told, around five million non-union workers would like a union to negotiate on their behalf, especially over issues such as redundancy, health and safety, sick pay entitlement, disciplinary matters, pay and pensions.

Many non-union workers, however, are resigned to the fact that while they might like to join a union, either their employer will not 'allow' them or the relevant union(s) is not interested. When unions attempt to organise small, non-union companies, owners/managers may victimise union activists or, as at Sew & Son, promote them (Rainnie, 1989:219; and Scott *et al.*, 1989:72–3). In the hotel and catering industry employees are well aware of management hostility towards trade unionism, and 'employees' perception of this hostility has a role in forming apparent psychological barriers to acceptance of the likely benefits of union membership and plays some part in generating a sense of both resignation and of the immutability of hotel and catering workers' lot in life' (Macaulay and Wood, 1992:27). Not only is there a sense of fatalism about the likely success of trade unions in dealing with hotel and catering employers, but any positive attitude towards trade unions is tempered by scepticism about the lack of interest so far shown by unions in the industry (ibid:26). Rainnie (1985a:219–22, 1989:133–41) paints a similar picture in the clothing industry, where union structures make it difficult for women to attend branch meetings (given the time and location), and male union officials of the NUTGW are often disinterested in women's needs and aspirations. The women's apathy towards the union is therefore 'rooted in an unholy alliance of the isolation of the steward from the union, the weakness of that union, the resulting weakness of workplace trade unionism, the position of women at work and the role of the family' (Rainnie, 1985a:222, 1989:141). Of course, in both hotels and catering and clothing, many of the problems identified could be overcome by the unions concerned. But could the employer be compelled to negotiate with the workforce?

Given the unitary outlook of the owners/managers of small firms, it is hard to imagine that many would voluntarily decide to grant union recognition. The majority would simply not countenance such a challenge to their cherished independence and authority, although Abbott's (1993:310) study of small service sector firms revealed that almost a third would accept a request for trade union recognition. Moreover as Curran and Stanworth (1981a:17) demonstrate in a study of printing and electronics, the managers of unionised firms 'were, on the whole, surprised at how relatively painless managing a unionised firm turned out to be and, in fact, often recognised some advantages from unionisation'. This finding is echoed by Scott *et al.* (1989:83), who conclude that 'small firms and unions each need on the one hand to be far less wary. On the other hand, there might be positive benefits from co-existence'. Handling disciplinary matters and the management of change in small, non-union firms are examples of areas where such firms might benefit from more formal, collectively determined procedures which provide rights of representation for the workforce (see also Freeman, 1995). As already noted, one reason why small firms do not grow, and therefore do not create the jobs that former Conservative governments longed for, is their inability to move from an informal employee relations system based on personal relations to a more formalised procedure: a principal reason why owners/managers do not expand their business is precisely because they perceive potential problems with staff (e.g. Ford, 1982:42). More formal procedures in the internal labour market, then, should not be automatically equated with inefficiency or a lack of flexibility but if anything, their opposite (see Chapter 3). At the same time, and equally important, an independent organisation can protect and promote employee rights. Unionisation, in other words, need not be a 'zero sum' process for the owner/manager. At present it is not only the non-union employee that suffers from management hostility and the apathy of many trade unions, but also the economy itself wherein small, non-union firms fail to stimulate economic growth.

Conclusion

The debate on, and indeed the practice of, non-unionism in the UK appears to be at a critical juncture. On the one hand, now that 'non-unionism has come out of the closet' (Flood and Turner, 1993:54), it has been suggested that 'the influence by example of non-union "companies of excellence" (e.g. IBM, Marks and Spencer) and the former Conservative government's treatment of unions in the public sector may be factors working to bring about changes in management attitudes towards unions through the course of time' (Beaumont, 1986:33). In other words the expansion of non-unionism in the 1980s and early 1990s might simply be the tip of the iceberg. On the other hand, given that research on union decline suggests that falling density is not irreversible, and given the fact that many unions have launched a number of initiatives to organise non-unionism's growing ranks, the outlook may be more optimistic for trade unions (see Green, 1992:456; Kelly, 1990, 1996; Kelly and Wadding-ton, 1995; Turnbull, 1997; and Chapter 5 above).

The idea that firms are following the example of IBM or Marks & Spencer is clearly ludicrous. The non-unionism promoted by Conservative governments during the 1980s and early 1990s was principally that found among small firms, where the government's aim was to remove 'restrictions' (including those imposed by trade unions) in order to encourage 'enterprise'. These companies are *not*, however, burdened by the law (e.g. Clifton and Tatton-Brown, 1979; Evans *et al.*, 1985; Ford, 1982; Scott *et al.*, 1989:84–90; and Westrip, 1982), as former Conservative governments suggested. In fact quite the opposite. The majority are either genuinely ignorant of the law, or choose to ignore or deliberately flout it (Ford, 1982:43–6; and Scott *et al.*, 1989:90). Put simply, 'Unorganised employment is now often unregulated employment' (Dickens and Hall, 1995:271).

Further erosion of employees' legal rights and protections in small, non-union firms is therefore more likely to encourage exploitation than enterprise. As Rainnie (1989:151) concludes, 'far from needing de-regulation, much *greater* control should be exercised over the wages and conditions provided by small firms. In short, there exists a crying need for a far more extensive and detailed regulatory framework for small firms than we have at present' (original emphasis). Statutory protection would certainly enhance the employment rights of non-union workers, but this would also require an effective system of enforcement. Trade unions could fulfil such a role. Indeed this is the message behind many union initiatives in recent years (e.g. the T&GWU's Link Up campaign discussed in Chapter 5 and the GMB's Fair Laws and Rights in Employment campaign). In addition to wielding the 'sword of justice', unions would also look after the 'vested interests' of non-union employees, increasing rates of pay and improving conditions of work. This is arguably of more immediate importance, as a great many non-union employees are among the 10 million Britons who earn poverty wages (see Chapter 3). But what about the owner/manager? Some would no doubt have to swallow their pride if they were to grant union recognition, and they would all have to surrender a degree of autonomy. But more formalised procedures would also benefit management: it would not only help to stabilise employee relations, but facilitate managed growth. As Scott *et al.* (1989:90) argue, 'it would be useful to dispel the myth that formalised, stable employment relationships based on a minimum legal framework, represent creeping bureaucratisation, the death of enterprise and damage to employment growth'. In sum, many non-union employees need effective collective representation. A great many owners/managers would benefit as well. So too, it must be added, would the economic and social health of the nation.

CHAPTER 10

The dynamics of industrial conflict

The ambulance workers' dispute, 1989–90

On strike?

An ambulance crew 'refused to deal with a newborn baby found abandoned in a ditch' declared the headline in the *Sun* on 23 November 1989. The ambulance unions were on strike. Or were they? 'We're very concerned about one thing', said Derek Turner, an ambulanceman at Deptford Station, 'the public think we're on strike. We're not on strike. All we're doing is what we are contracted to do' (quoted in the *Financial Times*, 23 September 1989). That meant working their 39-hour week (a ban on overtime) and 'working-to-rule'. The unions were demanding a pay increase large enough to restore parity with the fire service; a pay formula similar to that in the other emergency services (linking pay increases to the upper quartile average earnings for adult male manual workers); premium rates for overtime; improvements to holiday entitlement and long-service leave/pay; and a further reduction in the working week. The first two demands, a substantial pay rise and a pay formula, were the key issues. What incensed the ambulance workers was the unequal treatment, as they saw it, between themselves and the police and fire-fighters. As Eric Robinson, a 40-year-old ambulanceman with 15 years' service put it, 'we stand shoulder to shoulder with the police and fire service on jobs, but we don't stand shoulder to shoulder on pay. And yet the ambulance service handles more emergency calls each day than either the fire or police' (quoted in the *Financial Times*, 25 October 1989). They were, quite simply, 'third among equals' (Kerr and Sachdev, 1992).

Background to the dispute

During the Winter of Discontent in 1978–9, a period of widespread industrial unrest during the final months of the then Labour government's term of office, National Health Service (NHS) ancillary workers and ambulance crews had struck work for a pay increase that was well above the government's 5 per cent pay limit. In all subsequent disputes ambulance workers have demanded recognition as an emergency service, alongside the police and fire service, thereby securing a formula to guarantee automatic pay increases. Each time their claim has been refused on the grounds that ambulance crews spend only a small proportion of their time on emergency work, and that a pay formula would add to inflationary pressures within the economy. Thus despite a substantial pay increase following the 1979 action (well in excess of 20 per cent), further disputes followed in 1981 and 1982. The pay agreement of November 1985 brought a temporary respite, absorbing shift, weekend and bonus payments into an all-in salary. This put paid to the old structure of low hourly rates of pay, premium rates for overtime, and numerous incentive bonus schemes and allowances. Management wanted to eradicate various 'restrictive practices' designed to boost take-home pay under this system, such as 'manufactured overtime', in the expectation that this would 'result in a more professional service which would leave behind the mores of its indus-trial past' (Duncan Nichol, NHS Chief Executive, 1992:147). Coincidentally the resulting *hourly* equivalent pay of the new salary structure was now equal to that of a qualified fire-fighter with five years' experience. The unions sought to maintain this link in subsequent negotiations (Kerr and Sachdev, 1992:128), but management maintained that:

1. Ambulance staff can become qualified after 15 months; fire-fighters qualify in their fifth year.
2. Ambulance staff are subject to a standard working week of 39 hours (40 hours in 1986); fire-fighters 42 hours.
3. The due settlement date for the pay of ambulance staff is 1 April; for fire-fighters it is early November.
4. No NHS staff group has outside pay links (Nichol, 1992:147).

The unions failed to maintain the link. By 1989 an 11.14 per cent gap had opened up in the hourly rate between a qualified ambulance worker and that of a fire-fighter with over four years' experience (Kerr and Sachdev, 1992:128). Moreover average overtime hours, now paid at the standard rate, were 10 hours per week. Some workers, such as Julie Piecewska at the Deptford Station, worked 30 hours overtime a week in addition to the standard 39 hours in order to meet mortgage payments. Morale, as in 1979 (Clegg, 1979b:39), was dismally low, the symptom of both low pay (and status) among staff and the financial neglect of the service. Kent's seventeen stations, for example, had only forty defibrillators (the machines used to trace heart patterns and shock a heart into restarting) most of which had been paid for by charities and money raised through jumble sales. The inquiry into the disaster at the Hillsborough football stadium concluded that more lives would have been saved if more defibrillators had been available. The effect on staff morale was summed up by Mick Denyer, an ambulanceman for 19 years and the Kent convenor for the GMB:

> Why should we have to go round with a begging bowl for essential equipment? Morale in the service is at an all-time low. Apathy is the most used word. There is a cure – cash. Cash for the crews and cash for the equipment (quoted in the *Financial Times*, 7 September 1989).

Industrial action

Although the ambulance unions' objectives were conventional enough, the 'means to their ends was another matter' (Kerr and Sachdev, 1992:127). Industrial action began at midnight on 13 September 1989, following a four to one majority vote in favour of a ban on overtime and rest-day working in response to management's final offer of a 6.5 per cent increase in pay. The day before industrial action began, local authorities awarded manual workers an increase of between 8.8 and 9.2 per cent. The scene was thus set for a protracted struggle, especially as the ambulance unions had determined *not* to strike but to continue to answer all accident and emergency calls. 'There was a recognition that the techniques of industrial action in the manufacturing sectors (the strike, the picket line and go-slows) were not necessarily the most appropriate methods for the health service' (ibid:127). But the tactics adopted by the ambulance unions enabled management to hire taxis or to request patients to make their own way to hospital, thus negating the unions' action. By October the industrial action was stepped up, with a ban on non-urgent clerical work, rigid adherence to the 39-hour working week and refusal to transfer non-urgent patients from hospitals. When this too proved ineffective, a further escalation was agreed. From mid November all qualified ambulance crews trained to handle accident and emergency vehicles agreed to ban non-emergency work. It was envisaged that this would have an immediate effect, as most ambulance work involved the transportation of patients to and from hospital, outpatients and day centres (ibid:131–2).

Management responded with industrial action of its own, docking the pay of staff who refused to work normally. In London, crews were suspended for refusing to use radios in the way management wanted – a dispute, it appeared, about pressing or not pressing a radio button. Police and troops were now involved, as they had been in previous ambulance disputes (Morris, 1986). The cost to the Metropolitan Police alone was £100 000 per day to cover ambulance services. By mid December the Met had run up a bill of £3.5 million. It seemed to many people that this money would be better spent on a pay increase for the ambulance workers, after all this sum represented almost 2 per cent of the total wage bill for ambulance staff in 1987–8. But the government's position was unequivocal: 'Of all the things you can spend money on in a health care system, buying off strikes is about the worst' (Kenneth Clarke, Health Secretary, quoted in the *Financial Times*, 14 December 1989). And so the dispute continued into the new year. Ambulance staff continued to lose pay, the unions continued to pay out large sums of money in dispute benefit (which they could ill-afford), management continued to refuse to recognise the unions' demands, the government continued to pay the police to do the ambulance workers' jobs, and the public continued to endure considerable inconvenience.

The government's stance was nothing new. Throughout the 1980s the Thatcher government had made a virtue out of 'standing firm' in a succession of public sector disputes (see Chapter 6). The ambulance dispute was no different. In fact one of Kenneth Clarke's Health Department officials described the dispute as 'the miners' strike for the NHS' (*The Economist*, 16 December 1989). But on this occasion the strategy backfired in a quite spectacular fashion. As a subsequent report in *The Economist* (13 January 1990) pointed out, it was 'strange to relate, [that] Margaret Thatcher's government is being outmanoeuvred by a trade union'. In fact there were five unions (COHSE, GMB, NALGO, NUPE and the T&GWU) but only a single spokesperson, Roger Poole of NUPE, who – unfortunately for the right-wing tabloid press – was 'no dim, chain-smoking class warrior' (ibid). This was a conscious strategy on the part of the unions to prevent any differences between them, imaginary or otherwise, being exploited by journalists, management or the government. In contrast government ministers and backbench MPs appeared to be queuing up to send contradictory messages, a problem compounded by the brusque, combative approach adopted by the Secretary of State for Health, Kenneth Clarke (Kerr and Sachdev, 1992:134–5). One media management coup by the unions was that letters addressed to Mr Clarke by Roger Poole were carefully released to the media in time to catch the evening radio and TV news programmes, with the Secretary of State being asked to comment on these letters before he had even received them (Nichol, 1992:149). As the *Financial Times* reported on 5 January 1990,

Skilful tactics, and an emollient appearance on television, have earned public sympathy for the Chief union negotiator, Mr Roger Poole of the National Union of Public Employees (NUPE). Clumsiness, and an unfortunate use of terminology, have had the opposite effect on the popularity of Mr Clarke.

One such 'unfortunate use of terminology' was Mr Clarke's description of ambulance staff as merely 'professional drivers'. Such comments clearly jarred with the public's perception of ambulance crews as potential life-savers.

Mobilising public support

The unions were determined to cultivate the latent support for ambulance staff among the public and media alike, having learnt the lessons of the past that TV coverage of ugly confrontations with the police, or the more sombre pictures of ambulances standing idle while emergency calls went unanswered, would alienate public opinion. The unions 'were well aware that, if public opinion turned against them, the dispute was lost' (Kerr and Sachdev, 1992:140). In the end, perhaps the most remarkable aspect of the dispute was the massive and unwavering public support the ambulance staff received throughout the dispute (ibid; and Terry, 1991:97). Opinion polls regularly reported 80 per cent support among the general public for the ambulance crews (and even 60–70 per cent among Tory voters), while only 10 per cent were in favour of the government's stance. This was despite a government advertising campaign to put its case, costing £100 000. The public continued to queue up to make financial donations to the ambulance crews and to sign petitions of support. In fact a 4.5 million signature petition in support of the ambulance workers set a new world record as the largest petition ever to be presented.

The impasse was now complete: a government unwilling to provide additional funds for more pay (and arguably unable to do so without getting even more political egg on its face); unions enjoying massive public support but unable to finance the dispute indefinitely (and arguably unable to win the dispute without escalating industrial action still further and in the process running the risk of alienating the public); a management determined to keep wage costs down and unwilling to negotiate any pay formula to guarantee parity with other emergency services, but at the same time running the risk of damaging staff morale even further (thereby exacerbating, among other things, the problems of recruitment and retention faced in some areas, such as the South-East); and a workforce heartened by public support but increasingly frustrated by lack of progress, leading to divisions among the rank-and-file about the most appropriate tactics to deploy to win the dispute. As is often the case in such disputes, a settlement was only possible with the assistance of third party intervention (from ACAS) and a package that left plenty of scope for differing interpretations.

Management had already recast the 6.5 per cent offer over 12 months to 9 per cent over 18 months, but this had been rejected: 'In essence, the offer was unchanged: it was old wine in new bottles' (Kerr and Sachdev, 1992:136). Likewise the unions had withdrawn the claims for a shorter working week, longer holidays, service pay and service leave, but this had similarly been dismissed by management as 'an empty gesture since the unions knew that the management side had rejected these elements and was not likely to concede them because of the repercussive effects on other NHS staff groups' (Nichol, 1992:150). In the event the final settlement was a two-year agreement involving a 9 per cent consolidated increase from 1 March 1990 to 30 September 1990, and a further 7.9 per cent from 1 October 1990 to 30 March 1991. There was also a lump sum payment covering the period April 1989 to March 1990, skill/training allowances of between £150 and £500 per annum for staff with various paramedic skills, and an element of local pay flexibility. Arguably, the most notable feature of the deal was that it was exceptional in its complexity and ambiguity, enabling Roger Poole to claim to have 'driven a coach and horses' through the government's public sector pay policy, whereas Duncan Nichol maintained that it had added only slightly more than 13 per cent to the wage bill over two years.

Counting the cost

So who won the dispute? As the accounts of both management (Nichol, 1992:153–4) and unions (Kerr and Sachdev, 1992:139–41) make clear, it depends on whose bargaining objectives are considered. The government suffered a protracted period of political embarrassment and its short-term aim of weakening the health service unions and maintaining a 6.5 per cent pay norm was clearly unsuccessful. However the subsequent re-election of a Conservative government in 1992 (albeit with a different party leader) after an election campaign in which the NHS figured prominently, perhaps suggests that there was no lasting political damage. Health Service management were yet again able to stave off any agreement on a pay formula, and more importantly achieved a degree of flexibility in pay that would help them to 'square the circle' of solving recruitment and retention problems at the same time as making the NHS more cost-effective by introducing local pay bargaining. In fact the ambulance service has since been at the forefront of more decentralised pay bargaining in the new NHS trusts and the dispute accelerated the move towards a 'two-tier' ambulance service, with skilled paramedics handling emergency work while non-urgent work performed by patient transport staff, or what *The Economist* (16 December 1989) described as 'granny humping', was increasingly put out to private companies. The unions can claim to have secured a substantial pay increase for their members, at least in the context of government pay policy at the time, though they failed to secure a pay formula. More significant for the unions, perhaps, was 'the quality and effectiveness of its control and presentation, and for the way in which it reversed the 1980s "political calculus" of public sector disputes. By union – indeed, by any – standards the dispute was a public relations triumph' (Terry, 1991:105).

The rank-and-file's objectives were parity and a pay formula. In the end they achieved neither, and not surprisingly the gap between fire-fighters and ambulance staff has *not* subsequently been closed. The settlement was accepted in a workforce ballot by an overwhelming majority (over 80 per cent), but 'that result reflected a mixture of approval, weariness at the length of the dispute and recognition that it was the best deal achievable' (Kerr and Sachdev, 1992:139). Thus the agreement has done little to resolve the long-term malaise of the service. As Duncan Fowlie, an ambulanceman with 17 years' service reflected: 'When I joined the service, I felt I was looked up to. One of the most damaging things to come out of this dispute is that we now know exactly what our boss, Kenneth Clarke, thinks of us – and it's not very much' (quoted in the *Financial Times*, 24 February 1990).

Perhaps the real losers in this dispute, however, as management and the press are always keen to point out in public sector disputes, were the public, or in this case the patients (Nichol, 1992:153). As an editorial in the *Financial Times* on 26 February 1990 concluded, 'The human cost of the conflict has been such that neither side can properly be said to have won.' Nobody could put a precise figure on such costs, especially deaths arising from the dispute (ibid). As for the newborn baby abandoned in a ditch, that particular story subsequently proved to be totally unfounded.

Britain's changing strike pattern

Strikes are inherently complex and often dramatic events. Specific strikes, especially those in the public sector, invoke media and political comment, with employees and their trade unions usually being apportioned the blame. This was clearly evident, at least initially, during the ambulance workers' dispute, although on that occasion the rhetoric of the government and the sensationalism of some sections of the tabloid press clearly backfired. Most disputes, however, pass without press – let alone political – comment. Liverpool dockers, for example, who have been in dispute with MDHC since September 1995, have been ignored by the press and politicians alike (see Pilger, 1996). One of the few occasions when the dispute made the headlines was when the footballer Robbie Fowler, later dubbed the 'strikers' striker', lifted the revered crimson shirt of Liverpool FC after scoring his second goal against SK Brann in the Cup Winners' Cup, to reveal a T-shirt that read:

500 Liverpool

DO**CK**ERS

Sacked since September 1995

Even then the press were more interested in reporting the collision of 'passion and fashion', and the subsequent plight of the 'Toxteth scally' at a UEFA disciplinary hearing, than the interplay of 'power and politics' or the plight of the dockers and their families on the picket line. When industrial disputes do make the front pages or are debated in parliament, they are quickly forgotten. Invariably all they leave behind for public scrutiny is a statistical entry in *Labour Market Trends* or other government publications. The ambulance workers' dispute, for example, was registered as just one of 693 disputes that began in 1989, contributing to the loss of 487 000 working days and involving more than 100 000 workers (*Employment Gazette*, July 1991). Its wider significance – most notably as a public relations success for the unions – was thus submerged along with 692 other disputes that took place in 1989, both big and small, long and short, in public and private sectors, and involving white-collar, blue-collar or pink-collar workers. One consequence of compressing such diverse activities into just three figures, as Shalev (1978:1) points out, is that strike data have become 'some of the most over-abused and least understood of man's [*sic*] many attempts to freeze and condense richly dynamic social events into static, artificial, and misleadingly accurate arithmetic'.

Through the artificial and somewhat anaesthetic process of measurement and recording, we often lose sight of the actors involved in industrial disputes, their motives, the meanings they attach to such behaviour, and the immediate outcomes and wider ramifications of industrial action for management, labour and the state. And yet we cannot ignore the aggregate statistics. At best they are one of the few widely available measures of the trends in industrial conflict over time. At worst they are seized upon by the press and politicians alike as some kind of barometer for the general health of employee relations, be it good (few strikes) or bad (many strikes). The ambulance workers' dispute, for example, came at the end of what had been mooted in the press and on the Labour benches of parliament as a Summer of Discontent, nowhere near on the scale of the Winter of Discontent a decade earlier but nonetheless characterised by 'some of the most intractable and complex disputes of recent years' (Beardwell, 1990:121). Working days lost in the 12 months to August 1989 rose sharply to 4.6 million in comparison with 2.6 million to August 1988, and given that the 'litmus test of the Conservative government's objective of curbing the power of trade unions was strikes' (Kessler and Bayliss, 1992:207), this led some commentators to question the success of the government's industrial relations reforms (Beardwell, 1990:120–1). But other statistics were on hand to counter the view of any return of the 'British disease'. The final number of recorded stoppages in 1989, at only 693, was a postwar low. By 1993 the number had shrunk to just 203, the lowest calendar year total ever recorded (records began in 1891). Working days lost also declined dramatically, from over four million in 1989 to less than 0.3 million in 1994, another all-time low.

It is not uncommon for strike levels to fluctuate from one year to another. The number of working days lost is particularly susceptible to the influence of a few major strikes (just eighteen disputes in 1993, for example, accounted for 83 per cent of all working days lost). As already indicated, however, statistics can be used to discern trends in the number (frequency), duration (working days lost) and breadth (workers involved) of strikes over time. Thus the late 1960s and 1970s may be seen as a period of heightened industrial unrest compared with earlier postwar years, the 1980s and especially the 1990s. For some the decline in strike activity in recent years is not only a vindication of Conservative governments' employment law and labour market policies, but also indicates that 'strikes themselves are inefficient and outdated means of bargaining. The strike is ill-suited to advanced societies in which workers have valuable skills to sell in an efficiently functioning labour market' (Hanson and Mather, 1988:27). This interpretation must be rejected, however, on empirical, analytical and theoretical grounds. *Empirically*, there is the well-known problem of incomplete data: not all strikes are recorded. The docks dispute in Liverpool, for example, is not officially recorded as MDHC legally dismissed the dockers during an unofficial dispute (see Lavalette and Kennedy, 1996; and Saundry and Turnbull, 1996). A dispute that would have added over 60 000 working days lost to the official statistics in 1995, over 180 000 in 1996 and a similar figure in 1997, is simply ignored by government statisticians because there is no longer an employment relationship between the dockers and MDHC. Equally important, official statistics exclude all industrial action short of a work stoppage (such as work to rule).

Analytically, there is the problem of imputing behaviour from statistical data: the causes of behaviour cannot be inferred simply from a statistical datum (e.g. strikes have declined, *ipso facto* they are inefficient and no longer necessary) without empirical observation of the actual 'data' themselves (strikes and those taking part in strikes). When the data under examination are human beings, the manifestations of individual and collective actions cannot simply be assumed, if only because workers have the ability to learn and modify their behaviour in response to varying stimuli. Crucially, strikes can shape both the patterns and parameters of future industrial action: if strikes bring success, workers may be encouraged, or at least be less reticent, to withdraw their labour in subsequent disputes with their employer. As Cohn (1993) demonstrates, when unions develop a reputation for striking, employers are more likely to offer generous settlements. In fact, 'Winning or losing is less important than generating a reputation for militancy. Such a reputation can be obtained by showing a willingness to strike for striking's sake, even to the point of engaging in kamikaze assaults' (ibid:28). This strategy is only successful, however, in relation to short (*blitzkrieg*) strikes (ibid:216–18). When unions lose major (siege) disputes, the effect can be widespread demoralisation and greater reluctance to strike in the immediate future.

Theoretically, it is implicit in Hanson and Mather's (1988) argument that if strikes are unnecessary or pathological, then conflict can simply be attributed to misunderstanding or mischief. As the latter is usually attributed to shop-floor activists or trade unions, these authors argue for the abolition of *all* trade union immunities, placing them under common-law jurisdiction, on the assumption that this would lead to a further diminution of strike action (see Chapter 6). The only 'cause' of strikes would then be mistakes, misunderstandings or misfortune. As Graham Mather MEP has argued elsewhere, 'In a few years' time the strike will be seen as a distortion, an error and an unnecessary feature of any sensible bargaining relationship' (*Independent on Sunday*, 30 July 1995). Indeed it is not uncommon for management to explain strikes in these terms, as was the case in the ambulance workers' dispute. In the view of the NHS Chief Executive, the strike was not only unnecessary but could have been avoided had it not been for the misfortune of the (unexpected) absence of the staff-side secretary, which led to a six weeks' delay in presenting the initial pay offer for consultation (Nichol, 1992). By the time an offer was put to the members, inflation had risen and the offer was unacceptable. But such an explanation not only assumes that the offer would have been acceptable in the first place, it also ignores the *underlying* causes of unrest (morale, status and parity) in the ambulance service. The same criticism applies to similar arguments about the general decline of strikes, in which Hanson and Mather (1988), among others, not only ignore the diverse character of strike activity but more importantly the (unchanged) structural base of industrial conflict between employer and employee (discussed in Chapter 2).

Attention to such detail and the underlying causes of unrest produces a very different interpretation of recent trends. One of the most notable developments of recent years, for example, has been a shift in the locus of strike activity from the private to the public sector. Many of these disputes, including the ambulance dispute of 1989–90 and the recent strikes in the fire service (1995–7), are clearly political with a small 'p'. If nothing else, public opinion and the 'national interest' will tend to play a more prominent role in such disputes. But the most notable feature of the past decade is that behind the statistics published in the pages of the *Employment Gazette* and *Labour Market Trends* lie some of the most intense and bitter struggles of recent memory. Thus to extrapolate from a decline in the number of strikes to predict the eradication of industrial unrest is clearly facile. As many authors have noted (e.g. Durcan *et al.*, 1983:404–24; and Hyman, 1989b:197), it is possible to 'explain' strike trends over time, and the decline of strike activity during recent years, through the analysis of such *proximate* variables as the changing economic environment, the role of product and labour markets, bargaining structures and institutions, management initiatives, and the changing relationship between employees, their unions and the state. But the *underlying* causes of industrial conflict – the structural realities of economic relations within capitalist systems, the nature of the labour process, the division and distribution of income and wealth, and relations of power and control within and beyond the workplace – have remained fundamentally unaltered. Indeed changes to the distribution of income, the growing number of workers on low wages, the decline of trade union influence and many of the other developments outlined in previous chapters suggest that, if anything, the bases of conflicts of interest have been heightened over the past two decades. What needs to be explained are the various *manifestations* of such conflicts, including non-strike forms of dissension.

A central aim of this chapter, therefore, is to consider the dimensions, trends and character of strikes during the postwar period, with particular emphasis on the period since the late 1960s. By exploring the various explanations of strikes within this broader historical context and examining non-strike forms of conflict, it is possible to offer a more balanced evaluation of the nature of industrial conflict and its persistence in the face of government policy aimed at curbing strike activity. In doing so, the distinction between proximate or precipitating causes of strikes and the underlying causes of industrial unrest will be emphasised. Not only does this cast the 1980s and 1990s in a rather different light from that shed by many previous reviews of recent strike patterns, it also illustrates that strikes are not the only, or even the most important, form of industrial conflict. As Kornhauser *et al.* (1954:13) pointed out many years ago,

> A true understanding of industrial strife . . . demands consideration of related, less spectacular manifestations as well. It may even be suggested that the general object of study is not the labor dispute, the strike, or the lockout, but the total range of behavior and attitudes that express opposition and divergent orientations between industrial owners and managers on the one hand and working people and their organizations on the other hand.

In order to encapsulate such a wide range of behaviour it is necessary to move from the bases of conflict (why is conflict inevitable?) to specific forms of work organisation (why do patterns of conflict and accommodation vary across firms, industries and occupations?) and the meanings attached to any specific manifestation of industrial conflict by the parties involved (see Edwards, 1986:17; and Hyman, 1989b:71–5). In other words it is essential to go beyond the study of trends and statistics, and simple (mono-causal) explanations of strikes, to consider the actual *processes* of industrial conflict, especially at the workplace level where employees seek to achieve a degree of control over their working lives. First, however, we must consider the most (ab)used of all indicators of industrial conflict, the strike statistic.

Strikes: measurement and trends

Strikes have been defined as 'a temporary stoppage of work by a group of employees in order to express a grievance or enforce a demand' (Griffin, 1939:20). Thus the action involves those who sell their labour – *employees* rather than employers (who, as in the ambulance dispute, may engage in a range of industrial actions of their own); the employees intend to return to work after the strike is concluded (the stoppage is *temporary*); the workers have withdrawn their labour (a strike is a *stoppage* of work, unlike an overtime ban, work-to-rule or go-slow where labour is effectively withheld); the action is collective (involving a *group* of employees); and it is purposive or calculative (to *express* a grievance or *enforce* a demand). It is interesting and important to note that the involvement of trade unions is not seen as a defining character-istic, despite the commonplace association of unions and strikes. Strikes can and sometimes do involve non-union workers, although the mobilisation of collective interests is often difficult in the absence of union organisation.

In order to measure strike activity, as opposed to defining it as a form of social activity, the Office for National Statistics (ONS) records as a strike any stoppage of work due to an industrial dispute (that is, connected with the terms and conditions of employment) between employers and employees (or between one group of employees and another), that involves at least ten employees for at least one day or the loss of at least one hundred working days. Industrial disputes thus include strikes over such issues as pay, the duration and pattern of working hours, redundancy questions, working conditions and supervision, staffing and work allocation, dismissal and other disciplinary measures, and trade union matters such as demarcation disputes. Although the ONS uses these categories to define the 'principal cause' of a strike, in recognition of the fact that most strikes are multi-causal, in many cases a more appropriate term would be 'reason given for striking'. For example the dominance of pay disputes in the official statistics is perhaps a reflection of the fact that, in a market economy, work is fundamentally a means to an end (that end being income). Furthermore, in a dispute with several contributory causes it is often easier to simplify and articulate the discontent in monetary terms, thereby providing a common denominator to mobilise opposition to fight for improved wages rather than more diffuse goals such as better working conditions, less stringent supervision or more acceptable allocation procedures. Thus in the ambulance workers' dispute, status was a key issue, as the quotes from Mick Denyer and Duncan Fowlie cited above aptly testify, but in the event their grievances were expressed in pounds and pence, with wages used to 'represent a badge of status' (Hyman, 1989b:123).

Though the ambulance workers' dispute had significant political ramifications, it was nonetheless an 'industrial' dispute as defined by the ONS. In general, strikes that have explicitly political *ends*, rather than political implications, are excluded from official statistics, though the dividing line is not always clearcut (the last 'political' dispute to be excluded from the statistics occurred in 1986, resulting from a visit by an MP to the coal industry). Also excluded are many small/short disputes, or what Knowles (1952:xiv) described as 'the "frontier incidents" of industrial life'. Thus as the criteria for counting strikes reflect, not all strikes are recorded by the ONS, even when official data are available on small/short disputes (between 1949 and 1973, for example, the National Dock Labour Board recorded over 3100 strikes on the waterfront but fewer than 2300 were entered in the official statistics) (see Turnbull *et al.*, 1996:722). Furthermore, a proportion of strikes that actually qualify as such under the government's definition go unrecorded. For example, in a study of fifty plants Kelly and Nicholson (1980:27) found that of 183 known stoppages that met the official criteria, only 88 (43 per cent) were actually recorded in the *Employment Gazette*, while a further 91 stoppages lasting less than one day or involving fewer than ten workers were officially excluded. Major workplace industrial relations surveys have also demonstrated that official statistics miss around a third of all stoppages (Brown, 1981:97–101), a shortfall that is not only attributable to the very small size/ duration of some strikes but also to the fact that the data reported to the ONS come from management sources (and there is no statutory obligation to report stoppages). In the 1980 Workplace Industrial Relations Survey, for example, if only management reports of strikes among manual workers were counted then 27 per cent of all establishments recorded a stoppage over the previous year, compared with 34 per cent if strikes reported by either management or union respondents were counted (Daniel and Millward, 1983:215–16). No doubt managements sometimes forget or cannot be bothered to inform the relevant government department of a strike. On other occasions, however, management may be concerned about the company's public image (with the press, shareholders and the government) if they make known each and every dispute (for example a strike over a company violation of health and safety standards).

Two further issues relating to the statistics are worthy of note. First, disputes that do not result in a stoppage of work, such as an overtime ban or a work-to-rule, are not included in the statistics. To reinforce the point made earlier, the data refer to strikes, *not* industrial conflict – the latter might also include sabotage, the restriction of output, absenteeism, labour turnover and even accidents. Thus if we want to follow Kornhauser and his colleagues (1954:13) and explore the *total* range of behaviour and attitudes that express opposition and divergent interest between management and labour, we must look beyond the official statistics. Second, although the official statistics include 'lock-outs' (that is, where the employer prevents employees from working by locking the entrance to the place of work), no distinction is made between strikes and lock-outs in the actual statistics. In other words we do not know *who* caused the stoppage of work. Almost invariably, however, stoppages are attributed to employees in general and trade unions in particular, and the 'problem' of industrial conflict is consequently defined in managerial terms. Unions are cast as the villains while employers simply exercise 'managerial prerogative'. But as Hyman (1989b:184) notes,

> as well as the lock-out, conflict with the *employee* can take the form of plant closure, sackings, victimization, blacklisting, speed-ups, safety hazards, arbitrary discipline and so on. The routine practices of employers do not *count* as 'industrial conflict'; they are part of the normal, repressive reality of work (original emphasis).

At the same time, employees often attribute blame (the cause) for strike action to management (Batstone *et al.*, 1978:47–8). In the ambulance workers' dispute, for example, this centred on the management action of docking workers' pay – without just reason in the eyes of the workforce.

Official data must therefore be treated with caution, especially in an international context (see McCarthy, 1970). For example, of the OECD countries for which strike statistics are readily available, only two, the UK and the United States, exclude political strikes. Denmark and Germany impose a similar qualifying restriction of at least 100 working days lost, whereas Austria, Belgium, Italy, the Netherlands and Turkey impose no restrictions on size, while Finland, Greece and Spain require only that the dispute last one hour or more. In an international comparison for 1995, the UK had the fourth lowest strike rate (days lost per 1000 employees) out of twenty-four countries, but at least fifteen of these countries counted disputes that would not have been recorded in the UK (Sweeney and Davies, 1997). In the national context, however, official strike statistics provide a reasonable indication of trends over time, given that the criteria for inclusion have remained fairly constant, the accuracy of reporting strikes is unlikely to have changed (at least not on a systematic basis), and significant year-on-year variations tend to even out over the longer run. The statistics for the frequency, breadth and duration of strike activity in the UK are presented in Table 10.1. This illustrates the magnitude of these longer-term variations, especially with respect to the number of workers involved and working days lost. For the postwar period as a whole, it is possible to identify at least eight distinct phases or patterns of strike activity, each of approximately six years' duration.

The postwar peace, 1946–52

With the exception of 1951 there was a downward trend in strike activity during this period, and a virtual absence of national, large-scale, official stoppages. Coalmining accounted for around a third of all days lost, half the number of workers involved and over 60 per cent of all stoppages. Eight other industries accounted for over half of the remaining stoppages and nearly 70 per cent of the remaining time lost and workers involved (Durcan *et al.*, 1983:26–57). The socioeconomic consensus constructed by the Labour government (as discussed in Chapter 6) no doubt contributed to the postwar peace, but this period was still characterised by a 'depression mentality', possibly because many of the trade union leaders of the time had come to office during the interwar years. Union leaders, through the TUC, held together a firm anti-strike policy (Coates and Topham, 1988:234–5), which in many respects failed to meet the expectations of the rank-and-file (Cronin, 1979:138; and Hyman, 1989b:197).

The return of the strike, 1953–9

The downward trend of strikes was reversed during 1953, with the number of stoppages exceeding 2000 in 1955 and remaining above that level for the rest of the 1950s. This period also witnessed the return, after a 20-year absence, of the 'set-piece' strike: industry-wide stoppages conducted with the support of the national trade union(s) concerned. There were two national strikes in engineering and one each in shipbuilding and printing during this period. There was also a marked increase in the concentration of strike activity, with the eight most strike-prone industries, which collectively employed 20 per cent of all employees, accounting for 55 per cent of all stoppages and 84 per cent of all workers involved and working days lost (Durcan *et al.*, 1983:58–91).

The shopfloor movement, 1960–8

This period was marked by growth in the number of stoppages at the shopfloor level, with non-mining strikes passing the 1000 mark for the first

TABLE 10.1   Postwar strikes

Year	Frequency (number of strikes beginning in year)	Breadth (number of workers involved, 000s)	Duration (number of working days lost, 000s)
1946	2205	526	2158
1947	1721	623	2433
1948	1759	426	1944
1949	1426	434	1807
1950	1339	303	1389
1951	1719	379	1694
1952	1714	416	1792
Average 1946–52	**1698**	**444**	**1888**
1953	1746	1374	2184
1954	1989	450	2457
1955	2419	671	3781
1956	2648	508	2083
1957	2859	1359	8412
1958	2629	524	3462
1959	2093	646	5270
Average 1953–59	**2340**	**551**	**3950**
1960	2832	819	3024
1961	2686	779	3046
1962	2449	4423	5798
1963	2068	593	1755
1964	2524	883	2277
1965	2354	876	2925
1966	1937	544	1428
1967	2116	734	2787
1968	2378	2258	4690
Average 1960–68	**2372**	**1323**	**3189**
1969	3116	1665	6846
1970	3906	1801	10980
1971	2228	1178	13551
1972	2497	1734	23909
1973	2873	1528	7197
1974	2922	1626	14750
Average 1969–74	**2924**	**1589**	**12872**
1975	2282	809	6012
1976	2016	668	3284
1977	2703	1166	10142

Table 10.1 continued

Year	Frequency (number of strikes beginning in year)	Breadth (number of workers involved, 000s)	Duration (number of working days lost, 000s)
1978	2471	1041	9405
1979	2080	4608	29474
Average 1975–79	**2310**	**1658**	**11663**
1980	1330	834	11964
1981	1338	1513	4266
1982	1528	2103	5313
1983	1352	574	3754
1984	1206	1464	27135
1985	887	791	6402
Average 1980–85	**1274**	**1213**	**9806**
1986	1053	720	1920
1987	1004	887	3546
1988	770	790	3702
1989	693	727	4128
1990	620	298	1903
Average 1986–90	**828**	**684**	**3040**
1991	357	176	761
1992	240	148	528
1993	203	385	649
1994	203	107	278
1995	232	174	415
Average 1991–95	**247**	**198**	**526**

Source: *Employment Gazette* and *Labour Market Trends*.

time (1166 in 1980) and then almost doubling by the end of the period (2157 in 1968). Strike frequency had been dominated by the coalmining industry up to the late 1950s, whereafter the proportion of mining strikes fell from around three quarters of the total to less than 10 per cent by the end of the 1960s. A further indication of the 'contagion' rather than the 'concentration' of strike activity in this period was that no industries were completely strike free during the 1960s, as had been the case in previous periods. The strike pattern itself was now dominated by small, short, unofficial stoppages arising from shopfloor issues, with the virtual disappearance, yet again, of the national, official macro-stoppage (Durcan *et al.*, 1983:92–131). The latter, it appeared, 'took on some of the characteristics of a conjuror's prop: "Now you see it, now you don't"' (ibid:403). The prominence of the large-scale strike was to return thereafter, however, since which time it has rarely been out of the limelight.

The formal challenge, 1969–74

Legal controls had been imposed on pay increases in the mid-1960s, and by the end of the decade there were demands (and plans) for legislative restrictions on strikes from both major political parties (see Chapter 6). The turbulent period 1969–74 saw first the abandonment and then the reintroduction of legal controls on pay, the introduction and failure of the Industrial Relations Act 1971, and a significant increase in strike activity. Strikes spread to previously 'strike free' groups such as teachers, refuse collectors, hospital workers and postal workers, while long-quiescent groups in the steel, clothing and glass industry also resorted to strike action (see Coates and Topham, 1988:238). Not only did the macro-strike reappear, but the public rather than the private sector 'became the battleground for set piece confrontations' (Durcan *et al.*, 1983:132). These and subsequent public sector disputes are recorded in Table 10.2. With the introduction of incomes policies, the majority of strikes were now wage rather than non-wage disputes (from 1955 to 1964 the proportion of wage disputes was 47 per cent of the total, whereas from 1965 to 1974 it rose to 56 per cent), while greater legal intervention in employee relations sparked an unprecedented wave of political strikes involving around six million workers and accounting for the loss of over six million working days (ibid:170, 438; and Wigham, 1976:156–80). These strikes, which were excluded from official statistics, serve to highlight the intensity of formal trade union opposition and worker militancy towards government policy during this period. Working days lost had exceeded six million on only one previous occasion during the postwar years, in 1957, but surpassed this total in every year between 1969 and 1974. With the exception of 1976, this trend continued throughout the rest of the 1970s.

Containment and resurgence, 1975–9

With the election of a Labour government in 1974 and the establishment of a Social Contract with the trade unions, the TUC agreed to rigid pay restraint in 1975. More importantly, this policy was broadly supported at the workplace level. Strikes declined by almost a third in the space of two years, and in 1976

TABLE 10.2   Examples of major disputes in the public sector, 1970–95

		Workers involved		Days lost	
		(000s)	(% of annual total)	(000s)	(% of annual total)
1970	Local authority workers	122	6.8	1216	11.1
1971	Postal workers	180	15.3	6230	46.0
1972	Coal miners	308	17.8	10726	44.9
1973	Gas workers	23	1.5	304	4.2
	Hospital ancillaries	55	3.6	285	4.0
1974	Coalminers	258	15.9	5567	37.7
	Teachers (Scotland)	40	2.5	175	1.2
	Local authority clerical	3	0.2	111	0.8
1977	Firemen	30	2.8	1258	12.4
1979	Hospital and local authorities	1300	28.2	3200	10.9
	Civil service clerical	300	6.5	700	2.4
1980	Steel workers	140	16.8	8800	73.6
	Teachers (Scotland)	32	3.8	103	0.9
1981	Civil service	290	19.2	867	20.3
1982	Hospital workers	180	8.6	781	14.7
	Railway workers	–	–	900	16.9
1983	Water workers	35	6.1	766	20.4
	Social workers	4	0.7	52	1.4
1984	Coal miners	140	9.6	22300	82.2
1985	Coal miners (cont.)	113	14.3	4026	62.9
	Teachers (Scotland)	41	5.2	218	3.4
	Teachers (E & W)	162	20.5	604	9.4
1986	Postmen	9	1.3	31	1.6
	Teachers	–	–	310	16.1
1987	Teachers	158	17.8	123	3.5
	Civil servants	14	1.6	624	17.6
1988	Postmen	120	15.2	120	3.2
	Postmen	119	15.1	1036	28.0
	Civil servants	97	12.3	115	3.1
	Miners	19	2.4	135	3.6
1989	Local authority non-manuals	313	43.1	2004	48.5
	Ambulance workers	10	1.4	147	3.6
1990	Ambulance workers (cont)	106	35.6	340	17.9
1991	Council workers	27	15.3	102	13.4
1992	Lecturers	15	10.1	15	2.8
	Council workers	1	0.7	80	15.2
1993	Civil servants	162	42.1	162	25.0
1994	Railway workers	3	3.0	54	19.4
	College lecturers	22	20.3	63	22.7
1995	College lecturers (cont)	22	12.5	39	9.4

Sources: *Employment Gazette* and *Labour Market Trends*

there were fewer pay-related strikes than non-pay-related strikes for the first time since 1967. However incomes policies upset comparability and notions of fairness, especially among public sector workers, where pay policy was invariably enforced more tightly. As Davies (1979:220) has demonstrated, incomes policies tend to reduce pay disputes but increase non-pay strikes, and reduce pay strikes only at the expense of an upsurge when the policy is removed. Ultimately the Labour government's incomes policy was not so much removed as destroyed by a resurgence of conflict during 1977–9, especially in the winter of 1978–9. With real wages falling during a period of high inflation, a 'revival of struggle' was almost inevitable following the government's parsimonious pay limit of 5 per cent, imposed in the autumn of 1978 (Hyman, 1989b:198–9).

Coercive pacification, 1980–5

During the first half of the 1980s unemployment doubled, the Conservative government initiated a biennial legislative programme that was more restrictive than the Industrial Relations Act 1971, and many employers (with full state support) took on the unions. Many of the strikes that occurred were 'defensive' in character, often against redundancy, attacks on trade union organisation, speed-up at work or the erosion of real income (Hyman, 1989b:199–202). One illustration of this was that pay disputes declined from 58 per cent of the total during 1974–9 to 44 per cent during 1980–5. In manufacturing the number of strikes halved between 1979 and 1980, and the number of pay strikes fell by 60 per cent (compared with a 34 per cent decline in non-pay disputes). As a result 60 per cent of the total reduction in strike activity in 1979–80 was attributable to the reduction in pay strikes in manufacturing (Lyddon, 1994). Year after year in the early 1980s, major battles in the public sector were fought and invariably lost by the unions (steel in 1980, railways in 1982, water in 1983, coal in 1984–5), along with several major private sector disputes (for example print workers in 1983 and 1984). 'Major' disputes (involving 500 000 or more working days) accounted for a much higher proportion of total days lost in the 1980s than during the 1970s (*Employment Gazette*, May 1992), and largely accounted for the fact that 'days lost' declined to only the level of the 1960s (a time of increasing concern about the UK's 'strike problem'). The defeats for the trade unions, however, combined with the decline of pay disputes in the face of severe cash limits in the public sector, provided 'evidence of an erosion of the will to resist' (Hyman, 1989b:212). With the balance of power now firmly in the employers' favour, strikes appeared to have little chance of success. Unlike the 'contagion' effect of strikes in the 1960s and 1970s, the 1980s witnessed a 'negative demonstration' effect, especially after the miners' strike of 1984–5, which 'systematically undermined most workers' collective strength and confidence' (ibid:226). Yet conflict was never far from the surface. There was evidence, for example, of workers increasingly indulging in 'cut price' forms of industrial action such as overtime bans (Edwards, 1992:378; Milner, 1993). If workers did strike, it was increasingly for a shorter period, with a marked increase in what might be termed 'token stoppages' lasting no longer than a day.

Calculative bargaining, 1986–90

In 1985 the number of strikes fell below 1000 for the first time in the postwar period. But as unemployment declined and the economy enjoyed a mini (inflationary) boom, strikes once again rose above 1000 in both 1986 and 1987. Pay disputes continued to decline as a proportion of the total (now below 40 per cent), while the number of strikes lasting less than one day increased to almost half the total. At the same time a number of major set-piece confrontations took place (for example by telecommunications workers in 1987, postal workers in 1988, dockers and council workers in 1989, and engineering workers in 1990). Record bankruptcies and the fear of unemployment, however, clearly played a role in the overall 'damping down' of overt conflict, but so too did the rise of average earnings (for those in employment), suggesting that many workers did not 'need' to strike. Nevertheless data from the third Workplace Industrial Relations Survey reveal that there was an increase in the proportion of employees who took strike action for the first time during this period, despite the decline in both strike and non-strike action during the latter part of the decade (Millward *et al.*, 1992:292–4). The number of establishments affected by strike and non-strike action in each of the Workplace Industrial Relations Surveys (each based on a sample of around 2000 establishments) is reported in Table 10.3.

Legislation also played a part in the decline in strike activity. However, although the aim of successive Conservative governments was to curb trade union activities in general and strikes in particular, evidence of the effectiveness of the law during the late 1980s was by no means clear-cut (see Chapter 6). Secondary action, which was expressly targeted by legal restrictions, almost disappeared by the end of the 1980s (Millward *et al.*, 1992:358–9), and in a number of major disputes the law was used to great, if not decisive, effect (Evans, 1985, 1987; and *Labour Research*, September 1990). The dock strike of 1989 is a good example (see Chapter 6). In the ambulance workers' dispute the employers sought and obtained injunctions prohibiting action in five separate regional health authorities (*Labour Research*, April 1990). In other cases union representatives called off strike action after employers threatened

TABLE 10.3 Percentage of establishments affected by industrial action, 1980–90

	1980	*1984*	*1990*
Strike action	13	19	10
Non-strike action	16	18	5
Strike or non-strike action	22	25	12

Source: Millward *et al.* (1992:279).

to use the law, and union members were in some cases unwilling to strike through fear of entanglement with the law (*Labour Research*, September 1990). But in the majority of cases it appears that employers were reluctant to use (as opposed to threaten to use) the law.

Equally, it has been argued that the law has not only had a limited overall impact on the level of strike activity, but may have acted to increase worker solidarity in the event of a strike, given that the action would have been approved by a majority of the workforce in a democratic vote (Brown and Wadhwani, 1990; Elgar and Simpson, 1993; and Martin *et al.*, 1991). What is often overlooked is that ballots allowed both parties to put their position to a vote without a strike taking place. Indeed with ballots becoming increasingly integrated into trade union bargaining strategies and consultation with members (Millward *et al.*, 1992:298–301), they were available for use as a bargaining counter: once a ballot has been called and strike action approved, employers have to choose between meeting the union's demand or facing a strike (see Edwards, 1995b:455–6; Kessler and Bayliss, 1992:222; Martin *et al.*, 1991:202–3; and Undy *et al.*, 1996:240). In this context, then, strikes might be viewed as an indicator of union weakness as more powerful unions do not need to strike to secure their objectives: the threat of action is sufficient. Not only were more and more strikes preceded by a ballot, but in an increasing proportion of ballots the vote was in favour of strike action. And yet in a majority of cases no action took place. For example, in 89 per cent of the YES ballots in 1986 there was no subsequent strike action. Thus, as Brown and Wadhwani (1990) demonstrate, there may have been a decline in overt disruption but not necessarily a diminution of the impact of the strike *threat*. This is supported by the absence of any significant decline in the proportion of CBI member organisations who cited the threat of industrial action as an important factor in determining their annual wage increase (ibid). In short the decline in strike activity was neither indicative of a decline in industrial conflict nor of the demise of trade union power.

Economic pacification and legal (self) restraint, 1991–5

In the early 1990s the UK's strike pattern changed yet again, with the number of disputes, workers involved and working days lost all recording new postwar lows. Changes to the composition of the labour force, as documented in Chapter 3, most notably the decline of (former) strike-prone industries such as vehicle manufacturing, the virtual demise of coalmining and the substitution of non-union/casual labour for registered dockers on the waterfront clearly contributed to the decline in strike activity (see Edwards, 1995b:449–54). Moreover there were no 'large' disputes (involving the loss of more than 500 000 working days) and very few national disputes in this period. In fact the decentralisation of collective bargaining (Chapter 7) and privatisation of whole swathes of the public sector (Chapter 6) rendered the logistics and legality of national, official macro-stoppages problematic to say the least. In addition to these structural changes, two factors appear to have been instrumental to the reduction of industrial disputes in the 1990s, namely economic forces and legal constraints. As in the early 1980s, the economic recession of the 1990s had a significant impact on workers' willingness to strike. Unlike the Thatcher recession of 1980–1, however, the Major recession of 1990–3 had a more widespread impact on the south as well as the north of the country, and on white-collar as well as blue-collar workers. Thus whereas strikes in public services increased significantly in the 1980s compared with the 1970s, the number of disputes tumbled in the mid 1990s. More generally, the proportion of working days lost in pay disputes declined from three quarters of all days lost in the late 1980s to less than 40 per cent from 1991–5. In 1994 as many as one in eight larger companies in manufacturing and one in six firms in the service sector were reported to have introduced pay freezes lasting up to 12 months (ACAS, 1995:13). Disputes over redundancy issues accounted for 43 per cent of all working days lost at the height of the recession from 1991–3.

The reticence of workers to strike is illustrated by the increase in the proportion of short (token) stoppages (over half the total number of stoppages lasted just one day or less) and the increase in the number of collective conciliation cases undertaken by ACAS, following a sharp decline between 1987 and 1990 (although conciliation was still well below the number of cases handled in the 1970s and early 1980s). As in the late 1980s there were far more ballots for industrial action than actual strikes, which again raises the question of the role of the law in employee relations. Following the introduction of the Trade Union Reform and Employment Rights Act (see Chapter 6), ballots for industrial action must now be conducted through an independent body. In the two years following the introduction of the Act, 5487 ballots were conducted by the Electoral Reform Society and Unity Security Balloting Services, of which 73 per cent were in favour of strike action. Thus while there were just

435 strikes in 1994–5 there were over 4000 votes in favour of strike action, continuing the pattern of calculative bargaining established in the late 1980s. However the cumulative, and coercive, effects of the law cannot be discounted. Gall and McKay (1996), for example, have demonstrated that while the total number of injunctions brought against trade unions may have been relatively few in number (just 169 between 1983 and March 1996), a relatively high frequency of injunctions were related to the main provisions of each new Act immediately after its introduction. A decline in the *resort* to injunctions by employers, therefore, cannot be equated with a decline in the general *deterrent* effects of the body of statutory and case law established over the past eighteen years: 'employers have experimented with each of the provisions of a new Act . . . to obtain the remedy *they* required' (ibid:569, emphasis added), thereby setting the parameters and possibilities of 'lawful' industrial action. The most recent Tory legislation in particular 'seemed to be the beginning of a cat and mouse game in which unions started to wriggle from the law's clutches, only to be grabbed by a fresh set of statutory claws. In short, the art of the possible became an increasingly futile pastime' (Dunn and Metcalf, 1996:77). As Gall and McKay (1996:575) conclude,

> much of the 'real' influence of employment law may be, as it were, 'inside the minds' of union members and officials . . . the cautious attitudes of trade unionists and the threats to and use of the employment laws by the employers, have led to an atmosphere of self-imposed restraint.

Overview

Although the pattern of strike activity in the postwar period has been subdivided into (apparently) distinct periods, it should be borne in mind that in practice these phases both overlapped and displayed contradictory tendencies (Hyman, 1989b:198–9). Once again our analogy of a spiral is useful (see Chapter 1) to emphasise the interplay of both continuity and change, of movement and return within the cycle. In 1996, for example, although the total number of disputes remained at an historically low level, the number of working days lost increased sharply to over 1.3 million, largely as a result of major disputes in transport and communications (railways, London Underground and Royal Mail). As in 1989 the press were talking of another 'summer of discontent' and asking whether the British striker was making a comeback (Heery, 1997:97). Thus in contrast to the idea of a gradual demise of strike action (Hanson and Mather, 1988), various other authors have noted that, over the long run, strikes have tended to occur in waves, reflecting the fact that strike

Movements in various industries have generally been in the same direction and of at least comparable magnitude, as if orchestrated to one basic rhythm. That rhythm itself is unique: periodic explosions of militancy, or strike waves, have predominated over the long-term trajectory and short-term fluctuations (Cronin, 1979:49).

Each wave, however, was unique, an indicator 'of qualitative changes in the relations between workers and employers' (ibid:47). The fact that strikes have tended to fluctuate over time, both in the short and the long term, suggests that, among other things, the state of the economy exerts a significant impact on strike activity. But while the root cause of strike waves may be economic, their effects are deeply political:

> Strike waves are the nexus of the strategic interaction between workers, employers, and the state. The financial and legitimation crisis provoked by strike waves requires solutions at *both* the economic and political levels. Reactions by employers and the state to strike waves set the terms of class relations for years to come (Franzosi, 1995:347, original emphasis).

The object of study, then, is not simply the strike (statistic) but the changing nature of employment relations and the manifestation of (class) conflict in its many different guises.

Theories of strikes

Long-run waves in the pattern of strike action have been linked to the 'Kondratieff cycle' of industrial output, consisting of a long period of rapid growth (20–30 years) followed by an equally long phase of stagnation. Evidence from a number of countries suggests that strike waves correspond to the downturn of the Kondratieff cycle (as in 1968–74) when workers' expectations are still rising while employers face a crisis of profitability (Franzosi, 1995:339–40; and Screpanti, 1987). During the period of economic upswing, strikes are more frequent (workers are more confident) but of shorter duration (employers are often more willing to concede). The downswing, in contrast, is often a period in which industrial conflict evolves in a very irregular form, 'with high, short and scattered peaks of intensity emerging over a floor of depressed moods' (Screpanti, 1987:112). As Coates and Topham (1988:249–50) have observed,

> severe, large, prolonged strikes are associated with periods of economic dislocation and nascent slump, a time when workers' organizations are still strong, undefeated in major conflicts, and often when workers are most conscious of what they have to lose, in terms of living standards and job security.

At the same time, it is in such periods that employers are fighting to survive or protect their profit margins.

Although the economic cycle is widely acknowledged as impacting upon both the level and the character of strike action, the influence of economic variables is rarely straightforward. For example when unemployment is low, workers are likely to feel more confident and be prepared to strike more often, but equally employers might be more willing to concede to union demands without a strike. When unemployment is high and rising, workers are likely to be less confident, but in the face of employer initiatives to cut costs they may have more reason to strike, and if they do so may display considerable solidarity. As a result it is often argued that the general economic environment is more important as a 'background' variable. At a more disaggregated level, for example, it is evident that while the same macroeconomic conditions prevail across the economy, some industries experience an increase in strike activity while others experience a decline (Durcan *et al.*, 1983:404–5). Cronin (1979:179–87), however, illustrates that it is the interplay of labour *and* (international) product markets that is the crucial variable, as strike-prone industries are generally those that are 'thoroughly entangled' with economic fluctuations; those with a moderate strike-propensity are merely 'jostled' by the market; while those with very few strikes are largely 'sheltered' from the international market, producing mainly for domestic demand.

It has long been recognised that some industries and occupations are more prone to strike activity than others. While Cronin highlights the importance of international product markets in creating uncertainty and change, others have stressed the location of the worker in society. In a study of eleven countries Kerr and Siegel (1954) noted that miners, dockers, sailors, loggers and, to a much lesser extent, textile workers displayed the highest strike rates among different occupational/industrial groups. For Kerr and Siegel (1954:191–2) these workers,

> form isolated masses, almost a 'race apart'. They live in their own separate communities: the coal patch, the waterfront district, the logging camp, the textile town. These communities have their own codes, myths, heroes, and social standards. There are few neutrals in them to mediate the conflicts and dilute the mass. All people have grievances, but what is important is that all the members of each of these groups have the same grievances.

Furthermore, these groups tend to have strong union organisation, 'a kind of working-class party or even government for these employees, rather than just another association', while the strike itself 'is a kind of colonial revolt against far-removed authority, an outlet for accumulated tensions, and a substitute for occupational and social mobility' (ibid:193).

Over the years, however, this theory has been much discredited. In their study of strikes in France, for example, Shorter and Tilly (1974:349) demonstrated that most French strikers were not, by and large, marginal workers on the periphery of society: 'the most militant, effective workers are precisely those in the middle of the heterogeneous, swirling metropolis, not the isolated proletarians of the civic community'. Likewise the idea of strikes as a 'colonial revolt' explains little about the day-to-day conflicts over the wage–effort bargain that traditionally characterise the activity of strike-prone occupational groups such as miners and dockers. In a powerful critique, Edwards (1977) casts doubt on the measure of strike propensity used by Kerr and Siegel; the value of a typology, or more precisely a description of polar cases, which runs along two separate continua ('individual–mass' and 'isolation–integration') but leaves the 'middle ground' unresolved; and the fact that even among isolated masses such as miners and dockers, strike propensity varies considerably both within and between countries. As Turnbull *et al.* (1996) demonstrate, while dockers may have a deserved reputation for militancy, strike activity within the port transport industry has been characterised by persistent disputes in a minority of major ports, which have dominated the industry's overall strike pattern, and relative quiescence in the majority of ports where dockers, like colliers in a previous era (Church *et al.*, 1990) and their contemporaries in manufacturing (*Employment Gazette*, 1976:1219), have rarely struck work. Nonetheless it is not unusual for commentators to fall back on the isolated mass theory, or a variant of it, to explain, for example, the decline of strike activity during the 1980s:

> The work organization and work culture of manual labour in mine and mill, dock and railway, shipyard and engineering factory, were relatively conducive to a 'spontaneous' sense of solidarity. Shops and offices, schools and hospitals are significantly different work milieu, with labour processes which are often fragmented and isolated. Clerks and typists, nurses and teachers, supervisors and technicians, typically respond to a complexity of interests and pressures; and their responses are rarely informed by a reflex commitment to the ethics and traditions of the labour movement (Hyman, 1989b:229).

This is not to say that such workers will not strike. In fact, whereas almost 2.8 million workers employed in administration, health and banking were involved in strike action during the 1970s (including the Winter of Discontent), the comparable figure for the 1980s was 3.5 million (*Labour Research*, June 1992; and Lyddon, 1994). Rather it is the character and meaning of such strikes for those involved that is different.

Despite the criticisms, the idea of community and the sense of common purpose this engenders cannot be simply dismissed. Arguably, 'community' should not be invoked to explain strike *incidence* but rather to help understand the character of workplace relations, the connections between work and non-work activities, and ultimately the *processes* involved in strike action (Edwards, 1988; Turnbull, 1992; and Turnbull *et al.*, 1996). Such factors clearly play a role in the ability of some groups of workers both to mobilise and to sustain collective solidarity. Among dock workers, for example, once a decision had been taken to strike the dockers traditionally accepted this decision to a man, even if they disapproved of strikes in general or the particular issue at stake (Turnbull, 1992:299). On the waterfront, the connections between work and community were felt most forcibly by the blackleg, who would face ostracism and 'contrived accidents' at work while his family would share the same fear of opprobrium (ibid:299–300). The names and addresses of 'scabs' who crossed the picket line at the port of Liverpool in September 1995 were displayed in local pubs, and the wives of dockers dismissed by MDHC distributed leaflets to the neighbours of working dockers and regularly held vigils outside their homes.

Such militant solidarity was inextricably linked to the second factor identified by Kerr and Siegel (1954:195) in accounting for the interindustry propensity to strike, namely the character of the job and the worker. Again, strikes cannot simply be explained by the nature of technology (the monotony of the assembly line, the hazards of the pit, the ergonomics of the office) (see Edwards, 1983:224; and Gallie, 1978), but this is not to say that such factors are unimportant. In general, work that is skilled or dangerous, and especially both, often produces a high degree of emotional involvement in the work tasks. If workers see themselves in terms of their occupational role – because this offers the highest status and most flattering self-image – and/or subscribe to a value system that is set by their occupation, they are likely to develop a strong occupational culture (Turnbull, 1992:298). In the ambulance workers' dispute, for example, it was clear that the workers' occupational esteem and status had been belittled by the refusal of management and the government to accord them equal status with the police and fire services. This was not only an important grievance in itself but also played a key role in maintaining the solidarity of the ambulance workers throughout the six-month dispute. As with the notion of community, then, occupational culture helps to explain how strikes may be sustained by traditions of solidarity or occupational identity, rather than necessarily explaining why strikes take place or why the frequency of industrial action varies over time and place. The latter requires much closer attention to bargaining structures and institutions, management initiatives and worker responses.

A clear illustration of the importance attached to bargaining structures and institutions can be found in the work of the Royal Commission on Trade Unions and Employers' Associations (Donovan, 1968). One of the major conclusions of the Commission was that:

> The shortcomings of the industrial relations system emphasises how important and how general a failure there has been to devise institutions in keeping with changing needs. Unofficial strikes and other types of unofficial action are above all a symptom of this failure. This conviction is borne out by consideration of circumstances in all four industries which suffer most from unofficial strikes – coalmining, docks, shipbuilding and ship-repair and motors. In all these industries work group

organisation is exceptionally strong, fragmented bargaining has been the rule, and wage structures have been notoriously anarchic (1968:108).

Simply put, strikes will be more prevalent where employees possess the *means*, the *motivation* and the *opportunity* to strike (Clegg, 1979a:272–9). In the docks, for example, despite the fact that unofficial action was discouraged by the T&GWU, and despite too the fact that neither management nor the T&GWU recognised shop stewards until after decasualisation in 1967, dockers had always been able to act independently, and effectively, on the wharf, where any delay to shipping could be very costly (the means); as a result of casual employment and the irregular arrival of shipping, attributable to the trade cycle, seasonal variation and the vagaries of wind and wave, dockers' weekly earnings fluctuated widely (the motivation); and with work organised around small gangs, paid at a piece rate on jobs where no two cargoes were ever exactly alike (with respect to ship, gear, packaging, sequence of discharge, gang composition and ultimately the weather), there was ample scope for the negotiation and renegotiation of the wage–effort bargain (the opportunity) (see Turnbull and Sapsford, 1991; Turnbull, 1992; and Turnbull *et al.*, 1996). Similar features were evident in coalmining (Church *et al.*, 1990 and 1991; and Durcan *et al.*, 1983:240–71) and the car industry (Durcan *et al.* 1983:312–51; and Turner *et al.*, 1967).

As with many other explanations of strikes, this particular theory has a certain intuitive appeal and empirical purchase, at least for the strike-prone industries. Thus the movement from piece rates to a national day-wage system in the mining industry, most notably the National Powerloading Agreement of 1966, was associated with a decline in short, small, pit-level disputes. But while management reform initiatives clearly had an impact on at least one dimension of the strike pattern in coalmining, they met with far less success in other industries (Durcan *et al.*, 1983:412). Indeed industrial relations reform in many industries exacerbated rather than resolved conflicts of interest, suggesting that the initial explanation was inadequate (Edwards, 1983:224; and Turner *et al.*, 1977) and highlighting the importance of worker response to management initiatives. Put differently, strikes were not simply the outcome of various structural characteristics and economic conditions, as agency (the mobilisation of discontent by union activists) played a crucial intervening role. The port transport industry is a clear example of this, where rank-and-file dockers strongly resisted management reforms, government intervention and even the official policy of their own union (Turnbull, 1992; and Turnbull *et al.*, 1996). As Edwards (1992:386) has argued, it is crucial to consider the strategies of the two sides, the interaction between strategy and resources, and in particular the processes whereby background conditions become defined as resources that can be actively employed.

By linking the processes of strike action to the structural conditions of the economy and industry in general, and the workplace in particular, it is possible to construct an integrated analysis of the level and character of strike activity in specific industries (ibid:385–6; and Turnbull *et al.*, 1996). As discussed in Chapter 5 above, Batstone (1988) has provided a useful framework for looking at the power resources of capital and labour, and on the labour side he identifies three principal resources: disruptive capacity in the production process; scarcity value in the labour market; and political influence within the political arena. The extent to which workers possess and can wield these resources depends in turn on the structures and strategies of their trade union(s). The level of union membership (numbers and density) and the sophistication of union organisation play a key role (sophistication here refers to the number and quality of union representatives, especially at the shopfloor level, their relations with members and the resources and facilities available to them). Finally, the power resources of the parties are influenced by a series of contextual factors, namely the nature of labour and product markets, the form of the production process and its technology, the institutions of employee relations and the role of the state.

In the case of coalmining, rising oil prices during the 1970s enhanced the disruptive potential of the miners, while changes to collective bargaining arrangements and state involvement in industrial relations placed the National Union of Mineworkers (NUM) in a position of considerable political influence. These power resources were wielded with great effect in the first national coal strikes since the General Strike of 1926. In addition the disruptive and political influence of the NUM in 1972 and 1974 was backed up by effective union organisation and strategies, most notably the use of mass and flying pickets. In the ambulance workers' dispute, crews clearly had the power to disrupt the production process, but only for emergency work. It was only those with paramedic skills, and those in the South-East, who possessed real scarcity value in the labour market. But the ambulance workers were able to wield significant political influence, especially for such a numerically small group, effected by the organisation and sophistication of the unions' strategy. The (occupational) solidarity of the rank-and-file also played a crucial role, as did the strategy and (mis)management of the dispute by the employers and the government. But ultimately the various 'background conditions' to the dispute that were mobilised to great effect by the unions, in particular public sympathy and the political problems faced by the government at the time, were a *necessary* but not a *sufficient* condition for success:

> However skilfully Roger Poole of NUPE presented the case, however unified the unions, however strong public support, however much some local managers lost their nerve and agreed with the staff – none of this mattered. The action did not escalate to its logical finale [an all out strike] and therefore the government could always ride it out (Seifert, 1992:276).

Given that no two strikes are ever identical, a more integrated analysis of the level and character of strike activity across industries, occupations and individual workplaces allows not only the processes but also the meanings attached to such action to be analysed. Clearly a one-day strike in a factory or office differs markedly from a six-month dispute in an emergency service or a year-long pit strike. For some workers, striking is *part of* the day-to-day struggle of industrial life, for others it is almost *separate from* that struggle, a rare event entered into with considerable fear and trepidation. The docks and a small minority of manufacturing plants (Smith *et al.*, 1978:55) are good examples of the former, while many white-collar and professional occupations, along with highly competitive industries such as clothing and, to a lesser extent, the health service, are examples of the latter. The processes of industrial conflict will therefore vary from one organisation to another. Each has a 'negotiated order', the outcome of a dialectical interaction between social structure and social consciousness, but in some situations this engenders a high level of stability, in others it leads to heightened levels of conflict (Hyman, 1989b:71).

It is therefore essential to consider workplace relations in more detail, but in doing so to consider *all* manifestations of industrial conflict. In practice strikes are part of a continuum of behaviour, albeit the most visible or manifest example of industrial conflict. But they are not the only manifestation. In coalmining, for example, not only did the expression of strike action change over time (small, short, pit-level disputes giving way to large protracted, national stoppages), but there was an increase in absenteeism at precisely the same time. Thus absenteeism in coalmining was believed to have 'replaced strike action to some extent as the most reliable index and manifestation of discontent' (Handy, 1968:45). Although Handy linked the sharp increase in absenteeism to the impact of pit closures on morale, there was also a clear link to changes in the structure of collective bargaining and the movement away from piece-work payment systems negotiated at the pit level (Sapsford and Turnbull, 1993). As Hyman (1989b:58) has observed, 'attempts to suppress specific manifestations of conflict, *without removing the underlying causes of unrest*, may merely divert the conflict into other forms' (original emphasis). In other words, as one opportunity to express discontent was closed off (the short, small, pit-level strike), others were resorted to more frequently (national, industry-wide strikes and individual absence). In the words of Clark Kerr, 'the manifestation of hostility is confined to no single outlet. Its means of expression are as unlimited as the ingenuity of man [*sic*] (1964:170–1).

The forms and theory of industrial conflict

The bases of industrial conflict within capitalist economies – the structural antagonism that exists between employer and employee, both in the work place and beyond – have been examined in some detail in Chapter 2. The fundamental characteristics and tensions of the employment relationship, such as hierarchy and control, exploitation and resistance, need not be repeated here. Whatever else may have changed since the 1980s, the defining characteristics of the employment relationship remain unaltered. Thus the basic conflicts of interest that exist between employer and employee have neither been eroded nor eradicated. Indeed there is not even any evidence of 'them and us' attitudes having significantly weakened, either among workers (Edwards and Whitston, 1993:30–1; and Kelly and Kelly, 1991) or management (Waddington and Whitston, 1995b:416). What *has* changed, however, are the manifestations of industrial conflict. The growth of 'cut price' forms of collective action has already been noted. But what about individual or 'unorganised' forms of conflict? What about employer conflict with the employee, for instance over intensification of work in the office (Lane, 1988:77), the hospital (Bach, 1989) and elsewhere (Edwards and Whitston, 1991; and Waddington and Whitston, 1995b), which in some industries has been accompanied by an increase in accident rates and even deaths (Beaumont, 1995:42; Grunberg, 1986; *Labour Research*, September 1990, June 1991; and Nichols, 1990)? As has been noted, 'the tensions generated by a given work situation may cause workers either to go on strike, stay at home, hit the foreman, or smash (or be smashed by) the machine' (Hyman, 1982:403).

A major distinction between the many forms of industrial conflict is that absenteeism, turnover, sabotage and the like are regarded as forms of 'unorganised' conflict, where

workers typically respond to the oppressive situation in the only way open to them *as individuals*: by withdrawal from the source of discontent, or, in the case of certain forms of sabotage or indiscipline, by reacting against the immediate manifestation of oppression (Hyman, 1989b:56, original emphasis).

More specifically, such action is usually spontaneous, reactive and above all not borne out of any calculative strategy. 'Organized conflict, on the other hand, is far more likely to form part of a conscious strategy to change the situation which is identified as the source of discontent' (ibid). In reality, however, the dividing line between organised and 'unorganised' conflict is rarely so clear cut. How does one classify, for example, 'blue flu', a situation where all the officers of the New York Police Department report in sick on the same day? As Plowman *et al.* (1981:27) note, this has proved a very effective substitute for strike action. During the recent BA cabin crew strike nearly 2000 staff went on sick leave rather than participate in the official strike, largely because BA threatened disciplinary action against those who supported the dispute. The 'sick note strike', as it was later dubbed, continued throughout the summer of 1997, with 'illness' levels almost double the seasonal average. According to Martyn Bridger, general manager of BA's cabin services, many employees were 'taking their turn' to go sick, which resulted in flight cancellations and severe operational difficulties for the airline (*Daily Telegraph*, 7 August 1997; see also Chapter 4). Conversely, some spontaneous strikes display little calculative intent, with concrete demands only formulated *after* the walkout. Such stoppages, according to Hyman (1975:187), are more akin to mass absenteeism as the 'withdrawal from work' aspect predominates. Likewise absenteeism may not only be a purposive and positive path to various sorts of personal goals (Nicholson, 1977:238), but 'a stratagem in intergroup relations . . . a defensive or aggressive act in intergroup conflict' (Chadwick-Jones *et al.*, 1982:1). The fact that virtually every organisation has a known and accepted 'absence norm' suggests that absenteeism may be determined, or at least the boundaries defined, by cultural norms related to the social organisation of the workplace (that is, shared understandings about 'absence legitimacy', the custom and practice of employee behaviour and its control). In other words such behaviour may to some extent be organised by the work group (see Turnbull and Sapsford, 1992:293–6).

Of course absence from work may reflect many things other than conflict, and in general does not represent deliberate defiance. Again, however, whether such forms of behaviour can be taken as an expression of conflict with the employer depends both on the meanings attached to such behaviour (is absence, sabotage, pilfering, uncooperative behaviour, *inter alia*, viewed as a way of 'getting back' at management?), and on the structure of employer–employee relations (in any given workplace the expression of industrial conflict, in its many different forms, will be contingent on the pattern of labour control). On the world's airlines, for example, apparently innocuous and imperceptible behaviour such as the type of shoes being worn, the amount of jewellery, and even the colour of eye-shadow or underwear can all represent an expression of conflict and a means of 'getting back' at management as all these have been specified in the employee's contract (Hochschild, 1983:102–3, 126). More explicit is the effect of employer–employee relations and the pattern of labour control on the cabin crew's facial expressions:

> in the flight attendant's work, smiling is separated from its usual function, which is to express a personal feeling, and attached to another one – expressing a company feeling. The company exhorts them to smile more, and 'more sincerely', at an increasing number of passengers. The workers respond to the speed-up with a slowdown: they smile less broadly, with a quick release and no sparkle in the eye, thus dimming the company's message to the people. It is a war of smiles (ibid:127).

For other employees it is a war of words. Telephone sales personnel, for example, who are increasingly required to 'charm' customers over the phone, may proffer misleading information and a false name, leaving customers to ring back for 'Mike Rotch', 'Hugh Jass', 'Mike Hunt' or his brother, 'Eric'.

Instead of a charm offensive the company's employees indulge in offensive charm as a way of 'getting back' at management.

Unfortunately, 'unorganised' conflict, and the relationship between organised and unorganised conflict, has received remarkably little attention in either industrial sociology or industrial relations (Edwards and Scullion, 1984:547). While organised conflict is seen to be both formal and collective, and unorganised conflict both informal and individual, there is a considerable grey area in between. However there is sufficient research on absenteeism, sabotage, pilfering and other forms of employee behaviour such as turnover to locate such action along a continuum, illustrated in Figure 10.1, and to develop a theory of industrial conflict that focuses on the characteristics of workplace relations and the negotiation of the wage–effort bargain.

FIGURE 10.1   Forms of industrial conflict

At the collective end of the continuum in Figure 10.1, strikes are the most notable form of action organised by workers and/or their unions (on a more or less formal basis). Working to rule can often be as effective, as such action can cause considerable disruption to production and frustration for management, while the workforce continues to receive wages. Such action often precedes wage negotiation or strike action (Batstone *et al.*, 1978:41), as during the ambulance workers' dispute. During wage negotiations, it is not uncommon for workers to indulge in 'bureaucratic sabotage', choking the company's grievance and disputes procedures with numerous claims (many of which may be bogus) in order to put pressure on management to reach a more favourable pay settlement. Although most people associate sabotage with the wilful destruction of machinery (throwing a spanner into the works), Dubois (1979:14) defines sabotage as *any* form of action, even 'working without enthusiasm', that results in a loss of production, lower quality output or an inferior service. Thus sabotage might be active or passive, offensive or defensive, individual or collective, open or covert, spontaneous or organised (ibid:21). At the extreme, 'militant sabotage' – which is open, invariably collective and usually well-organised – may be rare, but it has been actively deployed by workers to exert control over the work process. Such action is not only a direct challenge to managerial authority, but aims to restructure social relationships and redistribute power. As Taylor and Walton (1971:243) point out, however, attempts to assert control through sabotage (as at the Fiat car plant in Turin, Italy, in 1969) are more often found where 'restrictions are placed upon the expression of dissatisfaction in industries with a history of militant activity'. Thus sabotage (ibid), and in particular absenteeism (Knowles, 1952:221), are often viewed as *alternatives* to strike activity, although there is evidence to suggest they may be *complementary* or *additive* forms of dissent (see for example Bean, 1975; P. K. Edwards, 1979; and Turnbull and Sapsford, 1992).

For some workers, however, apparently individual acts such as absenteeism are in fact highly organised and controlled on a collective basis. Not without reason, then, absence from work has been described as 'the silent strike' (Cook, 1990). In numerical terms absence from work is certainly as significant as strikes. In fact many more working days are lost from absence than from strikes (Jones, 1971:12; and Nicholson, 1977:237), and currently around 5–7 per cent of available working time for manual workers is lost due to absence (Edwards and Whitston, 1989:2) compared with much less than 1 per cent due to strikes. Absence among professional and white-collar workers has increased significantly in recent years, and it is estimated that absence from work now costs British business around £12 billion per annum (CBI, 1997). But is non-attendance an expression of conflict, either for the workforce as a whole or for specific work groups and/or individuals? Although a distinction is usually drawn between absence and absenteeism, where the former represents all permissible or excusable non-attendance while the latter implies deliberate or wilful non-attendance, in reality the distinction between the two is often blurred. The more important points, from the employers' perspective, are that, first, workers see absence through a very different 'moral lens', endorsing a range of types of absence that managers typically regard as illegitimate (Edwards and Whitston, 1993:45, 48). Second, *any* form of 'avoidance behaviour' challenges managerial control. Absenteeism represents 'a refusal to accept managerial logic and an assertion by the worker of control over when his or her labour power shall be expended' (Edwards and Scullion, 1982:128). For management, then, absenteeism is at best a minor (logistical) impediment to the efficient organisation of production, at worst a direct challenge to managerial control and the viability of the organisation itself (Turnbull and Sapsford, 1992:294).

For employees, 'avoidable' absence is rarely a *deliberate* policy of resistance. More usually it is a means of relieving tension and frustration with the work situation, rather than any attempt to change that situation, let alone to restructure power relations. However at times, and for some workers, absenteeism does represent an attempt to assert a greater degree of control over the labour process, a purposive activity that represents a direct challenge to managerial authority rather than simply a negative reaction to work pressures. Both forms of absence may represent conflict with the employer, but they have qualitatively different meanings for those involved, and qualitatively different behavioural consequences.

Where there are strong lateral ties between employees (strong horizontal integration) based on a strong 'occupational culture', as found among dockers, miners, shipbuilders or train drivers (see Edwards and Whitston, 1989:19; Nicholson and Johns, 1985:399; and Turnbull, 1992), and where hierarchical (low-trust) relations exist between management and workforce (weak vertical integration), it is not uncommon for workers to regard voluntary absence as an 'entitlement'. Moreover such workers will defend their *right* to 'have one off' even in the face of managerial discipline (Turnbull and Sapsford, 1992:295). Absence, in other words, is defiant of managerial control. Dockers, for example, traditionally engaged in highly organised forms of absence, taking it in turns to 'have one off', and resisted managerial attempts to discipline any one individual (gang member) for absenteeism on the grounds that such action constituted random victimisation. The same applies to pilfering, which among dockers was also a highly organised activity (Mars, 1974). As with absence, dockers would steal in groups, according to their own rules, and would penalise their own deviants. Like refuse collectors, dock gangs displayed considerable order and internal control, maintained through a well-established hierarchy, earning the label 'wolves' as they worked (hunted) and stole (killed) in packs (Mars, 1982:31–2).

As with absenteeism, pilfering is arguably more costly than strikes. In fact pilfering and fiddling costs British companies an estimated £14 million a day, or £5 billion per annum (*The Independent*, 8 August 1992). Highly organised, collective forms of pilfering, however, are comparatively rare. More common-place are situations where employees need the support of the group in order to steal, but like vultures they act on their own when at the feast (Mars, 1982:2). Travelling salesmen and bread roundsmen are good examples, rely-ing on information and support from colleagues in order to 'work the fiddle', but acting in isolation for much of their actual work. This clearly takes us into the grey (middle) area of Figure 10.1 and presents considerable analytical problems (see Edwards, 1986:255). The boundary or dividing line between organised and unorganised, formal and informal activity is particularly difficult to locate. In order to protect piece rates, for example, workers might establish output norms and discipline 'rate busters'. Controls are informal and individuals might refuse to conform, even when 'sent to Coventry'. More stringent collective controls are difficult to impose, however, as it is 'illegiti-mate' to discipline somebody for producing too much. The more significant point about such activity is that it is contrary to management control and direction of the labour process. Factory workers are often adept at deceiving management regarding the maximum effort or pace of work possible and are therefore able to 'make out' (Roy, 1954).

Output control, in its many guises, is essentially a calculative activity, an attempt to shift the wage–effort bargain in the employee's favour. Similarly absence from work can take on 'calculative' overtones, especially in a low-trust work environment where employees' involvement in their work is limited to an essentially economic exchange (time versus money). The absence culture that develops is therefore determined, in large part, by calculation

(Nicholson and Johns, 1985:402–3), as are acts of sabotage. Again, the narrow conception of sabotage as a form of destruction is too limited as it can also include the production of goods below acceptable levels of quality (Dubois, 1979; and Edwards, 1986:249). In other words, workers might indulge in illicit or illegal activities to facilitate the work process, such as running machines above recommended speeds or using improper tools or materials in order to increase output and earn more money, but such activity is against the interests of management as it can result in costly machine downtime and/or substandard production. Organisation and even the connivance of supervisors is implicit in such activity (see Taylor and Walton, 1971), although it is *individuals* who are punished, or even dismissed, for such actions.

Thus an important distinction between organised and (supposedly) unorganised forms of conflict is that, whatever the degree of organisation involved, in the latter case it is ultimately the individual that will be subject to discipline, and any group support for the individual concerned is more likely to be implicit rather than explicit. The employee's union, for example, is unlikely to condone the destruction of machinery, calculative absence, pilfering or even making out. At the extreme, where conflict is almost entirely unorganised, informal and individual, it is more than likely that unions will not be represented at all. The absence of union organisation, as was demonstrated in the case of Sew & Son and the other non-union firms discussed in Chapter 9, is a key feature of many workplaces characterised by high levels of employee turnover (quits). The physical isolation of employees at such companies makes organised activity difficult, as does the imposition of direct forms of control and the strict adherence to management rules. Thus for supermarket check-out operators, shop assistants and many (female) machinists, patterns of isolation and subordination in their work is reflected in, for example, the nature of fiddling, where employees indulge in such activity on their own initiative and receive no group support either to perform such acts or when detected. The only collective dimension of such 'donkey' jobs (so-called because they are generally arduous, monotonous, repetitive and isolated) is that employees rarely accuse each other of fiddling. Beyond that, as a supermarket cashier cited by Mars (1982:68) points out, 'there are absolutely no alliances or anything like that'.

It is also commonplace for employee resentment at the impositions created by working in a supermarket or other repetitive jobs to be expressed through sickness and absence, which tend to be higher than normal (Hill and Trist, 1962:38; and Mars, 1982:31). According to Nicholson and Johns (1985:402–3), where management rules prevail, or where there is a dependent or paternalistic culture, voluntary absence from work is regarded as a form of deviant behaviour (consistent, of course, with the unitarist attitude of most managers). But it is difficult to distinguish between avoidable and unavoidable absence as non-attendance is more usually a means of relieving tension and frustration at work. Likewise it is difficult to distinguish between accidental and intentional acts of sabotage. Such spontaneous acts of resistance can still be purposeful and positive for the employee – to let off steam or take a break – and at the same time can present problems for management.

Running throughout this analysis of industrial conflict has been a focus on the on-going process of negotiation over the wage–effort bargain, the frontier of control that exists in all organisations. As employees attempt to redefine the wage–effort bargain or redraw the frontier of control, they come into conflict with their employer. Clearly the pattern of negotiation and confrontation differs markedly from one organisation to the next, with important consequences for the different forms of overt conflict – be it strikes, work-to-rule, sabotage, pilferage, absenteeism or whatever – and whether such action is organised or unorganised, collective or individual. In order to differentiate the many possible patterns, Edwards (1986:226–7) classifies workplaces according to three characteristics of workers' approaches and organisation:

- *Militant* – the extent to which workers perceive themselves as having interests that are opposed to or inconsistent with the interests of management, and act accordingly.
- *Collective* – the degree to which an individual or collective orientation exists.
- *Organisation* – the extent to which a collective orientation is translated into collective organisation.

Using these characteristics, Edwards identifies four possible types of workplace, listed in Table 10.4.

As with other classifications, Table 10.4 is comprised of idealised and simplified types. Some cases will therefore fall between types, and there is a good deal of variation within each type. Nonetheless there is a clear synergy between, for example, a Type 1 workplace and 'donkey' fiddles, 'spontaneous' sabotage and absence which reflects an attempt to relieve the frustrations of work. Strikes in these organisations, if they do occur, are more likely to be *separate from* rather than an integrated part of day-to-day struggles. At the other end of the spectrum, one finds a synergy between a Type 4 workplace and 'wolf pack' fiddles and collectively imposed absence norms. For workers in such organisations, strikes are more likely to be *part of* the day-to-day struggle over the wage–effort bargain. Within Type 2 and 3 workplaces more calculative forms of pilferage, absence and sabotage may be found, but the fact that significant variation exists across these two Types is indicative of the problems encountered in defining, and delineating, the different forms of conflict located in the grey (middle) area of Figure 10.1.

In each and every case, however, once it is recognised that the wage–effort bargain is indeterminate, as was demonstrated in Chapter 2, then it must be

TABLE 10.4   Classification of characteristics of workplace relations

	Militant	*Collective*	*Organisational*
TYPE 1	NO	NO	NO
TYPE 2	YES	NO	NO
TYPE 3	YES	YES	NO
TYPE 4	YES	YES	YES

TYPE 1 – is very common, especially in organisations in highly competitive industries. Many of these industries employ female labour and have a strict system of supervision (direct control), as at Sew & Son (Chapter 9), but the key feature is the absence of resources among workers to make their demands effective against the demands of management. Also in this group, however, are organisations where sophisticated paternalism is the dominant management style, as at Marks & Spencer and IBM.

TYPE 2 – these workplaces are often characterised by militant individualism, where workers negotiate with management over rates and assert their right to plan their own work (thereby exercising considerable influence over effort).

TYPE 3 – in these workplaces there is collective negotiation over the effort bargain (unlike Type 1), but controls are often informal or limited to exploiting managerial leniency. In other words, negotiation rarely develops into organised pressure to shift the frontier of control in workers' favour on a more permanent basis.

TYPE 4 – where the workforce exercises substantial control over the effort bargain, sustained through tight union organisation, control is exercised against management and over the workers as well (as on the docks).

Source: Adapted from Edwards (1986:227–34).

acknowledged that the struggle for control is an inevitable condition in *all* workplaces. That struggle may take the form of peaceful bargaining, or it may erupt into long and bitter strikes. The first step in the understanding of industrial conflict is therefore to recognise its many and varied forms. The second is to identify the meanings and purposes attached to workplace behaviour by the workers involved in order to determine whether such behaviour can be construed as an expression of conflict. Finally, just as 'to admit the rationality of strikes is to accept that strikers have a case: that genuine deprivations underlie industrial conflict' (Hyman, 1989b:118–19), the same can be said of all other forms of conflict. To throw a spanner in the works or to go absent may not be as rational as to strike, since it brings only temporary relief and is unlikely to change either the immediate work situation or the frontier of control, except perhaps in the short term. But in some situations it may be the only option available and as such the most rational thing to do in the circumstances. To restate the point made earlier, it is facile to argue that industrial conflict has abated in recent years without first undertaking not only a more detailed look at the strike statistics themselves but also (of equal, if not more importance) to consider the many other possible expressions of dissatisfaction and dissent.

Conclusion

To seek an understanding of the nature of conflict within work organisations is to grapple with a complex phenomenon. While much analysis focuses on strike statistics that provide a ready 'index' of conflict, these data can offer a misleading picture. In recent years, for example, there has been a tendency to equate the decline in officially recorded strikes with a decline (or even the demise) of industrial conflict. Not only does this ignore the intensity of conflict and bitterness of feelings invoked in many strike situations, it ignores the diverse nature of both strikes and other forms of industrial conflict. The ambulance workers' dispute, for example, was just one of many prolonged and bitter public sector disputes over the past two decades. At the start of the dispute the crews used non-strike action to press their claims, while the subsequent failure of the strike to secure the workers' principal objectives suggests a continuation of the discontent, ill-feeling and poor morale that were at the root of the dispute. In this chapter we have therefore cautioned against any suggestion that industrial conflict has 'withered away', emphasising instead the many and varied forms of industrial conflict, the importance of both attitudes and behaviour, and the influence of a diverse range of structural, contextual and individual factors, both within the workplace and beyond. In particular we have argued for a greater appreciation of the underlying (and continuing) sources of tension and conflict within contemporary work organisations, and an awareness that the business cycle, collective bargaining structures, pay systems and the like are as much a consequence as a cause of industrial conflict.

PART 4

SUMMARY AND CONCLUSIONS

CHAPTER 11

The future direction of employee relations

Change and continuity

With more than half a million enterprises spread across scores of industries, attempts to draw general conclusions about the current state of employee relations, not to mention possible future directions, must necessarily be a cautious activity. And ever more so with the recent election of a Labour government. In the foregoing chapters, however, we have sought to take account of some of the main aspects of this diversity. The case studies, for example, have purposely been drawn from the public and private (and recently privatised) sectors, as well as from services and manufacturing, domestic and foreign-owned enterprises, unionised and non-unionised settings and, in our case of Sew & Son in Chapter 9 and the discussion of union recruitment activities in Chapter 5, smaller as well as larger establishments. What these cases and the wider analysis underline are the dangers of drawing too simple or overgeneralised conclusions: conclusions, for example, about whether employee relations in the recent past have been characterised by change *or* continuity, and whether individualism has *or* has not become the defining principle of employee relations in contemporary UK organisations.

In practice, as we have seen, the colours in the landscape of employee relations run into one another: policies and practices are diverse, with developments occurring at different paces in different (and in some cases, opposite) directions, or even not at all. Tradition and a reluctance to change are evident in employee relations practices in the same way that new departures and breaks with the past are evident. This should hardly take us by surprise. Employee relations are, after all, arrangements that are constructed and maintained by people, and the diverse characteristics of human nature – inertia, reluctance and resistance to change, as well as forthrightness, risk and a desire to move on – will be reflected in the social arrangements that groups of people establish. At the same time, those same social arrangements derive from an employment relationship whose essential characteristics are basically little changed: there still exists an asymmetry of power, an indeterminacy surrounding the wage–effort bargain, and an interdependency between the parties. The ensuing patterns of conflict, accommodation and cooperation produce an underlying continuity, but at the same time present both opportunities and constraints for all the principal actors in employee relations (management, labour and the state). Thus at one level employee relations appears to have changed inexorably, while at the same time one is struck by a sense of *déjà vu*. In 1981 there would have been few workers still in employment who had lived or worked through the depression of the interwar years, yet all our readers today will have lived through two recessions during which unemployment exceeded three million. Nothing has changed yet everything is different: as we twist around the spiral of capitalist economic development we experience progression and return, never a return to exactly the same point but always to a place that is familiar.

The twin forces of change and continuity are evident in several developments and issues that have emerged from the diverse and contradictory patterns of employee relations practice. These are of interest both in their own right and as possible signposts to future trends. To illustrate these it is not necessary to rehearse all the arguments of the previous chapters, but it may be useful to summarise aspects of change and continuity for the three main actors in employee relations – management, trade unions and the state – and in particular to explore likely developments in government policy in the coming years. Following this, the chapter examines one further future development in employee relations, namely closer European integration to which the new Labour government is committed.

Management, unions and the state

Management

In terms of management's role in employee relations over the past two decades, a persistent theme has been their attempt to reconstruct forms of labour control and develop a new employee relations style. This has included attempts to ring-fence the power of the trade union voice – particularly the national union organisation – within the company. This objective can be seen to underlie, for example, debates within the union movement on the most appropriate relationship (cooperation or confrontation) between management and labour (see Chapter 5), in the way many companies (including Nissan, Chapter 8) have sought to (re)define the role of employee representatives in consultative rather than bargaining terms, and in the way (as in British Steel, Chapter 7) attempts have been made to reduce or eliminate the significance of national collective bargaining frameworks (and national union influence) in favour of more localised activity, where attention is focused much more directly on plant performance. In addition there has been a renewed emphasis on communicating the company's 'message'. Compared with the 1970s, however, it became apparent during the 1980s and 1990s that an increasing number of managers were keen to define this message and its operational implications as suitable topics for information and possibly even consultation, but not as a subject for joint regulation. Changes brought about in the nature of collective relations, and in particular a tendency for consultation to replace negotiation as the *modus operandi* of these arrangements when dealing with work-related issues, coupled with a burgeoning of new forms of communicating directly with employees, reflected this management view.

Yet while various changes in management's attitude and approach to employee relations can be identified, a strong element of continuity is also evident. In part this reflects those organisations where, for a variety of reasons (including a general satisfaction with their current operation), employee relations have not undergone the sorts of change evidenced elsewhere. A more fundamental source of continuity, however, is the persistence of a pragmatic and opportunistic approach to employee relations that elicits compliance rather than active cooperation from the workforce. The fact that management increasingly desire the latter but usually secure the former does not mean that they have abandoned cooperation as an objective (except perhaps in certain areas of the public sector, at least during particular periods). In fact the opposite is true. The language of 'continuous improvement' and 'total quality management' sets great store by the need to secure the active cooperation, contribution and knowledge of the workforce. Similarly, in such dictums as 'employees are our most valuable asset', the rhetoric if not yet the reality of human resource management represents an acknowledgement that it is only through the active cooperation of the workforce that productivity, quality and ultimately profitability can be sustained. Hence in this key respect the central managerial problematic – that of securing a surplus product *and* the cooperation of the workforce – remains much the same as in the past. Management's basic objective in any employee relations policy is still to secure and maintain a predictable, productive and cost-effective labour force.

At various points throughout this book we have examined the different ways in which management rely on workforce cooperation and the various ways in which employee relations policies and procedures are used to secure that cooperation. Furthermore, in our study of British Airways (Chapter 4) we examined how, in some contexts, management's need for cooperation has gone beyond the requirement to secure simply manual or mental labour, to a need to also elicit emotional labour: the self-subordination of employees' own emotions in the interests of 'customer satisfaction'. Clearly the requirement for employees to suppress their own emotions during the performance of their work role is not a new phenomenon. What is new, however, is the emphasis now placed on customer care as a particular source of competitive advantage. Indeed in a system where all airline staff greet their customers with a 'genuine' smile, it becomes *imperative* that management secure an active emotional contribution from their own workforce. The importance of employee cooperation and contribution is a prominent feature of our other cases: the importance of *kaizen* at Nissan, for example, and skill reorganisation activities at British Steel. Over the years Marks & Spencer appears to have been adept at securing such cooperation from its workforce, although as we have seen the foundations for such cooperation are extremely high levels of dependency on the part of M&S employees and the subordination of employee interests at supplier companies such as Sew & Son.

Yet, to reiterate, while at one level there appears to be widespread recognition among management of the need to gain greater commitment and secure the active cooperation of its workforce, at another level management has failed to realise that cooperation by putting employee relations on a more stable and longer-term footing. This is illustrated by the way in which UK management, compared with some of their European counterparts, have sought to pursue greater workforce flexibility in recent years. The argument of several European commentators is that the search for flexibility in the UK has been essentially 'defensive' or short term (see for example Boyer, 1988; Brunhes, 1989; and Rojot, 1989). Such flexibility is primarily an *ad hoc*, short-term, low-labour-cost response to fluctuations in demand. The use of temporary and short-term contracts, hire and fire practices and high rates of overtime working may be seen to typify this response. In contrast 'offensive' or long-term flexibility strategies are characterised by greater proactivity, with an emphasis on achieving an adaptable rather than a low-cost labour force. Training, retraining and the multiskilling of employees are central to these notions of long-term flexibility (Blyton and Morris, 1992:121). The absence of an adequate training ethos in the UK, coupled with an emphasis on cost reduction (rather than productivity enhancement) as the central competitive strategy, are among the factors creating reliance on short-term rather than longer-term flexibility strategies.

The short-term horizon of most flexibility strategies in the UK reflects a broader preoccupation with the short rather than the longer term, and in particular the primacy of short-term financial performance as the measure of organisational success. Saunders *et al.* (1992:192–3) note that UK companies display a unique form of financial myopia, in stark contrast with European firms. A recent survey, for example, found that UK (and US) managers rank the importance of profitability for shareholders first and employee satisfaction last, whereas in continental Western Europe (in particular Germany and France) the opposite is true (*Observer*, 23 June 1996; see also Hutton, 1996). The Labour government has expressed a commitment to reducing short-termism through, for example, tax changes to encourage long-term share-holding, statutory reporting of long-run indicators of corporate strength, and companies demonstrating a 'public interest' basis for any hostile takeovers. On their own, however, such changes are unlikely to break the vicious spiral of cost-cutting that plagues UK industry. Stakeholding, as opposed to share-holding, where property rights are qualified by a mutual set of claims from employees, government, suppliers and other interested parties (for exampole local communities), requires a legal and financial 'architecture' that allows companies to develop bonds of trust and cooperation with the various stakeholders in the company (see Kay, 1993). Given that trust between management and labour does not evolve organically from the corporate architecture of deregulation, as all the data from *British Social Attitudes* surveys and other sources would appear to suggest, then greater regulation of the labour market and labour management is evidently called for.

The problem of short-termism in approaches to flexibility and other management policies is that they are self-reinforcing. For example, if labour is not only treated as expendable but is also paid a comparatively low wage (such that it is always likely to be dissatisfied and in search of improved remuneration elsewhere), there is an increased likelihood that management will be discouraged from investing in high levels of training. For any specialist skills they require they will prefer, where possible, to 'poach' employees from elsewhere rather than train up their own workers or new recruits (Henley and Tsakalotos, 1992). The outcome, therefore, is inadequate training, both in quantity and quality. For capital as a whole such a policy is inherently irrational, as firms are confronted by labour shortages for skilled labour even in the midst of mass unemployment, but for individual capitalists it is evidently rational given the prevailing socioeconomic context (or what Kay calls the prevalent corporate architecture). Put differently, management often adopt irrational policies for rational reasons. This is perhaps the greatest failing of deregulation and new human resource management policies, namely the assumption that firms are 'islands' and that as long as top executives are committed to progressive personnel policies then everything will fall into place. But unless other firms in the same industry or sector adopt similar policies, firms that invest in their human resources run the risk of losing skilled labour. To prevent such 'free rider' and 'market failure' problems requires, first, a view of the workforce as a long-term investment and an important stakeholder in the future of the organisation, and second, an element of compulsion. The state can facilitate both, via more proactive employment policies in the public sector (a return to the 'good employer' model) and compulsory training for the private sector (perhaps via a training levy or similar policies).

Long-term commitment and motivation on the part of workers will only be secured if management are prepared to offer jobs that are stable, well paid, interesting and ones in which their employees' views are adequately represented. Considerable lip-service has been paid by management to the importance of building long-term relationships grounded on trust and commitment, but in reality the reciprocity required to build a genuine improvement in employee relations is often more notable by its absence. Managers have been clearer about what they require from employees (productivity, commitment, contribution) and the means to secure those outcomes (e.g. work intensification, cost minimisation, marginalisation of trade union influence, performance-related pay, teamwork and the like) but are far less convincing when it comes to what they are offering in return, other than a job and a wage. Some companies, such as Blue Circle, are even offering jobs *in return for* a wage: workers 'gain' job security, or more precisely a five-year commitment to 'no *compulsory* redundancies', while employers secure lower costs as a result of a pay freeze and greater flexibility. Such agreements, heralded by the Labour Party as an example of 'social partnership', are simply the inevitable outcome of 'partnership' in a deregulated market where employees' interests are neither guaranteed by law nor recognised by right, and where consequently they have nothing to 'trade' but the remuneration of their labour. Of course employment is important, and all the more so in times of high unemployment in countries such as the UK, where income support for the unemployed is comparatively low. But if the defining features of many jobs continue to be insecurity, low pay, inadequate representation, poor training and unsatisfying work, then any attempt to build employee commitment and more stable employee relations will be undermined by their shallow foundations. It is little wonder that most firms have been unable to establish a coherent and consistent employee relations style, nor that they should encounter workforce opposition when they attempt to increase efficiency. 'Management attitudes' are now the principal source of grievance in UK workplaces (Waddington and Whitston, 1995b:432–3), which not even HRM can alleviate (Beaumont, 1995:43).

The argument here, then, is that there is a greater need for consistency and reciprocity in managerial policy towards employees and employee relations. In the longer term, the securing of high-quality, productive work from motivated employees will be more likely via the creation of a highly skilled workforce afforded greater discretion and employed in better-paid jobs, than by continued adherence to a cost-minimisation strategy based on low-skilled, low-paid work. Indeed the trajectory of international competition is increasingly towards non-price factors such as quality, specification and service, which requires regulation, not deregulation, of labour markets (see Figure 3.2). A report commissioned by the Department of Trade and Industry (DTI) highlighted the importance of such non-price factors, noting that while the UK's cost base may now be competitive by world standards, UK firms have failed to develop new products. The 'hole in the heart' of UK manufacturing, according to the report, is management, who are poorly educated, ill-trained and consistently fail to turn technology into competitive products (*The Sunday Times*, 14 March 1993).

These flaws in UK industry will take decades to remove, and they will not be redressed without proactive labour market policies. The starting point, as the DTI report suggests, must be education and training, both for management and the workforce. For today's markets, productivity-enhancing rather than cost-minimising approaches to manufacturing are more likely to deliver high value added goods. A stronger productive base would in turn support the growing service sector of the economy. Competitive edge, in other words, can be constructed on the basis of workers' skills, flexibility, innovation and adaptability, creating a matrix of high value added products, high wages, high productivity and high levels of investment (in both physical and human assets). Trade unions can play a positive role in such a matrix (see Streeck, 1987, 1992).

Trade unions

Among trade unions too there is evidence of significant continuities as well as change. Like management's approach to employee relations, there is similar evidence that individual unions and the TUC are lacking sufficiently consistent, coordinated (and coordinating) policies. The challenges facing the unions are widely recognised, both within and outside the labour movement: a decline in membership, a managerial attack on the role of unions within the workplace, increased legal circumscription of trade union action and internal organisation, political exclusion, the need to appeal to new sections of the workforce, and the difficulty of developing new policies and initiatives during periods of economic recession, which inevitably focus most union attention on job protection issues. Recognition of these problems is one thing. Action and resolution is, however, another. As Terry (1991:111) argues, 'A decade of Thatcherism may have strengthened strategic *thinking* among both unions and managers: what it simultaneously seems to have done is to have weakened the capacity to implement those strategies' (original emphasis).

Hence, just as management struggle to control the social relations of production in the face of persistent (and inherent) confrontations with labour and the instability created by competition, so too do the very forces that have undermined trade union power, most notably economic recession, make the task of recovery all the more difficult. If nothing else, the drain on union finances puts them in a Catch 22 situation: unions desperately need to recruit more members, but do not have sufficient resources to mount effective organising and recruitment campaigns, especially in those industries and firms where the potential for membership growth is greatest. Even where unions are able to build up membership and support, recalcitrant employers can still refuse to grant recognition.

What makes the developments and challenges of the past decade or so all the more significant, however, is the evident lack of coordination within sections of the union movement itself. In part this reflects the historic weakness of the TUC as a confederating body – a weakness that contrasts, for example, with the corresponding confederations in some European countries, for example Austria, Germany and Scandinavia (Henley and Tsakalotos, 1992:572) (though several union confederations in Norway, Sweden and elsewhere have been weakened over the last decade, with a growing proportion of union members belonging to organisations not affiliated to the central confederation – see Hyman, 1991a:627). More significant in the UK, however, is the problem of inter-union rivalry over potential members, a problem that derives largely from historical structure and the absence of any 'industrial logic' in many union mergers. This has exacerbated the overall lack of coordination within the union movement, and rendered organisation and recruitment in the non-union sector ('distant expansion') all the more problematic. The short-termism that bedevils managerial policy and practice is thus echoed in trade union strategies for membership recovery, in particular the effort being put into merger discussions and 'sweetheart' single union deals, rather than a more concerted campaigning effort for membership recruitment in new areas of employment and hitherto poorly organised industries. Admittedly these latter activities are riskier and far more expensive in terms of union time and money, but in the longer run they are likely to create a more enduring basis for independent trade union organisation. As we discussed in Chapter 5, the adoption of an 'organising model' is designed precisely to circumvent some of these long-standing problems, but by its very nature is a time-consuming and resource-intensive process.

The impact of managerial strategies on trade union activity and action is more pervasive than is often appreciated. Most notably, the emphasis on cost minimisation has contributed to the unions' problem of dwindling finances (Willman, 1989). Higher wage levels, particularly if coupled with an increased willingness to devote a higher proportion of wages to union subscriptions, could enable unions to establish more effective provision in such areas as membership enquiries, the training of representatives, the buying-in of outside expertise and the funding of adequate research departments to facilitate, among other things, the development of more proactive policies on work-related issues. The benefits of greater financial resources on the research capability of individual trade unions in Germany such as IG Metall, as well as the activities of the main German confederated body, the Deutscher Gewerkschaftsbund (DGB), attest to the possibilities and potential of a more adequately resourced trade union movement. In the absence of significantly higher subscription income, an even greater premium is placed on unions deploying their resources effectively. This can not be achieved by competing with other unions for the same groups of workers, nor primarily by redistributing existing memberships by mergers and amalgamations, but rather by determining how unions can organise and work cooperatively to gain membership and influence in new areas of employment and develop their role in areas where recognition has already been secured. There are today a great many employees who would benefit from union representation, particularly those workers employed by small, non-union companies. Moreover the evidence suggests that many would actually join a union if given the opportunity (either by the union engaging in recruitment activity or the employer being willing to grant recognition). In a democratic society, employees should not be denied this right.

International research suggests that if UK trade unions could combine central and decentral organisation – effective representative structures at both the national and the workplace level – then their prospects for the future would doubtless improve (see Boyer, 1995; and Hancké, 1993). While the organising model discussed in Chapter 5 might redress weaknesses at the workplace level, unions are hoping to be led out of the political wilderness by the incoming Labour government and thereby reassert greater national influence. The TUC is certainly hoping to become a 'partner' in the reconstruction of UK society, suggesting that unions should no longer 'be seen as part of Britain's problem but as part of the solution to the country's problems. . . . At the national level partnership means Government discussing issues with employers and trade unions on a fair and open basis where a common approach can reap dividends' (TUC, 1997:1). For many, sentiments such as these smack of old-style corporatism. But New Labour is determined *not* to turn back the clock. If the UK is to move from a 'liberal' to a 'corporatist' economic system – as reflected in Labour's commitment to the 'social market' – then such a move, as depicted in Figure 6.1, will be predicated on a weak trade union movement, a 'pure' rather than a 'bargained' form of corporatism.

The state

The state's approach to employee relations has been characterised by a similar short-termism to that pervading management and, to a lesser extent, trade union thinking on employee relations. Of course these outlooks are not unrelated; management and unions are functioning in a labour market shaped by public policy and an economy subject to the stop–go cycle of economic (mis)management. In Chapter 6 we examined how the state's guiding principle throughout the 1980s and early 1990s has been one of deregulating labour markets and removing 'obstacles' to the free operation of market forces. In this approach the key obstacle to be removed or diminished has been that of trade union influence, leading to an erosion by legislative action, strike defeats, unemployment and the termination of the union's role in policy-making bodies. As we have noted, the competitive strategy advanced by successive Conservative governments centred on cost reduction, particularly the achievement and maintenance of the lowest possible labour costs. In turn the emphasis on cost reduction rather than productivity enhancement drove a set of other policies: for example, besides policies aimed at reducing trade union influence, there was inadequate public funding of education, training and retraining. The upshot was the reinforcement of a comparatively low-skill, low-productivity, low-wage and technologically backward economy, particularly in comparison with most of the UK's Western European competitors.

One of the central problems with this strategy was its ineffectiveness. The cost of maintaining many millions of workers in low-paid employment, and millions more with no job at all, was not offset by general economic success. On the contrary, the depressed state of economic activity, high rates of unemployment, weakness of the currency, balance of payments deficits and general inadequacy of social welfare provision, all attest to a policy that was intrinsically flawed. It still costs the government around £9000 per annum to pay for each unemployed worker, for example, and so it is hardly surprising that the social security budget is over £70 billion and rising. The government now loses £3.5 billion per annum in revenue as a result of denationalisation, even though it afforded the Treasury an income of almost £90 billion in one-off payments between 1979 and 1997 (based on current prices). In fact privatisation revenues tracked the rise in the previous governments' so-called 'rescue' spending (social security, health and social services) and the fall in 'renewal' spending (education, training, transport and housing).

One of the most notable features of the UK's economic management is the degree to which key aspects of policy and practice are out of step with other European economies – countries that by most indices are performing more successfully than is currently the case in the UK. While countries such as the Netherlands and Germany have built up extensive social protection and legal rights for employees, including the right to organise, bargain, receive information and take strike action, the UK has moved in the opposite direction, removing statutory protections from particular groups of workers, opposing European proposals aimed at safeguarding the interests of various (and often vulnerable) groups of workers, and weakening trade unions' ability to adequately and effectively represent the interests of employees. In the same way, while the vast majority of European countries operate with either minimum wage legislation or full collective bargaining coverage, in the UK (and Ireland) a significant proportion of the workforce remain unprotected (Bazen and Benhayoun, 1992). The result is a wider dispersion of wages in the UK than in any of its EU counterparts, and a higher proportion in low-paid employment (ibid:625; see also Chapter 3 above). The Labour government is, of course, committed to a national minimum wage, the Social Chapter, and a statutory union recognition procedure (although the latter is unlikely to take effect until the next millennium). But Labour is also committed to retaining much of the previous Tory governments' employment and trade union legislation (as a result the UK will still have some of the toughest labour laws in the Western world). The Labour government is also keen to retain the 'flexibility' of UK labour markets in order to create jobs and attract inward investment.

However, despite the attraction of the UK as a low-cost, off-shore location for Asian investment (and even that of other European countries), in a world characterised by increasing global trade and the transnational organisation of production, a competitive strategy based on cheap labour costs in any Northern European country seems a likely act of folly. The Conservatives failed to recognise either the inability of UK capital to compete on labour costs with many newly industrialising countries, or the centrality of identifying areas of potential competitive advantage and growth from a higher-trained, more skilled workforce (which is central to the policy of the current Labour government). The main shortcoming of the state's labour market strategy during the 1980s and 1990s was not that it led to the UK becoming 'the Taiwan of Europe' as some observers suggested, but that it was impossible to maintain even this position in the face of the strong cost-based competition from Taiwan itself. There is no long-term security in a competitive strategy based on low-investment, low-cost, low-skill, low-technology, low-value-added products. There will invariably be countries that can manufacture and export mass-produced, low-technology goods to the market more cheaply than the UK. It is alarming that the structure of the UK economy now resembles that of a semi-peripheral country, specialising in sectors that are not research intensive (Overbeek, 1990).

Although the Labour government has prioritised education and training, fairness at work and social partnership, whether (functional) flexibility, productivity, and committed work relationships can germinate in soil that has been exhausted by the removal of individuals' legal protections, an undermining of collective representation and a failure to provide adequately funded education and training provision for the past two decades or more, is open to question. Outside the UK it has been more widely recognised that a truly adaptable workforce stems from secure rather than insecure employment relationships (see Figure 3.2). According to Dore (1986), for example, the life-time employment system enjoyed by (a proportion of) workers in Japan, while appearing a potential source of rigidity, has in practice yielded a high degree of flexibility, due to the reciprocal exchange of job security for acceptance of internal mobility and flexibility within the organisation. Similar arguments are evident in Europe, signalled for instance in the support for the EU draft Directive on 'atypical' workers, which is designed to define the rights of part-time and temporary workers (Due *et al.*, 1991:96–9). The Conservative government opposed this Directive on the grounds that it would inhibit employers' flexibility, whereas other countries supported it on the grounds that a better paid and better protected part-time workforce would be more committed and more willing to be flexible: a flexibility based on the foundation rather than the absence of security.

In the UK, the widespread absence of high-trust relationships in employee relations is a profound obstacle to the more effective development of those relations (Fox, 1974). But it is difficult to see how that trust can be developed and endure given attitudes that denigrate collectivism as a component of employee relations, something to be discouraged and marginalised wherever possible. As we discuss below, collectivism *is* compatible with efficiency, as European examples attest. Of course it remains to be seen whether the Labour government will be able to put employee relations on a sounder footing through the establishment of a positive system of legal rights for employees – the right to information, to organise, to bargain and to strike. Some of Labour's proposals are vague if not contradictory – advocating partnership and fairness at work, for example, whilst retaining (external) labour market flexibility and Tory employment laws on union governance and strike action, two of the key channels for effective union and employee 'voice' within organisations. As we discussed in Chapter 6, UK employees currently have no right to bargain or to strike; in the latter case there are merely a series of limited immunities that under certain circumstances prevent legal action being brought against trade unions or strike organisers. In contrast the typical situation in Europe (though the precise position varies somewhat from country to country) is that these employee rights are seen by the state as legitimate and indeed *necessary* elements in the effective functioning of employee relations.

Summary

In tracing the development of employee relations through the 1980s and 1990s, the conjunction of a number of factors has clearly been influential. These factors include economic recession, high (and continuing) unemployment, the weakened power of labour (both individual and collective), and the policies of Conservative governments that viewed unions as too strong and the labour force as too protected for the efficient working of market forces. Thus as managers sought to respond to markets that were generally more competitive, and in seeking to adapt their organisations accordingly (via, for example, acquisitions and disacquisitions, mergers, joint ventures, technological change, product development and relocation), they were able to operate in a labour market that had fewer 'restrictions' and protections deriving from either statutory regulation or trade union power.

Many of the structural features that are shaping, and constraining, employee relations in the UK – from the globalisation of capital and the prevalence of shareholder as opposed to stakeholder interests, to the nature and functioning of labour markets and the historical legacy of union organisation – will continue to exert a powerful influence in the early years of the next millennium. An important factor in coming years, already briefly discussed in Chapter 8, will be that of closer European integration. Given the previous government's 'opt out' from the Social Chapter, Europe appears to many commentators and practitioners to have exerted only a modest impact on the control and administration of the employment relationship. Will the Labour government's enthusiasm for a social Europe change all this?

Extending employee relations to Europe?

Any analysis of the influence of increasing European integration on employee relations within member states and individual companies must remain tentative. Not only is the UK government's orientation towards Europe in a state of transition, but the attitudes of member states as a whole towards the EU's social agenda appear to be in a state of flux as contrasting arguments are put forward regarding the merits of, on the one hand, establishing minimum levels of protection for employees within the EU and, on the other hand, the competitive dangers of failing to lower social charges and increase labour flexibility within the EU. Under the Conservative government of John Major, the UK 'opted out' of the social policy aspects of the Maastricht Treaty, which limited the application of regulations introduced under the Social Chapter programme to the other member states. During the period that the UK opt-out was in force, two employment-related Directives were introduced, one concerning the introduction of European Works Councils in 'Community-scale undertakings', and the other the provision of (unpaid) parental leave for either parent in employment. The incoming Labour government expressed greater commitment to the philosophy underlying the Social Chapter, which it signed up to (cancelling the UK's opt-out) soon after gaining power in 1997. In the short term this means that the terms of the European Works Council and Parental Leave Directives will apply in the UK. It also signals the end of the UK government's opposition to other employment-related agreements, notably the Working Time Directive, which came into force in 1996 and regulates maximum weekly hours, the maximum length of shifts, minimum rest periods and annual holidays (IDS, 1996). In addition to the application of these Directives, which have their origin in the European Commission, the European Court of Justice has made a number of significant judgements affecting employee rights in the UK, for example in relation to work of equal value (Rubinstein, 1984) and the requirement to give part-time workers the same qualifying period as their full-time counterparts with respect to statutory employment rights concerning, for example, redundancy pay and unfair dismissal compensation (Dickens, 1995:209). Overall, and incrementally, over time these various provisions will represent significant additions to basic employee rights and protections in Europe in general, and the UK in particular.

These various developments notwithstanding, it is important to note that to date the track record of the European Union in the area of employment and employee relations has been at best modest. In areas such as employee rights to information, and the development of employee representation at company board level, for example, long-standing proposals for change have made little headway at the European level (see Chapter 8). Overall, past experiences of concerted employer opposition (voiced both by employers' associations and major multinational corporations), the watering-down of Directives and the failure of individual member states and companies to comply with EU regulations, signal a need for extreme caution in anticipating any future scale and pace of development.

Analysis of the possible impact of Europe on employee relations is also complicated by the fact that European integration is not taking place in a vacuum, but against the background of the specific economic, political and social contexts of its member states. Perhaps the biggest of these issues is that occurring largely outside the current EU borders, involving the removal of the frontiers between Eastern and Western Europe in the late 1980s and early 1990s, and the continuing economic problems and political instabilities of a number of former Eastern European countries. Assistance in meeting the costs of reconstruction, and the future role of the EU within a unified Europe, will continue to form a major focus for much of the efforts of EU member states in coming years. Within the EU itself, the political context prevailing in individual member states will similarly exert a critical influence on the extent and form of development of the social agenda within Europe.

Equally important, however, will be the overall level of economic activity, and in particular the level of unemployment arising not least from the reconstruction activity that has been identified as a key feature of European economic integration in the face of increasing competition from outside the EU (Ramsay, 1991:543). Clearly the power of organised labour to secure greater influence at the organisational, national and supranational levels has been undermined by slow economic growth. The continuing high level of unemployment will also affect the degree to which EU institutions prioritise employment-generation issues, compared with defining and protecting the rights of those already in employment. Also, in spite of greater interaction between trade unions within Europe (Martinez Lucio and Weston, 1996) and the recent growth of the trade union 'Euro-demo' in Paris, Brussels and elsewhere against company plant closure announcements (*Financial Times*, 17 March 1997; and *The Irish Times*, 28 March 1997), unemployment levels in general, and related issues of job protection in particular, are likely to stimulate a greater inward-looking (and thereby less of a pan-European) orientation among trade unions and employees within individual member states: what Ramsay (1991:548) has termed 'the chronic vulnerability of unions to nationalism'. Thus for both the EU institutions and the various trade union organisations, the amount of attention given to extending employee rights and representation within the EU is likely to be greater during periods of low or declining unemployment, compared with when unemployment is high and/ or increasing.

Yet despite the restricted impact that the EU has had on employment relations within member states since the 1960s, and despite the factors that make the prediction of developments uncertain, there are several indications that closer European ties are likely to play an increasingly important role in shaping the employee relations systems of individual countries and companies. It is to these that we now turn.

The Social Charter and Social Chapter

Employment issues within the EU were given fresh impetus in the late 1980s and 1990s in the form of the Community Charter of Fundamental Social Rights (the 'Social Charter'), adopted at the Strasbourg summit in 1989 by all members except the UK. This and the accompanying Action Programme which contains forty-seven proposals for implementation, sought improved rights regarding social and employment protection. However, while reference is made in the Charter to specific aspects of employment, such as equal treatment, health and safety protection and the right to information, consultation and participation, as Ramsay (1991:555) points out, some of the points remain 'extraordinarily vague', not least due to the attempt to make the Charter principles applicable under different systems of national legislation and practice (see also Addison and Siebert, 1992).

The principles of the Social Charter, which were subsequently endorsed in a separate annex (the 'Social Chapter') to the 1991 Maastricht Treaty, contained several important elements, notably the extension of qualified majority voting (QMV) as the basis for a wider range of decision making beyond health and safety issues to cover working conditions, worker information and consultation rights, gender equality and assistance for the unemployed (Addison and Siebert, 1992:510). In addition it was recognised that the UK's decision to opt out of the social policy aspects of the Maastricht Treaty precluded it from impeding the development in the other eleven states of those social policy issues decided by QMV. The eleven countries agreed to the general objectives of 'the promotion of employment, improved living and working conditions, proper social protection, dialogue between management and labour, the development of human resources with a view to lasting high employment, and the combating of social exclusion' (extract from Annex IV of the Maastricht Treaty 1991). Before Maastricht, rights of interest to employees required unanimous agreement among the EU members, and in practice most were blocked by individual states (particularly the UK). However, as Grahl and Teague (1992b:524) and others have argued, QMV increased the likelihood that many of the draft Directives long held up in the European Council, or some equivalent measures, would reach the EU statute books in the foreseeable future.

One measure that gained approval under QMV was the European Works Council (EWC) Directive. As discussed in Chapter 8, under the terms of this Directive, 'Community-scale undertakings' are required to establish European works councils to act as the basis for informing and consulting with employee representatives on the company's plans and any proposals relevant to employee interests. Multinational companies are required to provide information to their EWC on at least an annual basis, covering such areas as the company's structure, its economic and financial situation, probable developments in the business, its current and likely future employment situation, and investment prospects. Consultation will be required where management proposals are likely to entail serious consequences for the interests of employees (Addison and Siebert, 1992:501; see also Bercusson, 1997; Hall, 1992; and Chapter 8 above).

As the EWC Directive only came into force in September 1996, followed by a period in which firms were required to set up the necessary works council machinery, it remains too early to tell whether in the long term such consultative mechanisms will play a major or a minor role in the development of employee relations in general, and in extending the rights of employees in multinational companies in particular. According to Bercusson (1997:4) at least 1200 multinationals are covered by the Directive. Among these a number of prominent UK firms have already established Europe-wide committees that include their UK employees, even though until 1997 they could have refused to do so under the terms of the UK opt-out. Thus companies such as United Biscuits (UB), for example, established a European Consultative Council in 1994 to cover its 23 000 employees employed in the UK and Europe. The UB Council consists of twenty employee representatives (each serving on the Council for three years), who are accompanied to the meetings by four full-time trade union officials, together with senior human resource managers and representatives from central and divisional management (Industrial Relations Services, 1994:4). The UB Council meets annually to pursue a 'transnational dialogue' on issues such as group performance, overall strategy, jobs and employment policy, and other employee issues. However the Council specifically excludes issues that are subject to national or local negotiation (ibid).

The establishment of similar EWCs is on-going and to date little assessment has been made of the utility of such committees. However there are grounds for concern that, in some cases at least, such committees may be no more than 'window dressing', precluding the most important issues. In the UK, for example, employee representatives of another European works council, established in 1995 by the textile group Coats Viyella, were 'outraged' that details of job losses, factory closures and the decision to move existing work from the UK to other countries was not disclosed to or discussed within its European council (Littlefield, 1996). A more prominent failure to consult involved the car maker Renault, which in February 1997 announced the closure of its Vilvoorde plant near Brussels, without having consulted its 3100-strong workforce or their union representatives (*Financial Times*, 28 February 1997, 6 March 1997). This action appears to contravene EU Directives on works councils and collective redundancies by failing to warn workers at the plant before the closure announcement. However if Renault were to be found guilty in the Belgian courts of a breach of EU rules, the maximum fine of 20 million Belgian francs (around £400 000) is insignificant compared with both the 850 million French francs (over £90 million) that Renault says it will save by transferring the production to other Renault plants, and the 11 million ECU (£8.2 million) in government aid that the company has applied for to carry out additional investment in its Valladolid plant in Spain (*Financial Times*, 7 March 1997). More generally, the firm's willingness to ignore EU law on procedures for consultation must cast doubt on the long-term robustness of existing regulations governing consultation and information within multi-national organisations.

Yet despite the restricted nature of the EWC Directive, the question mark over employers' respect for its authority, and the (at best) minor way in which the EWC provisions counter the considerable imbalances between employer and employed in multinational companies, the Directive may nonetheless be seen to have a particular symbolic importance. For not only is the EWC Directive 'threatening to those who believe in the uninhibited right to manage as the driving force of the "free" market' (Ramsay, 1991:558), but it also emphasises the importance of worker rights within the EU, and in particular it endorses the legitimacy of collective representation at a time when, in the UK at least, almost two decades of Conservative policy acted wholly in favour of individualism and sought to undermine the role of collective representation.

In addition Marginson (1992) has argued that irrespective of EU Directives, the creation of a single European market is likely to further encourage some firms to organise aspects of their employee relations on a Europe-wide basis. However, as Marginson also notes, such developments are more likely in certain types of organisation than others, in particular those companies which already operate with a single management structure within Europe and a divisional structure organised internationally along product group lines rather than by national subsidiaries. A predisposition to introduce Europe-wide information and consultation arrangements is also more likely in those organisations where growth has occurred via greenfield developments (thus facilitating a common approach to employee management) rather than through acquisitions and mergers (ibid:537). Furthermore, just as the logic of TQM, JIT and other production techniques requires a greater emphasis on management communicating the importance of quality to employees and securing employee contribution via different forms of involvement, so too corporations organised on a Europe-wide basis are increasingly likely to emphasise the importance of employee compliance to broad organisational changes, and commitment to intrafirm 'customers' in other locations, which might be advanced through greater Europe-wide communication channels.

While it is possible that consultation and information arrangements will be developed, there remains little prospect of cross-national collective bargaining within Europe. Though joint union–employer committees exist in several industrial sectors, including coal, steel and transport, employers' associations and multinational employers have been highly resistant to the idea of transnational bargaining. On the contrary, multinationals have shown a clear preference for 'divide and rule' policies towards workforces in different European locations. Attempts to control unions via 'coercive comparisons', threats of relocation and an unwillingness to divulge disaggregated financial information have been more prominent than any willingness to contemplate cross-national collective bargaining arrangements or to foster links between employee representative bodies at different locations. Differences in national legislation, the tendency for some countries to be dominated by multi-employer industry bargaining arrangements (in contrast with countries such as the UK where bargaining is more decentralised), the ideological conflicts between different union confederations in Europe and the incipient national-ism of many employees and unions – particularly when faced with economic insecurity – have further acted (and continue to act) to restrict any develop-ment towards transnational bargaining (see Enderwick, 1984; Marginson, 1992; Marginson and Sisson, 1994, 1996; and Northrup and Rowan, 1979).

Trade unions in Europe

Despite the lack of development (or prospect) of cross-border collective bargaining, there has been some (albeit limited) increase in the extent to which trade unions are interacting at the European level. Industry-wide union committees have been established in several industries and act as potentially important exchanges of information, not only in relation to the terms and conditions prevailing in different national contexts, but also as regards trade union policies and effective union strategies in their dealings with employers. An example of cross-national information exchange was evident in the 1989–91 campaign for shorter working hours in the UK engineering industry. The tactics deployed by the Confederation of Shipbuilding and Engineering Unions (CSEU) – in particular the use of selective strike action in companies operating within interlinked production chains, together with the introduction of a national strike levy to compensate those taking part in strike action – closely matched the strategy followed by the CSEU's German counterpart, IG Metall, during its earlier campaign for shorter hours in the mid 1980s (Blyton, 1992b). The exchange of information between the UK and German unions was facilitated by the former leader of the AEU (now the AEEU), Bill Jordan, who also held the Presidency of the European Metalworkers' Federation at the time of the UK dispute, and by informal meetings held between the unions prior to the first strike ballots in Britain (ibid:427). In addition the economic success of the German engineering industry in the latter half of the 1980s was cited by the CSEU to counter UK employer claims that a reduction in hours would necessarily be associated with a decline in competitiveness. As UK unions are increasingly keen to point out, an improvement in employees' working conditions – whether in the form of shorter hours, higher pay, better conditions or greater legal protection – is not necessarily incompatible with greater efficiency, but can in fact provide the foundation for higher productivity, greater flexibility and the more effective introduction and exploitation of technological innovations.

Overall, however, the picture cannot yet be characterised as one of individual unions gaining significant strength from closer European ties. In general, many (though not all) trade union movements in Europe have been weakened by membership decline during the 1980s and 1990s, and this has placed organisational and financial constraints on the development of international contact and collaboration. Moreover, in a period of economic restructuring and job insecurity, unions have been unwilling to sacrifice national sovereignty (and self-interest) for the cause of international solidarity. As a result the development of cross-national links between unions remains predominantly (though with one or two notable exceptions) at the level of information exchange rather than any stronger expressions of cross-border support (though the growth of the 'Euro-demo' may herald a change in this). This lack of solidarity should hardly come as a surprise given the conflicts and lack of unanimity among trade unions within the same company, let alone the unions in a single national confederation such as the TUC. Moreover if cross-national solidarity is based ultimately on a willingness and an ability to mobilise strike action in support of fellow unionists in another country, as the legislation currently stands such sympathy action would be unlawful in several European countries, including the UK, Germany and the Netherlands (Industrial Relations Services, 1989; O'Higgins, 1986).

In other individual cases too, closer European integration appears to have had little effect on the ability of unions to resist employer action. Grahl and Teague (1992a), for example, cite the cases of the ISTC in the late 1970s and the NUM during the 1984–5 strike as examples of UK unions failing to develop a sufficiently European orientation in the fight against plant closures and mass redundancies. In the case of the steelworkers, for example, Grahl and Teague note the tendency of European joint union–management committees for the ISTC to support UK employers in attempting to minimise the impact of closures in the UK, rather than a willingness to join forces with other unions to resist or seek to mitigate the restructuring programme as a whole. Even at times of sustained economic growth, the degree of international union development has been comparatively modest. Hyman (1991a:632) points to the 'high degree of differentiation among European trade union movements in terms of structure, ideology, and levels of organisation' as seriously hampering any development of combined influence. At times of major economic restructuring, recession and high unemployment, trade unions (and the employees they represent) have persistently shown a strong tendency to think even more parochially. With unemployment in the EU standing at over 18 million, there is little likelihood of a major change in this attitude, all the more so given the continued resistance of multinational employers to contemplate transnational bargaining arrangements. However, just as in management–union relations there are possibilities for the development of more extensive information and consultation arrangements at the European level, so too in inter-union relations the possibilities exist for greater assistance and exchange of information. The sector union committees already in existence, the prospects for greater inter-union contact on some form of European works councils, and the demonstration effect of the value of cooperation, such as exhibited in the UK engineering dispute, point to the possibility of somewhat closer links in the future, with consequences for the amount of information available to individual unions and greater awareness of possible strategies to be considered in the pursuit of union claims (see Martinez Lucio and Weston, 1996).

A European demonstration effect?

It is evident from the foregoing discussion that a number of variables limit our ability to predict the effect of closer European integration on employee relations. Several factors can potentially intervene to influence the extent and pace of change. Despite these uncertainties, however, and despite the past record of the EU with regard to employment policy, it seems likely that European integration will have a positive rather than a negative effect on employee relations policies and practices within member states in coming years.

In addition to any direct effects in the UK following the termination of its 'opt-out', European integration could exert a more indirect, 'demonstration' effect on employee relations in the UK, with elements of employee relations approaches from continental Europe gaining influence within the UK. Certainly aspects of these approaches are being embraced by some trade unions, most notably the GMB in its 'New Agenda' policies. During the 1980s and early 1990s the major demonstration effects on employee relations in the UK came from Japan and North America. In part these were imported via direct inward investment from these countries (by major companies such as Nissan, Sony, Hewlett Packard and IBM). In addition much of the managerial language that has become commonplace in recent years has drawn heavily on experiences and examples from these countries: for example in the thinking behind TQM and JIT in Japan and in the management language and practice of HRM in the United States. The influence of these ways of thinking are evident in contemporary UK employee relations – not least in the way single-union agreements became more common, particularly on greenfield sites, and how US-style HRM is consistent with the previous UK Conservative government's emphasis on individualism rather than collectivism in employee relations, and in the emphasis on communications and involvement rather than bargaining and joint decision-making (see Blyton and Turnbull, 1992).

However, examples from Europe demonstrate that collectivism and social protection on the one hand, and economic success and efficiency on the other, are not mutually exclusive, and that such policies can operate successfully in systems where collectivism rather than individualism is still regarded as a central organising principle for employee relations. Countries such as Germany demonstrate a greater acceptance of trade unions as legitimate members of the national body-politic, and works councils are highly regarded 'social partners' within the enterprise. The significance of works councils in Germany attests to the ability of management to work successfully with collective bodies that have the right to codetermination as well as to consultation and information (see Beaumont, 1995). Furthermore, countries such as Germany and Sweden demonstrate that high levels of social protection are not an inevitable hindrance to efficiency, as appears to have been the view of recent UK governments and employers. On the contrary, the more secure employment and social protection provided in these European countries has improved efficiency to a much greater extent than the short-term, solely cost-driven approaches to competitiveness that have been more evident in the UK.

A final word

A common adage is that management gets the trade unions and employee relations it deserves. This maxim has been demonstrated at numerous points in the foregoing chapters. If the employment relationship is characterised by insecurity and mistrust, this hardly augurs well for employee relations. Add to this the attempts over the past two decades to undermine collective rights and representation, then the foundations of employee relations look shaky indeed. For seeking to reject collectivism is to disregard one of the fundamental characteristics of the employment relationship – namely the common experience of work within any organisation and the interdependencies that exist between workforce and management. The individualism of the 1980s is already widely seen as an historic failure. There is growing recognition of not only the legitimacy but also the efficacy of collective interest representation, both within the UK and in the pan-European context. That two decades of attack on trade unions has not broken them is testament both to their resilience as organisations and the asymmetry inherent in the employment relationship, which gives rise to collective interests and the need for those to be articulated through independent representation.

In the past, too many employees have suffered from inadequate trade union support, poor management policies and the state's economic mismanagement. Unless the principal actors in employee relations adopt a longer-term perspective and recognise the legitimacy of collective representation, the benefits of an expanded floor of employee rights and the value of much wider involvement and joint regulation of the employment relationship, then many employees will continue to be the victims of low-paid and unrewarding work. This situation is surely unsustainable for the state, unsatisfactory for management and unacceptable for millions of employees.

Case readings

To enable readers to explore the background of the cases used to introduce the chapters in Parts 2 and 3, additional reading on each of the seven cases is provided below. Brief comments on the references are also provided to indicate the main issues covered and perspectives adopted by the respective authors. Where appropriate, details of the web site of the case organisation are also listed.

Part 2

Chapter 4

General accounts of the history of British Airways are provided by Corke (1986) and Campbell-Smith (1986). More specific analysis of employee relations in BA, and the changes introduced in the 1980s and 1990s, are provided by Colling (1995a), Heller (1992), Höpfl (1993), Höpfl *et al.* (1992) and Goodstein (1990). The latter's account is subject to a scathing critique by a former BA manager (Tate, 1991). Gil (1990), ITF (1992) and Cappelli (1995a) offer international perspectives on management strategy in the industry, in particular attempts to cut costs and improve quality of service, while Hochschild (1983) focuses on the management of 'emotional labour'.
http://www.british-airways.com/

Chapter 5

Coates and Topham (1991) provide an excellent historical account of the formation of the T&GWU, while Snape (1994a) and Fisher (1995) consider the more recent policy of the Union. Recent T&GWU publications emphasise the importance of the organising model to the Union's current recruitment activities, which are discussed in more detail by Turnbull (1997). The contrasting case for union servicing is made by Bassett and Cave (1993). The TUC has also produced a number of useful reports on union organising (for example TUC 1996a, 1997). More general reviews of union organising and recruitment campaigns are provided by Mason and Bain (1991) and Snape (1994b), while Gallie (1996) and Whitston and Waddington (1994) consider the reasons why

employees join trade unions. The pros and cons of union moderation versus union militancy are discussed by, *inter alia*, Bacon and Storey (1996), Kelly (1996) and Kelly and Waddington (1995).
http://www.tgwu.org.uk/

Chapter 6

The history of employee relations in the UK docks is chronicled by Turnbull *et al.* (1992), who also provide a detailed account of the state's involvement in the industry (see also Turnbull, 1993) and of the 1989 national dock strike. The law played a key role in the defeat of the dockers in 1989 (see Simpson, 1989), but there were arguably more important long-term, structural forces at work that more adequately account for the collapse of worker solidarity during the strike (see Turnbull, 1992). The arguments for deregulation can be found in the former Conservative government's White Paper (Department of Employment, 1989), although a more engaging critique is provided by David Davis MP (1988). Proponents of abolition have subsequently claimed that deregulation was a success (for example Dale, 1991; *Employment Gazette*, July 1990; and Finney, 1990), although more detailed and comprehensive analysis suggests a very different picture (Evans *et al.*, 1993; Saundry and Turnbull, 1996, 1997; Turnbull, 1991b, 1993; Turnbull and Wass, 1995; and Turnbull and Weston, 1993a, b and c).

Part 3

Chapter 7

The contemporary development of employee relations at British Steel is examined in more detail in Blyton (1992c, 1993). The more recent of these also provides greater background information on the development of employee relations prior to the series of changes in the 1980s. Other sources of historical material and analysis include Docherty (1983), Bowen (1976) and Upham (1980, 1990). For an account of the managerial thinking behind these recent changes, see Avis (1990), while for a trade union perspective see Docherty (1983) and Bacon *et al.* (1996). The particular events surrounding the national steel strike are also well documented in Docherty, and by Hartley *et al.* (1983). A comparative examination of the work organisation changes can be found in Morris *et al.* (1992). There is also a substantial body of literature on the North American and European steel industry. On the former see Hoerr (1988), while on the latter see Franz (1991) and Houseman (1991). Broader-based reports on the world steel industry can be found in Yachir (1988) and ILO (1992).
http://www.britishsteel.co.uk/

Chapter 8

The managerial perspective on the development of employee relations at Nissan is well described in *The Road to Nissan*, written by the company's former UK Personnel

Director, Peter Wickens (1987). This can usefully be read in conjunction with the main critique of Nissan's approach and philosophy written by Garrahan and Stewart (1992), who argue that Nissan's emphasis on 'quality, flexibility and teamwork' should in fact be read as 'control, exploitation and surveillance' (ibid:59). For a more summary account of work organisation and employee relations at Nissan, see Oliver and Wilkinson (1992), who include the company as one of several cases of Japanese firms operating in the UK. For a more general discussion of recent developments in employee involvement, see Hyman and Mason (1995), Marchington (1992, 1994, 1995), Marchington *et al.* (1992) and Ramsay (1992).
http://www.nissan-europe.com/index.html

Chapter 9

The structure, operations and management of Marks & Spencer are explored in detail by Tse (1985), ranging from buyer–supplier relations, human relations policy and wider corporate responsibility to the community. Lord Sieff (1986) provides his own account of M&S in his memoirs. The M&S philosophy of 'good human relations' is summarised in a short article by Lord Sieff (1984) in *Personnel Management*, and is elaborated in more detail in his book *On Management* (1990). Turnbull and Wass (1998) offer a critique of 'Marksist management' and explore employee perceptions of sophisticated paternalism in a major high street retail store. Employee relations in small, non-union clothing firms such as Sew & Son that manufacture for M&S are discussed in a series of articles by Rainnie (1984, 1985a, 1985b) and his more general text on *Industrial Relations in Small Firms* (1989).
http://www.marks-and-spencer.com/

Chapter 10

Contrasting accounts of the ambulance workers' dispute are provided by NHS chief executive Duncan Nichol (1992), and Kerr and Sachdev (1992), research officers with NUPE (the principal union involved in the dispute). Nichol presents an essentially unitarist account of the strike, while Kerr and Sachdev emphasise the importance of union cooperation, strategy and public opinion during the dispute. A more general account of employee relations in the health service is provided by Seifert (1992). For a recent and thorough review of industrial conflict in the UK, see Edwards (1992). An excellent analysis of the most important theories of industrial conflict is provided by Franzosi (1995).

Bibliography

Abbott, B. (1993) 'Small Firms and Trades Unions in Services in the 1990s', *Industrial Relations Journal*, 24(4):308–17.

ACAS (1995) *Annual Report 1994*, London: ACAS.

Ackers, P., Marchington, M., Wilkinson, A. and Goodman, J. (1992) 'The Use of Cycles? Explaining Employee Involvement in the 1990s', *Industrial Relations Journal*, 23(4): 268–83.

Ackers, P., Smith, C. and Smith, P. (1996) 'Against All Odds? British Trade Unions in the New Workplace', in P. Ackers, C. Smith and P. Smith (eds), *The New Workplace and Trade Unionism: Critical Perspectives on Work and Organization*, London: Routledge, 1–40.

Adams, R.J. and Meltz, N.M. (1993) *Industrial Relations Theory: Its Nature, Scope and Pedagogy*, Metuchen: IMLR Press.

Addison, J.T. and Siebert, W.S. (1992) 'The Social Charter: Whatever Next?', *British Journal of Industrial Relations*, 30(4): 495–513.

Adeney, M. and Lloyd, J. (1986) *The Miners' Strike, 1984–85: Loss Without Limit*, London: Routledge & Kegan Paul.

Ahlstrand, B.W. (1990) *The Quest for Productivity: A Case Study of Fawley After Flanders*, Cambridge: Cambridge University Press.

Ahlstrand, B. and Purcell, J. (1988) 'Employee Relations Strategy in the Multi-Divisional Company', *Personnel Review*, 17(3): 3–11.

Aldington, Lord (1986) 'Britain's Manufacturing Industry', *Royal Bank of Scotland Review*, (151): 3–13.

Amin, A. and Dietrich, M. (1990) 'From Hierarchy to "Hierarchy": The Dynamics of Contemporary Corporate Restructuring in Europe', paper presented at the European Association for Evolutionary Political Economy Conference, Florence.

Andrews, M. and Naylor, R. (1994) 'Declining Union Density in the 1980s: What Do Panel Data Tell Us?', *British Journal of Industrial Relations*, 32(3): 413–31.

Anthony, P.D. (1994) *Managing Culture*, Milton Keynes: Open University Press.

Armstrong, P. (1984) 'Competition Between the Organisational Professions and the Evolution of Management Control Strategies', in K. Thompson (ed.), *Work, Employment and Unemployment*, Milton Keynes: Open University Press, 97–120.

Ascher, K. (1987) *The Politics of Privatisation: Contracting Out Public Services*, Basingstoke: Macmillan.

Ashworth, M. and Forsyth, P. (1984) *Civil Aviation Policy and the Privatisation of British Airways*, Report Series No.12, London: Institute for Fiscal Studies.

Atkinson, J. (1984) 'Manpower Strategies for Flexible Organisations', *Personnel Management*, August: 28–31.

Atkinson, T. (1996) *Incomes and the Welfare State*, Cambridge: Cambridge University Press.

Auerbach, S. (1988) 'Injunction Procedure in the Seafarers' Dispute', *Industrial Law Journal*, 17(4): 227–38.

Auerbach, S. (1990) *Legislating for Conflict*, Oxford: Clarendon Press.

Avis, R. (1990) 'British Steel: A Case of the Decentralization of Collective Bargaining', *Human Resource Management Journal*, 1(1): 90–9.

Bach, S. (1989) 'Too High a Price to Pay? A Study of Competitive Tendering for Domestic Services in the NHS', *Warwick Papers in Industrial Relations*, no. 25, IRRU, University of Warwick.

Bach, S. and Winchester, D. (1994) 'Opting Out of Pay Devolution? Prospects for Local Pay Bargaining in UK Public Services', *British Journal of Industrial Relations*, 32(2): 263–82.

Bacon, N., Blyton, P. and Morris, J. (1996) 'Among the Ashes: Trade Union Strategies in the UK and German Steel Industries', *British Journal of Industrial Relations*, 34(1): 25–50.

Bacon, N. and Storey, J. (1996) 'Individualism and Collectivism and the Changing Role of Trade Unions', in P. Ackers, C. Smith and P. Smith (eds), *The New Workplace and Trade Unionism: Critical Perspectives on Work and Organization*, London: Routledge, 41–76.

Bacon, R. and Eltis, W. (1978) *Britain's Economic Problem: Too Few Producers*, London: Macmillan.

Bailey, R. (1994) 'Annual Review Article 1993: British Public Sector Industrial Relations', *British Journal of Industrial Relations*, 32(1): 113–36.

Bailey, R. (1996) 'Public Sector Industrial Relations', in I. Beardwell (ed.), *Contemporary Industrial Relations: A Critical Analysis*, Oxford: Oxford University Press, 121–50.

Bain, G. S. (1970) *The Growth of White Collar Unionism*, Oxford: Clarendon.

Bain, G. S. (1986) 'Introduction to a Symposium on the Role and Influence of Trade Unions in a Recession', *British Journal of Industrial Relations*, 24(2): 157–9.

Bain, G. S. and Clegg, H. A. (1974) 'Strategy for Industrial Relations Research in Great Britain', *British Journal of Industrial Relations*, 12(1): 91–113.

Bain, G. S. and Elsheikh, F. (1976) *Union Growth and the Business Cycle*, Oxford: Blackwell.

Bain, G. S. and Elsheikh, F. (1980) 'Unionisation in Britain: An Inter-Establishment Analysis Based on Survey Data', *British Journal of Industrial Relations*, 18(2): 169–78.

Bain, G. S. and Price, R. (1983) 'Union Growth: Dimensions, Determinants and Destiny', in G. S. Bain (ed.), *Industrial Relations in Britain*, Oxford: Blackwell, 3–33.

Bamber, G. J. and Whitehouse, G. (1992) 'International Data on Economic, Employment and Human Resource Issues', *International Journal of Human Resource Management*, 3(2): 347–70.

Bannock, G. and Daly, M. (1990) 'Size Distribution of UK Firms', *Employment Gazette*, May: 255–8.

Bassett, P. (1986) *Strike Free: New Industrial Relations in Britain*, London: Macmillan.

Bassett, P. (1988) 'Non-Unionism's Growing Ranks', *Personnel Management*, March: 44–7.

Bassett, P. and Cave, A. (1993) *All for One: The Future of the Unions*, London: Fabian Society.

Bate, P. and Murphy, A. J. (1981) 'Can Joint Consultation Become Employee Participation?', *Journal of Management Studies*, 18(4): 389–409.

Batstone, E. (1984) *Working Order: Workplace Industrial Relations Over Two Decades*, Oxford: Blackwell.

Batstone, E. (1986) 'Labour and Productivity', *Oxford Review of Economic Policy*, 2(3): 32–43.

Batstone, E. (1988) 'The Frontier of Control', in D. Gallie (ed.), *Employment in Britain*, Oxford: Blackwell, 218–47.

Batstone, E., Boraston, I. and Frenkel, S. (1977) *Shop Stewards in Action: The Organization of Workplace Conflict and Accommodation*, Oxford: Blackwell.

Batstone, E., Boraston, I. and Frenkel, S. (1978) *The Social Organization of Strikes*, Oxford: Blackwell.

Bazen, S. and Benhayoun, G. (1992) 'Low Pay and Wage Regulation in the European Community', *British Journal of Industrial Relations*, 30(4): 623–38.

Beadle, R. (1995) 'Opting Out of Pay Devolution? The Prospects for Local Pay Bargaining in UK Public Services: A Comment', *British Journal of Industrial Relations*, 33(1): 137–42.

Bean, R. (1975) 'The Relationship Between Strikes and "Unorganised" Conflict in Manufacturing Industries', *British Journal of Industrial Relations*, 17(1): 95–8.

Beardwell, I. (1990) 'Annual Review Article 1989', *British Journal of Industrial Relations*, 28(1): 113–28.

Beardwell, I. (1996) 'How Do We Know How It Really Is? An Analysis of the New Industrial Relations', in I. Beardwell (ed.), *Contemporary Industrial Relations: A Critical Analysis*, Oxford: Oxford University Press, 1–10.

Beatson, M. (1993) 'Trends in Pay Flexibility', *Employment Gazette*, September: 405–28.

Beaumont, P. B. (1986) 'Management Opposition to Union Organisation: Researching the Indicators', *Employee Relations*, 8(5): 31–8.

Beaumont, P. (1987) *The Decline of Trade Union Organisation*, London: Croom Helm.

Beaumont, P. (1990) *Change in Industrial Relations*, London: Routledge.

Beaumont, P. B. (1992a) 'Annual Review Article 1991', *British Journal of Industrial Relations*, 30(1): 107–25.

Beaumont, P. B. (1992b) *Public Sector Industrial Relations*, London: Routledge.

Beaumont, P. B. (1995) *The Future of Employment Relations*, London: Sage.

Beaumont, P. B. and Cairns, L. (1987) 'New Towns – A Centre of Non-Unionism?', *Employee Relations*, 9(4): 14–15.

Beaumont, P. B. and Harris, R. I. D. (1988a) 'High Technology Industries and Non-Union Establishments in Britain', *Relations Industrielles*, 43(4): 829–46.

Beaumont, P. B. and Harris, R. I. D. (1988b) 'Non-Union Establishments in Britain: The Spatial Pattern', *Employee Relations*, 10(4): 13–16.

Beaumont, P. B. and Harris, R. I. D. (1989) 'The North–South Divide in Britain: The Case of Trade Union Recognition', *Oxford Bulletin of Economics and Statistics*, 51(4): 413–28.

Beaumont, P. B. and Harris, R. I. D. (1990) 'Union Recruitment and Organising Attempts in Britain in the 1980s', *Industrial Relations Journal*, 21(4): 274–86.

Beaumont, P. B. and Harris, R. I. D. (1992) ' "Double-Breasted" Recognition Arrangements in Britain', *International Journal of Human Resource Management*, 3(2): 267–83.

Belanger, J. (1987) 'Job Control After Reform: A Case Study of British Engineering', *Industrial Relations Journal*, 18(1): 50–62.

Bercusson, B. (1997) *European Works Councils – Extending the Trade Union Role*, London: Institute of Employment Rights.

Best, M. (1990) *The New Competition*, Cambridge: Polity.

Beynon, H. (1984) *Working for Ford*, 2nd edn, Harmondsworth: Penguin.

Bird, D., Kirosingh, M. and Stevens, M. (1992) 'Membership of Trade Unions in 1990', *Employment Gazette*, April: 185–90.

Bird, D., Stevens, M. and Yates, A. (1991) 'Membership of Trade Unions in 1989', *Employment Gazette*, June: 337–43.

Bishop, M., Kay, J. and Mayer, C. (eds) (1994) *Privatisation and Economic Performance*, Oxford: Oxford University Press.

Bitner, M. J. Booms, B. M. and Stanfield Tetreault, M. (1990) 'The Service Encounter: Diagnosing Favorable and Unfavorable Incidents', *Journal of Marketing*, 54(1): 71–84.

Blackburn, R. A. (1990) 'Small Firms and Sub-Contracting: What is it and Where', paper presented at the Conference on Self-Employment, Essex.

Blackwell, R. and Lloyd, P. (1989) 'New Managerialism in the Civil Service: Industrial Relations under the Thatcher Administration', in R. Mailly, S. J. Dimmock and A. S. Sethi (eds), *Industrial Relations in the Public Services*, London: Routledge, 68–113.

Blackwell, R. and Terry, M. (1987) 'Analysing the Political Fund Ballots: A Remarkable Victory or the Triumph of the Status Quo?', *Political Studies*, 35(4):623–42.

Blyton, P. (1980) *Organizing Heterogeneous Employees Within A White Collar Union*, Unpublished PhD Thesis, Sheffield University.

Blyton, P. (1981) 'Cross National Currents in Joint Consultation', in R. Mansfield and M. Poole (eds), *International Perspectives on Management and Organization*, Farnborough: Gower, 59–66.

Blyton, P. (1989) 'Working Population and Employment', in R. Bean (ed.), *International Labour Statistics*, London: Routledge, 125–43.

Blyton, P. (1992a) 'Flexible Times? Recent Developments in Temporal Flexibility', *Industrial Relations Journal*, 23(1): 26–36.

Blyton, P. (1992b) 'Learning from Each Other: The Shorter Working Week Campaigns in the German and British Engineering Industries', *Economic and Industrial Democracy*, 13(3): 417–30.

Blyton, P. (1992c) 'Steel: A Classic Case of Industrial Relations Change in Britain', *Journal of Management Studies*, 29(5): 635–50.

Blyton, P. (1993) 'Steel', in A. Pendleton and J. Winterton (eds), *Public Enterprise in Transition: Industrial Relations in State and Privatized Corporations*, London: Routledge, 166–84.

Blyton, P. and Bacon, N. (1997) 'Re-casting the Occupational Culture in Steel: Some Implications of Changing from Crews to Teams in the UK Steel Industry', *The Sociological Review*, 45(1): 79–101.

Blyton, P., Franz, H. W., Morris, J. and Bacon, N. (1993) *Work Reorganization in the UK and German Steel Industries*, final report, London: Anglo-German Foundation.

Blyton, P. and Morris, J. (1992) 'HRM and the Limits of Flexibility', in P. Blyton and P. Turnbull (eds), *Reassessing Human Resource Management*, London: Sage, 116–30.

Blyton, P., Nicholson, N. and Ursell, G. (1981) 'Job Status and White Collar Members Union Activity', *Journal of Occupational Psychology*, 54(1): 33–45.

Blyton, P. and Turnbull, P. (1994) *The Dynamics of Employee Relations*, 1st edn, Houndmills: Macmillan.

Blyton, P. and Turnbull, P.(eds) (1992) *Reassessing Human Resource Management*, London: Sage.

Blyton, P. and Turnbull, P. (1996) 'Confusing Convergence: Industrial Relations in the European Airline Industry – A Comment on Warhurst', *European Journal of Industrial Relations*, 2(1): 7–20.

Bolton, J. (1971) *Report of the Committee of Enquiry on Small Firms*, Cmnd 4811, London: HMSO.

Bonavia, M. R. (1987) *The Nationalisation of British Transport: The Early History of the British Transport Commission, 1948–53*, London: Macmillan.

Booth, A. (1983) 'A Reconsideration of Trade Union Growth in the United Kingdom', *British Journal of Industrial Relations*, 21(3): 379–91.

Booth, A. (1989) 'The Bargaining Structure of British Establishments', *British Journal of Industrial Relations*, 27(2): 225–34.

Booth, C. (1902) *Life and Labour of the People in London*, London: Macmillan.

Bowen, P. (1976) *Social Control in Industrial Organisations*, London: Routledge & Kegan Paul.

Bowles, S. (1985) 'The Production Process in a Competitive Economy: Walrasian, Neo-Hobbesian, and Marxian Models', *American Economic Review*, 75(1): 16–36.

Boyer, R. (ed.) (1988) *The Search for Labour Market Flexibility*, Oxford: Clarendon Press.

Boyer, R. (1995) 'The Future of Unions: Is the Anglo-Saxon Model a Fatality, or Will Contrasting National Trajectories Persist?', *British Journal of Industrial Relations*, 33(4): 545–56.

Brannen, P., Batstone, E., Fatchett, D. and White, P. (1976) *The Worker Directors: A Sociology of Participation*, London: Hutchinson.

Bratton, J. (1992) *Japanization at Work: Managerial Studies for the 1990s*, London: Macmillan.

Braverman, H. (1974) *Labor and Monopolgy Capital: The Degradation of Work in the Twentieth Century*, New York: Monthly Review Press.

Brewster, C. J., Gill, C. G. and Richbell, S. (1983) 'Industrial Relations Policy: A Framework for Analysis', in K. Thurley and S. Wood (eds), *Industrial Relations and Management Strategy*, Cambridge: Cambridge University Press, 66–72.

Brown, R. K. (1988) 'The Employment Relationship in Sociological Theory', in D. Gallie (ed.), *Employment in Britain*, Oxford: Blackwell, 33–66.

Brown, W. (ed.) (1981) *The Changing Contours of British Industrial Relations: A Survey of Manufacturing Industry*, Oxford: Blackwell.

Brown, W. (1983) 'British Unions: New Pressures and Shifting Loyalties', *Personnel Management*, October: 48–51.

Brown, W. (1993) 'The Contraction of Collective Bargaining in Britain', *British Journal of Industrial Relations*, 31(2): 189–200.

Brown, W., Marginson, P. and Walsh, J. (1995) 'Management: Pay Determination and Collective Bargaining', in P. Edwards (ed.), *Industrial Relations: Theory and Practice in Britain*, Oxford: Blackwell, 123–50.

Brown, W. and Nolan, P. (1988) 'Wages and Labour Productivity: The Contribution of Industrial Relations Research to the Understanding of Pay Determination', *British Journal of Industrial Relations*, 26(3): 339–61.

Brown, W. and Wadhwani, S. (1990) 'The Economic Effects of Industrial Relations Legislation', *National Institute Economic Review*, (131): 57–70.

Brown, W. and Walsh, J. (1991) 'Pay Determination in Britain in the 1980s: The Anatomy of Decentralization', *Oxford Review of Economic Policy*, 7(1): 44–59.

Brown, W. and Wright, M. (1994) 'The Empirical Tradition in Workplace Bargaining Research', *British Journal of Industrial Relations*, 32(2): 153–64.

Brunhes, B. (1989) 'Labour Flexibility in Enterprises: A Comparison of Firms in Four European Countries', in Organisation for Economic Cooperation and Development (ed.), *Labour Market Flexibility: Trends in Enterprises*, Paris: OECD, 11–36.

Buchanan, R. T. (1992) 'Measuring Mergers and Concentration in UK Unions, 1910–1988', *Industrial Relations Journal*, 23(4): 304–15.

Bullock Committee of Inquiry (1977) *Report on Industrial Democracy*, London: HMSO.

Burawoy, M. (1979) *Manufacturing Consent: Changes in the Labor Process Under Monopoly Capitalism*, Chicago: University of Chicago Press.

Burrell, G. (1992) 'Back to the Future: Time and Organization', in M. Reed and M. Hughes (eds), *Rethinking Organization*, London: Sage, 165–83.

Burrows, R. and Curran, J. (1989) 'Sociological Research on Service Sector Small Businesses: Some Conceptual Considerations', *Work, Employment & Society*, 3(4): 527–39.

Byrne, D. (1986) *Waiting for Change*, London: Low Pay Unit.

Cameron, K. S. (1994) 'Investigating Organizational Downsizing – Fundamental Issues', *Human Resource Management*, 33(2): 183–8.

Campbell, M. and Daly, M. (1992) 'Self-Employment into the 1990s', *Employment Gazette*, June: 269–92.

Campbell-Smith, D. (1986) *The British Airways Story: Struggle for Take-Off*, London: Coronet Books.

Cappelli, P. (1985a) 'Competitive Pressures and Labor Relations in the Airlines Industry', *Industrial Relations*, 25(4): 316–38.

Cappelli, P. (1985b) 'Theory Construction in IR and some Implications for Research', *Industrial Relations*, 24(1): 90–112.

Cappelli, P. (ed.) (1995a) *Airline Labor Relations in the Global Era*, Ithaca: ILR Press.

Cappelli, P. (1995b) 'Rethinking Employment', *British Journal of Industrial Relations*, 33(4): 563–602.

Carley, M. (1995) 'Talking Shops or Serious Forums?', *People Management*, 13 July: 26–31.

Carlzon, J. (1987) *Moments of Truth*, New York: Harper and Row.

Carruth, A. and Disney, R. (1988) 'Where Have Two Million Trade Union Members Gone?', *Economica*, 55(1): 1–19.

Caulkin, S. (1995) 'Take Your Partners', *Management Today*, February: 26–30.

CBI (1988) *The Structure and Process of Pay Determination in the Private Sector: 1979–1986*, London: Confederation of British Industry.

CBI (1997) *Managing Absence in Sickness and in Health*, London: CBI.

Chadwick, M. G. (1983) 'The Recession and Industrial Relations: A Factory Approach', *Employee Relations*, 5(5): 5–12.

Chadwick-Jones, J. K., Nicholson, N. and Brown, C. (1982) *Social Psychology of Absenteeism*, New York: Praeger.

Charles, R. (1973) *The Development of Industrial Relations in Britain 1911–1939*, London: Hutchinson.

Church, R., Outram, Q. and Smith, D. N. (1990) ' British Coal Mining Strikes 1893–1940: Dimensions, Distribution and Persistence', *British Journal of Industrial Relations*, 28(2): 329–49.

Church, R., Outram, Q. and Smith, D. N. (1991) 'The Isolated Mass Revisited: Strikes in British Coal Mining', *Sociological Review*, 39(1): 55–87.

Clark, J. (ed.) (1993) *Human Resource Management and Technical Change*, London: Sage.

Claydon, T. (1989) 'Union Derecognition in Britain in the 1980s', *British Journal of Industrial Relations*, 27(2): 214–24.

Claydon, T. (1996) 'Union Derecognition: A Re-Examination', in I. Beardwell (ed.), *Contemporary Industrial Relations: A Critical Analysis*, Oxford: Oxford University Press, 151–74.

Clegg, C., Nicholson, N., Ursell, G., Blyton, P. and Wall, T. (1978) 'Managers' Attitudes Towards Industrial Democracy', *Industrial Relations Journal*, 9(3): 4–17.

Clegg, H. A. (1976) *Trade Unionism Under Collective Bargaining*, Oxford: Blackwell.

Clegg, H. A. (1979a) *The Changing System of Industrial Relations in Great Britain*, Oxford: Blackwell.

Clegg, H. A. (1979b) *Local Authority and University Manual Workers, NHS Ancillary Staffs, and Ambulancemen*, Report no. 1, London: HMSO.

Clegg, H. A. (1985) *A History of British Trade Unions Vol. 2: 1911–33*, Oxford: Oxford University Press.

Clegg, H. A. (1990) 'The Oxford School of Industrial Relations', *Warwick Papers in Industrial Relations*, no. 31, IRRU, University of Warwick.

Clegg, H. A. and Chester, T. E. (1954) 'Joint Consultation', in A. Flanders and H. A. Clegg (eds), *The System of Industrial Relations in Great Britain*, Oxford: Blackwell, 323–64.

Clegg, H. A., Fox, A. and Thompson, A. F. (1964) *A History of British Trade Unionism Since 1889*, vol. 1, Oxford: Clarendon Press.

Cliff, T. (1970) *The Employers' Offensive*, London: Pluto.

Clifton, R. and Tatton-Brown, C. (1979) *Impact of Employment Legislation on Small Firms*, Research Paper no. 6, London: Department of Employment.

Coates, D. (1980) *Labour in Power?*, London: Longman.

Coates, D. (1994) *The Question of UK Decline: The Economy, State and Society*, Hemel Hempstead: Harvester Wheatsheaf.

Coates, D. and Hillard, J. (eds) (1986) *The Economic Decline of Modern Britain: The Debate Between Left and Right*, Brighton: Wheatsheaf Books.

Coates, K. (ed.) (1976) *The New Worker Cooperatives*, Nottingham: Spokesman Books.

Coates, K. and Topham, T. (1988) *Trade Unions in Britain*, London: Fontana.

Coates, K. and Topham, T. (1991) *The Making of the Transport and General Workers' Union Volume One: The Emergence of the Labour Movement*, Oxford: Blackwell.

Cohn, S. (1993) *When Strikes Make Sense – And Why: Lessons From Third Republic French Coal Miners*, New York: Plenum.

Cole, G. D. H. (1923) *Workshop Organisation*, Oxford: Clarendon Press.

Collard, R. and Dale, B. (1989) 'Quality Circles', in K. Sisson (ed.), *Personnel Management in Britain*, Oxford: Blackwell, 356–77.

Colling, T. (1995a) 'Experiencing Turbulence: Competition, Strategic Choice and the Management of Human Resources in British Airways', *Human Resource Management Journal*, 5(5): 18–32.

Colling, T. (1995b) 'Renewal or Rigor Mortis? Union Responses to Contracting in Local Government', *Industrial Relations Journal*, 26(2): 134–45.

Collis-Squires, N. (1977) 'An Investigation of the National Dock Labour Scheme as an Example of Statutory Joint-Control of an Industry', LL.M thesis, University of Warwick.

Commons, J. R. (1919) *Industrial Goodwill*, New York: Arno Press.

Constable, J. and McCormick, R. (1987) *The Making of British Managers*, London: British Institute of Management.

Conyon, M. J. (1995) 'Directors' Pay in the Privatized Utilities', *British Journal of Industrial Relations*, 33(2): 159–71.

Cook, F. G., Clark, S. C., Roberts, K. and Semeonoff, E. (1975) 'White and Blue Collar Attitudes to Trade Unionism and Social Class', *Industrial Relations Journal*, 6(4): 47–58.

Cook, P. (1990) 'The Silent Strike: Causes and Solutions', Address to the Conference on Absenteeism and Employee Turnover, Centre for Industrial Relations and Labour Studies, University of Melbourne.

Corke, A. (1986) *British Airways: The Path to Profitability*, London: Frances Pinter.

Cornfield, K. G. (1979) *Product Design*, London: National Economic Development Office.

Cornwall, J. (1977) *Modern Capitalism, Its Growth and Transformation*, Oxford: Martin Robertson.

Coutts, K. and Godley, W. (1989) 'The British Economy Under Mrs. Thatcher', *Political Quarterly*, 60(2): 137–51.

CPA (1991) *Dock Labour Compensation Scheme*, Committee of Public Accounts, thirty-first report, HC 196, London: HMSO.

Crafts, N. (1991) 'Reversing Relative Economic Decline? The 1980s in Historical Perspective', *Oxford Review of Economic Policy*, 7(3): 81–98.

Craig, A. (1986) *The System of Industrial Relations in Canada*, 2nd edn, Scarborough, Ont: Prentice-Hall.

Craig, C., Garnsey, E. and Rubery, J. (1985) *Payment Structures and Smaller Firms*, Research Paper no. 48, London: Department of Employment.

Cregan, C. and Johnston, S. (1990) 'An Industrial Relations Approach to the Free Rider Problem: Young People and Trade Union Membership in the UK', *British Journal of Industrial Relations*, 28(1): 84–104.

Cressey, P. and MacInnes, J. (1980) 'Voting for Ford: Industrial Democracy and the Control of Labour', *Capital and Class*, (11): 5–33.

Cronin, J. E. (1979) *Industrial Conflict in Modern Britain*, London: Croom Helm.

Cross, M. (1988) 'Changes to Working Practices in UK Manufacturing 1981–88', *Industrial Relations Review and Report*, no. 415, May: 2–10.

Crouch, C. (ed.) (1979) *State and Economy in Contemporary Capitalism*, London: Croom Helm.

Crouch, C. (1982a) *The Politics of Industrial Relations*, 2nd edn, London: Fontana.

Crouch, C. (1982b) *Trade Unions: The Logic of Collective Action*, London: Fontana.

Crouch, C. (1995) 'The State: Economic Management and Incomes Policy', in P. Edwards (ed.), *Industrial Relations: Theory and Practice in Britain*, Oxford: Blackwell, 229–54.

Cully, M. and Woodland, S. (1996) 'Trade Union Membership and Recognition: An Analysis of Data for the 1995 Labour Force Survey', *Labour Market Trends*, May: 215–24.

Curran, J. (1990) 'Re-thinking Economic Structure: Exploring the Role of the Small Firm and Self Employment in the British Economy', *Work, Employment & Society*, 4 (special issue): 125–46.

Curran, J. and Burrows, R. (1986) 'The Sociology of Petit Capitalism: A Trend Report', *Sociology*, 20(2): 265–79.

Curran, J. and Stanworth, J. (1981a) 'Size of Workplace and Attitudes to Industrial Relations in the Printing and Electronics Industries', *British Journal of Industrial Relations*, 19(1): 14–25.

Curran, J. and Stanworth, J. (1981b) 'The Social Dynamics of the Small Manufacturing Enterprise', *Journal of Management Studies*, 18(2): 141–58.

Currie, R. (1979) *Industrial Politics*, Oxford: Clarendon Press.

Dabscheck, B. (1983) 'Of Mountains and Routes Over Them: A Survey of Theories of Industrial Relations', *Journal of Industrial Relations*, 25(4): 485–506.

Dahrendorf, R. (1956) *Class and Class Conflict in Industrial Societies*, London: Routledge & Kegan Paul.

Dale, I. (1991) *The End of the Dock Labour Scheme – An Interim Appraisal*, London: Aims of Industry.

Dale, I. and Kerr, J. (1995) 'Small and Medium-Sized Enterprises: Their Numbers and Importance to Employment', *Labour Market Trends*, December: 461–66.

Daly, A., Hitchens, D. M. W. N. and Wagner, K. (1985) 'Productivity, Machinery and Skills in a Sample of British and German Manufacturing Plants', *National Institute Economic Review*, February: 48–61.

Daly, M. (1990) 'The 1980s – A Decade of Growth in Enterprise', *Employment Gazette*, November: 553–65.

Daly, M. (1991) 'The 1980s – A Decade of Growth in Enterprise', *Employment Gazette*, March: 109–29.

Daniel, W. W. (1985) 'The First Job Taken by the Unemployed Compared with those they Lost', *Policy Studies*, 6(1): 38–58.

Daniel, W. W. (1987) *Workplace Industrial Relations and Technical Change*, London: Frances Pinter.

Daniel, W. W. and Millward, N. (1983) *Workplace Industrial Relations in Britain: The DE/PSI/SSRC Survey*, London: Heinemann.

Darlington, R. (1994) *The Dynamics of Workplace Unionism: Shop Stewards' Organization in Three Merseyside Plants*, London: Mansell.

Dash, J. (1969) *Good Morning Brothers!*, London: Lawrence & Wishart.

Dastmalchian, A., Blyton, P. and Adamson, R. (1991) *The Climate of Workplace Relations*, London: Routledge.

Davies, A. (1986) *Industrial Relations and New Technology*, London: Croom Helm.

Davies, R. J. (1979) 'Economic Activity, Incomes Policy and Strikes – A Quantitative Analysis', *British Journal of Industrial Relations*, 17(2): 205–23.

Davies, R. J. (1983) 'Incomes and Anti-Inflation Policy', in G. S. Bain (ed.), *Industrial Relations in Britain*, Oxford: Blackwell, 419–55.

Davis, D. (1988) *Clear the Decks – Abolish the National Dock Labour Scheme*, Policy Study No.101, London: Centre for Policy Studies.

Dawson, P. and Webb, J. (1989) 'New Production Arrangements: The Totally Flexible Cage?', *Work, Employment & Society*, 3(2): 221–38.

Deaton, D. (1985) 'Management Style and Large-Scale Survey Evidence', *Industrial Relations Journal*, 16(2): 67–71.

Deaton, D. and Beaumont, P. (1980) 'The Determinants of Bargaining Structure: Some Large Scale Evidence for Britain', *British Journal of Industrial Relations*, 18(2): 202–16.

Delbridge, R. and Trunbull, P. (1992) 'Human Resource Maximization: The Management of Labour under Just-in-Time Manufacturing Systems', in P. Blyton and P. Turnbull (eds), *Reassessing Human Resource Management*, London: Sage, 56–73.

Delbridge, R., Turnbull, P. and Wilkinson, B. (1992) 'Pushing Back the Frontiers: Management Control and Work Intensification Under JIT/TQM Factory Regimes', *New Technology, Work and Employment*, 7(2): 97–106.

Deming, W. E. (1982) *Quality, Productivity and Competitive Position*, Cambridge, Mass: MIT Press.

Deming, W. E. (1986) *Out of Crisis*, Cambridge: Cambridge University Press.

Demos (1995) *The Time Squeeze*, London: Demos Quarterly.

Denman, J. and McDonald, P. (1996) 'Unemployment Statistics from 1881 to the Present Day', *Labour Market Trends*, January, 5–18.

Department of Employment (1985) *Employment: The Challenge for the Nation*, Cmnd 9474, London: HMSO.

Department of Employment (1989) *Employment in the Ports – The Dock Labour Scheme*, Cm 664, London: HMSO.

Department of Employment (1991) *Industrial Relations in the 1990 – Proposals for Further Reform of Industrial Relations and Trade Union Law*, Cm 1602, London: HMSO.

Department of Employment (1992) 'Historical Supplement 3, Employment Statistics', *Employment Gazette*, 100(6), June.

Devlin, Lord (1965) *Final Report of the Committee of Inquiry Under the Rt. Hon. Lord Devlin into Certain Matters Concerning the Port Transport Industry*, Cmnd 2734, London: HMSO.

Dickens, L. (1995) 'UK Part-Time Employees and the Law – Recent and Potential Developments', *Gender, Work and Organization*, 2(4): 207–15.

Dickens, L. and Hall, M. (1995) 'The State: Labour Law and Industrial Relations', in P. Edwards (ed.), *Industrial Relations: Theory and Practice in Britain*, Oxford: Blackwell, 255–303.

Dickens, L., Jones, M., Weekes, B. and Hart, M. (1985) *Dismissed: A Study of Unfair Dismissal and the Industrial Tribunal System*, Oxford: Blackwell.

Dickson, T., McLachlan, H. V., Prior, P. and Swales, K. (1988) 'Big Blue and the Unions: IBM, Individualism and Trade Union Strategy', *Work, Employment & Society*, 2(4): 506–20.

Disney, R. (1990) 'Explanations of the Decline in Trade Union Density in Britain: An Appraisal', *British Journal of Industrial Relations*, 28(2): 165–78.

Disney, R., Gosling, A. and Machin, S. (1995) 'British Unions in Decline: Determinants of the 1980s Fall in Union Recognition', *Industrial & Labor Relations Review*, 48(3): 403–19.
Docherty, C. (1983) *Steel and Steelworkers: The Sons of Vulcan*, London: Heinemann.
Donovan. (1968) Royal Commission on Trade Unions and Employers' Associations 1965–68, *Report*, Cmnd 3623, London: HMSO.
Dore, R. (1986) *Flexible Rigidities*, London: Athlone.
Dore, R. (1988) 'Rigidities in the Labour Market', *Government & Opposition*, 23(4): 393–412.
Dore, R. (1989) 'Where are We Now: Musings of an Evolutionist', *Work, Employment & Society*, 3(4): 425–46.
Dore, R. (1992) 'Japanese Capitalism, Anglo-Saxon Capitalism: How Will the Darwinian Contest Turn Out?', Centre for Economic Performance, OP.4, London School of Economics.
Drucker, P. (1974) *Management: Tasks, Responsibilities, Practice*, London: Heinemann.
Dubois, P. (1979) *Sabotage in Industry*, Harmondsworth: Penguin.
Due, J., Madsen, J. S. and Stroby-Jensen, C. (1991) 'The Social Dimension: Convergence or Diversification of IR in the Single European Market', *Industrial Relations Journal*, 22(2): 85–102.
Dunlop, J. T. (1958) *Industrial Relations Systems*, New York: Holt.
Dunn, S. (1990) 'Root Metaphor in the Old and New Industrial Relations', *British Journal of Industrial Relations*, 28(1): 1–31.
Dunn, S. (1993) 'From Donovan to . . . Wherever', *British Journal of Industrial Relations*, 31(2): 169–87.
Dunn, S. and Metcalf, D. (1996) 'Trade Union Law Since 1979', in I. Beardwell (ed.), *Contemporary Industrial Relations: A Critical Analysis*, Oxford: Oxford University Press, 66–98.
Dunn, S. and Wright, M. (1994) 'Maintaining the "Status Quo"? An Analysis of the Contents of British Collective Agreements, 1979–1990', *British Journal of Industrial Relations*, 32(1): 23–46.
Dunning, J. H. (1976) *United States Industry in Britain*, London: Wilton House.
Durcan, J. W., McCarthy, W. E. J. and Redman, G. P. (1983) *Strikes in Post-War Britain: A Study of Stoppages of Work Due to Industrial Disputes, 1946–73*, London: George Allen & Unwin.
Dyer, L., Lipsky, D. and Kochan, T. (1977) 'Union Attitudes Towards Management Co-operation', *Industrial Relations*, 16(2): 163–72.
Edgeworth, F. Y. (1881) *Mathematical Psychics*, London: Kegan Paul.
Edwardes, M. (1983) *Back from the Brink*, London: Collins.
Edwards, P. K. (1977) 'A Critique of the Kerr-Siegel Hypothesis of Strikes and the Isolated Mass: A Study of the Falsification of Sociological Knowledge', *Sociological Review*, 25(3): 551–74.
Edwards, P. K. (1979) 'Strikes and Unorganised Conflict: Some Further Considerations', *British Journal of Industrial Relations*, 13(1): 95–8.
Edwards, P. K. (1983) 'The Pattern of Collective Industrial Action', in G. S. Bain (ed.), *Industrial Relations in Britain*, Oxford: Blackwell, 209–34.
Edwards, P. K. (1986) *Conflict at Work: A Materialist Analysis of Workplace Relations*, Oxford: Blackwell.
Edwards, P. K. (1987) *Managing the Factory*, Oxford: Blackwell.
Edwards, P. K. (1988) 'Patterns of Conflict and Accommodation', in D. Gallie (ed.) *Employment in Britain*, Oxford: Blackwell, 187–217.
Edwards, P. K. (1992) 'Industrial Conflict: Themes and Issues in Recent Research', *British Journal of Industrial Relations*, 30(3): 361–404.

Edwards, P. K. (1995a) 'From Industrial Relations to the Employment Relationship: The Development of Research in Britain', *Relations Industrielles*, 50(1): 39–65.

Edwards, P. K. (1995b) 'Strikes and Industrial Conflict', in P. Edwards (ed.), *Industrial Relations: Theory and Practice in Britain*, Oxford: Blackwell, 434–60.

Edwards, P. K. and Bain, G. S. (1988) 'Why are Trade Unions Becoming More Popular? Unions and Public Opinion in Britian', *British Journal of Industrial Relations, 26(3): 311–26*.

Edwards, P. K., Hall, M., Hyman, R., Marginson, P., Sisson, K., Waddington, J. and Winchester, D. (1992) 'Great Britain: Still Muddling Through', in A. Ferner and R. Hyman (eds), *Industrial Relations in the New Europe*, Oxford: Blackwell, 1–68.

Edwards, P. K. and Scullion, H. (1982) *The Social Organisation of Industrial Conflict*, Oxford: Blackwell.

Edwards, P. K. and Scullion, H. (1984) 'Absenteeism and the Control of Work', *Sociological Review*, 32(3): 547–72.

Edwards, P. K. and Whitston, C. (1989) 'Industrial Discipline, the Control of Attendance, and the Subordination of Labour: Towards an Integrated Analysis', *Work, Employment and Society*, 3(1): 1–28.

Edwards, P. K. and Whitston, C. (1991) 'Workers are Working Harder: Effort and Shopfloor Relations in the 1980's', *British Journal of Industrial Relations*, 29(4): 593–601.

Edwards, P. K. and Whitston, C. (1993) *Attending to Work: The Management of Attendance and Shopfloor Order*, Oxford: Blackwell.

Edwards, R. (1979) *Contested Terrain: The Transformation of the Workplace in the Twentieth Century*, London: Heinemann.

Elgar, J. and Simpson, B. (1993) 'The Impact of the Law on Industrial Disputes in the 1980s', in D. Metcalf and S. Milner (eds), *New Perspectives on Industrial Disputes*, London: Routledge, 70–114.

Elger, T. (1990) 'Technical Innovation and Work Reorganisation in British Manufacturing in the 1980s: Continuity, Intensification or Transformation', *Work, Employment and Society*, 4 (special issue): 67–101.

Elliott, J. (1978) *Conflict or Cooperation: The Growth of Industrial Democracy*, London: Kogan Page.

Emerson, M. (1988) 'Regulation or Deregulation of the Labour Market', *European Economic Review*, 32(2): 775–817.

Enderwick, P. (1984) 'The Labour Utilisation Practices of Multinationals and Obstacles to Multinational Collective Bargaining', *Journal of Industrial Relations*, 26(3): 345–64.

Evans, N., MacKay, D., Garratt, M. and Sutcliffe, P. (1993) *The Abolition of the Dock Labour Scheme*, Research Series No.14, London: Employment Department.

Evans, S. (1985) 'The Use of Injunctions in Industrial Disputes', *British Journal of Industrial Relations*, 23(1): 133–7.

Evans, S. (1987) 'The Use of Injunctions in Industrial Disputes, May 1984–April 1987', *British Journal of Industrial Relations*, 25(3): 419–35.

Evans, S. (1990) 'Free Labour and Economic Performance: Evidence from the Construction Industry', *Work, Employment & Society*, 4(2): 239–52.

Evans, S., Ewing, K. and Nolan, P. (1992) 'Industrial Relations and the British Economy in the 1990s: Mrs Thatcher's Legacy', *Journal of Management Studies*, 29(5): 571–89.

Evans, S., Goodman, J. and Hargreaves, L. (1985) *Unfair Dismissal Law and Employment Practice in the 1980s*, Research Paper no. 53, London: Department of Employment.

Ewing, K. D. (1989) *Britain and the ILO*, London: Institute of Employment Rights.

Ewing, K. D. (1991) *The Right to Strike*, Oxford: Clarendon Press.

Ewing, K. and Napier, B. (1986) 'The Wapping Dispute and Labour Law', *Cambridge Law Journal*, 45(2): 285–303.

Fairbrother, P. (1983) *The Politics of Union Ballots*, London: Workers' Educational Association.

Fairbrother, P. (1996) 'Workplace Trade Unionism in the State Sector', in P. Ackers, C. Smith and P. Smith (eds), *The New Workplace and Trade Unionism: Critical Perspectives on Work and Organization*, London: Routledge, 110–48.

Farnham, D. and Giles, L. (1995) 'Trade Unions in the UK: Trends and Counter-Trends Since 1979', *Employee Relations*, 17(2): 5–22.

Farnham, D. and Pimlott, J. (1990) *Understanding Industrial Relations*, 4th edn, London: Cassell.

Fells, R. E. (1989) 'The Employment Relationship, Control and Strategic Choice in the Study of Industrial Relations', *Labour and Industry*, 2(3): 470–92.

Felstead, A. (1993) *Franchising At Work*, London: Routledge.

Ferner, A. (1989) 'Ten Years of Thatcherism: Changing Industrial Relations in British Public Enterprises', *Warwick Papers in Industrial Relations*, no. 27, IRRU, University of Warwick.

Ferner, A. (1991) 'Changing Public Sector Industrial Relations in Europe', *Warwick Papers in Industrial Relations*, no. 37, IRRU, University of Warwick.

Ferner, A. and Colling, T. (1991) 'Privatization, Regulation and Industrial Relations', *British Journal of Industrial Relations*, 29(3): 391–409.

Ferner, A. and Colling, T. (1995) 'Privatization and Marketization', in P. Edwards (ed.), *Industrial Relations: Theory and Practice in Britain*, Oxford: Blackwell, 491–514.

Fevre, R. (1986) 'Contract Work in the Recession', in K. Purcell, S. Wood and S. Allen (eds), *The Changing Experience of Employment*, London: Macmillan, 18–34.

Fevre, R. (1987) 'Subcontracting in Steel', *Work, Employment & Society*, 1(4): 509–27.

Filipcova, B. and Filipec, J. (1986) 'Society and Concepts of Time', *International Social Science Journal*, (107): 19–32.

Fine, B. (1990) 'Scaling the Commanding Heights of Public Enterprise Economics', *Cambridge Journal of Economics*, 14(2): 127–42.

Fine, B. and Harris, L. (eds) (1985) *The Peculiarities of the British Economy*, London: Lawrence & Wishart.

Fine, B. and O'Donnell, C. (1985) 'The Nationalised Industries', in B. Fine and L. Harris (eds), *The Peculiarities of the British Economy*, London: Lawrence & Wishart, 147–66.

Finegold, D. and Soskice, D. (1988) 'The Failure of Training in Britain: Analysis and Prescription', *Oxford Review of Economic Policy*, 4(3): 21–53.

Finney, N. (1990) 'Repeal of the National Dock Labour Scheme: Britain's Ports in an Era of Industrial Relations Change', *Employee Relations*, 12(4): 10–16.

Finniston, M. (1980) *Report of the Committee of Inquiry into the Engineering Profession*, Cmnd 7794, London: HMSO.

Fisher, J. (1995) 'The Trade Union Response to HRM in the UK: The Case of the TGWU', *Human Resource Management Journal*, 5(3): 7–23.

Flanders, A. (1964) *The Fawley Productivity Agreements: A Case Study of Management and Collective Bargaining*, London: Faber.

Flanders, A. (1965) *Industrial Relations: What is Wrong with the System?*, London: Faber.

Flanders, A. (1975) *Management and Unions: The Theory and Reform of Industrial Relations*, London: Faber & Faber.

Flanders, A. and Clegg, H. A. (1954) *The System of Industrial Relations in Great Britain*, Oxford: Blackwell.

Flood, P. and Turner, T. (1993) 'Human Resource Strategy and the Non-Union Phenomenon', *Employee Relations*, 15(6): 54–66.

Ford, J. (1982) 'Who Breaks the Rules? The Response of Small Businesses to External Regulation', *Industrial Relations Journal*, 13(3): 40–9.

Foulkes, F. K. (1981) 'How Top Nonunion Companies Manage Employees', *Harvard Business Review*, September–October: 90–6.

Fox, A. (1966) 'Industrial Sociology and Industrial Relations', *Royal Commission Research Paper No. 3*, London: HMSO.

Fox, A. (1974) *Beyond Contract: Work, Power and Trust Relations*, London: Faber

Fox, A. (1985) *History and Heritage*, London: Allen & Unwin.

Franz, H. W. (1991) 'Quality Strategies and Workforce Strategies in the European Steel Industry', in P. Blyton and J. Morris (eds), *A Flexible Future? Prospects for Employment and Organization*, Berlin: Walter de Gruyter, 259–73.

Franzosi, R. (1995) *The Puzzle of Strikes: Class and State Strategies in Postwar Italy*, Cambridge: Cambridge University Press.

Fredman, S. and Morris, G. (1989) 'The State as Employer: Setting a New Example', *Personnel Management*, August: 25–9.

Freeman, R. B. (1995) 'The Future for Unions in Decentralized Collective Bargaining Systems: US and UK Unionism in an Era of Crisis', *British Journal of Industrial Relations*, 33(4): 519–36.

Freeman, R. and Pelletier J. (1990) 'The Impact of Industrial Relations Legislation on British Union Density', *British Journal of Industrial Relations*, 28(2): 141–64.

Friedman, A. L. (1977) *Industry and Labour: Class Struggle at Work and Monopoly Capitalism*, London: Macmillan.

Friedman, A. L. (1987) 'The Means of Management Control and Labour Process Theory: A Critical Note on Storey', *Sociology*, 21(2): 287–94.

Fry, G. K. (1988) 'The Thatcher Government, the Financial Management Initiative and the New Civil Service', *Public Administration*, 66(1): 1–20.

Gall, G. (1994) 'The Rise of Single Table Bargaining in Britain', *Employee Relations*, 16(4): 62–71.

Gall, G. and McKay, S. (1994) 'Trade Union Derecognition in Britain, 1988–1994', *British Journal of Industrial Relations*, 32(3): 433–48.

Gall, G. and McKay, S. (1996) 'Research Note: Injunctions as a Legal Weapon in Industrial Disputes', *British Journal of Industrial Relations*, 34(4): 567–82.

Gallagher, C., Daly, M. and Thomason, J. (1990) 'The Growth of UK Companies 1985–87 and their Contribution to Job Generation', *Employment Gazette*, February: 92–8.

Gallie, D. (1978) *In Search of the New Working Class: Automation and Social Integration within the Capitalist Enterprise*, Cambridge: Cambridge University Press.

Gallie, D. (1996) 'Trade Union Allegiance and Decline in British Urban Labour Markets', in D. Gallie, R. Penn and M. Rose (eds), *Trade Unionism in Recession*, Oxford: Oxford University Press, 140–74.

Gallie, D., Penn, R. and Rose, M. (1996) 'The British Debate on Trade Unionism: Crisis and Continuity', in D. Gallie, R. Penn and M. Rose (eds), *Trade Unionism in Recession*, Oxford: Oxford University Press, 1–32.

Gallie, D. and Rose, M. (1996) 'Employer Policies and Trade Union Influence', in D. Gallie, R. Penn and M. Rose (eds), *Trade Unionism in Recession*, Oxford: Oxford University Press, 33–64.

Garrahan, P. and Stewart, P. (1992) *The Nissan Enigma: Flexibility at Work in a Local Economy*, London: Cassell.

Gil, A. (1990) 'Air Transport Deregulation and its Implications for Flight Attendants', *International Labour Review*, 129(3): 317–31.

Gintis, H. (1976) 'The Nature of Labor Exchange and the Theory of Capitalist Production', *Review of Radical Political Economics*, 8(2): 36–54.

Godfrey, G. and Marchington, M. (1996) 'Shop Stewards in the 1990s: A Research Note', *Industrial Relations Journal*, 27(4): 339–44.

Goffee, R. and Scase, R. (1982) ' "Fraternalism" and "Paternalism" as Employer Strategies in Small Firms', in G. Day, L. Caldwell, K. Jones, D. Robbins and H. Rose (eds), *Diversity and Decomposition in the Labour Market*, Aldershot: Gower, 107–24.

Goffee, R. and Scase, R. (1995) *Corporate Realities: The Dynamics of Large and Small Organisations*, London: Routledge.

Goodman, J. (1984) *Employment Relations in Industrial Society*, Oxford: Philip Allan.

Goodman, J. (1996) 'Annual Review Article 1995', *British Journal of Industrial Relations*, 34(1): 151–69.

Goodstein, L. D. (1990) 'A Case Study in Effective Organizational Change Toward High Involvement Management', in D. B. Fishman and C. Cherniss (eds), *The Human Side of Corporate Competitiveness*, Newbury Park CA: Sage, 171–200.

Gordon, D. M. (1976) 'Capitalist Efficiency and Socialist Efficiency', *Monthly Review*, (3): 19–39.

Gordon, D. M., Edwards, R. and Reich, M. (1982) *Segmented Work, Divided Workers: The Historical Transformation of Labor in the United States*, Cambridge: Cambridge University Press.

Gosling, A. and Machin, S. (1992) 'Trade Unions and Wage Dispersion in UK Establishments, 1980–90', mimeo, University College London.

Gospel, H. F. (1992) *Markets, Firms, and the Management of Labour in Modern Britain*, Cambridge: Cambridge University Press.

Gospel, H. F. and Palmer, G. (1993) *British Industrial Relations*, 2nd edn, London: Routledge.

Goss, D. M. (1988) 'Social Harmony and the Small Firm: A Reappraisal', *Sociological Review*, 36(1): 114–32.

Goss, D. M. (1991) 'In Search of Small Firm Industrial Relations', in R. Burrows (ed.), *Deciphering the Enterprise Culture: Entrepreneurship, Petty Capitalism and the Restructuring of Britain*, London: Routledge, 152–75.

Grahl, J. and Teague, P. (1992a) *Industrial Relations and European Integration*, London: Lawrence & Wishart.

Grahl, J. and Teague, P (1992b) 'Integration Theory and European Labour Markets', *British Journal of Industrial Relations*, 30(4): 515–27.

Green, F. (1990) 'Trade Union Availability and Trade Union Membership in Britain', *Manchester School of Economic and Social Studies*, 58(4): 378–94.

Green, F. (1992) 'Recent Trends in British Trade Union Density: How Much of a Compositional Effect?', *British Journal of Industrial Relations*, 30(3): 445–58.

Gregg, P. and Wadsworth, J. (1995) 'A Short History of Labour Turnover, Job Tenure, and Job Security. 1975–93', *Oxford Review of Economic Policy*, 11(1): 73–90.

Gregg, P. and Yates, A. (1991) 'Changes in Wage-Setting Arrangements and Trade Union Presence in the 1980s', *British Journal of Industrial Relations*, 29(3): 361–76.

Gregory, M. (1996) *Dirty Tricks*, London: Warner.

Griffin, J. I. (1939) *Strikes*, New York: Columbia University Press.

Griffith, J. A. (1981) *The Politics of the Judiciary*, 2nd edn, London: Fontana.

Grönroos, C. (1984) 'A Service Quality Model and its Marketing Implications', *European Journal of Marketing*, 18(4): 36–44.

Grunberg, L. (1986) 'Workplace Relations in the Economic Crisis: A Comparison of a British and French Automobile Plant', *Sociology*, 20(4): 503–30.

Guest, D. (1987) 'Human Resource Management and Industrial Relations', *Journal of Management Studies*, 24(5): 503–21.

Guest, D. (1989) 'Human Resource Management: Its Implications for Industrial Relations and Trade Unions', in J. Storey (ed.), *New Perspectives on Human Resource Management*, London: Routledge, 41–55.

Guest, D. (1991) 'Personnel Management: The End of Orthodoxy?', *British Journal of Industrial Relations*, 29(2): 149–76.

Guest, D. and Hoque, K. (1993) 'The Mystery of the Missing Human Resource Manager', *Personnel Management*, June: 40–1.

Guest, D. and Hoque, K. (1994) 'The Good, The Bad and the Ugly: Employment Relations in New Non-Union Workplaces', *Human Resource Management Journal*, 5(1): 1–14.

Guille, H. (1984) 'Industrial Relations Theory: Painting by Numbers', *Journal of Industrial Relations*, 26(4): 484–95.

Gunnigle, P. and Brady, T. (1984) 'The Management of Industrial Relations in the Small Firm', *Employee Relations*, 6(5): 21–4.

Hakim, C. (1989a) 'Identifying Fast Growing Firms', *Employment Gazette*, January: 29–41.

Hakim, C. (1989b) 'New Recruits to Self-Employment in the 1980s', *Employment Gazette*, June: 286–97.

Hakim, C. (1990) 'Core and Periphery in Employers' Workforce Strategies: Evidence from the 1987 ELUS Survey', *Work, Employment & Society*, 4(2): 157–88.

Hall, M. (1992) 'Behind the European Works Council Debate: The European Commission's Legislative Strategy', *British Journal of Industrial Relations*, 30(4): 547–66.

Hall, M., Carley, M., Gold, M., Marginson, P. and Sisson, K. (1995) *European Works Councils: Planning for the Directive*, London: Eclipse.

Hamel, G. and Prahalad, C. K. (1994) *Competing for the Future*, Boston, MA: Harvard Business School Press.

Hamil, S. (1993) *Britain's BEST Employers? A Job Hunter's Guide*, London: Kogan Page.

Hampden-Turner, C. and Trompenaars, A. (1994) *The Seven Cultures of Capitalism*, London: Piatkus.

Hancké, B. (1993) 'Trade Union Membership in Europe, 1960–1990: Rediscovering Local Unions', *British Journal of Industrial Relations*, 31(4): 593–613.

Handy, C. (1984) *The Future of Work*, Oxford: Blackwell.

Handy, C. (1987) *The Making of Managers*, London: Manpower Services Commission/ National Economic Development Council/British Institute of Management.

Handy, C., Gordon, C., Gow, I. and Randlesome, C. (1988) *Making Managers*, Oxford: Pitman.

Handy, L. J. (1968) 'Absenteeism and Attendance in the British Coal-Mining Industry: An Examination of Post-War Trends', *British Journal of Industrial Relations*, 6(1): 27–50.

Hanson, C. G. and Mather, G. (1988) *Striking Out Strikes: Changing Employment Relations in the British Labour Market*, Hobart Paper 110, London: Institute of Economic Affairs.

Harbison, F. H. (1954) 'Collective Bargaining and American Capitalism', in A. Kornhauser, R. Dubin, and A. M. Ross (eds), *Industrial Conflict*, New York: McGraw-Hill, 270–79.

Harris, C. (1988) *Redundancy and Recession in South Wales*, Oxford: Blackwell.

Harris, L. (1986) 'Working-Class Strength: A Counterview', in D. Coates and J. Hillard (eds), *The Economic Decline of Modern Britain: The Debate Between Left and Right*, Brighton: Wheatsheaf Books, 264–6.

Hart, T. J. (1993) 'Human Resource Management – Time to Exorcize the Militant Tendency', *Employee Relations*, 15(3): 29–36.

Hartley, J., Kelly, J. and Nicholson, N. (1983) *Steel Strike: A Case Study in Industrial Relations*, London: Batsford.

Hayek, F. A. (1979) *Law, Legislation and Liberty*, London: Routledge & Kegan Paul

Hayek, F. A. (1984) *1980s Unemployment and the Unions*, London: Institute of Economic Affairs.

Heery, E. (1997) 'Annual Review Article 1996', *British Journal of Industrial Relations*, 35(1): 87–109.

Heery, E. and Kelly, J. (1994) 'Professional, Participative and Managerial Unionism: An Interpretation of Change in Trade Unions', *Work, Employment & Society*, 8 (1): 1–22.

Heller, R. (1992) 'How BA Engineered its Turnround', *Management Today*, September: 50–5.

Hendry, C. (1990) 'The Corporate Management of Human Resources under Conditions of Decentralization', *British Journal of Management*, 1(2): 91–103.

Henley, A. and Tsakalotos, E. (1992) 'Corporatism and the European Labour Market after 1992', *British Journal of Industrial Relations*, 30(4): 567–86.

Herzberg, F. (1966) *Work and the Nature of Man*, Cleveland: World Publishing.

Hibbett, A. (1991) 'Employee Involvement: A Recent Survey', *Employee Gazette*, December: 659–64.

Hickson, D. J., Butler, R. J., Cray, D., Mallory, G. R. and Wilson, D. C. (1985) *Top Decisions: Strategic Decision-Making in Organisations*, Oxford: Blackwell.

Hill, C. W. L. and Pickering, J. F. (1986) 'Divisionalisation, Decentralisation and Performance of Large UK Companies', *Journal of Management Studies*, 23(1): 26–50.

Hill, J. M. M. and Trist, E. L. (1962) *Industrial Accidents, Sickness and Other Absences*, London: Tavistock Institute.

Hill, S. (1991) 'Why Quality Circles Failed but Total Quality Management Might Succeed', *British Journal of Industrial Relations*, 29(4): 541–68.

Hinton, J. (1973) *The First Shop Stewards Movement*, London: Allen & Unwin.

Hochschild, A. R. (1983) *The Managed Heart: Commercialization of Human Feeling*, Berkeley: University of California Press.

Hoel, B. (1982) 'Contemporary Clothing Sweatshops', in J. West (ed.), *Work, Women and the Labour Market*, London: Routledge & Kegan Paul, 80–98.

Hoerr, J. P. (1988) *And the Wolf Finally Came: The Decline of the American Steel Industry*, Pittsburgh: University of Pittsburgh Press.

Holmes, J. (1986) 'The Organization and Locational Structure of Production Subcontracting', in A. J. Scott and M. Storper (eds), *Production, Work and Technology*, London: Allen & Unwin, 80–106.

Höpfl, H. (1992) 'Death of a Snake-Oil Salesman: The Demise of the Corporate Life-Lie', paper presented at the Employment Research Unit annual conference, Cardiff Business School.

Höpfl, H. (1993) 'Culture and Commitment: British Airways', in D. Gowler, K. Legge and C. Clegg (eds), *Case Studies in Organizational Behaviour and Human Resource Management*, London: Paul Chapman, 117–38.

Höpfl, H., Smith, S. and Spencer, S. (1992) 'Values and Valuations: The Conflicts Between Cultural Change and Job Cuts', *Personnel Review*, 21(2): 24–38.

House of Lords (1985) *Report from the Select Committee on Overseas Trade*, London: HMSO.

Houseman, S. R. (1991) *Industrial Restructuring with Job Security: The Case of European Steel*, Cambridge, Mass: Harvard University Press.

Howells, D. (1981) 'Marks and Spencer and the Civil Service: A Comparison of Culture and Methods', *Public Administration*, 59(3): 337–52.

Hudson, R. and Sadler, D. (1989) *The International Steel Industry: Restructuring, State Policies and Localities*, London: Routledge.

Hutton, W. (1996) *The State We're In*, London: Vintage.

Hyman, J. and Mason, B. (1995) *Managing Employee Involvement and Participation*, London: Sage.

Hyman, R. (1975) *Industrial Relations: A Marxist Introduction*, London: Macmillan.

Hyman, R. (1978) 'Pluralism, Procedural Consensus and Collective Bargaining', *British Journal of Industrial Relations*, 16(1): 16–40.

Hyman, R. (1981) 'Green Means Danger? Trade Union Immunities and the Tory Attack', *Politics and Power*, (4): 128–45.

Hyman, R. (1982) 'Pressure, Protest, and Struggle: Some Problems in the Concept and Theory of Industrial Conflict', in G. B. J. Bomers and R. B. Peterson (eds), *Conflict Management and Industrial Relations*, Boston: Kluwer Nijhoff, 401–22.

Hyman, R. (1987a) 'Strategy or Structure? Capital, Labour and Control', *Work, Employment & Society*, 1(1): 25–55.

Hyman, R. (1987b) 'Trade Unions and the Law: Papering Over the Cracks?', *Capital and Class*, (31): 93–113.

Hyman, R. (1989a) *The Political Economy of Industrial Relations: Theory and Practice in a Cold Climate*, London: Macmillan.

Hyman, R. (1989b) *Strikes*, 4th edn, London: Macmillan.

Hyman, R. (1991a) 'European Unions: Towards 2000', *Work, Employment & Society*, 5(4): 621–39.

Hyman, R. (1991b) 'Trade Unions and the Disaggregation of the Working Class', mimeo, IRRU, University of Warwick.

Hyman, R. (1992) 'Industrial Relations Research: The European Dimension', *Research Review, IRRU Newsletter*, 10, Spring: 6–9.

Hyman, R. (1994) 'Theory and Industrial Relations', *British Journal of Industrial Relations*, 32(2): 165–80.

Hyman, R. (1995) 'The Historical Evolution of British Industrial Relations', in P. Edwards (ed.), *Industrial Relations: Theory and Practice in Britain*, Oxford: Blackwell, 27–49.

Hyman, R. and Elger, T. (1981) 'Job Controls, the Employers' Offensive and Alternative Strategies', *Capital and Class*, (15): 115–49.

Ibbs, R. (1988) *Improving Management in Government: The Next Steps*, London: HMSO.

IDE (1981) *Industrial Democracy in Europe*, Oxford: Clarendon Press.

IEA (1978) *Trade Unions: Public Goods or Public 'Bads'*, London: Institute of Economic Affairs.

ILO (1981) *Employment Effects of Multinational Enterprises in Industrialised Countries*, Geneva: International Labour Office.

ILO (1992) *Recent Developments in the Iron and Steel Industry*, Geneva: ILO.

Incomes Data Services (IDS) (1996) 'UK To Toe the Line on Working Time Limits', *Employment Europe*, (413): 26–8.

Industrial Relations Services (1989) *The Regulation of Industrial Conflict in Europe*, London: Industrial Relations Services.

Industrial Relations Services (1994) 'First British European Works Councils Established', *IRS Employment Trends*, (574): 4–7.

Ingham, G. (1970) *Size of Industrial Organisation and Worker Behaviour*, Cambridge: Cambridge University Press.

Ingram, P. N. (1991a) 'Changes in Working Practices in British Manufacturing Industry in the 1980s: A Study of Employee Concessions Made During Wage Negotiations', *British Journal of Industrial Relations*, 29(1): 1–13.

Ingram, P. N. (1991b) 'Ten Years of Manufacturing Wage Settlements: 1979–89', *Oxford Review of Economic Policy*, 7(1): 93–106.

IRRR (1992) 'Single Union Deals in Perspective', *Industrial Relations Review and Report*, (523): 7–15.

IRRR (1993) 'Single Union Deals Survey: 1', *IRS Employment Trends 528*, January: 3–15.

ISR (1996) *Employee Satisfaction: Tracking European Trends*, London: International Survey Research.

ITF (1992) *The Globalisation of the Civil Aviation Industry, and its Impact on Aviation Workers*, London: International Transport Workers' Federation.

Jackson, M. P. (1991) *An Introduction to Industrial Relations*, London: Routledge.

Jackson, M. P., Leopold, J. W. and Tuck, K. (1993) *Decentralization of Collective Bargaining: An Analysis of Recent Experience in the UK*, Houndmills: Macmillan.

James, K. M. (1989) 'A Case of the Emperor's Clothes', *Training and Development*, October: 18.

Jones, R. M. (1971) *Absenteeism*, Manpower paper no. 4, London: HMSO.

Joseph, Sir Keith (1986) 'Solving the Union Problem is the Key to Britain's Recovery', in D. Coates and J. Hillard (eds), *The Economic Decline of Modern Britain: The Debate Between Left and Right*, Brighton: Wheatsheaf Books, 98–105.

Juran, J. M. (1979) *Quality Control Handbook*, New York: McGraw Hill.

Juran, J. M. (1988) *Juran on Planning for Quality*, New York: Free Press.

Kahn-Freund, O. (1959) 'Labour Law', in M. Ginsberg (ed.), *Law and Opinion in England in the 20th Century*, London: Stevens, 215–63.

Kahn-Freund, O. (1972) *Labour and the Law*, London: Stevens & Sons.

Kaldor, N. (1966) *Causes of the Slow Rate of Growth in the United Kingdom*, Cambridge: Cambridge University Press.

Kaufman, B. (1993) *The Origins and Evolution of the Field of Industrial Relations in the United States*, Ithaca, NY: ILR Press.

Kay, J. (1993) *The Foundations of Corporate Success*, Oxford: Oxford University Press.

Kay, J. (1997) 'Stakeholding', *CentrePiece*, 2(1): 22–4.

Keenoy, T. (1985) *Invitation to Industrial Relations*, Oxford: Blackwell.

Keenoy, T. (1991) 'The Roots of Metaphor in the Old and New Industrial Relations', *British Journal of Industrial Relations*, 29(2): 313–28.

Keenoy, T. (1992) 'Constructing Control', in J. F. Hartley and G. M. Stephenson (eds), *Employment Relations: The Psychology of Influence and Control at Work*, Oxford: Blackwell, 91–110.

Keenoy, T. and Noon, M. (1992) 'Employment Relations in the Enterprise Culture: Themes and Issues', *Journal of Management Studies*, 29(5): 561–70.

Keep, E. and Mayhew, K. (1995) *The British System of Vocational Education and Training: A Critical Analysis*, Oxford: Oxford University Press.

Keep, E. and Rainbird, H. (1995) 'Training', in P. Edwards (ed.), *Industrial Relations: Theory and Practice in Britain*, Oxford: Blackwell, 515–42.

Kelly, J. (1987) 'Trade Unions Through the Recession 1980–84', *British Journal of Industrial Relations*, 25(2): 275–82.

Kelly, J. (1988) *Trade Unions and Socialist Politics*, London: Verso.

Kelly, J. (1990) 'British Trade Unionism 1979–89: Change, Continuity and Contradictions', *Work, Employment & Society*, 4 (special issue): 29–65.

Kelly, J. (1994) 'Does the Field of Industrial Relations Have a Future?', mimeo, London School of Economics.

Kelly, J. (1996) 'Union Militancy and Social Partnership', in P. Ackers, C. Smith and P. Smith (eds), *The New Workplace and Trade Unionism: Critical Perspectives on Work and Organization*, London: Routledge, 77–109.

Kelly, J. and Bailey, R. (1989) 'British Trade Union Membership, Density and Decline in the 1980s: A Research Note', *Industrial Relations Journal*, 20(1): 54–61.

Kelly, J. and Heery, E. (1989) 'Full-time Officers and Trade Union Recruitment', *British Journal of Industrial Relations*, 27(2): 196–213.

Kelly, J. and Heery, E. (1994) *Working for the Union: British Trade Union Officers*, Cambridge: Cambridge University Press.

Kelly, J. and Kelly, C. (1991) '"Them and Us": Social Psychology and "The New Industrial Relations"', *British Journal of Industrial Relations*, 29(1): 25–48.

Kelly, J. and Nicholson, N. (1980) 'Strikes and Other Forms of Industrial Action', *Industrial Relations Journal*, 11(5): 20–31.

Kelly, J. and Waddington. J. (1995) 'New Prospects for British Labour', *Organization*, 2(3/4): 415–26.

Kerr, A. and Sachdev, S. (1992) 'Third Among Equals: An Analysis of the 1989 Ambulance Dispute', *British Journal of Industrial Relations*, 30(1): 127–43.

Kerr, C. (1964) *Labor and Management in Industrial Society*, New York: Doubleday.

Kerr, C. and Siegel, A. (1954) 'The Interindustry Propensity to Strike – An International Comparison', in A. Kornhauser, R. Dubin and A. M. Ross (eds), *Industrial Conflict*, New York: McGraw Hill, 189–212.

Kessler, I. (1991) 'Workplace Industrial Relations in Local Government', *Employee Relations*, 13(2): 3–31.

Kessler, I. and Purcell, J. (1995) 'Individualism and Collectivism in Theory and Practice: Management Style and the Design of Pay Systems', in P. Edwards (ed.), *Industrial Relations: Theory and Practice in Britain*, Oxford: Blackwell, 337–67.

Kessler, S. and Bayliss, F. (1992) *Contemporary British Industrial Relations*, London: Macmillan.

Kessler, S. and Bayliss, F. (1995) *Contemporary British Industrial Relations*, 2nd edn, London: Macmillan.

Kilpatrick, A. and Lawson, T. (1980) 'On the Nature of Industrial Decline in the UK', *Cambridge Journal of Economics*, 4(1): 85–102.

Kinnie, N. (1992) 'From IR to HR? Change and Continuity in Industrial Relations – A Longitudinal Case', paper presented to Employment Research Unit Conference, Cardiff Business School, September.

Klein, J. (1989) 'The Human Cost of Manufacturing Reform', *Harvard Business Review*, March-April: 60–6.

Knowles, K. G. J. C. (1952) *Strikes: A Study in Industrial Conflict*, Oxford: Blackwell.

Kornhauser, A., Dubin, R. and Ross, A. M. (eds) (1954) *Industrial Conflict*, New York: McGraw Hill.

Labour Research Department (1996) *Part of the Union: The Challenge of Recruiting and Organising Part-Time Workers*, London: Trades Unions Congress.

Lamb, H. and Percy, S. (1987) 'Big Mac is Watching You', *New Society*, 82(1293): 15–17.

Lane, C. (1988) 'New Technology and Clerical Work', in D. Gallie (ed.), *Employment in Britain*, Oxford: Blackwell, 67–101.

Lane, T. (1982) 'The Unions: Caught on the Ebb Tide', *Marxism Today*, September: 6–13.

Lavalette, M. and Kennedy, J. (1996) *Solidarity on the Waterfront: The Liverpool Lock Out of 1995/96*, Birkenhead: Liver Press.

Layard, R., Mayhew, K. and Owen, G. (1994) *Britain's Training Deficit*, Aldershot: Avebury.

Lazonick, W. (1978) 'The Subjection of Labor To Capital: The Rise of the Capitalist System', *Review of Radical Political Economics*, 10(1): 1–31.

Legge, K. (1988) 'Personnel Management in Recession and Recovery: A Comparative Analysis of What the Surveys Say', *Personnel Review*, 17(2): 1–72.

Legge, K. (1995) *Human Resource Management: Rhetorics and Realities*, Houndmills, Macmillan.

Leopold, J. W. (1986) 'Trade Union Political Funds: A Retrospective Analysis', *Industrial Relations Journal*, 17(4): 287–303.

Leopold, J. W. (1997) 'Trade Union Political Fund Ballots and the Labour Party', *British Journal of Industrial Relations*, 35(1): 23–38.

Lewin, K. (1958) 'Group Decisions and Social Change', in E. E. Maccoby, T. M. Newcomb and E. L. Hartley (eds), *Readings in Social Psychology*, New York: Holt, Rinehart and Winston, 97–211.

Lewis, P. (1989) 'The Unemployed and Trade Union Membership', *Industrial Relations Journal*, 20(4): 271–9.

Lewis, R. (1983) 'Collective Labour Law', in G. S. Bain (ed.), *Industrial Relations in Britain*, Oxford: Blackwell, 361–92.

Lewis, R. (ed.) (1986) *Labour Law in Britain*, Oxford: Blackwell.

Lewis, R. (1990) 'Strike-Free Deals and Pendulum Arbitration', *British Journal of Industrial Relations*, 28(1): 32–56.

Lewis, R. (1991) 'Reforming Industrial Relations: Law, Politics and Power', *Oxford Review of Economic Policy*, 7(1): 60–75.

Lewis, R. and Simpson, B. (1981) *Striking a Balance? Employment Law After the 1980 Act*, Oxford: Martin Robertson.

Littlefield, D. (1996) 'Works Council Snub Infuraites Employees', *People Management*, 2 May: 5.

Littler, C. and Salaman, G. (1984) *Class at Work*, London: Batsford.

Lockwood, D. (1966) 'Sources of Variation in Working Class Images of Society', *Sociological Review*, 14(3): 249–67.

Lowe, J. (1992a) ' "Locating the Line": The Front-Line Supervisor and Human Resource Management', in P. Blyton and P. Turnbull (eds), *Reassessing Human Resource Management*, London: Sage, 148–68.

Lowe, J. (1992b) 'Teambuilding via Outdoor Training: Experiences from a UK Automotive Plant', *Human Resource Management Journal*, 2(1): 42–59.

Lyddon, D. (1994) 'Recent British Strike Trends', British Universities Industrial Relations Association, mimeo, University of Keele.

Macaulay, I. R. and Wood, R. C. (1992) 'Hotel and Catering Industry Employees' Attitudes Towards Trade Unions', *Employee Relations*, 14(3): 20–8.

Macfarlane, A. (1982) 'Trade Union Growth, the Employer and the Hotel and Restaurant Industry: A Case Study', *Industrial Relations Journal*, 13(4): 29–43.

MacInnes, J. (1985) 'Conjuring Up Consultation: The Role and Extent of Joint Consultation in Post-War Private Manufacturing Industry', *British Journal of Industrial Relations*, 23(1): 93–113.

MacInnes, J. (1987) *Thatcherism at Work: Industrial Relations and Economic Change*, Milton Keynes: Open University Press.

Mackay, L. (1986) 'The Macho Manager: It's no Myth', *Personnel Management*, January: 25–7.

Mangham, I. and Silver, M. (1986) *Management Training: Context and Practice*, London: Economic and Social Research Council.

Marchington, M. (1980) *Responses to Participation at Work*, Farnborough: Gower.

Marchington, M. (1982) *Managing Industrial Relations*, Maidenhead: McGraw Hill.

Marchington, M. (1987) 'A Review and Critique of Research on Developments in Joint Consultation', *British Journal of Industrial Relations*, 25(3): 339–52.

Marchington, M. (1989) 'Joint Consultation in Practice', in K. Sisson (ed.), *Personnel Management in Britain*, Oxford: Blackwell, 378–402.

Marchington, M. (1992) *Managing the Team*, Oxford: Blackwell.

Marchington, M. (1994) 'The Dynamics of Joint Consultation', in K. Sisson (ed.), *Personnel Management: A Comprehensive Guide to Theory and Practice in Britain*, Oxford: Blackwell: 662–93.

Marchington, M. (1995) 'Involvement and Participation', in J. Storey (ed.), *Human Resource Management: A Critical Text*, London: Routledge, 280–305.

Marchington, M., Goodman, J., Wilkinson, A. and Ackers, P. (1992) *New Developments in Employee Involvement*, Research Series No.2, Sheffield: Employment Department.

Marchington, M. and Harrison, E. (1991) 'Customers, Competitors and Choice: Employee Relations in Food Retailing', *Industrial Relations Journal*, 22(4): 286–99.

Marchington, M. and Parker, P. (1990) *Changing Patterns of Employee Relations*, Hemel Hempstead: Harvester Wheatsheaf.

Marginson, P. (1992) 'European Integration and Transnational Management-Union Relations in the Enterprise', *British Journal of Industrial Relations*, 30(4): 529–45.

Marginson, P., Armstrong, P., Edwards, P. K., Purcell, J. and Hubbard, N. (1993) 'The Control of Industrial Relations in Large Companies: An Initial Analysis of the Second Company Level Industrial Relations Survey', *Warwick Papers in Industrial Relations*, no. 45, IRRU, University of Warwick.

Marginson, P. Edwards, P. K., Martin, R., Purcell, J. and Sisson, K. (1988) *Beyond the Workplace: Managing Industrial Relations in Multi-Plant Enterprises*, Oxford: Blackwell.

Marginson, P. and Sisson, K. (1994) 'The Structure of Transnational Capital in Europe: The Emerging Euro-company and its Implications for Industrial Relations', in R. Hyman and A. Ferner (eds), *New Frontiers in European Industrial Relations*, Oxford: Blackwell, 15–51.

Marginson, P. and Sisson, K. (1996) 'Multinational Companies and the Future of Collective Bargaining: A Review of the Research Issues', *European Journal of Industrial Relations*, 2(2): 173–97.

Marglin, S. (1974) 'What do Bosses do? The Origins and Function of Hierarchy in Capitalist Production', in A. Gorz (ed.), *The Division of Labour*, Brighton: Harvester Press, 13–54.

Mars, G. (1974) 'Dock Pilferage', in P. Rock and M. McIntosh (eds), *Deviance and Control*, London: Tavistock, 109–28.

Mars, G. (1982) *Cheats At Work: An Anthropology of Workplace Crime*, London: George Allen & Unwin.

Marsden, D. and Thompson, M. (1990) 'Flexibility Agreements and their Significance in the Increase in Productivity in British Manufacturing Since 1980', *Work, Employment & Society*, 4(1): 83–104.

Marsden, R. (1982) 'Industrial Relations: A Critique of Empiricism', *Sociology*, 16(2): 232–50.

Marsh, A. (1982) *Employee Relations Policy and Decision Making*, London: Confederation of British Industry.

Marshall, A. (1930) *Principles of Economics*, 8th edn, London: Macmillan.

Marshall, Sir Colin, (1989) 'How British Airways was Privatized', in E. Butler and M. Price (eds), *The Manual on Privatization: Mainspring of World Development in the 1990's*, London: Adam Smith Institute, 71–7.

Martin, R., Fosh, P., Morris, H., Smith, P. and Undy, R. (1991) 'The Decollectivisation of Trade Unions? Ballots and Collective Bargaining in the 1980s', *Industrial Relations Journal*, 22(3): 197–208.

Martin, R., Smith, P., Fosh, P., Morris, H. and Undy, R. (1995) 'The Legislative Reform of Union Government 1979–94', *Industrial Relations Journal*, 26(2): 146–55.

Martinez Lucio, M. (1993) 'The Post-Office', in A. Pendleton and J. Winterton (eds), *Public Enterprise in Transition: Industrial Relations in State and Privatized Corporations*, London: Routledge, 22–43.

Martinez Lucio, M. and Weston, S. (1992) 'Human Resource Management and Trade Union Responses: Bringing the Politics of the Workplace Back into the Debate', in P. Blyton and P. Turnbull (eds), *Reassessing Human Resource Management*, London: Sage, 215–32.

Martinez Lucio, M. and Weston, S. (1996) *Employee Networking and European Works Councils*, London: Anglo-German Foundation.

Marx, K. (1972) *Contribution to the Critique of Political Economy*, Chicago: Charles H. Kerr.

Marx, K. (1976) *Capital*, vol. 1, Harmondsworth: Penguin.

Marx, K. and Engels, F. (1975) *Articles on Britain*, Moscow: Progress Publishers.

Maslow, A. H. (1943) 'A Theory of Human Motivation', *Psychological Review*, 50: 370–96.

Mason, B. and Bain, P. (1991) 'Trade Union Recruitment Strategies: Facing the 1990s', *Industrial Relations Journal*, 22(1): 36–45.

Mason, B. and Bain, P. (1993) 'The Determinants of Trade Union Membership in Britain: A Survey of the Literature', *Industrial & Labor Relations Review*, 46(2): 332–51.

Mason, C. (1991) 'Spatial Variations in Enterprise: The Geography of New Firm Formation', in R. Burrows (ed.), *Deciphering Enterprise Culture: Entrepreneurship, Petty Capitalism and the Restructuring of Britain*, London: Routledge, 74–106.

Massey, D. (1984) *Spatial Divisions of Labour*, London: Macmillan.

Massey, D. (1988) 'What's Happening to UK Manufacturing?', in J. Allen and D. Massey (eds), *The Economy in Question*, London: Sage, 45–90.

Mayhew, K. (1985) 'Reforming the Labour Market', *Oxford Review of Economic Policy*, 1(2): 60–79.

Mayhew, K. (1991) 'The Assessment: The UK Labour Market in the 1980s', *Oxford Review of Economic Policy*, 7(1): 1–17.

Mayo, E. (1933) *The Human Problems of an Industrial Civilisation*, New York: Macmillan.

McCarthy, T. (1988) *The Great Dock Strike 1889*, London: Weidenfeld & Nicolson.

McCarthy, W. E. J. (1967) *The Role of Shop Stewards in British Industrial Relations*, Royal Commission on Trade Unions and Employers' Associations, Research Paper no.1, London: HMSO.

McCarthy, W. E. J. (1970) 'The Nature of Britain's Strike Problem: A Reassessment of Arguments in the Donovan Report and a Reply to H. A. Turner', *British Journal of Industrial Relations*, 8(3): 224–36.

McCarthy, W. E. J. (1987) 'The Case for a More Balanced Framework of Labour Law', *Warwick Papers in Industrial Relations*, no. 14, IRRU, University of Warwick.

McCarthy, W. E. J. (1991) *Towards 2000: A Consultative Document*, London: Trades Union Congress.

McCarthy, W. E. J. (1992) 'Time to Move On: Or Reflections on Forty Years of Industrial Relations Research', Research Review, *IRRU Newsletter*, 10, Spring: 2–5.

McCarthy, W. E. J. (1994) 'Of Hats and Cattle: Or the Limits of Macro-Survey Research in Industrial Relations', *Industrial Relations Journal*, 25(4): 315–22.

McCarthy, W. E. J., Parker, P. A. L., Hawes, W. R. and Lumb, A. L. (1971) *The Reform of Collective Bargaining at Plant and Company Level*, London: Department of Employment/HMSO.

McGregor, D. (1960) *The Human Side of Enterprise*, New York: McGraw-Hill.

McIlroy, J. (1988) *Trade Unions in Britain Today*, Manchester: Manchester University Press.

McIlroy, J. (1995) *Trade Unions in Britain Today*, 2nd edn, Manchester: Manchester University Press.

McLoughlin, I. (1996) 'Inside the Non-Union Firm', in P. Ackers, C. Smith and P. Smith (eds), *The New Workplace and Trade Unionism: Critical Perspectives on Work and Organization*, London: Routledge, 301–23.

McLoughlin, I. and Gourlay, S. (1992) 'Enterprise Without Unions: The Management of Employee Relations in Non-Union Firms', *Journal of Management Studies*, 29(5): 669–91.

Mellor, M., Hannah, J. and Stirling, J. (1988) *Worker Co-operatives in Theory and Practice*, Milton Keynes: Open University Press.

Melman, S. (1958) *Decision-Making and Productivity*, London: Blackwell.

Mesher, J. and Sutcliffe, F. (1986) 'Industrial Action and the Individual', in R. Lewis (ed.), *Labour Law in Britain*, Oxford: Blackwell, 243–71.

Metcalf, D. (1989) 'Water Notes Dry Up: The Impact of the Donovan Reform Proposals and Thatcherism at Work on Labour Productivity in British Manufacturing Industry', *British Journal of Industrial Relations*, 27(1): 1–31.

Metcalf, D. (1991) 'British Unions: Dissolution or Resurgence?', *Oxford Review of Economic Policy*, 7(1): 18–32.

Miliband, R. (1969) *The State in Capitalist Society*, London: Weidenfeld & Nicolson

Millward, N. (1994) *The New Industrial Relations?*, London: PSI.

Millward, N. and Stevens, M. (1986) *British Workplace Industrial Relations 1980–84*, Aldershot: Gower.

Millward, N., Stevens, M., Smart, D. and Hawes, W. R. (1992) *Workplace Industrial Relations in Transition*, Aldershot: Dartmouth.

Milner, S. (1993) 'Overtime Bans and Strikes: Evidence on Relative Incidence', *Industrial Relations Journal*, 24(3): 201–10.

Milner, S. (1995) 'The Coverage of Collective Pay-setting Institutions in Britain, 1895–1990', *British Journal of Industrial Relations*, 33(1): 69–91.

Minford, P. (1985) *Unemployment: Cause and Cure*, 2nd edn, Oxford: Blackwell.

Morris, G. (1986) *Strikes in Essential Services*, London: Mansell.

Morris, J., Blyton, P., Bacon, N. and Franz, H. W. (1992) 'Beyond Survival: The Implementation of New Forms of Work Organization in the UK and German Steel Industries', *International Journal of Human Resource Management*, 3(2): 307–29.

Morris, T. and Wood, S. (1991) 'Testing the Survey Method: Continuity and Change in British Industrial Relations', *Work, Employment & Society*, 5(2): 259–82.

MSF (1996) *How Organising Works: A Manual for Fulltime Officials and Organisers*, London: Manufacturing, Science, and Finance.

NACAB (1993) *Job Insecurity: CAB Evidence on Employment Problems in the Recession*, London: National Association of Citizens Advice Bureaux.

Neale, A. (1992) 'Are British Workers Pricing Themselves out of Jobs? Unit Labour Costs and Competitiveness', *Work, Employment & Society*, 6(2): 271–85.

New, C. C. and Myers, A. (1986) *Managing Manufacturing Operations in the UK, 1975–1985*, London: British Institute of Management.

Newell, H. (1993) 'Exploding the Myth of Greenfield Sites', *Personnel Management*, January: 20–3.

Nichol, D. (1992) 'Unnecessary Conflict: NHS Management's View of the 1989–90 Ambulance Dispute', *British Journal of Industrial Relations*, 30(1): 145–54.

Nichols, T. (ed.) (1980) *Capital and Labour: Studies in the Capitalist Labour Process*, London: Fontana.

Nichols, T. (1986) *The British Worker Question: A New Look at Workers and Productivity in Manufacturing*, London: Routledge & Kegan Paul.

Nichols, T. (1990) 'Industrial Safety in Britain and the 1974 Health and Safety at Work Act: The Case of Manufacturing', *International Journal of the Sociology of Law*, 18(3): 317–42.

Nichols, T. and O'Connell Davidson, J. (1991) 'Privatisation and Economism: An Investigation Amongst "Producers" in Two Privatised Public Utilities in Britain', paper presented at the Employment Research Unit annual conference, Cardiff Business School.

Nicholson, N. (1977) 'Absence Behaviour and Attendance Motivation: A Conceptual Synthesis', *Journal of Management Studies*, 14(3): 231–52.

Nicholson, N. and Johns, G. (1985) 'The Absence Culture and the Psychological Contract – Who's in Control of Absence', *Academy of Management Review*, 10(3): 397–407.

Nicholson, N., Ursell, G. and Blyton, P. (1980) 'Social Background, Attitudes and Behaviour of White-Collar Shop Stewards', *British Journal of Industrial Relations*, 18(2): 231–39.

Nolan, P. (1983) 'The Firm and Labour Market Behaviour', in G. S. Bain (ed.), *Industrial Relations in Britain*, Oxford: Blackwell, 291–310.

Nolan, P. (1989) 'Walking on Water? Performance and Industrial Relations under Thatcher', *Industrial Relations Journal*, 20(2): 81–92.

Nolan P. and Brown, W. (1983) 'Competition and Workplace Wage Determination', *Oxford Bulletin of Economics and Statistics*, 45(3): 269–87.

Noon, M. and Blyton, P. (1997) *The Realities of Work*, Basingstoke: Macmillan.

Northrup, H. R. and Rowan, R. L. (1979) *Multinational Collective Bargaining Attempts*, Philadelphia: University of Pennsylvania Press.

Oakland, J. S. (1989) *Total Quality Management*, Oxford: Butterworth-Heinemann.

OECD (1994a) *Economic Outlook*, July, Paris: Organisation for Economic Cooperation and Development.

OECD (1994b) *The OECD Jobs Study: Evidence and Explanations*, Paris: Organisation for Economic Cooperation and Development.

OECD (1996) *Economic Outlook*, July, Paris: Organisation for Economic Cooperation and Development.

Offe, C. and Ronge, V. (1982) 'Theses on the Theory of the State', in A. Giddens and D. Held (eds), *Classes, Power and Conflict*, London: Macmillan, 249–56.

Offe, C. and Wiesenthal, H. (1980) 'Two Logics of Collective Action: Theoretical Notes on Social Class and Organisational Form', *Political Power and Social Theory*, 1: 67–115.

Ogbonna, E. (1992) 'Organisational Culture and Human Resource Management: Dilemmas and Contradictions', in P. Blyton and P. Turnbull (eds), *Reassessing Human Resource Management*, London: Sage, 74–96.

Ogbonna, E. and Wilkinson, B. (1988) 'Corporate Strategy and Corporate Culture: The Management of Change in the UK Supermarket Industry', *Personnel Review*, 17(6): 10–14.

Ogbonna, E. and Wilkinson, B. (1990) 'Corporate Strategy and Corporate Culture: The View from the Checkout', *Personnel Review*, 19(4): 9–15.

Ogden, S. (1981) 'The Reform of Collective Bargaining: A Managerial Revolution?', *Industrial Relations Journal*, 12(4): 30–42.

Ogden, S. (1982) 'Bargaining Structure and the Control of Industrial Relations', *British Journal of Industrial Relations*, 20(2): 170–85.

Ogden, S. (1993) 'Water', in A. Pendleton and J. Winterton (eds), *Public Enterprise in Transition: Industrial Relations in State and Privatized Corporations*, London: Routledge, 134–65.

Ogden, S. (1994) 'The Reconstruction of Industrial Relations in the Privatized Water Industry', *British Journal of Industrial Relations*, 32(1): 67–84.

Ogden, S. G. (1995) 'Transforming Frameworks of Accountability: The Case of Water Privatization', *Accounting, Organizations & Society*, 20(2/3): 193–218.

Ogden, S. and Anderson, F. (1995) 'Representing Customers' Interests: The Case of the Privatized Water Industry in England and Wales', *Public Administration*, 73(4): 535–59.

Ogden, S. and Watson, R. (1996) 'The Relationship Between Changes in Incentive Structures, Executive Pay and Corporate Performance: Some Evidence from the Privatised Water Industry in England and Wales', *Journal of Business Finance & Accounting*, 23(5&6): 721–51.

O'Higgins, P. (1986) 'International Standards and British Labour Law', in R. Lewis (ed.), *Labour Law in Britain*, Oxford: Blackwell, 572–94.

Oliver, N. and Wilkinson, B. (1992) *The Japanization of British Industry*, 2nd edn, Oxford: Blackwell.

Organising Works (1995) *Organising Works*, no. 2, Melbourne: Organising Works.

Organising Works (1996) *Organising in Everything We Do – A Manual on the Craft of Organising and Recruitment*, Melbourne: Organising Works.

Overbeek, H. (1990) *Global Capitalism and National Decline: The Thatcher Decade in Perspective*, London: Unwin Hyman.

Owen Smith, E. (1971) *Productivity Bargaining: A Case Study in the Steel Industry*, London: Pan.

Panitch, L. (1981) 'Trade Unions and the Capitalist State', *New Left Review*, (125): 21–43.

Parkin, F. (1971) *Class, Inequality and Political Order*, London: MacGibbon & Kee.

Parsons, T. (1952) *The Social System*, London: Routledge & Kegan Paul.

Pateman, C. (1970) *Participation and Democratic Theory*, London: Cambridge University Press.

Pavitt, K. (ed.) (1980) *Technical Innovation and British Economic Performance*, London: Macmillan.

Payne, C. (1989) 'Trade Union Membership and Activism Among Young People in Britain', *British Journal of Industrial Relations*, 27(1): 111–32.

Pearson, P. and Quiney, M. (1992) *Poor Britain: Poverty, Inequality and Low Pay in the Nineties*, London: Low Pay Unit.

Pendleton, A. (1991a) 'Integration and Dealignment in Public Enterprise Industrial Relations: A Study of British Rail', *British Journal of Industrial Relations*, 29(3): 411–26.

Pendleton, A. (1991b) 'Workplace Industrial Relations in British Rail: Change and Continuity in the 1980s', *Industrial Relations Journal*, 22(3): 209–21.

Pendleton, A. and Winterton, J. (eds) (1993) *Public Enterprise in Transition: Industrial Relations in State and Privatized Corporations*, London: Routledge.

Peters, T. and Waterman, R. (1982) *In Search of Excellence*, New York: Harper Row.

Phillips, G. and Whiteside, N. (1985) *Casual Labour: The Unemployment Question in the Port Transport Industry, 1880–1970*, Oxford: Clarendon.

Phizacklea, A. (1987) 'Minority Women and Economic Restructuring', *Work, Employment & Society*, 1(3): 309–25.

Pickard, J. (1990) 'Engineering Tools Up for Local Bargaining', *Personnel Management*, March: 40–3.

Pilger, J. (1996) 'They Never Walk Alone', *Guardian Weekend*, 23 November, 14–23.

Piore, M. and Sabel, C. (1984) *The Second Industrial Divide: Prospects for Prosperity*, New York: Basic Books.

Plowman, D. H., Deery, S. J. and Fisher, C. H. (1981) *Australian Industrial Relations*, Sydney: McGraw Hill.

Pollert, A. (1988) 'Dismantling Flexibility', *Capital and Class*, (34): 42–75.

Ponak, A. M. and Fraser, C. R. P. (1979) 'Union Activists' Support for Joint Programs', *Industrial Relations*, 18(2): 197–209.

Pond, C. (1983) 'Wages Councils, the Unorganised and the Low Paid', in G. S. Bain (ed.), *Industrial Relations in Britain*, Oxford: Blackwell, 179–208.

Poole, M. (1981) *Theories of Trade Unionism*, London: Routledge & Kegan Paul.

Poole, M. (1986) 'Managerial Strategies and "Styles" in Industrial Relations: A Comparative Analysis', *Journal of General Management*, 12(1): 40–53.

Poole, M. (1988) 'Industrial Relations Theory and Management Strategies', *International Journal of Comparative Labour Law and Industrial Relations*, 4(1): 11–24.

Poole, M. and Jenkins, G. (1996) *Back to the Line? A Survey of Managers' Attitudes to Human Resource Management Issues*, London: Institute of Management.

Poole, M. and Mansfield, R. (1992) 'Managers' Attitudes to Human Resource Management: Rhetoric and Reality', in P. Blyton and P. Turnbull (eds), *Reassessing Human Resource Management*, London: Sage, 200–14.

Poole, M. and Mansfield, R. (1993) 'Patterns of Continuity and Change in Management Attitudes and Behaviour in Industrial Relations, 1980–1990', *British Journal of Industrial Relations*, 31(1): 11–35.

Poole, M., Mansfield, R., Blyton, P. and Frost, P. (1981) *Managers in Focus*, Aldershot: Gower.
Popham, P. (1992) 'Turning Japanese', *The Independent Magazine*, 12 September: 24–30.
Porter, M. E. (1990) *The Competitive Advantage of Nations*, New York: Free Press.
Purcell, J. (1982) 'Macho Managers and the New Industrial Relations' *Employee Relations*, 4(1): 3–5.
Purcell, J. (1987) 'Mapping Management Styles in Employee Relations', *Journal of Management Studies*, 24(5): 533–48.
Purcell, J. (1989) 'The Impact of Corporate Strategy on Human Resource Management', in J. Storey (ed.), *New Perspectives on Human Resource Management*, London: Routledge, 67–91.
Purcell, J. (1991) 'The Rediscovery of the Management Prerogative: The Management of Labour Relations in the 1980s', *Oxford Review of Economic Policy*, 7(1): 33–43.
Purcell, J. and Ahlstrand, B. (1989) 'Corporate Strategy and the Management of Employee Relations in the Multi-Divisional Company', *British Journal of Industrial Relations*, 27(3): 396–417.
Purcell, J. and Ahlstrand, B. (1994) *Human Resource Management in the Multi-Divisional Firm*, Oxford: Oxford University Press.
Purcell, J. and Gray, A. (1986) 'Corporate Personnel Departments and the Management of Industrial Relations: Two Case Studies in Ambiguity', *Journal of Management Studies*, 23(2): 205–23.
Purcell, J., Marginson, P., Edwards, P. and Sisson, K. (1987) 'The Industrial Relations Practices of Multi-Plant Foreign-Owned Firms', *Industrial Relations Journal*, 18(2): 130–37.
Purcell, J. and Sisson, K. (1983) 'Strategies and Practice in the Management of Industrial Relations', in G. S. Bain (ed.), *Industrial Relations in Britain*, Oxford: Blackwell, 95–120.
Rainnie, A. F. (1984) 'Combined and Uneven Development in the Clothing Industry: The Effects of Competition on Accumulation', *Capital and Class*, (22): 141–56.
Rainnie, A. F. (1985a) 'Is Small Beautiful? Industrial Relations in Small Clothing Firms', *Sociology*, 19(2): 213–24.
Rainnie, A. F. (1985b) 'Small Firms, Big Problems: The Political Economy of Small Businesses', *Capital and Class*, (25): 140–68.
Rainnie, A. F. (1989) *Industrial Relations in Small Firms: Small Isn't Beautiful*, London: Routledge.
Rainnie, A. F. (1991) 'Small Firms: Between the Enterprise Culture and "New Times" ', in R. Burrows (ed.), *Deciphering the Enterprise Culture: Entrepreneurship, Petty Capitalism and the Restructuring of Britain*, London: Routledge, 176–99.
Ram, M. (1991) 'Control and Autonomy in Small Firms: The Case of the West Midlands Clothing Industry', *Work, Employment & Society*, 5(4): 601–19.
Ram, M. (1994) *Managing to Survive: Working Lives in Small Firms*, Oxford: Blackwell.
Ramsay, H. (1977) 'Cycles of Control', *Sociology*, 11(3): 481–506.
Ramsay, H. (1980) 'Phantom Participation: Patterns of Power and Conflict', *Industrial Relations Journal*, 11(3): 46–59.
Ramsay, H. (1983) 'Evolution or Cycle? Worker Participation in the 1970s and 1980s', in C. Crouch and F. Heller (eds), *Organisational Democracy and Political Processes*, London: Wiley, 203–26.
Ramsay, H. (1991) 'The Community, the Multinational, its Workers and Their Charter: A Modern Tale of Industrial Democracy?', *Work, Employment & Society*, 5(4): 541–66.
Ramsay, H. (1992) 'Commitment and Involvement', in B. Towers (ed.), *The Handbook of Human Resource Management*, Oxford: Blackwell, 208–37.
Ramsay, H., Pollert, A. and Rainbird, H. (1992) 'A Decade of Transformation? Labour Market Flexibility and Work Organisation in the United Kingdom', in Organisation

for Economic Cooperation and Development (ed.), *New Directions in Work Organisation: The Industrial Relations Response*, Paris: OECD, 169–95.

Ray, G.F. (1987) 'Labour Costs in Manufacturing', *National Institute Economic Review*, 2(120): 71–4.

Reed, M. and Anthony, P. (1992) 'Professionalizing Management and Managing Professionalization: British Management in the 1980s', *Journal of Management Studies*, 29(5): 591–613.

Reynolds, L.G. (1956) *Labor Economics and Labor Relations*, Englewood Cliffs, NJ: Prentice-Hall.

Ricardo, D. (1817) *Principles of Political Economy and Taxation* (1965 edition), London: Dent.

Richardson, R. and Rubin, M. (1992) 'The Shorter Working Week in Engineering: Surrender Without Sacrifice?', working paper no. 270, Centre for Economic Performance, London School of Economics.

Ritzer, G. (1996) *The McDonaldization of Society*, 2nd edn, Thousand Oaks, CA: Pine Forge.

Rojot, J. (1989) 'National Experiences in Labour Market Flexibility', in Organisation for Economic Cooperation and Development (ed.), *Labour Market Flexibility: Trends in Enterprises*, Paris: OECD, 37–60.

Rose, M. (1975) *Industrial Behaviour: Theoretical Developments Since Taylor*, Harmondsworth: Penguin.

Rose, M. and Jones, B. (1984) 'Management Strategy and Trade Union Response', in D. Knights, H. Willmott and D. Collinson (eds), *Job Redesign*, London: Heinemann, 81–106.

Rowthorn, B. (1986) 'The Passivity of the State', in D. Coates and J. Hillard (eds), *The Economic Decline of Modern Britain: The Debate Between Left and Right*, Brighton: Wheatsheaf Books, 264–6.

Roy, D. (1954) 'Efficiency and the Fix: Informal Inter-group Relations in a Piecework Machine Shop', *American Journal of Sociology*, 60(3): 255–66.

Rubenowitz, S., Norrgren, F. and Tannenbaum, A.S. (1983) 'Some Social Psychological Effects of Direct or Indirect Participation in Ten Swedish Companies', *Organization Studies*, 4(3): 243–59.

Rubery, J. (1987) 'Flexibility of Labour Costs in Non-Union Firms', in R. Tarling (ed.), *Flexibility in Labour Markets*, London: Academic Press, 59–83.

Rubery, J. (1988) 'Employers and the Labour Market', in D. Gallie (ed.), *Employment in Britain*, Oxford: Blackwell, 251–80.

Rubery, J. (1995) 'The Low-Paid and the Unorganized', in P. Edwards (ed.), *Industrial Relations: Theory and Practice in Britain*, Oxford: Blackwell, 543–68.

Rubery, J., Tarling, R. and Wilkinson, F. (1987) 'Flexibility, Marketing and the Organisation of Production', *Labour and Society*, 12(1): 131–51

Rubinstein, M. (1984) *Equal Pay for Work of Equal Value*, London: Macmillan.

Salamon, M. (1987) *Industrial Relations: Theory and Practice*, London: Prentice Hall.

Salmans, S. (1980) 'Mixed Fortunes at M&S', *Management Today*, November: 67–73.

Salsbury, P.L. (1993) 'Memorandum from Marks and Spencer', House of Commons Employment Committee of Inquiry, *The Future of the Unions*, London: HMSO.

Sapper, S. (1991) 'Do Members' Services Packages Influence Trade Union Recruitment', *Industrial Relations Journal*, 22(4): 309–16.

Sapsford, D. (1981) *Labour Market Economics*, London: George Allen & Unwin.

Sapsford, D. and Turnbull, P. (1993) 'Research Note: Organized and "Unorganized" Conflict in the British Coal-mining Industry, 1947–83', *International Journal of Manpower*, 14(9): 6–63.

Saunders, J., Brown, M. and Laverick, S. (1992) 'Research Notes on the Best British Companies: A Peer Evaluation of Britain's Leading Firms', *British Journal of Management*, 3(4): 181–95.

Saundry, R. and Turnbull, P. (1996) 'Mêlée on the Mersey: Contracts, Competition and Labour Relations on the Docks', *Industrial Relations Journal*, 27(4): 275–88.

Saundry, R. and Turnbull, P. (1997) 'Private Profit, Public Loss: The Financial and Economic Performance of UK Ports', *Maritime Policy & Management*, 24(4): 319–34.

Sayer, A. and Walker, R. (1992) *The New Social Economy: Reworking the Division of Labour*, Oxford: Blackwell.

Scase, R. (1982) 'The Petty Bourgeoisie and Modern Capitalism: A Consideration of Recent Theories', in A. Giddens and G. Mackenzie (eds), *Social Class and the Division of Labour*, Cambridge: Cambridge University Press, 148–61.

Scase, R. (1995) 'Employment Relations in Small Firms', in P. Edwards (ed.), *Industrial Relations: Theory and Practice in Britain*, Oxford: Blackwell, 569–95.

Scott, A. (1994) *Willing Slaves? British Workers Under Human Resource Management*, Cambridge: Cambridge University Press.

Scott, M., Roberts, I., Holroyd, G. and Sawbridge, D. (1989) *Management and Industrial Relations in Small Firms*, Research Paper no. 70, London: Department of Employment.

Screpanti, E. (1987) 'Long Cycles in Strike Activity: An Empirical Investigation', *British Journal of Industrial Relations*, 25(1): 99–124.

Seifert, R. (1990) 'Prognosis for Local Bargaining in Health and Education', *Personnel Management*, August: 54–7.

Seifert, R. (1992) *Industrial Relations in the NHS*, London: Chapman & Hall.

Sewell, G. and Wilkinson, B. (1992) 'Employment or Emasculation? Shopfloor Surveillance in a Total Quality Organization', in P. Blyton and P. Turnbull (eds), *Reassessing Human Resource Management*, London: Sage, 97–115.

Shalev, M. (1978) 'Lies, Damned Lies, and Strike Statistics: The Measurement of Trends in Industrial Conflict', in C. Crouch and A. Pizzorno (eds), *The Resurgence of Class Conflict in Western Europe Since 1968*, vol. 1, National Studies, London: Macmillan, 1–19.

Shorter, E. and Tilly, C. (1974) *Strikes in France, 1830–1968*, Cambridge: Cambridge University Press.

Shutt, J. and Whittington, R. (1987) 'Fragmentation Strategies and the Rise of Small Units: Cases from the North West', *Regional Studies*, 21(1): 13–23.

Sieff, M. (1984) 'How I See the Personnel Function', *Personnel Management*, December: 28–30.

Sieff, M. (1986) *Don't Ask the Price: The Memoirs of the President of Marks & Spencer*, London: Weidenfield & Nicolson.

Sieff, M. (1990) *Marcuss Sieff on Management: The Marks & Spencer Way*, London: Weidenfield & Nicolson.

Simpson, B. (1986) 'Trade Union Immunities', in R. Lewis (ed.), *Labour Law in Britain*, Oxford: Blackwell, 161–94.

Simpson, B. (1989) 'The Summer of Discontent and the Law', *Industrial Law Journal*, 18(4): 234–41.

Sinclair, D. M. (1996) 'The Importance of Gender for Participation in and Attitudes to Trade Unionism', *British Journal of Industrial Relations*, 27(3): 239–52.

Sisson, K. (1983) 'Employers' Organisations', in G. S. Bain (ed.), *Industrial Relations in Britain*, Oxford: Blackwell, 121–34.

Sisson, K. (1984) 'Changing Strategies in Industrial Relations', *Personnel Management*, May: 24–7.

Sisson, K. (1987) *The Management of Collective Bargaining: An International Comparison*, Oxford: Blackwell.

Sisson, K. (ed.) (1989) *Personnel Management in Britain*, Oxford: Blackwell.

Sisson, K. (1993) 'In Search of HRM', *British Journal of Industrial Relations*, 31(2): 201–10.

Sisson, K. (1994) 'Personnel Management: Paradigms, Practice and Prospects', in K. Sisson (ed.), *Personnel Management: A Comprehensive Guide to Theory and Practice in Britain*, Oxford: Blackwell, 3–50.

Sisson, K. and Brown, W. (1983) 'Industrial Relations in the Private Sector: Donovan Revisited', in G. S. Bain (ed.), *Industrial Relations in Britain*, Oxford: Blackwell, 137–54.

Sisson, K. and Marginson, P. (1995) 'Management: Systems, Structures and Strategy', in P. Edwards (ed.), *Industrial Relations: Theory and Practice in Britain*, Oxford: Blackwell, 89–122.

Slichter, S. H. (1941) *Union Policies and Industrial Management*, Washington DC: Brookings Institute.

Smith, C., Child, J. and Rowlinson, M. (1990) *Reshaping Work: The Cadbury Experience*, Cambridge: Cambridge University Press.

Smith, C. T. B., Clifton, R., Makeham, P., Creigh, S. W. and Burn, R. V. (1978) *Strikes in Britain*, Department of Employment, Manpower Paper 15, London: HMSO.

Smith, G. B. (1990) 'Co-Makership: The Japanese Success Story in a British Environment', *International Journal of Quality and Reliability Management*, 7(2): 7–14.

Smith, M. (1986) 'UK Manufacturing Output and Trade Performance', *Midland Bank Review*, Autumn: 8–16.

Smith, P., Fosh, P., Martin, R., Morris, H. and Undy, R. (1993) 'Ballots and Union Government in the 1980s', *British Journal of Industrial Relations*, 31(3): 365–82.

Smith, P. and Morton, G. (1990) 'A Change of Heart: Union Exclusion in the Provincial Newspaper Sector', *Work, Employment & Society*, 4(1): 105–24.

Smith, P. and Morton, G. (1993) 'Union Exclusion and the Decollectivization of Industrial Relations in Contemporary Britain', *British Journal of Industrial Relations*, 31(1): 97–114.

Snape, E. (1994a) 'Reversing the Decline? The TGWU's Link-Up Campaign', *Industrial Relations Journal*, 25(3): 222–33.

Snape, E. (1994b) 'Union Organizing in Britain: The Views of Local Full-Time Officials', *Employee Relations*, 16(8): 48–62.

Snape, E. (1995) 'The Development of "Managerial Unionism" in Britain: A Research Note', *Work, Employment & Society*, 9(3): 559–68.

Spilsbury, M., Hoskins, M., Ashton, D. J. and Maguire, M. J. (1987) 'A Note on the Trade Union Patterns of Young Adults', *British Journal of Industrial Relations*, 25(2): 267–74.

Sproull, A. and MacInnes, J. (1987) 'Patterns of Union Recognition in Scottish Electronics', *British Journal of Industrial Relations*, 25(3): 335–8.

Stafford, A. (1961) *A Match to Fire the Thames*, London: Hodder & Stoughton.

Stephenson, G., Brotherton, C., Delafield, G. and Skinner, M. (1983) 'Size of Organisation, Attitudes to Work and Job Satisfaction', *Industrial Relations Journal*, 14(2): 28–40.

Stevens, J. and MacKay, R. (1991) *Training and Competitiveness*, London: Kogan Page.

Storey, J. (1985) 'The Means of Management Control', *Sociology*, 19(2): 193–211.

Storey, J. (ed.) (1989) *New Perspectives on Human Resource Management*, London: Routledge.

Storey, J. (1992) *Developments in the Management of Human Resources: An Analytical Review*, Oxford: Blackwell.

Storey, J. (ed.) (1995) *Human Resource Management: A Critical Text*, London: Routledge.

Storey, J. and Bacon, N. (1993) 'Individualism and Collectivism: Into the 1990s', *International Journal of Human Resource Management*, 4(3): 665–84.

Storey, J. and Sisson, K. (1993) *Managing Human Resources and Industrial Relations*, Buckingham: Open University Press.

Strauss, G. and Feuille, P. (1978) 'Industrial Relations Research: A Critical Analysis', *Industrial Relations*, 17(3): 259–77.

Streeck, W. (1987) 'Industrial Relations and Industrial Change: The Restructuring of the World Automobile Industry in the 1970s and 1980s', *Economic and Industrial Democracy*, 8(4): 437–62.

Streeck, W. (1988) 'Comment on Ronald Dore, "Rigidities in the Labour Market"', *Government & Opposition*, 23(4): 413–23.

Streeck, W. (1992) *Social Institutions and Economic Performance: Studies of Industrial Relations in Advanced Capitalist Economies*, London: Sage.

Sweeney, K. (1996) 'Membership of Trade Unions in 1994: An Analysis Based on Information from the Certification Officer', *Labour Market Trends*, February: 49–54.

Sweeney, K. and Davies, J. (1997) 'International Comparisons of Labour Disputes in 1995', *Labour Market Trends*, April: 129–34.

T&GWU (1995a) *Organising for Strength: Organisers' Manual*, London: Transport & General Workers' Union.

T&GWU (1995b) *The Administrative Report of the 36th Biennial Delegate Conference*, London: Transport & General Workers' Union.

T&GWU (1996) *Organiser's Bulletin*, Winter, London: Transport & General Workers' Union, Region 1.

Tate, B. (1991) 'Book Review – The Human Side of Corporate Competitiveness, by D.B. Fishman and C. Cherniss (eds)', *Human Resource Management Journal*, 1(4): 110–12.

Taylor, B., Elger, T. and Fairbrother, P. (1991) 'Work Relations in Electronics: What Has Become of Japanisation in Britain?', paper presented to the 9th Annual Labour Process Conference, UMIST, 10–12 April.

Taylor, L. and Walton, P. (1971) 'Industrial Sabotage: Motives and Meanings', in S. Cohen (ed.), *Images of Deviance*, Harmondsworth: Penguin, 219–45.

Terry, M. (1983) 'Shop Steward Development and Managerial Strategies', in G.S. Bain (ed.), *Industrial Relations in Britain*, Oxford: Blackwell, 67–91.

Terry, M. (1991) 'Annual Review Article 1990', *British Journal of Industrial Relations*, 29(1): 97–112.

Terry, M. (1995) 'Trade Unions: Shop Stewards and the Workplace', in P. Edwards (ed.), *Industrial Relations: Theory and Practice in Britain*, Oxford: Blackwell, 203–28.

Terry, M. and Edwards, P.K. (eds) (1988) *Shopfloor Politics and Job Controls: The Post-War Engineering Industry*, Oxford: Blackwell.

Thirlwall, A.P. (1982) 'De-Industrialisation in the United Kingdom', *Lloyds Bank Review*, (144): 22–37.

Thomas, B.J. (1994) 'The Privatization of United Kingdom Seaports', *Maritime Policy & Management*, 21(2): 135–48.

Thomas, M. (1985) 'In Search of Culture: Holy Grail or Gravy Train', *Personnel Management*, September: 24–7.

Thompson, P. and McHugh, D. (1990) *Work Organisations: A Critical Introduction*, London: Macmillan.

Thomson, I. (1996) 'Employee Participation at Work: The European Dimension', *European Access*, 5: 39–47.

Tillsley, C. (1994) 'Employee Involvement: Employees' Views', *Employment Gazette*, June: 211–6.

Tse, K.K. (1985) *Marks & Spencer: Anatomy of Britain's Most Efficiently Managed Company*, Oxford: Pergamon.

TUC (1988) *Meeting the Challenge*, first report of Special Review Body, London: Trades Union Congress.

TUC (1989) *Organizing for the 1990s*, second report of Special Review Body, London: Trades Union Congress.

TUC (1996a) *A Five Million Strong Challenge*, London: Trades Unions Congress.

TUC (1996b) *Testament of Youth: A Manifesto for Young Workers*, London: Trades Unions Congress.

TUC (1997) *Partnership for Progress: Next Steps for the New Unionism*, London: Trades Union Congress.

Turnbull, P. (1988a) 'Leaner and Possibly Fitter: The Management of Redundancy in Britain', *Industrial Relations Journal*, 19(3): 201–13.

Turnbull, P. (1988b) 'The Economic Theory of Trade Union Behaviour: A Critique', *British Journal of Industrial Relations*, 26(1): 99–118.

Turnbull, P. (1988c) 'The Limits to "Japanisation" – Just-in-Time, Labour Relations and the UK Automotive Industry', *New Technology, Work and Employment*, 3(1): 7–20.

Turnbull, P. (1991a) 'Buyer-Supplier Relations in the UK Automotive Industry', in P. Blyton and J. Morris (eds), *A Flexible Future? Prospects for Employment and Organization*, Berlin: Walter de Gruyter, 169–89.

Turnbull, P. (1991b) 'Labour Market Deregulation and Economic Performance: The Case of Britain's Docks', *Work, Employment & Society*, 5(1): 17–35.

Turnbull, P. (1991c) 'Trade Unions and Productivity: Opening the Harvard "Black Boxes"', *Journal of Labor Research*, 12(2): 135–50.

Turnbull, P. (1992) 'Dock Strikes and the Demise of the Dockers' "Occupational Culture"', *Sociological Review*, 40(2): 294–318.

Turnbull, P. (1993) 'Docks', in A. Pendleton and J. Winterton (eds), *Public Enterprise in Transition: Industrial Relations in State and Privatized Corporations*, London: Routledge, 185–210.

Turnbull, P. (1997) 'Organising Works in Australia – Will it Work in Britain?', mimeo, University of Cardiff.

Turnbull, P., Morris, J. and Sapsford, D. (1996) 'Persistent Militants and Quiescent Comrades: Intra-Industry Strike Activity on the Docks, 1947–89', *Sociological Review*, 44(4): 710–45.

Turnbull, P. and Sapsford, D. (1991) 'Why Did Devlin Fail? Casualism and Conflict on the Docks', *British Journal of Industrial Relations*, 29(2): 237–57.

Turnbull, P. and Sapsford, D. (1992) 'A Sea of Discontent: The Tides of Organised and "Unorganised" Conflict on the Docks', *Sociology*, 26(2): 291–309.

Turnbull, P. and Wass, V. (1994) 'The Greatest Game No More – Redundant Dockers and the Demise of "Dock Work"', *Work, Employment & Society*, 8(4): 487–506.

Turnbull, P. and Wass, V. (1995) '"The Great Dock and Dole Swindle": Accounting for the Costs and Benefits of Port Transport Deregulation and the Dock Labour Compensation Scheme', *Public Administration*, 73(4): 513–34.

Turnbull, P. and Wass, V. (1997a) 'Job Insecurity and Labour Market Lemons: The (Mis)Management of Redundancy in Steel Making, Coal Mining and Port Transport', *Journal of Management Studies*, 34(1): 27–51.

Turnbull, P. and Wass, V. (1998) 'Marksist Management: Sophisticated Human Relations in a High Street Retail Store', *Industrial Relations Journal*, 29(2) (forthcoming).

Turnbull, P. and Weston, S. (1992) 'Employment Regulation, State Intervention and the Economic Performance of European Ports', *Cambridge Journal of Economics*, 16(4): 385–404.

Turnbull, P. and Weston, S. (1993a) 'Cooperation or Control? Capital Restructuring and Labour Relations on the Docks', *British Journal of Industrial Relations*, 31(1): 115–34.

Turnbull, P. and Weston, S. (1993b) 'The British Port Transport Industry, Part 1. Operational Structure, Investment and Competition', *Maritime Policy & Management*, 20(2): 109–20.

Turnbull, P. and Weston, S. (1993c) 'The British Port Transport Industry, Part 2. Employment, Working Practices and Productivity', *Maritime Policy & Management*, 20(3): 181–95.

Turnbull, P., Woolfson, C. and Kelly, J. (1992) *Dock Strikes: Conflict and Restructuring in Britain's Ports*, Aldershot: Avebury.

Turner, H. A., Clack, G. and Roberts, G. (1967) *Labour Relations in the Motor Industry*, London: George Allen & Unwin.

Turner, H. A., Roberts, G. and Roberts, D. (1977) *Management Characteristics and Labour Conflict*, Cambridge: Cambridge University Press.

Undy, R., Ellis, V., McCarthy, W. E. J. and Halmos, A. M. (1981) *Change in Trade Unions: The Development of UK Unions Since the 1960s*, London: Hutchinson

Undy, R., Fosh, P., Morris, H., Smith, P. and Martin, R. (1996) *Managing the Unions: The Impact of Legislation on Trade Union Behaviour*, Oxford: Clarendon Press.

United Nations (1996) *Human Development Report*, Geneva: United Nations.

Upchurch, M. and Donnelly, E. (1992) 'Membership Patterns in USDAW 1980–1990: Survival as Success?', *Industrial Relations Journal*, 23(1): 60–8.

Upham, M. (1980) 'British Steel: Retrospect and Prospect', *Industrial Relations Journal*, 11(1): 5–21.

Upham, M. (1990) 'Passages on the Path to Privatisation: The Experience of British Steel', *Industrial Relations Journal*, 21(2): 87–97.

Ursell, G. (1983) 'The Views of British Managers and Shop Stewards on Industrial Democracy', in C. Crouch and F. Heller (eds), *Organisational Democracy and Political Process*, Chichester: Wiley, 327–52.

Ursell, G. and Blyton, P. (1988) *State, Capital and Labour: Changing Patterns of Power and Dependence*, London: Macmillan.

Ursell, G., Wall, T., Clegg, C., Lubbock, J., Blyton, P. and Nicholson, N. (1980) 'Shop Stewards Attitudes Towards Industrial Democracy', *Industrial Relations Journal*, 11(1): 22–30.

Vandamme, J. (ed.) (1986) *Employee Consultation and Information in Multinational Corporations*, London: Croom Helm.

Waddington, J. (1988) 'Business Unionism and Fragmentation Within the TUC', *Capital and Class*, (36): 7–15.

Waddington, J. (1992) 'Trade Union Membership in Britain 1980–1987: Unemployment and Restructuring', *British Journal of Industrial Relations*, 30(2): 287–324.

Waddington, J. (1995) *The Politics of Bargaining: The Merger Process and British Trade Union Structural Development, 1892–1987*, London: Mansell.

Waddington, J. and Whitston, C. (1995a) 'Trade Unions: Growth, Structure and Policy', in P. Edwards (ed.), *Industrial Relations: Theory and Practice in Britain*, Oxford: Blackwell, 151–202.

Waddington, J. and Whitston, C. (1995b) 'Work Intensification and Grievances at Unionised Workplaces in the UK', *Industrielle Beziehungen*, 2(4): 414–43.

Wall, T. D. and Lischeron, J. A. (1977) *Worker Participation: A Critique of the Literature and Some Fresh Evidence*, Maidenhead: McGraw Hill.

Walsh, J. (1993) 'Internalization v. Decentralization: An Analysis of Recent Developments in Pay Bargaining', *British Journal of Industrial Relations*, 31(3): 409–32.

Walton, R. E. and McKersie, R. B. (1965) *A Behavioural Theory of Labor Negotiations*, New York: McGraw-Hill.

Warhurst, R. (1995) 'Converging on HRM? Change and Continuity in European Airlines' Industrial Relations', *European Journal of Industrial Relations*, 1(2): 259–74.

Webb, S. and Webb, B. (1920) *The History of Trade Unionism 1866–1920*, London: Longman.

Wedderburn, Lord (1972) 'Labour Law and Labour Relations in Britain', *British Journal of Industrial Relations*, 10(2): 270–90.

Wedderburn, Lord (1989) 'Freedom of Association and Philosophies of Labour Law', *Industrial Law Journal*, 18(1): 1–38.

Weekes, B. C. M., Mellish, M., Dickens, L. and Lloyd, J. (1975) *Industrial Relations and the Limits of Law: The Industrial Effects of the Industrial Relations Act, 1971*, Oxford: Blackwell.

Welch, R. (1991) 'The Legal Mystification of Industrial Relations', *Employee Relations*, 13(4): 9–15.

Westrip, A. (1982) 'Effects of Employment Legislation on Small Firms', in D. Watkins, J. Stanworth and A. Westrip (eds), *Stimulating Small Firms*, Aldershot: Gower, 32–66.

Wheeler, D. (1997) *The Stakeholder Corporation*, London: Pitman.

Whipp, R. and Clark, P. (1986) *Innovation and the Auto Industry*, London: Frances Pinter.

Whitston, C. and Waddington, J. (1992) 'Why Sign Up? New Trade Union Members' Reasons for Joining', *IRRU Research Review*, University of Warwick, (6): 2–4.

Whitston, C. and Waddington, J. (1994) 'Why Join a Union?', *New Statesman & Society*, 18 November, 36–8.

Wickens, P. (1985a) 'Management Philosophy: Nissan Style', discussion paper, Trent Business School, Trent Polytechnic.

Wickens, P. (1985b) 'Nissan: The Thinking Behind the Union Agreement', *Personnel Management*, August: 18–21.

Wickens, P. (1987) *The Road to Nissan: Flexibility, Quality, Teamwork*, London: Macmillan.

Wigham, E. (1976) *Strikes and the Government, 1983–1974*, London: Macmillan.

Wilkinson, A. and Willmott, H. (eds) (1995) *Making Quality Critical: New Perspectives on Organizational Change*, London: Routledge.

Wilkinson, B. and Oliver, N. (1990) 'Obstacles to Japanization: The Case of Ford UK', *Employee Relations*, 12(1): 17–21.

Wilkinson, F. and White, M. (1994) 'Product-Market Pressures and Employers' Response', in J. Rubery and F. Wilkinson (eds), *Employer Strategy and the Labour Market*, Oxford: Oxford University Press, 111–37.

Williams, K., Williams, J. and Haslam, C. (1987) *The Breakdown of Austin Rover*, Leamington Spa: Berg.

Williams, K., Williams, J., Haslam, C. and Wardlow, A. (1988) 'Facing up to Manufacturing Failure', Aberystwyth Economic Papers, OP.15, University of Wales College of Aberystwyth.

Willis, P. E. (1977) *Learning to Labour*, London: Saxon House.

Willman, P. (1986) 'Labour Relations Strategy at BL Cars', in S. Tolliday and J. Zeitlin (eds), *The Automobile Industry and its Workers*, Cambridge: Polity Press, 305–27.

Willman, P. (1989) 'The Logic of "Market-Share" Trade Unionism: Is Membership Decline Inevitable?', *Industrial Relations Journal*, 20(4): 260–70.

Willman, P. (1996) 'Merger Propensity and Merger Outcomes Among British Unions, 1986–1995', *Industrial Relations Journal*, 27(4): 331–8.

Willman, P. and Cave, A. (1994) 'The Union of the Future: Super-Unions or joint Ventures?', *British Journal of Industrial Relations*, 32(3): 395–412.

Willman, P. and Morris, T. (1995) 'Financial Management and Financial Performance in British Trade Unions', *British Journal of Industrial Relations*, 32(2): 289–98.

Wilson, D. F. (1972) *Dockers: The Impact of Industrial Change*, London: Fontana/Collins.

Wilson, R. H. H. (1995) 'Corporate Restructuring in the Final Phase of Deregulation: A View from the Melting Pot', in P. Cappelli (ed.), *Airline Labor Relations in the Global Era*, Ithaca: ILR Press, 223–30.

Winchester, D. (1983a) 'Industrial Relations in the Public Sector', in G. S. Bain (ed.), *Industrial Relations in Britain*, Oxford: Blackwell, 155–78.

Winchester, D. (1983b) 'Industrial Relations Research in Britain', *British Journal of Industrial Relations*, 21(1): 100–14

Winchester, D. (1988) 'Sectoral Change and Trade-Union Organization', in D. Gallie (ed.), *Employment in Britain*, Oxford: Blackwell, 493–518.

Winchester, D. and Bach, S. (1995) 'The State: The Public Sector', in P. Edwards (ed.), *Industrial Relations: Theory and Practice in Britain*, Oxford: Blackwell, 304–34.

Winkler, J. T. (1974) 'The Ghost at the Bargaining Table: Directors and Industrial Relations', *British Journal of Industrial Relations*, 12(2): 191–212.

Wood, S. (1982) (ed.), *The Degradation of Work?*, London: Hutchinson.

Wood, S. and Kelly, J. (1982) 'Taylorism, Responsible Autonomy and Management Strategy', in S. Wood (ed.), *The Degradation of Work?*, London: Hutchinson, 74–89.

Worrell, D. L., Davidson, W. N. and Sharma, V. M. (1991) 'Layoff Announcements and Stockholder Wealth', *Academy of Management Journal*, 34(3): 662–78.

Wray, D. (1996) 'Paternalism and its Discontents: A Case Study', *Work, Employment & Society*, 10(4): 701–15.

Wright, M. (1996) 'The Collapse of Compulsory Unionism? Collective Organization in Highly Unionized British Companies' 1979–91', *British Journal of Industrial Relations*, 34(4): 497–513.

Yachir, F. (1988) *The World Steel Industry Today*, London: Zed.

Yeandle, D. and Clark, J. (1989) 'Growing a Compatible IR Set-up', *Personnel Management*, July: 36–9.

Young, H. (1989) *One of Us*, London: Pan Books.

Zeithaml, V. A. Parasuraman, A. and Berry, L. L. (1985) 'Problems and Strategies in Services Marketing', *Journal of Marketing*, 49(2): 33–46.

Author index

Subject index

CHESTER COLLEGE LIBRARY